CONCORDIA COLLEGE LIBRARY
2811 N. E. HOLMAN ST.
PORTLAND, OREGON 97211

BIBLICAL FAITH
AND SOCIAL ETHICS

BIBLICAL
FAITH and
SOCIAL ETHICS

E. Clinton Gardner
ASSOCIATE PROFESSOR OF CHRISTIAN SOCIAL ETHICS
EMORY UNIVERSITY

HARPER & ROW, PUBLISHERS
New York and Evanston

BJ
1251
G28

BIBLICAL FAITH AND SOCIAL ETHICS

Copyright © 1960 by E. Clinton Gardner

Printed in the United States of America

All rights in this book are reserved.
No part of the book may be used or reproduced
in any manner whatsoever without written per-
mission except in the case of brief quotations
embodied in critical articles and reviews. For
information address Harper & Row, Publishers,
Incorporated, 49 East 33 Street, New York
16, N.Y.

G–M

Library of Congress catalog card number: 60–7003

To Ruth, Edward, Marilyn, and Arnold

10.7.65 Clark H.

23514

CONTENTS

vii

PART IV: CHRISTIAN ETHICS AND SOCIETY

CONCORDIA COLLEGE LIBRARY
2811 N. E. HOLMAN ST.
PORTLAND, OREGON 97211

ACKNOWLEDGMENTS

While it is impossible to record the names of all of those who have provided the seed and the sunshine and rain which have made the present book possible, the author wishes to acknowledge his special indebtedness to Professor H. Richard Niebuhr, of the Divinity School of Yale University, for his stimulating lectures, his understanding counsel, his patient guidance, and his encouragement during the author's sojourn at Yale both as a seminarian and as a graduate student. The extent of this indebtedness is obvious to those who are acquainted with Professor Niebuhr either through his classroom teaching or through his writings. While the author's gratitude is not so obvious, it is nonetheless real.

The author is also conscious of the debt of appreciation which he owes to many other teachers at Yale and Vanderbilt and to his students in social and Christian ethics at North Carolina State College and the Candler School of Theology. His interest in ethics has been quickened by both teachers and students, and both have contributed important insights which have found their way into the present book.

A special word of gratitude is due the administrative officials of Emory University—especially Dean William R. Cannon, of the Candler School of Theology—for arranging a leave from teaching responsibilities in order that the task of writing the present volume might be undertaken.

The indebtedness of the author to a wide range of scholars in the fields of theology, ethics, and the social sciences is indicated by references to many of their works in footnotes. It is hoped that these references will serve as introductions and guides to some of the most relevant literature in the field. The author is grateful to the publishers of *Religion in Life* and *Theology Today* for permission to make use of the substance of the following articles which have previously appeared in these journals: "Rethinking the Protestant Doctrine of Vocation," *Religion in Life*, XXV, no. 3 (Summer, 1956); "The Role of Law and Moral Principles in Christian Ethics," *Religion in Life*, XXVIII, no. 2 (Spring, 1959); and "Justice and Love," *Theology Today*, XIV, no. 2 (July, 1957).

Finally, the author wishes to express his deep appreciation to his wife for her encouragement, her patience, and her assistance; for it has been she who in a very real sense has performed the greater labor by assuming an extra portion of parental responsibility and enduring the curtailment of family life necessitated by the present task.

E. CLINTON GARDNER

Emory University
New Year's Day, 1960

PART I
INTRODUCTION

chapter 1

THE FIELD OF ETHICS

ETHICS AS A CRITICAL STUDY OF MORALITY

ETHICS may be defined as the critical study of morality. It consists of a systematic analysis of the nature of the moral life of man, including both the standards of right and wrong by which his conduct may be guided and the goods toward which it may be directed. On the one hand, ethics is concerned with the practical moral choices which men make; and on the other hand, it is concerned with the ideal goals and principles which they acknowledge to place a claim upon them.

The study of ethics rests upon the assumption that man is both free and responsible. Unless man is free in a very real sense, he cannot be held responsible for his acts; and, if he is not responsible for them, it is meaningless to speak of them as having ethical significance. If his actions were determined by the same kind of factors which condition the behavior of physical objects, it would be idle to talk about moral obligation, duty, praise, blame, and even truth. This does not imply, however, that ethics presupposes a thoroughgoing indeterminism in the area of human action. Indeed, such an assumption would make the moral choice equally as meaningless as would the assumption of a complete determinism. Ethics assumes that moral choices are not mere matters of chance; they are not fortuitous and completely unpredictable. A person whose actions were free in this sense would not be a good man. He would have no stability of character, and there would be no basis for confidence that his future actions would be of a certain kind, either good or bad. Moral choices, therefore, are not so much undetermined as they are the product of a different kind of causation than that which governs the behavior of purely physical phenomena. They are the result not so much of biological or external compulsion as of the apprehension of the right and the good. In the words of William Temple, moral freedom "is not absence of determination; it is spiritual determination as distinct from mechanical or even organic determination. It is determination by what seems good as contrasted with determination by irresistible compulsion."[1] Moral freedom means the capacity for self-determination in the sense that man is free to choose the ends, the goals and values, which he will seek, and free to accept or to reject the demands of duty.

Ethics presupposes freedom and responsibility; and ethics is by the same token concerned, directly or indirectly, with all of man's free acts. It is concerned with all of his decisions and choices and evaluations. It is concerned, for example, with the aesthetic judgments which man makes insofar as these involve decisions concerning the use of time and energy and a choice as to whether or not one should seek to develop his aesthetic capacities either for his personal enrichment and enjoyment or for the enrichment of human life as a whole. Similarly, ethics is concerned with the choices and evaluations which are made in the pursuit of science and philosophy insofar as the former involve decisions concerning the value of these disciplines, the nature of the motivation which one has for engaging in them, and the use to which the resulting knowledge should be put. Moral activity is inescapable so long as man remains *man* as distinct from an automaton or a mere biological organism. He is engaged in moral conduct both in his activity as an individual in direct, "one-to-one" relationships with other individuals and in his activity as a member of countless groups through which he is related to large numbers of other persons who are also members of the same groups or are affected by these groups. Ethics pertains to all of man's activities which may meaningfully be praised or blamed. It is concerned with all of his behavior to which the concepts of "duty," "ought," and "the good" are relevant. It pertains to the choice of means as well as to the choice of ultimate ends. It is concerned with behavior which stems out of habit (getting up at four o'clock or at seven o'clock in the morning, the way one dresses, how fast one drives, how regularly one attends the meetings of the civic

[1] William Temple, *Nature, Man and God*, London, Macmillan and Co., Ltd., 1934, p. 229.

club to which he belongs) and ignorance insofar as a person is responsible for his ignorance (not knowing better how to rear one's children or vote) as well as to decisions and choices that are extremely complex (what should be the specific terms of the next contract between labor and management?). Thus it is clear that what often passes for the entire concern of ethics—behavior relating to such patterns as sex, alcohol, and gambling—is only a part of morality, and it will become more evident as we proceed that this constitutes only a comparatively minor part at that. It should also be clear that there is no escape from moral decisions either by way of inaction or by way of self-destruction. Inaction in effect supports the *status quo,* and the decision "not to be" is obviously one of the most fateful ethical choices any person can make.

Traditional treatments of ethics deal with the analysis of two major concepts, the *right* and the *good.* The concept of right involves the notions of duty, of moral law, and of imperatives; the concept of good involves the idea of goods or ends to be aimed at. In the former case the ideal life for man is envisaged as obedience to law, in the latter case as the satisfaction of desire and the achievement of ends. In the first instance ethics raises the question, What is my duty? In the second instance it asks, What is the highest good? Some ethical thinkers—Immanuel Kant, for example—have held that the question concerning the right is primary; others—e.g., Aristotle—have considered the question concerning the good to be the more important. But in the end, as Professor Ross reminds us, "both the notion of right and the notion of good are implied in the study of moral questions, and any one who tries to work with one only will sooner or later find himself forced to introduce the other."[2] Thus, while Kant sought to describe the whole duty of man in terms of an analysis of the implications of the concept of duty, without introducing the notion of goods to be aimed at, he was forced to argue that certain acts are wrong on the ground that they produced bad results. And, while Aristotle based his ethics primarily upon the notion of a good or an end to be achieved, when he discussed particular virtues such as courage he treated them as being right in relationship to the final good of human life (happiness and well-being).[3]

[2] Sir W. David Ross, *Foundations of Ethics,* Oxford, Clarendon Press, 1939, p. 5.
[3] *Nicomachean Ethics,* Bk. III.

ETHICS AND THE SOCIAL SCIENCES

Ethics differs from the social sciences as well as from the physical sciences both as regards its special field of inquiry and as regards its methodology, but it is far more closely related to the former disciplines than it is to the latter. The social sciences and ethics are both concerned with the analysis of human behavior, and both must therefore take account of the fact that man is free and unpredictable in a way in which atoms and molecules and planets are not free. The physical scientist restricts his investigations to those phenomena the behavior of which he assumes can be explained in terms of causal laws which can be empirically verified; such laws describe the conditions under which certain results are always found. The social scientist and the ethicist, on the other hand, are concerned with the investigation and analysis of various aspects of *human* behavior; and each assumes that man has a certain amount of freedom. Thus the social scientist tends to describe social causation in terms of statistical laws and correlations which indicate the degree of probability that one phenomenon (e.g., juvenile delinquency) will be found wherever another phenomenon (e.g., homes that are broken by divorce) is present rather than in terms of positive laws which describe invariant relationships between certain phenomena. The social scientist must allow for many variables, or uncontrolled factors, in social situations; and for this reason he cannot predict how a particular individual or group will behave under certain specified conditions but only how a certain number of individuals or groups will behave. The ethicist, as we have seen, assumes that man is free—within limits, of course—and therefore responsible for his actions.

But while ethics resembles the social sciences in that each of these disciplines is concerned with human behavior, the former differs from the latter in that it is concerned with different aspects of this behavior and also in that it employs a different method of analysis. Psychology, for example, is an empirical science and as such it deals with the observable facts of psycho-physical behavior and seeks to discover cause-effect relationships in terms of which certain types of behavior can be understood and on the basis of which the effects of these behavior patterns may be predicted. Ethics, on the other hand, is a normative discipline in the sense that it is primarily concerned with the question as to which goals people ought to pursue and what their motivations ought to be. Yet there is a close relationship between psychology and ethics. On the one hand, psychology sheds a great deal of light upon the ethical problem insofar as questions of motivation and the effects of the choice of particular ends or goals are concerned; but, on the other hand, the decisions of psychologists as to what aspects of human behavior they choose to investigate and the direction in which they seek to influence the personalities of their clients involve ethical considerations of the utmost importance. Psychological facts about human behavior are important, but they are never completely coercive for human choices. On the contrary, the discovery of these facts opens up new possibilities for future choices, and the problem of deciding which of these possibilities should be chosen is essentially a moral problem.[4] Psychology as an empirically oriented discipline helps clarify the nature of man's psychic needs and the complexity of the motives involved in his behavior, but it does not provide an answer to the crucial moral question: What is man's true good and toward what goals ought his decisions and actions be directed?

Similarly, sociology is also an empirical science. It analyzes the patterns of behavior and the value systems—the folkways and mores —of different cultures. It is concerned both with the description of the raw data of human experience and with the analysis and interpretation of the theoretical significance of this data. It not only describes the values which are held in a particular society but it also examines the extent to which the actual behavior of a society is consistent with its acknowledged values and goals. Yet sociology as such is not concerned with the ethical question: How *ought* the patterns of behavior which are adjudged normative in a particular culture themselves be changed? Ethics is greatly indebted to sociology for a deeper understanding of the complexity and interrelated character of social problems, for a deeper insight into the extent and manner in which the individual is influenced both for good and for evil by his culture, and for a more precise understanding of the techniques of social change and social control; but sociology does not provide a substitute for ethics. The task of moral evaluation, or choosing between cultural norms, is of a different order from the empirical one; for here we are faced with the question: How ought the customary, conventional morality be changed? This question—like the one re-

[4] See Philip Wheelwright, *A Critical Introduction to Ethics,* New York, The Odyssey Press, rev. ed., 1949, pp. 44–47.

garding the use to which psychological data shall be put—may be ignored or prejudged, but it cannot ultimately be escaped.

That the social sciences cannot be as completely divorced from ethics as was formerly assumed is being increasingly recognized by many psychologists and sociologists themselves. One of the clearest illustrations of the readiness of social scientists to acknowledge their a priori value assumptions is found in the literature on race relations which has appeared in this country in the last two decades.[5] Many of the publications in this field are ostensibly concerned almost completely with the accumulation of quantitative data and seek to provide analyses of the problem that are objective and "scientific." On the other hand, however, many students of race relations clearly recognize that the problem is essentially a moral rather than an empirically factual one although they may declare that the prerogative of making a priori judgments as to which values are right and which are wrong lies outside of the realm of the social sciences and although they may for this reason seek to avoid making any such evaluations.[6]

But an increasing number of writers who are primarily social scientists are coming to acknowledge the a priori character of the assumptions which underlie their concern with problems in the field of race relations and their belief that the democratic values of equality and justice represent desirable norms in intergroup relations. Thus even in the title of his book on race relations, *The More Perfect Union,* Robert MacIver suggests that his concern is to discover a social policy which will give fuller expression to the ideal of a democratic community; and he deplores the tendency on the part of social scientists generally to assume "that a more precise knowledge of the facts will of itself provide the answer to our question. . . . The unfortunate consequence is that generally the most scientific studies convey no message to the framers of social policy while the mass of exhortatory or advisory literature has no sure foundation in

[5] Cf. Waldo Beach, "A Theological Analysis of Race Relations" in Paul Ramsey, ed., *Faith and Ethics,* New York, Harper & Brothers, 1957. See especially pp. 205–209. Another particularly striking example of the recognition of the value judgments underlying the study of a major contemporary social problem is found in the literature on juvenile delinquency. In this connection see, e.g., Milton L. Barron, *The Juvenile in Delinquent Society,* New York, Alfred A. Knopf, 1954, Introduction, pp. xviii–xix; Lowell Juilliard Carr, *Delinquency Control,* New York, Harper & Brothers, rev. ed., 1950, pp. 35–36.

[6] Cf. Gunnar Myrdal, *An American Dilemma,* New York, Harper & Brothers, 1944, Introduction, pp. l–li.

scientific knowledge."[7] George Eaton Simpson and J. Milton Yinger, in *Racial and Cultural Minorities,* similarly acknowledge their belief in the goal of "complete integration," by which they mean that "situation where each individual will be judged and treated as an individual and not in any way as a member of a *supposed* or functionless group."[8] And Brewton Berry apparently agrees with those who hold that "a completely disinterested social science is impossible of achievement," although he believes that the sociologist should discipline himself to be as objective as possible in his investigation of social problems.[9]

In view of the inescapable involvement of the social sciences in making presuppositions of an ethical nature and also in view of the dependence of ethics upon these disciplines for an understanding of the cultural limitations and influences which inevitably affect all ethical judgments and choices, the relationship of ethics to the social sciences may best be described as a complementary—or perhaps more accurately as a dialectical—relationship. This is clearly the case insofar as social ethics as opposed to individualistically conceived personal ethics is concerned. Social ethics may be defined as "the study of *what is* in the light of *what ought to be.*" Viewed in these terms, the social scientist's distinctive contribution to the determination of social policy lies in the contribution which he makes to a more adequate understanding of *what is* whereas the distinctive task of the ethicist is to provide a normative framework in terms of which the empirical and theoretical data supplied by the social sciences can be evaluated. On the one hand, the social scientist cannot escape making ethical decisions despite his efforts to be objective; and, on the other hand, the ethicist ends up being moralistic and socially irrelevant insofar as he refuses to take account of the full range of empirical data made available by the social sciences in the prescriptions which he gives for dealing with specific social problems.

[7] Robert MacIver, *The More Perfect Union,* New York, The Macmillan Company, 1948, pp. 17–18. See also Appendix 2, on "Social Science and Social Action."

[8] George Eaton Simpson and J. Milton Yinger, *Racial and Cultural Minorities: An Analysis of Prejudice and Discrimination,* New York, Harper & Brothers, rev. ed., 1958, pp. 726–727.

[9] Brewton Berry, *Race and Ethnic Relations,* 2nd ed. of *Race Relations,* Boston, Houghton Mifflin Company, 1958, ch. I, especially pp. 21–22.

PHILOSOPHICAL AND THEOLOGICAL ETHICS

Our definition of ethics as the critical study of morality indicates the manner in which ethics may be viewed as a branch of philosophy which undertakes a systematic examination of the moral life. As such it analyzes and evaluates the various conceptions of the good life which men hold, and it raises important metaphysical and theological questions about the significance of the moral experience for man's understanding of his own nature and the nature of the universe in which he lives. What are the implications of the belief that the supreme intrinsic good lies in the enjoyment of the greatest possible amount of pleasure for the individual agent? Does the universe support this quest? Is the universe indifferent to justice? Or, what is the significance of man's experience of obligation or his sense of duty? What is the source of this obligation? Why does man find it difficult to do his duty? What is the price he pays for failure to assent to its demands? Does an analysis of the moral life either prove or support belief in God and in immortality?[10] If so, to what kind of God does it point, and what is the nature of the immortality which it suggests?

On the one hand, an analysis of the moral life—freedom, good, evil, duty, for example—sheds a great deal of light upon metaphysical and theological issues; but, on the other hand, the metaphysical and theological assumptions which the moralist makes as he examines the field of ethics also influence his understanding and analysis of the moral life. Thus, the philosophical hedonist begins his inquiry into the nature of moral activity with a conception of the nature of man which makes it possible for him to conclude that pleasure is the highest good for man. The self-realizationist is able to conclude that the greatest good for man lies in the fullest possible development of the powers and potentialities of the self because of certain assumptions which he makes about the nature of man and his relationship to the universe. Similarly, Kant's analysis of the moral life is greatly influenced by his assumption that reason constitutes the best method which ethics can employ and by his conviction that humanity—not just the self or an intellectual elite—is good. The Christian moralist likewise approaches the study of ethics with a particular set of assumptions about the nature of man, the universe, and God. He

[10] Cf. A. E. Taylor, *The Faith of a Moralist*, London, Macmillan & Co., Ltd., 1937.

seeks to understand the moral life—freedom, obligation, the good, the ultimate significance of morality—in terms of this faith, and the conclusions he draws concerning man's duties and true good are determined in large measure by the content of this faith. Thus, the theologian and the moral philosopher are alike in this respect, viz., that both base their systems of ethics upon assumptions which are not derived from reason and which are ultimately undemonstrable in terms of reason. But the fact that they use different sets of assumptions is of far-reaching importance and explains in large part the differences between the contents of the moralities which they recommend.

This does not mean, however, that one who approaches the study of ethics from the standpoint of Christian faith is not interested in analyses of the moral life which are made from other standpoints or that he has nothing to learn from them. Yet there has been a disturbing tendency among some recent Protestant theologians to dismiss all philosophical systems of ethics as being practically useless to the Christian moralist. One of the most influential representatives of this tendency to reject secular systems of ethics is Emil Brunner. In *The Divine Imperative,* Brunner analyzes several systems of philosophical ethics and concludes that, although each contains some elements of truth, each also has its own special defects and is filled with contradictions which arise out of man's sinfulness.[11] Even the elements of truth which each system contains are distorted and twisted because they are held in isolation from the complete truth which has its unity in God. The elements of truth which are embodied in each system can be properly apprehended, according to Brunner, only when they are revealed to man through the Divine action and apprehended in faith. Hence, not only is every rational system of ethics filled with contradictions, but the attempt to construct a synthetic ethic is also hopeless. In a word, the picture presented by systems of moral philosophy is, according to Brunner, that of "a heap of ruins."[12] But this does not really constitute a serious loss for the Christian, he believes, because Christian faith gives *"the* answer, the *only* answer, and the *whole* answer to the ethical problem."[13]

Despite the fact that the judgment which Brunner pronounces upon

[11] Emil Brunner, *The Divine Imperative,* trans. by Olive Wyon, New York, The Macmillan Company, 1942, chs. V and IX.
[12] *Ibid.,* p. 67.
[13] *Ibid.,* p. 51.

philosophical ethics is almost entirely negative, he himself has been strongly influenced by Kant's ethic of duty, as even the title of his great work on Christian ethics suggests.[14] That he has been influenced by other types of secular morality in the area of political and social thought is indicated by the place which he gives to a modified concept of "natural law" in his treatment of the notion of justice in *Justice and the Social Order*[15] as well as by the appeal which he makes to this idea in *The Divine Imperative* to show both that monogamy is an "order of creation" and that "normally the external guidance of family life belongs to the husband."[16]

Brunner's repudiation of philosophical ethics stems out of his tendency, on the one hand, to set up too sharp a dichotomy between reason and revelation as methods of knowing moral truth and his tendency, on the other hand, to interpret the Christian ethic as an ethic without "content" in the sense that the content of the commandment to love the neighbor must be discovered anew in each situation through the guidance of the Spirit.[17] According to Brunner, the Christian cannot be guided by any moral "principle" in his effort to discover what love for the neighbor requires at a particular time; rather, he must learn this in each new situation by opening himself up to the claims of the neighbor and listening in faith for the Divine Command to be addressed to him in terms of the specific action which is required in a particular moment of decision. In his rejection of principles of duty and value Brunner ignores the need which all finite and sinful men, including Christians, have for guidance in making ethical decisions. It is true that he qualifies this complete rejection of moral principles and rules when he comes to discuss the place of the moral law of the Old and New Testaments. Since this law is based upon revelation rather than upon secular reason, he considers it valuable as a guide to Christian conduct. (See Chapter 7, pp. 194–196.) Beyond this concession, however, he fails to take seriously the need for the guidance offered by the best insights of reason in those areas of life concerning which we have no specific guidance in Scripture (or, for

[14] *The Divine Imperative* is the title given the English translation of the original volume which appeared in German under the title *Das Gebot und die Ordnungen: Entwurf einer protestantisch-theologischen Ethik*, 2nd ed. The German title means literally "The Command and the Orders: an Outline of a Protestant Theological Ethic."

[15] Emil Brunner, *Justice and the Social Order*, trans. by Mary Hottinger, London, Lutterworth Press, 1949, pp. 47–49.

[16] *The Divine Imperative*, pp. 345 ff., 380.

[17] *Ibid.*, pp. 82–84.

that matter, where the literal law of Scripture is obviously inconsistent with the demands of Christian faith and love) and where the possibility of making the right decision depends in large part upon competent technical knowledge. Jesus and the writers of the New Testament never intended to deal systematically and comprehensively with all of the problems of modern life; and, from the beginning, Christians have had to draw upon the best moral wisdom of their day to help them relate the demands of Christ to the requirements of life in society. Moreover, in their analysis of the demands of Christ as well as those of society they have had to make use of the methods and tools of philosophical ethics. Such analysis has been necessary in order to make the *content* of their conduct consistent with the faith and love out of which their desire to serve their neighbors has stemmed.[18] The extent to which it has been possible to achieve such a consistency between faith and practice has largely depended upon the extent to which Christians have been able to discern the complexity of their moral choices, upon their ability to analyze the competing duties and goods at stake in particular choices, and upon their capacity to relate these duties and goods to the will of God.

While the Christian moralist can learn much from philosophical ethics about principles of duty and the nature and interrelationships of values, he cannot simply take over the insights which he gains from these systems in the form in which they appear in secular morality. Such insights cannot be added *as they are understood in these systems* to a list of Christian duties or goods which would otherwise be incomplete and therefore offer inadequate guidance for conduct. The effort to do this constitutes the fundamental weakness of Thomistic ethics. St. Thomas Aquinas assumed that the moral virtues of Aristotle—prudence, temperance, fortitude, and justice—could be taken over into Christian ethics as they were understood by Aristotle and that Christian ethics merely added onto this natural morali[t] theological virtues, viz., faith, hope, and love, which could be only by revelation. What St. Thomas failed to see was the fac apart from Christian faith the moral virtues of Aristotelian are understood quite selfishly and that if they are to become Chr n virtues they must be converted or transformed by being related rst of all to God rather than primarily to the good-for-the-self.

[18] George F. Thomas, *Christian Ethics and Moral Philosophy,* New York, Charles Scribner's Sons, 1955, pp. 388–390.

When the Christian moralist merely takes over certain insights from secular systems of morality without revising them or transforming them, the result is an attempted synthesis of elements which are essentially incompatible. Brunner rightly rejects every such eclectic synthesis as a distortion of Christian ethics, but he wrongly supposes that this is the only way in which the Christian moralist can employ moral philosophy. Christian ethics cannot simply add such graces as faith, hope, and love to a certain group of secular virtues either as a crown or as a postscript; but it can make use of natural morality, whether of the marketplace or of the philosophers, by reinterpreting the latter in the light of Christian faith and using it in the service of Christian love.

St. Augustine is perhaps the most influential representative of this method of relating Christian morality to moral philosophy in Christian history. He was one of the first Christian theologians to take seriously the implications of Christian faith and love insofar as these are related to the demands which life in human society entails; and he sought to determine what Christian love demands in terms of man's social responsibility by drawing upon the ethical, political, and scientific thought of his culture and transforming it by love in the service of God.[19] Augustine had himself been attracted to the Greek and Roman philosophers before his conversion to Christianity, but when he examined the moral virtues which they recommended from the standpoint of his new faith, he saw that these were perverted by pride and idolatry; hence, he referred to them as "splendid vices." But Augustine did not therefore conclude that new Christian virtues were to be substituted for the virtues of the philosophers; rather, the latter were to be transformed by love and reoriented toward God. "Temperance," writes Augustine, describing the classical Greek virtues when they have been thus reoriented toward God rather than the self, "is love keeping itself entire and incorrupt for God; fortitude is love bearing everything readily for the sake of God; justice is love, serving God only, and therefore ruling well all else, as subject to man; prudence is love making a right distinction between what helps it toward God and what might hinder it."[20] Similarly, as we have indicated, the political wisdom and entire culture of natural man

[19] For an excellent exposition of the conversionist motif in Augustine see H. Richard Niebuhr, *Christ and Culture,* New York, Harper & Brothers, 1951, pp. 206 ff.

[20] St. Augustine, "On the Morals of the Catholic Church," in Whitney J. Oates, ed., *Basic Writings of St. Augustine,* New York, Random House, 1948, ch. XV.

is to be converted and redirected toward God. It is to be transformed, not replaced by a special natural science, or a special political science, or a special logic which has been revealed to the Christian. Rather, all of this wisdom which is the product of human reason is to be reoriented and redirected by being given its true "center," viz., God. This true center can be known only by faith, and apart from it all of man's reasoning is off-center. When this true center is restored through faith, then and only then is man able to reason properly. As Augustine puts the matter, "I believe in order that I may understand." But Augustine also could not understand without using his reason both to understand his faith and to determine what it meant to love the neighbor in Roman society. Moreover, he could understand the latter only if he made use of the moral and political wisdom of Christian and non-Christian thinkers alike who had wrestled with the nature of man's political life on the basis of wider knowledge and experience in these areas than he had had. Similarly, the contemporary Christian cannot know what is required of him in the name of love for God and the neighbor in these areas unless he makes use of the guidance provided by specialists in these fields.

Admittedly, the task of Christian ethics would be far easier if either, on the one hand, the Christian could accept the insights of natural reason uncritically and add them to that which he knows by faith or if, on the other hand, he could repudiate them altogether. Both of these methods of relating Christian ethics to secular ethical thought are unsatisfactory, however, for the reasons which we have indicated. Because the Christian moralist needs guidance derived from reason to help provide the "content" of Christian ethics, he must make use of moral philosophy; but because man can reason rightly about his duties to his fellowmen and about the values which enrich human life only when all of his reasoning has its unifying principle in God, the Christian must transform these insights. Hence, the proper relationship between Christian ethics and philosophical ethics is that of the transformation of the latter by the former. This is the only satisfactory way to maintain the integrity of Christian ethics while recognizing the necessity of making use of principles derived from reason to guide the Christian in the discovery of what love requires in concrete moral choices.[21]

[21] For a fuller treatment of the relationship of Christian ethics to secular ethical thought, see Thomas, *op. cit.*, ch. 17.

THE STANDPOINT OF THE PRESENT ANALYSIS
OF CHRISTIAN ETHICS

While Christian ethics must make use of philosophical ethics to provide *part* of the content of morality, Christian ethics is clearly independent of secular systems of morality in the sense that the former is not based upon the latter. On the contrary, Christian ethics is based upon Christian theology and derives its *distinctive* content from this source. In the long run the moral teaching of Christianity stands or falls with Christian faith. This is true despite the common assumption that the ethical teaching may be accepted by those who reject the Christian faith.

The task to which we have set ourselves in the present study, therefore, is that of examining the moral life as this is viewed from the standpoint of Christian faith. Our task would be far easier if the ethical teachings of Christianity could be divorced from this faith and summarized independently of it, as Thomas Jefferson sought to do when he compiled a collection of the moral teachings of Jesus and as those of our contemporaries do who look to Jesus only as the supreme moral teacher. But, as E. F. Scott points out, it is ultimately impossible to separate the ethic of Jesus from his religious faith, for Jesus was not primarily a moralist: "Jesus was something else than a lawgiver or a reformer. He came with a message from God, and his ethic has no meaning apart from his religion."[22] Hence, one cannot understand the moral teaching of Christianity if he merely collects Jesus' ethical counsel found in the Sermon on the Mount and elsewhere in the Gospels, whether one interprets these teachings as laws to be literally fulfilled or as principles for general guidance. Whether we wish to do so or not, whether we are interested in theology or not, if we would understand the ethical teaching of Jesus we must seek to understand it in the context of his religious message.

Our task is further complicated by the fact that there are many types of Christian theology. Jesus did not formulate a system of theology just as he did not formulate a system of ethics, but theology is an inescapable task of the Church as it seeks to understand the significance of Jesus and his relationship to God and to man. Obviously, the interpretation of Christian ethics which one offers will depend

---

[22] E. F. Scott, *The Ethical Teaching of Jesus,* New York, The Macmillan Company, 1924, xii.

upon the particular theology which one holds. The present study undertakes to interpret Christian ethics from the standpoint of the basic tenets of classical or traditional Christianity. It rests upon the belief that, despite the many theologies which are represented by different denominations and historical schools, there are certain basic, underlying convictions about God as Creator, as Judge, and as Redeemer and about man as created in the image of God, as actually wayward and fallen but confronted with the promise of forgiveness and of renewal, upon which there is general agreement and which offer the Christian guidance in the moral life. That there is in our day increasing recognition of this unity which transcends the less significant differences is indicated by the growing strength of the ecumenical movement as exemplified in the National Council of the Churches of Christ in the United States of America and in the World Council of Churches.

The present interpretation of Christian ethics is offered, therefore, not as a definitive treatment of the subject but rather as one approach to Christian ethics.[23] The task of formulating a Christian ethic is a continuous, on-going one, which in the very nature of the case can never be completed. On the one hand, it involves the constant reformulation of any particular statement of this ethic as advances are made in theology, which provides its base; and, on the other hand, it involves a continuing effort to gain a more adequate understanding of human need and society, especially in view of the rapid changes which are taking place throughout the whole social order, and the constant need for each believer finally to discover the specific content of this ethic in terms of the uniqueness as well as the universality of each moral situation. In view of this fact as well as the more obvious limitations of the writer, we have set for ourselves the far more modest task of examining, within these limitations, the relationship of biblical faith to moral conduct. More specifically, the purpose of the present study is to inquire into the source and the content of Christian morality. The mood of the present analysis is that of interpretation rather than argument. The intent of the author is not to debate with other philosophical systems but rather to examine the way the moral life looks from the standpoint of Christian faith. Only when the Christian moral teaching is thus understood on its

Theme

[23] For a description and analysis of five major types of theological ethics see Niebuhr, *op. cit.* Cf. Albert C. Knudson, *The Principles of Christian Ethics,* New York, Abingdon-Cokesbury Press, 1943, ch. II.

own terms is one in a position to choose fairly between it and competing views on the basis of their relative adequacy to the facts of the moral life.

The aim of the present study, therefore, is to help the interested student come to grips with the basic issues and problems of morality as these appear in the light of Christian faith. It is hoped that the student will be led to pursue the issues that are raised here by reference to other interpretations of Christian ethics. Finally, the reader should perhaps be warned in advance that he will find here no code or set of rules which will tell him what the Christian must do in order to lead the good life. Rather, he will be pointed to a faith which enables him to act spontaneously and freely where the rules break down or are lacking.

RECOMMENDED READINGS

Brunner, Emil, *The Divine Imperative,* trans. by Olive Wyon, New York, The Macmillan Company, 1942, chs. IV–IX, XV–XVI.

Casserley, J. V. Langmead, *Morals and Man in the Social Sciences,* London, Longmans, Green & Co., 1951.

Holbrook, Clyde A., *Faith and Community,* New York, Harper & Brothers, 1959, ch. V.

Knudson, Albert C., *The Principles of Christian Ethics,* New York, Abingdon-Cokesbury Press, 1943, ch. I.

Niebuhr, H. Richard, *Christ and Culture,* New York, Harper & Brothers, 1951, chs. I, VI.

Niebuhr, Reinhold, "Christian Faith and Social Action," in *Christian Faith and Social Action,* John A. Hutchison, ed., New York, Charles Scribner's Sons, 1953.

Pike, James A., *Doing the Truth,* Garden City, New York, Doubleday & Company, 1955, chs. I–V.

Ramsey, Paul, *Basic Christian Ethics,* New York, Charles Scribner's Sons, 1950, ch. VI.

Ramsey, Paul, "The Transformation of Ethics," in *Faith and Ethics,* Paul Ramsey, ed., New York, Harper & Brothers, 1957, ch. V.

Thomas, George F., *Christian Ethics and Moral Philosophy,* New York, Charles Scribner's Sons, 1955, ch. 17.

Titus, Harold H., *Ethics for Today,* New York, American Book Company, 2nd ed., 1947, chs. I, VII–VIII, XIII, XV.

Wheelwright, Philip, *A Critical Introduction to Ethics,* New York, The Odyssey Press, rev. ed., 1949, chs. 1–2.

PART II
THE DEVELOPMENT OF CHRISTIAN ETHICS

chapter 2

_____

THE OLD TESTAMENT
BACKGROUND

THE OLD TESTAMENT IN RELATION
TO THE NEW TESTAMENT

"THE Bible," writes Professor H. Richard Niebuhr, "has always been and will doubtless remain the chief source book for the study of Christian ethics."[1] It is equally certain that the Old Testament has always been and will remain the one most indispensable guide for the study of the New Testament. For just as a knowledge of the Bible is necessary for an understanding of the thought of later theologians so a knowledge of the religious and ethical teaching of the Old Testament is necessary for an understanding of that of the New. That the closeness of this relationship has been recognized by Christians from the beginning is shown by the many references in the New Testament itself to the fulfillment of the hopes and promises of the Old in the person of Jesus, who is proclaimed to be the Christ, and by the fact that the Church early accepted the books included in both the Old and New Testaments as canonical.[2]

Both the Old and the New Testaments are parts of a continuous record of God's self-disclosure of His nature and will to Israel and

[1] Waldo Beach and H. Richard Niebuhr, *Christian Ethics,* New York, The Ronald Press Company, 1955, p. 10.
[2] The Canon of the Old Testament as we know it in the Authorized Version and most modern translations, including the Revised Standard Version, is the Hebrew Canon as adopted by the rabbinical Synod at Jamnia about 90 A.D. The New Testament was fixed in the form in which we now have it by the close of the fourth century, A.D.

the world, and as such they belong together. Christians believe that God's self-disclosure was most complete in the events centering about the life, death, and resurrection of Jesus of Nazareth. For this reason the Church included in the Canon of the New Testament only those writings which it considered most reliable as accounts of the events and most authoritative as interpretations of the generally accepted faith as that was understood by the Church at large. Thus, special importance was attached to the writings of the apostles and their associates. This did not mean that God had ceased to reveal Himself to men, but rather that the climax of His historical revelation was reached in the events associated with Jesus, and that His subsequent revelation becomes recognizable and intelligible only in relation to the biblical account of His revelatory action in Christ.

The close relationship that exists between the Old and the New Testaments as two parts of an on-going drama of revelation suggests that there is a fundamental unity between the two. And yet this unity is frequently overlooked by those who are more forcibly impressed with the wide diversity of religious and moral thought which is found in the Bible. There are indeed a wide variety of conceptions of God and a wide diversity of moral standards reflected in the sixty-six books of the Bible. For example, there are the two different accounts of creation in the first two chapters of Genesis, and these narratives reflect somewhat different conceptions of God. The message of Amos is different from that of Hosea. There are fundamental differences in the scales of values held by different men and at different times. The writer of the Fifty-eighth Psalm prays for the punishment of the wicked as a reward for the righteous, whereas the writer of the fifty-third chapter of Isaiah exalts the suffering servant who vicariously takes upon himself the sin of the unrighteous. The contrast between the moral teachings of the Old and New Testaments is presented in especially sharp focus in the Sermon on the Mount, where Jesus is represented as setting his requirements over against those which had been taught "to the men of old." Thus, Jesus declares, "You have heard that it was said to the men of old, 'You shall not kill; and whoever kills shall be liable to judgment.' But I say to you that every one who is angry with his brother shall be liable to judgment; whoever insults his brother shall be liable to the council, and whoever says, 'You fool!' shall be liable to the hell of fire" (Matt. 5:21–22).[3] And

[3] Unless otherwise indicated, all biblical references are to the Revised Standard Version.

in place of the ancient law of vengeance, "an eye for an eye and a tooth for a tooth," Jesus puts the new demand, "Do not resist one who is evil" (Matt. 5:38–39).

But it is easy to exaggerate the diversity within the Bible. When this is done, one of two things generally happens. On the one hand, those who look uncritically to the Bible for proof-texts in support of their positions find themselves in hopeless controversy as to which particular teaching is to be taken as the absolute authority. Thus some groups of Christians appeal to Jesus' statement about nonresistance to support their position of pacifism while others appeal to Paul's injunction to obey the state to support their participation in military service (Matt. 5:39; Rom. 13:1–7). On the other hand, an exaggerated emphasis upon the differences between the moral standards found in Scripture has frequently been used by those who seek to attack the Bible in an effort to show that it is inconsistent and therefore unreliable as an ethical guide. The resulting confusion in the minds of those who are unacquainted with critical methods of biblical study and with the deeper meaning of the biblical revelation is easy to understand, but it is difficult to justify. Upon more careful examination it becomes increasingly clear that the unity of the Scriptures both in their moral and in their religious teachings is far more significant and impressive than their diversity. The perception of this underlying unity depends, however, upon a genuine participation in the biblical story, and an effort to understand it first of all in its own terms as a single continuous account "of the historical action of God seeking the reconciliation of man and God, the human and the divine, the creature and the Creator."[4] Viewed in this light, the Bible is seen to be a "coherent unity," and its unity is found to lie in its central themes and underlying presuppositions. That this unity is presupposed in the New Testament is suggested by Jesus' warning in the Sermon on the Mount, "Think not that I have come to abolish the law and the prophets; I have come not to abolish them but to fulfill them" (Matt. 5:17), and by his summary of the law in two commandments: "And he said to him, 'You shall love the Lord your God with all your heart, and with all your soul, and with all your mind. This is the great and first commandment. And a second is like it, You shall love your neighbor as yourself. On these two commandments depend all the law and the prophets'" (Matt. 22:37–40).

[4] B. Davie Napier, *From Faith to Faith*, New York, Harper & Brothers, 1955, p. xvii.

It is suggested also by the Matthean account of the life of Jesus in terms of the latter's relationship to prophecy and by the opening verses of The Letter to the Hebrews: "In many and various ways God spoke of old to our fathers by the prophets; but in these last days he has spoken to us by a Son, whom he appointed the heir of all things, through whom also he created the world" (Heb. 1:1–2).

CHARACTERISTICS OF HEBREW MORALITY

If we would understand the underlying unity of biblical ethics, we must seek to discover the major ideas and themes which run throughout the Old and New Testaments, and our understanding of this unity as well as of the diversity within this unity will be deepened if we trace the development of these ideas in certain of the more important documents representing different periods in biblical history. Thus, our first task is to identify the major characteristic themes of biblical morality. In subsequent sections of the present chapter we shall attempt to trace briefly their development in selected writings of the Old Testament. The following two chapters will seek to clarify the relationship of the ethics of Jesus and Paul to these continuing themes.

The first major characteristic of Hebrew ethical thought that impresses itself upon one as he examines the morality of the prophets, of the lawgivers, of the sages, and of the New Testament is the fact that it is *theocentric or God-centered*. Indeed, so closely is the morality of the Hebrews related to their religion that they "seldom distinguished between ethics and religion" and from an early time their religion was "shot through with an ethical quality."[5] God is the source of all moral requirements and the highest good. Biblical ethics differs in this regard from those types of moral philosophy which look to human nature or to human happiness or the perfection (realization) of the self as the basis of man's moral requirements. The latter concerns are also reflected in the Bible, but they are not primary. The Ten Commandments are prefaced with the declaration, "And God spake all those words, saying, 'I am the Lord your God, who brought you out of the land of Egypt, out of the house of bondage' " (Exod. 20:1–2). The commandments which follow are not viewed as ethical in themselves, but they acquire ethical significance as the terms of a

[5] Hinckley G. Mitchell, *The Ethics of the Old Testament*, Chicago, The University of Chicago Press, 1912, p. 15.

covenant which God makes with Israel. The fulfillment of these commandments indicated that the Hebrews were loyal to God; disregard of them indicated their disloyalty. Indeed, so much are the religious and moral elements in the Decalogue of one piece that the prophets do not hesitate to speak of the worship of other gods, which was forbidden by the first article of the covenant, as adultery (Hos. 1:2; Jer. 3:1 ff.; Ezek. 23:1 ff.). Similarly, Micah equates human duty with God's requirements: "He has showed you, O man, what is good; and what does the Lord require of you but to do justice, and to love kindness, and to walk humbly with your God?" (Mic. 6:8). The divine source of ethical norms and values is always at least implicit in the wisdom literature, where it is acknowledged that the origin of the ethical insight is religious faith: "The fear of the Lord is the beginning of wisdom, and the knowledge of the Holy One is insight" (Prov. 9:10; cf. Job 28:28).[6] And, as we have already noticed, Jesus relates the two commandments which he gives in a very close way. Taken together they summarize "the law and the prophets," both of which ground man's duties in God's will, and the second commandment is declared to be "like" the first.

The close relationship between the ethical and religious teaching of the Bible suggests that the fundamental unifying element in its ethical thought is God. Biblical ethics is an ethic of the worship of one God. In the earlier stages of Hebrew history the existence of other gods was assumed; but, at least so far as Israel was concerned, after the time of Moses (c. 1200 B.C.) there was only one God to whom Israel was to be loyal and whose will was binding upon her. And when the monotheism which was implicit in the monolatry of Moses had become fully developed after the Babylonian Exile, Jesus and the writer of the latter part of Isaiah considered themselves in the tradition of the early Hebrew servants of Yahweh. It is the God of Abraham and of Isaac and of Jacob whom Jesus worships. The one living God of Israel is the unifying source of the moral requirements that rest upon man and the highest good or value for man.

A second major characteristic of Hebrew morality is *its imperative tone*. Insofar as the distinction between those types of ethical thought which begin with the consideration of man's duty and those which begin with the consideration of the ultimate end or goal to be achieved through human conduct is valid, biblical ethics clearly be-

---

[6] In this connection see also Otto J. Baab, *The Theology of the Old Testament*, New York, Abingdon-Cokesbury Press, 1949, pp. 68–75.

longs in the former grouping. It is primarily concerned with the question, "What is right?" rather than with the question, "What is man's chief good?" It begins with reminding men of their duties, stemming primarily out of a covenant relationship with God, rather than with the formulation of ideal goods which men are free to compare disinterestedly and from which they are free to choose as they see fit. The characteristic mood of all of the great summaries of Hebrew morality is the imperative. "You shall not steal" (Exod. 20:15). "You shall be holy . . ." (Lev. 19:2). "You shall love the Lord your God. . . ." "You shall love your neighbor . . ." (Matt. 22:37, 39). Even Micah's summary of the ethical teaching of the Old Testament, a summary which has also been widely used to represent the essence of biblical morality, while it employs the indicative mood and uses the word "good," speaks of God's requirements; and thus its intent is also imperative: "He has showed you, O man, what is good; and what does the Lord require of you but to do justice, and to love kindness, and to walk humbly with your God?" (Mic. 6:8).

In the third place, biblical morality is *concerned with persons and communities of persons* rather than with ideals and patterns in the abstract. Its emphasis is upon those acts which affect the neighbor and Israel, not upon justice and love as virtues in themselves. Western ethical thought has in general developed along much more abstract lines than the thought of Israel. As Professor Muilenburg points out, such terms as *personality, experience, conscience, history, virtue,* and the *summum bonum* are alien to the vocabulary of Israel, although the realities to which these point are dealt with at every turn.[7] The Ten Commandments are concerned with conduct that affects persons, including the primary Person to whom man is related in his decisions and his activity. It is not truthfulness as such which is demanded but only truthfulness toward the neighbor. The prophets are intensely interested in justice and mercy, but their concern is not with the "ideal" justice and mercy of some utopian dream but rather with justice and mercy as embodied in the decisions and actions of men in a sinful society. Truth and justice and mercy are things that are required to be *done* (cf. John 3:21). The whole law is frequently summarized in terms of love of neighbor (Rom. 13:8, 10; Gal. 5:14; John 13:34–35; 15:12, 17; I John 3:11; 4:7; II John 1:5; Jas. 2:8),

---

[7] James Muilenburg, "The Ethics of the Prophet," in *Moral Principles of Action*, Ruth Nanda Anshen, ed., New York, Harper & Brothers, 1952, p. 527.

but even love is not required in itself but only as related to God and the neighbor. No action is viewed as being right simply on account of the way in which it affects the self.

A fourth outstanding feature of biblical ethics is its *equalitarianism* in its estimate of human worth. The Hebrews are more impressed with the fundamental equality among men than with their differences. God has made all; He cares for all, and He seeks to redeem all. Hence the slave and the widow and the orphan must be cared for; they must be treated with justice and mercy, for this is the way in which God deals with all men, and this is the kind of conduct which He requires of men in their dealings with each other. The Holiness Code required that all Hebrew slaves were to be set free each fiftieth year, and the land was also to be redistributed in the year of jubilee (Lev. 25:10, 23–28). In the time of harvest, the owner of the land was to leave some of the fruit of the fields for the poor to glean. "And you shall not strip your vineyard bare, neither shall you gather the fallen grapes of your vineyard; you shall leave them for the poor and for the sojourner" (Lev. 19:10; cf. Ruth 2). Similarly, in the wisdom literature the claims of the needy are recognized: "A righteous man knows the rights of the poor" (Prov. 29:7). "If I have rejected the cause of my manservant or my maidservant, when they brought a complaint against me; what then shall I do when God rises up? When he makes inquiry, what shall I answer him? Did not he who made me in the womb make him? And did not one fashion us in the womb?" (Job 31:13–15). Similarly, in the suffering servant passages in Isaiah and in the example and teaching of Jesus the claims of the transgressors and those who are despised and lost are singled out in the most striking terms as the ones to whom the children of God owe a special service because their need is great and not because they merit more or will be able to repay anything at all. God shows no partiality (Acts 10:34) and He requires that men shall show no special deference to the rich (Jas. 2:9). Or again, "There is neither male nor female: for ye are all one in Christ Jesus" (Gal. 3:28).

Finally, Hebrew ethics is distinguished from other types of ethics in its emphasis upon *salvation from evil* rather than aspiration after the good. Israel's hope is in God rather than in man. God is represented as disclosing Himself to Moses as the "healer" of Israel (Exod. 15:26), whom He has adopted as His "first-born" (Exod. 4:22). The writer of the Ninety-fifth Psalm breaks forth in praise, "Let us make a joyful noise to the rock of our salvation" (Ps. 95:1). Hezekiah offers thanksgiving to God for deliverance: "Thou hast held back my life from the pit of destruction; for thou hast cast all my sins behind thy back" (Isa. 38:17). The writer of the early chapters of Isaiah looks for a coming "savior" (Isa. 19:20), but it is the unknown prophet of the Babylonian exile who sets forth the theme that God is Israel's Redeemer and Saviour in the clearest terms found anywhere in the Old Testament. Again and again he speaks of God as Israel's Redeemer (Isa. 41:14; 43:14; 44:6, 24; 47:4; 48:17; 49:7, 26; 54:5, 8), and describes Him as her Saviour (Isa. 43:3, 11; 45:15, 21; 46:4, 13; 49:8, 26; 51:5, 6, 8; 52:7, 10). Thus, Jehovah says to Israel, "Fear not, for I have redeemed you. . . . For I am the Lord your God, the Holy One of Israel, your Savior" (Isa. 43:1, 3). God will save Israel "with an everlasting salvation" (Isa. 45:17). And the testimony of the New Testament is that in Jesus this promise of salvation has been fulfilled. He "will save his people from their sins" (Matt. 1:21). In the synagogue at Nazareth Jesus declared that the promise of deliverance of Isaiah 61:12 was fulfilled in himself. Elsewhere Jesus is spoken of as "the Lamb of God, who takes away the sin of the world!" (John 1:29). The gospel is the "power of God for salvation" (Rom. 1:16). Those who are in Christ Jesus have been liberated by his Spirit from "the law of sin and death" (Rom. 8:1–2). Indeed, the entire New Testament is of one voice in proclaiming as the gospel message the good news that the long-awaited Messiah has come and that the promised salvation is now made possible through faith.[8]

THE COVENANT CODE

Perhaps the earliest piece of Hebrew legislation in the Old Testament is the document found in Exodus 20:22–23:33. This is generally referred to as the Covenant Code, and it is believed to have been formulated in the period of the early Hebrew monarchy, probably in the ninth century. It reflects the social and economic conditions of a relatively simple society quite different from that in which the later prophets lived. The society for which this set of laws was formulated was also relatively less advanced than that for which the Babylonian

---

[8] Cf. H. Wheeler Robinson's declaration to the effect that not only is it true that the "supreme and unifying theme of the Old Testament is God, as Creator, Ruler, and Redeemer" but this is also true of the Bible as a whole (*Inspiration and Revelation in the Old Testament*, Oxford, Clarendon Press, 1946, p. 148).

Code of Hammurabi, which is closely related to the Covenant Code, was designed.[9]

There are two types of requirements set forth in the Covenant Code: the unconditional "Words" and the conditional "Ordinances."[10] The former appear as unqualified, direct demands addressed to the second person; the latter are introduced by conditional clauses and consist of directions to judges who are charged with the dispensation of justice. Typical of the first type of commandment, or the "Words," are the following: "You shall not make gods of silver to be with me" (Exod. 22:23); "You shall be men consecrated to me" (Exod. 20:23); "You shall not pervert the justice due to your poor in his suit" (Exod. 23:6); "You shall not oppress a stranger" (Exod. 23:9); "You shall serve the Lord your God" (Exod. 23:25). Typical of the second type of commandment, or the "Ordinances," are such provisions as these: "When you buy a Hebrew slave, he shall serve six years, and in the seventh he shall go out free, for nothing" (Exod. 21:2); "When a man strikes his slave, male or female, with a rod and the slave dies under his hand, he shall be punished" (Exod. 21:20); "If you lend money to any of my people with you who is poor, you shall not be to him as a creditor, and you shall not exact interest from him" (Exod. 22:25). While the "Words" and the "Ordinances" are so interwoven that it is sometimes difficult to distinguish between the two, in general, the beginning and the end of the Covenant Code consist of the "Words" whereas the central section is composed of the "Ordinances." And, as Professor H. Richard Niebuhr points out, it is significant that the similarities between the Book of the Covenant and the Babylonian law are found almost exclusively in the conditional "Ordinances" while the similarities, in content as well as in form, between the early Hebrew code and the later utterances of the prophets (as well as those of Jesus as recorded in the Sermon on the Mount) are confined to the unconditional "Words." "It is in the latter that what is distinctive of ancient and later Israelite morality appears most clearly."[11]

The Covenant Code, like the Ten Commandments which immediately precede it, is ascribed to God as its author, and Moses is

[9] J. M. P. Smith, *The Origin and History of Hebrew Law,* Chicago, The University of Chicago Press, 1931, p. 18.

[10] The terms "The Words" and "The Ordinances" as designations for these two types of laws are derived from the declaration that Moses "told the people all the words of the Lord and all the ordinances" (Exod. 24:3).

[11] Beach and Niebuhr, *op. cit.,* p. 18.

assigned the role of mediator of the law to the Israelites.[12] Since God, not Moses, is the author of the law, its provisions are requirements of deity rather than of man. They are considered to be part of a covenant, or agreement between God and the Hebrews. Jehovah had chosen the Hebrews to be "his people"; He had promised to continue to protect and bless them even as He had when He delivered them out of bondage in Egypt. On their side, they had solemnly pledged themselves to be faithful to God, and this commitment meant that they would do His will. Yahweh had revealed Himself as a jealous God whose first requirement was that they should not worship any other gods. They were not to turn to Yahweh only when other gods failed or in time of pestilence and crisis; they were not to worship Him in order to use Him in some magical way for the pursuit of their human ends; they were not to worship Him with their lips and altars and sacrifices only; but they were to obey Him and serve Him in their economic activities such as lending money and sowing and harvesting, in their political affairs through the establishment of justice, and in their treatment even of the dumb animals, as well as in their cultic practices such as building altars and offering sacrifices.

This is the underlying assumption, the starting point, of biblical morality. Hebrew ethics begins, not with the demand for loyalty of the self to itself or even to society, but "with the assumption that those to whom it is addressed are bound to God and that God has bound himself to them."[13] This God is understood primarily in terms of personal will. God is absolutely trustworthy and faithful; His will is constant. And, as already noted, the God of Israel is one God in the practical sense that His will is normative for all of Israel's life. Neither in the Covenant Code nor in their other early literature were the Hebrews concerned with speculative monotheism, with the question as to whether other gods whom other peoples worshiped had any real existence; they were concerned only with practical monotheism, with the import of the requirement that they worship and serve only Yahweh.

The imperative character of the morality of the Covenant Code has already been indicated by what has been said about the two types of laws of which the document is composed. Consideration has also been given to the fact that there is an extremely close relationship between the worship of God and the service of the neighbor so that religion

---

[12] Napier, *op. cit.,* pp. 194–195.
[13] Beach and Niebuhr, *op. cit.,* p. 18.

and morality are inseparable, but an additional word is needed to indicate the extent to which the Covenant Code is concerned with the needs of one's neighbors rather than with idealistic or abstract norms of truth and justice. Thus, it is not interest which is categorically prohibited but interest on a poor man's loan (Exod. 22:25). It is not the taking of a pledge that is condemned but rather the taking of a man's garment in pledge and keeping it overnight when he has nothing else in which to sleep (Exod. 22:26, 27). The kind of justice which is required is not the justice of abstract or speculative reason, whereby each man is to be rewarded according to his merit or his "due," but rather a justice that is partial to those who are in special need. God is particularly attentive to their cry, even as He hearkened to the cry of the Israelites when they were in bondage in the land of Egypt. Thus, in the Covenant Code, and particularly in the "Words," the weak, the poor, foreigners, widows, orphans, and even animals that are in distress are singled out as the objects of special concern. It is in this particular solicitude for the distressed and the weak that the content of the Covenant Code differs most strikingly from the Code of Hammurabi. Such consideration is demanded in the name of justice, not merely recommended as an expression of charity. "You shall not afflict any widow or orphan" (Exod. 22:22). "If you see the ass of one who hates you lying under its burden, you shall refrain from leaving him with it, you shall help him lift it up" (Exod. 23:5). "You shall not oppress a stranger" (Exod. 23:9). Justice is not an abstract ideal, but it gets its content from the requirements of the neighbor under God. Likewise, certain ritual injunctions are given a humanitarian reference. Thus, the Sabbatical year is to be observed "that the poor of your people may eat; and what they leave the wild beasts may eat" (Exod. 23:11). Similarly, one reason that is given for observing the seventh day is not that it is dedicated to God but rather "that your ox and your ass may have rest, and the son of your bondmaid, and the alien, may be refreshed" (Exod. 23:12).[14] Thus, while it is true that other of the "Words" deal exclusively with religious rituals—the building of altars and the offering of sacrifices, for example—it is clear that the one God who demands the religious rites and sacrifices also demands social justice in the courts and in the economic practices of the community.

The equalitarianism of the Covenant Code has been suggested in

[14] Cf. Deuteronomy 5:12–15; contrast Exodus 20:8–11; 31:15; 35:2.

what has been said about the concept of justice which directs special concern to the needy and distressed. The latter have rights which are just as inviolable as those of the wealthy and comfortable. This recognition is most strikingly expressed in the concern for the rights of the slaves even though slavery itself is an accepted institution (Exod. 21:2–6, 7–11, 20–21, 26–27, 32).

Finally, the characteristic concern of Hebrew morality with salvation from evil is suggested by the very ratification of the covenant. Jehovah had delivered the Israelites out of bondage, and their acceptance of the covenant was at once an act of gratitude to Him for deliverance and also an act of entrusting themselves with their future to Him. Their reliance henceforth was to be, not upon themselves and their aspirations for themselves, but upon God, who had chosen them and delivered them out of bondage and who promised to continue to bless them if they would keep His commandments (Exod. 23:20–22). But, on the other hand, if they did not keep His commandments, God would punish them and even visit them with destruction (Exod. 22:20, 23–24; 23:21).

THE EIGHTH-TO-THE-SIXTH-CENTURY PROPHETS

In contrast to the simple conditions of a primitive agricultural society which are presupposed in the Covenant Code, the economic conditions and international involvements of the Hebrews in the time of the great prophets of the eighth to the sixth centuries were quite complex.[15] Amos, for example, whose prophecies date from the middle of the eighth century, addresses himself to people who are engrossed in the trade and speculation and bargaining of a commercial economy (Amos 8:4–6) and to people who own private strongholds, summer houses, and winter houses (Amos 3:10–11, 15). Cities have developed, and a leisure class has appeared in marked contrast to the poor of the land whom they are oppressing (Amos 6:4–6; 8:4–6). Instead of crude altars of earth, these folk have elaborate shrines with local priests and daily sacrifices (Amos 3:14; 4:4–5; 5:21–23; 7:10; 8:10). And they find themselves involved in wars with foreign powers so that these nations, and not just the aliens who are residing in Israel, must be related to God's will and sovereignty (Amos 1 and 2).

[15] See R. B. Y. Scott, *The Relevance of the Prophets,* New York, The Macmillan Company, 1947, pp. 160 ff.

That the moral teaching of the prophets is theocentric is clearly indicated by the characteristic manner in which they speak of themselves as being called and commissioned by God to be His mouthpieces and speak in His behalf to Israel. Thus when Amaziah, the priest of Bethel, admonishes Amos to go back to Judah and prophesy there, Amos tells him plainly why he must speak out in Bethel: "The Lord took me from following the flock, and the Lord said to me, 'Go, Prophesy to my people Israel.' Now therefore hear the word of the Lord" (Amos 7:15, 16). The word of the Lord is for Jeremiah as "a burning fire shut up in my bones" (Jer. 20:9). "And the Lord said to Isaiah, 'Go forth to meet Ahaz . . . at the end of the conduit of the upper pool on the highway to the Fuller's Field, and say to him . . .'" (Isa. 7:3).

While Amos, Hosea, Micah, and Isaiah are sometimes referred to as "the ethical prophets of the eighth century" because of their special emphasis upon God's demand for right conduct from His worshippers, these prophets were far from being more interested in ethics than they were in religion.[16] Their ethical teaching, as important as it is, was almost incidental, for they were first of all religious prophets. As Professor Snaith declares, "their insistence upon right conduct was religious in its origin, and at root was never anything else than religious."[17] Their moral teaching was derived from their understanding of God, who had revealed Himself to them as a righteous God, rather than from some rationalistic theory of virtue and the highest good for man, or from mere enthusiasm for the ideal of human equality, or some conception of the solidarity of mankind based upon such essentially humanistic notions as the organic nature of society and the prudential concept of "one world or none." The God of the prophets is not "the god of virtue" of philosophical ethical theories in the sense that He will see that human conceptions of virtue ultimately triumph; rather, He is the God whose nature reveals the ultimate norm by which all human ideals and conduct are being judged. God comes first; but because God is righteous, the prophets cannot be His spokesmen without making clear what His righteous will demands in terms of human conduct.

That prophetic morality is theocentric is further indicated by the prophets' understanding of human evil in terms of sin. *Sin* is es-

---

[16] Norman H. Snaith, *The Distinctive Ideas of the Old Testament,* London, The Epworth Press, 1944, p. 59.
[17] *Ibid.*

sentially a religious term as opposed to such categories as *offense,* *wrongdoing, immorality, vice,* and *crime.* In the Old Testament the concept has two main meanings: (1) an impersonal conception associated with taboo and (2) the personal conception of disobedience to God or rebellion against God. Under the first usage come the notions of "unclean," "accursed," and "holy."[18] The personal conception of sin as disobedience to God is far more characteristic of the Old Testament, however, and in the New Testament the impersonal conception has dropped out entirely. The conception of Israel's relationship to God in personal terms underlies both the covenant and the law even though the latter came to give increasing prominence to ritual and ceremonial requirements. As a result of the growing emphasis upon the importance of ritual, the prophets were led to protest against the tendency to confuse the formal and often irrational elements in the ceremonial law with God's moral and social demands. Thus Amos, for example, described God as hating and despising the ceremonial feasts and sacrifices which had been used to cover up Israel's disobedience to His demand for justice: "I hate, I despise your feasts, and I take no delight in your solemn assemblies. Even though you offer me your burnt offerings and cereal offerings, I will not accept them, and the peace offerings of your fatted beasts I will not look upon. Take away from me the noise of your songs; to the melody of your harps I will not listen. But let justice roll down like waters, and righteousness like an ever-flowing stream" (Amos 5:21–24).

Within the context of the meaning of sin as disobedience to God, the term is used in two more specific senses: (1) the basically ethical sense of transgressing a moral law and (2) the basically religious sense of rebellion against God. In the former case the essential consideration is the ethical concern that a code—albeit a code given by God—has been broken. In the latter case the essential concern is that the personal relationship between man and God has been estranged. A nonreligious person may speak of stealing as a transgression, but such an act has meaning as rebellion against God, as turning away from God's sovereign will, only to one who thinks in essentially religious terms. That this is the way the "ethical prophets" thought of sin is indicated by their characteristic use of the Hebrew word *pesha',* which means "rebellion" as well as "transgression," the latter being the word which is frequently used in the English transla-

[18] Millar Burrows, *An Outline of Biblical Theology,* Philadelphia, The Westminster Press, 1946, p. 165.

tions of the Old Testament.[19] Amos announces God's judgment upon the nations for their "rebellions" (Amos 1:3, 6, 9, 11, 13; 2:1, 4, 6)[20] against Him. That this is the primary meaning of sin for Amos is further indicated by his complaint that the people have not "returned" unto the Lord (Amos 4:6, 8, 9, 10, 11). Similarly, Hosea speaks of Israel as having "forsaken the Lord" (Hos. 4:10), of the Ephraimites as having "dealt faithlessly" with God (Hos. 6:7), and of their princes as "rebels" (Hos. 9:15). "Woe to them (the Ephraimites), for they have strayed from me! Destruction to them, for they have rebelled against me!" (Hos. 7:13). Here again Israel is called upon to "return to the Lord" (Hos. 6:1), for she has "stumbled because of (her) iniquity" (Hos. 14:1). Isaiah opens his prophecy with this charge against Israel: "Hear, O heavens, and give ear, O earth; for the Lord has spoken: 'Sons have I reared and brought up, but they have rebelled against me'" (Isa. 1:2). Similarly, Jeremiah in the seventh century accused Judah of having rebelled against God (Jer. 4:17) and of having "a stubborn and rebellious heart" (Jer. 5:23). Hananiah is charged with having "uttered rebellion against the Lord" (Jer. 28:16) and Babylon with having "proudly defied" God (Jer. 50:29). Likewise, the postexilic writer of the sixty-fifth chapter of Isaiah portrays God as spreading out His hands "to a rebellious people" (Isa. 65:2).

If the prophets are at one with the Covenant Code in deriving their morality from their convictions about the nature of God, the former go beyond the latter in two important ways which affect their moral teachings. In the first place they reflect a more fully developed monotheism, and in the second place they are convinced that the supreme requirement that God places upon man is that of justice. Although the acceptance of Yahweh as the sole God of Israel dates from the time of Moses, most modern scholars agree that the form of religion which he established was monolatry rather than monotheism.[21] Speculative or theoretical monotheism was first clearly enunciated in the Old Testament period by Second Isaiah (Isa. 45:21; 46:9–11); yet the faith of the eighth-century prophets included the conviction that Yahweh controlled all nations and used them for His purposes (Isa. 10:5–19; cf. Amos 6:14). While other factors contributed to the growth of a greater awareness of the monotheistic character of the

[19] Cf. Snaith, *op. cit.*, p. 64.
[20] R.S.V., "transgressions."
[21] Burrows, *op. cit.*, p. 57.

Hebrew faith, the culmination of this development came about as the result of the prophetic interpretation of history and the subsequent confirmation of this interpretation by the historical sequence of events. Not only had Yahweh punished the Gentile nations, Amos and his successors declared, but He would not spare even His chosen people. Jerusalem itself would be destroyed, notwithstanding the presence of the Temple therein (Jer. 9:11; Mic. 3:12). Hence, when the southern kingdom fell in 586 B.C., the way was prepared to accept this destruction of Judah herself as the punishment of Yahweh for her rebellion against Him rather than as the work of Marduk, the god of Babylon, who otherwise would have appeared to have overthrown Yahweh (Lam. 1:18; 2:17; 3:37–39; cf. Jer. 44:1–30). The experience of national disaster vindicated the prophets' moral interpretation of history, and their majestic understanding of God's sovereignty together with their deeper insight into the nature of His justice made possible the emergence of a monotheism that was distinctly ethical in character. Thus, during the exile in Babylon, Second Isaiah represented God as declaring, "There is no other god beside me, a righteous God and a Savior" (Isa. 45:21). Yahweh declares "the end from the beginning" and foretells things that are yet to be done; His counsel shall stand, and He will accomplish His purpose; He calls "a bird of prey from the east (and) the man of (His) counsel from a far country" (Isa. 46: 9–11).

The God whose will is sovereign among the nations as well as within Israel demands of all alike justice and righteousness; He cannot be bribed by sacrifices and peace offerings and rituals (Amos 5:21–24; Mic. 3:9–12). Profiteering, commercial dishonesty, and the oppression of the poor and needy are strongly condemned (Amos 8:4–6; cf. Mic. 6:10 ff.). Indeed, special concern is demanded for the widow and the orphan and for the poor and the needy. This does not mean, however, that there is a double standard of morality in that the needy are to receive better things and that actions that are condemned in the rich are to be condoned in the poor.[22] Rather, there is one standard for all, but since in actual practice the needy and the poor do not receive equal treatment with the powerful and the rich, they are singled out for special concern because their need is especially great. They have no redress in the courts, for the judges are unjust. Either the oppressors are themselves the judges or they control the latter through their influence and bribes. Hence the whole

[22] Snaith, *op. cit.*, p. 69.

Hebrew community is obligated to champion the cause of the oppressed, the fatherless, and the widow (Mic. 3:1; Jer. 21:12; cf. Isa. 26:9).

The accusations which the prophets make both against individuals and against nations are concrete and specific rather than abstract and general. Gaza has "carried into exile a whole people to deliver them up to Edom" (Amos 1:6). Ephraim has multiplied "falsehood and violence" and made "a bargain with Assyria" and carried oil to Egypt (Hos. 12:1). Israel will be punished because her inhabitants "sell the righteous for silver and the needy for a pair of shoes—they . . . trample the head of the poor into the dust of the earth, and turn aside the way of the afflicted" (Amos 2:6, 7). Or, again, in Israel there is "swearing, lying, killing, stealing, and committing adultery; they break all bounds and murder follows murder" (Hos. 4:2). The false prophets lead the people astray crying, "Peace" when they should be proclaiming judgment (Mic. 3:5, 8). The merchants of the city mete out dishonest weights and give scanty measures (Mic. 6:10, 11).

The prophets frequently speak of the justice which God requires of Israel in terms of her obligation to be faithful to the covenant. The covenant does not mean that Israel can rely upon this act of God's favor to guarantee her special privilege and protection against her enemies and security against internal decay. Accordingly God sternly rebukes and warns Israel: "You only have I known of all the families of the earth; therefore I will punish you for all your iniquities" (Amos 3:2). Israel has played the harlot (Hos. 3:1). She has worshipped other gods. She has not kept the requirements of the covenant. The "controversy" that God has with Israel is that there is "no faithfulness" in the land (Hos. 4:1). Therefore the day of the Lord will be "darkness, and not light" (Amos 5:18).

Despite the fact that the prophets see God's fundamental requirement as justice, and judgment as the reward for injustice, they nevertheless see the divine mercy as transcending the divine wrath. The judgment of God is not cancelled, but neither is it His final word. Israel has been like an unfaithful bride and deserves only punishment, but Yahweh promises to keep her as His bride because of His great love for her: "I will betroth you to me for ever; I will betroth you to me in righteousness and in justice, and in steadfast love, and in mercy. I will betroth you to me in faithfulness . . ." (Hos. 2:19, 20). Even Amos, who is perhaps the sternest and most relentless of all the prophets in his insistence upon the divine justice, holds out the hope that God may yet be gracious to a remnant of Joseph if this remnant will desist from evil and seek good (Amos 5:14–15).[23] Micah sees God's will ultimately triumphing in Israel. He will pardon her iniquity, for He "does not retain his anger for ever because he delights in stead-fast love" (Mic. 7:18). The new covenant which Jeremiah foretells is a covenant of mercy in a degree to which the old covenant was not, for the former will be written upon the hearts of men and they shall all know Him "from the least of them to the greatest . . . for I will forgive their iniquity, and I will remember their sin no more" (Jer. 31:31–34). But it is the unknown prophet of the Babylonian exile who most clearly sees God acting redemptively in order to save His people for His own sake: "For my name's sake I defer my anger, for the sake of my praise I restrain it for you, that I may not cut you off" (Isa. 48:9). The servant of the Lord will suffer vicariously for the wicked, and as the result of his chastisement many will be accounted righteous and healed (Isa. 53:5, 11). Israel has been chosen, not for special privilege, but to be "as a light to the nations, that my salvation may reach to the end of the earth" (Isa. 49:6). A new and eternal covenant based upon mercy will be instituted, and salvation will be freely offered to all peoples: "Turn to me and be saved, all the ends of the earth! For I am God, and there is no other. . . . 'To me every knee shall bow, every tongue shall swear' " (Isa. 45:22, 23; cf. 55:3; 56:6–8).

OTHER IMPORTANT DEVELOPMENTS

THE GROWTH OF LAW

During the earlier part of Jeremiah's ministry a great reformation of Judaism was instituted under the leadership of King Josiah in 621 B.C. The Temple had fallen into neglect, and Josiah gave orders that it be repaired. In this process there was discovered in the Temple a code of law which the king made the basis of his effort to purify the

[23] Cf. Burrows, *op. cit.,* p. 147; and Bernhard W. Anderson, *Rediscovering the Bible,* New York, Association Press, 1951, p. 115. However, some other commentators, it should be noted, view Amos 5:15 as either a later addition to the original text or as only a "logical concession" rather than a hope. See Scott (*op. cit.,* p. 129), for an expression of the latter view. Similarly, Robinson says that Amos 5:15 "anticipates Isaiah's characteristic doctrine of the righteous remnant" (*The Abingdon Bible Commentary,* New York, Abingdon-Cokesbury Press, 1929, p. 780). Amos 9:8–15 is clearly a later addition.

worship of Yahweh. This code has been preserved in Deuteronomy 12–26 and is known as the Deuteronomic Code. Evidently this was not a collection of entirely new laws but rather a revision and expansion of the Covenant Code which we have already examined. As such it reflects the social, economic, political, and religious conditions in Israel in the seventh century.

Insofar as the Deuteronomic Code deals with matters which were treated in the earlier Covenant Code the revised system of legislation manifests a somewhat less sympathetic attitude toward foreigners, a greater concern for detail in the elaboration of the law, more solicitude for the poor and the weak and offenders, and a greater concern with ritual than does the original system. On the one hand, the Deuteronomic Code specifically authorizes the taking of interest from foreigners (Deut. 23:20). On the other hand, it reflects a more highly developed and consistent humanitarian concern than does the Covenant Code. While both sets of laws prohibit keeping a man's cloak overnight as security for a loan, the later code also prohibits taking a mill or an upper millstone in pledge since the family would be left without means of preparing food (Deut. 24:6). Also, according to the Deuteronomic law, the Hebrew poor are to be aided by having their debts released (Deut. 15:1–3). The fields, vineyards, and olive trees are not to be gleaned too clean, for some of their yield is to be left for the sojourner, the widow, and the orphan. Women fare better in some respects than they did in the Covenant Code. Women slaves as well as men are to be set free every seventh year and sent out with liberal provision for their necessities (Deut. 15:12–15). A man may divorce his wife, but only if he gives her a written bill of divorcement, and then she may remarry (Deut. 24:1–2). There is an effort to qualify the *lex talionis* in the case of homicide in that provision is made for cities of refuge to which those guilty of accidental homicide may flee (Deut. 19:1–10).

Among the laws in the Deuteronomic Code dealing with new subjects the most important is the requirement that all public worship and sacrifice be centralized in the Temple at Jerusalem. This reform was apparently aimed at the worship of the Baalim, or agricultural deities of Canaan, which had continued, despite the Decalogue and the eighth-century prophets, in local shrines all over the country. The resulting centralization of worship in the Temple brought increased power and prestige to the priests as a privileged class. Other provisions of the law deal with such matters as clean and unclean animals, the payment of tithes, the conduct of the king, the waging of war, and marriage to foreigners.

On the whole the Deuteronomic Code represented an effort to fit the Covenant Code to the needs of a new day, and as such it reflects the impact of the prophets who had appeared in the interim between the two sets of legislation. Amos and Hosea, for example, had denounced the practice of religious prostitution (Amos 2:7, 8; Hos. 4:14), and the Deuteronomic Code prohibits it (Deut. 23:17). Similarly, it prohibits any juggling of weights and measures (Deut. 25:13–16) and the removal of the landmark of one's neighbor (Deut. 19:14; 27:17). Both the prophets and the Deuteronomic law sought to purify the worship of Yahweh, for both held that national survival depended upon the faithful worship of the God of Israel, but the law differed from the prophets in the importance it attached to ritual correctness. Indeed, in this respect it ran directly counter to the protests of the prophets, who had seen the extent to which ritualism had become a screen for injustice and consequently an abomination to God. The prophets had emphasized the ethical character of the worship which God required. The Deuteronomic Code, on the other hand, dealt at great length with such matters as clean and unclean foods, tithes, sacrifices, and the annual religious feasts. Moreover, the requirements relating to these were placed on the same level of importance as the requirement of justice in the life of the community. Thus the Deuteronomic Code, while attempting to perform the same basic task as the prophets, contributed through its emphasis upon ritualism to the undoing of the work of the prophets.[24]

A third major code of law, found in Leviticus 17–26, is known as the Holiness Code because of its special stress upon the holiness of Yahweh. This collection of legislation is conventionally dated from the sixth century. In it the emphasis upon ritual is carried much further than in either of the earlier codes. The interests that were of so great concern to the prophets are almost crowded out by the attention that is given to form and ceremony. Compared with the Deuteronomic Code, the Holiness Code gives a much smaller place to humanitarian and philanthropic interests. However, concern for

---

[24] It should not be forgotten, however, that these ritualistic requirements of the law of Israel helped keep the Jews from losing their religious identity with the loss of their national independence. Nevertheless, they also laid the basis for the growth of pharisaism and fanatical intolerance against adherents to other faiths. Cf. Georgia Harkness, *The Sources of Western Morality*, New York, Charles Scribner's Sons, 1954, p. 133.

Yahweh's holiness frequently issues in even higher social and ethical demands than are found in either of the earlier systems of law. Yahweh's holiness includes righteousness, and for this reason the people must be righteous as well as ceremonially pure. Thus, the remarkable chapter, Leviticus 19, which is sometimes referred to as the highest development of ethics in the Old Testament, begins: "You shall be holy; for I the Lord your God am holy" (Lev. 19:2). As in the Deuteronomic Code, provision is made for the poor and the sojourners to glean after the harvest (Lev. 19:9–10), and wages of the hired servant are not to be withheld over night (Lev. 19:13; cf. Deut. 24:15). Hatred of one's brother and vengeance against fellow Israelites are forbidden (Lev. 19:17–18). Here is found the commandment which Jesus lifted up as the second requirement of the whole law: "You shall love your neighbor as yourself" (Lev. 19:18). Even the foreigner who is sojourning in the land is to be treated as a native son; moreover, he is to be loved as oneself (Lev. 19:34). But here, also, even more than in the other sets of legislation, a host of petty requirements are set alongside of these great provisions for social justice. Thus, no flesh with blood in it is to be eaten (Lev. 19:26), and men are not to mar the edges of their beards (Lev. 19:27). Similarly, tattoo marks are forbidden in one breath, and in the next the practice of making one's daughter a harlot is condemned (Lev. 19:28, 29).

THE GROWTH OF INDIVIDUALISM

The earlier thought of the Hebrews, whether in law or in prophecy, had assumed the social solidarity of the Israelites. The loyalty of the nation as a whole to Yahweh was the important thing. The people as a whole were righteous or sinful; they kept the covenant or they played the harlot. The nation as a whole prospered or was punished; it would survive or it would be destroyed. And not only was the fate of each individual bound up with that of the entire community, but the fate of subsequent generations was also determined by the righteousness or sinfulness of the fathers, for Yahweh was a jealous God, "visiting the iniquity of the fathers upon the children to the third and the fourth generation of those who hate me, but showing steadfast love to thousands of those who love me and keep my commandments" (Exod. 20:5–6; cf. 34:7; Deut. 5:9–10). With the coming of Jeremiah and Ezekiel, however, the importance of the individual person's conduct and destiny began to receive greater attention. Jeremiah beheld a vision of a future in which men "shall no longer say, 'The fathers have eaten sour grapes, and the children's teeth are set on edge.' But every one shall die for his own sin; each man who eats sour grapes, his teeth shall be set on edge" (Jer. 31:29–30).[25] God will make a new covenant with his people: "I will put my law within them, and I will write it upon their hearts; and I will be their God, and they shall be my people" (Jer. 31:33). Isaiah of the Exile spoke of a remnant that would return unto God and be saved. But Ezekiel expressed the principle of individual responsibility most fully perhaps when he declared, "The soul that sins shall die. The son shall not suffer for the iniquity of the father, nor the father suffer for the iniquity of the son; the righteousness of the righteous shall be upon himself, and the wickedness of the wicked shall be upon himself" (Ezek. 18:20). Many of the Psalms gave poetic expression to the worth and responsibility of the individual (e.g., Psalms 1, 15, 19, 23). Finally, concern for the fate of the person found expression in the doctrine of the resurrection of the dead which was taken for granted by the Pharisees in the New Testament but which had developed very late in the Old Testament. Thus an increasing concern for the value and destiny of the individual marked the later thought of the Hebrews, but this emphasis never became so exclusive that concern for the value and well-being of the community was left out of account.[26]

THE CHANGING CONCEPTION OF DIVINE JUSTICE

The conviction underlying all biblical thought and conduct is the faith that God is sovereign and that He is just. Earlier Hebrew law and prophecy had made the further assumption that the divine justice consisted of rewarding good deeds and punishing evil ones in a way that was proportionate to the good and evil which men do, but this second assumption was in time seen to run counter to Israel's experi-

[25] Deuteronomy 24:16, in which the principle of individual responsibility is also recognized, is apparently a late addition to the Deuteronomic Code.

[26] Cf. Napier, *op. cit.,* p. 208. Even in the postexilic period of the Priestly Code, according to Professor Napier, "concern for the faithful community, for the persons in its devoted membership, is undiminished. Postexilic law just as ardently sought the well-being, the fulfilment, the salvation of the community as did the earlier law. But the dual emphasis has given way to a single primary stress: fulfilment lies in consuming devotion to cult and ritual."

ence. The wicked were seen to prosper at the expense of the righteous (Jer. 12:1–4; Ps. 73:1–14; 94:1–7; Hab. 1:2–4). The innocent were seen to suffer (Job 1–3, 29–31; Jer. 15:15–18), and Jerusalem had "received from the Lord's hand double for all her sins" (Isa. 40:2). The later prophets, Job, and some of the psalmists were thus led to reject the earlier notion that piety is rewarded in this life in terms of material prosperity. They maintained the conviction, however, that God is sovereign in this world and that He is just and righteous although His ways are so majestic and sublime that they are unfathomable by mortal man (Job 38:1–42, 6; Isa. 55:8, 9). God's justice will ultimately triumph, and its nature will be made plain (Ps. 73:16–22; Isa. 40, 41). Suffering cannot be rightly understood as divine punishment for man's transgressions; rather, it must be seen as part of a process whereby the souls of men are disciplined and tested (Deut. 8:2–5; Ps. 118:18; Prov. 3:11–12) and as the vicarious suffering of the innocent for the guilty (Isa. 52:13–53, 12). Despite the fact that faith in the resurrection of the dead had not clearly emerged as yet, these later writers gave increasingly fuller expression to the fundamental Hebrew faith in the unity and justice of God's rule, and they came more and more to understand the righteousness of God in terms of His mercy and forgiveness rather than in terms of justice conceived of as reward or punishment.

THE RISE OF APOCALYPTICISM

The fortunes of Israel among the nations and the failure of the message of the prophets and the lawgivers and sages to bring about peace and justice contributed to a deepening sense of the force and persistence of evil in the world and in human nature. As their monotheism became more explicit, the prophets saw all of the nations as subject to the one God and yet all as being in rebellion against Him. Evil had affected all so deeply that none deserved to be spared in the day of God's judgment. Hosea, it is true, expressed the hope that Israel might return unto the Lord; but Amos foresaw only the possibility that a repentant remnant of Israel might be spared (Amos 5:15). Similarly, Isaiah (Isa. 1:9; 10:20–22), Jeremiah (Jer. 44:28; cf. Jer. 31:31–34),[27] Micah (Mic. 4:6–8), and Zechariah (Zech. 8:6, 11 ff.) believed that only a remnant would be saved. Malachi

---

[27] Jeremiah's promise of a new covenant applies only to a holy remnant.

was so baffled by the prevalence of evil among his people that he cried out in anguish, "Have we not all one father? Has not one God created us? Why then are we faithless to one another, profaning the covenant of our fathers?" (Mal. 2:10). And if the prophet of the Babylonian exile proclaimed the salvation of Yahweh in more universal terms, both in the sense that Yahweh's intent was to save all men and also in the sense that he spoke of many Gentile servants of Yahweh as being drawn together from the ends of the earth, his greater hope rested not upon a smaller conception of evil but upon his greater faith that God Himself would transform and redeem those who would respond to His love and receive His mercy. Finally, attention should be called to the fact that the postexilic emphasis upon ritual law reflected a pessimism concerning the overcoming of evil in the national life while at the same time the centrality of the mercy seat as the most sacred object within the holy of holies vividly symbolized the ultimate dependence of man upon God's mercy for redemption from sin.

But the basic faith that God is sovereign and that He is just remained steadfast even while the conception of the radical nature of evil in man and in society deepened, and in the period immediately preceding the advent of Jesus there developed a new type of literature which we call the apocalypse and which is represented in the Old Testament by the book of Daniel and in the Apocrypha by such books as Enoch and II Esdras.[28] The prophets had looked for the establishment of a new age upon earth rather than for an otherworldly kingdom; but as the Hebrews continued to be oppressed and the anticipated day of their national restoration did not dawn, the conviction developed that the world was under the dominion of demonic superhuman powers which were also in rebellion against God.[29] Deliverance from these sinister powers, the apocalyptists believed, could come only through the intervention of God Himself. He would destroy the old world in a great catastrophic act and institute the new age. This event would be accompanied by the resurrection of the dead who would appear along with the living at the last judgment, after which the righteous would receive their eternal reward

[28] Examples of this form of literature in the New Testament are Mark 13 and the book of Revelation.

[29] Cf. Ephesians 6:12: "We are not contending against flesh and blood, but against the principalities, against the powers, against the world rulers of this present darkness, against the spiritual hosts of wickedness in the heavenly places."

and the wicked would be punished or destroyed. Sometimes God was pictured as acting directly to inaugurate this new age. At other times, as in the book of Enoch, He was pictured as acting indirectly through a heavenly being called the "Son of Man" (cf. Dan. 7:13). The imagery which these writers used was highly symbolic and frequently bizarre, but in essence it represented an intensification and universalization of the prophetic view of the history of Israel as a drama of rebellion, chastisement, and redemption. If the apocalyptists viewed evil as being more powerful and more universal than many of their predecessors, they also understood the power of God as being greater and the fulfillment of His purpose for the redeemed as being even more sublime and equally sure. God's complete victory over the powers of darkness would entail the transformation of the earth itself and the destruction of the powers of darkness which hold it in thrall. Hence, the emphasis in the description of the divine victory is upon a new earth rather than a restored national kingdom. Pessimism concerning this world because of the power of evil is accompanied by a profound optimism concerning God's final triumph over evil and the working out of His purpose for history. The apocalyptists add very little to the ethical insights of their forerunners, but they give eloquent testimony to an imperishable hope that springs from a profound faith in God who is the righteous Lord of history.

RECOMMENDED READINGS

Beach, Waldo, and Niebuhr, H. Richard, eds., *Christian Ethics,* New York, The Ronald Press Company, 1955, ch. I.

Burrows, Millar, *An Outline of Biblical Theology,* Philadelphia, The Westminster Press, 1946.

Eichrodt, Walther, *Man in the Old Testament,* London, Student Christian Movement Press, Ltd., 1951.

Harkness, Georgia, *The Sources of Western Morality,* New York, Charles Scribner's Sons, 1954, chs. V–VI.

Mitchell, Hinckley G., *The Ethics of the Old Testament,* Chicago, The University of Chicago Press, 1912.

Muilenburg, James, "The Ethics of the Prophet," in *Moral Principles of Action,* Ruth Nanda Anshen, ed., New York, Harper & Brothers, 1952.

Napier, B. Davie, *From Faith to Faith,* New York, Harper & Brothers, 1955, chs. II, IV–V.

Robinson, H. Wheeler, *Inspiration and Revelation in the Old Testament,* Oxford, Clarendon Press, 1946.

Scott, R. B. Y., *The Relevance of the Prophets,* New York, The Macmillan Company, 1947, chs. V–VIII.

Smith, J. M. P., *The Moral Life of the Hebrews,* Chicago, The University of Chicago Press, 1923.

Smith, J. M. P., *The Origin and History of Hebrew Law,* Chicago, The University of Chicago Press, 1931.

Snaith, Norman H., *The Distinctive Ideas of the Old Testament,* London, The Epworth Press, 1944.

chapter 3

JESUS AND THE KINGDOM OF GOD

INHERITED CONCEPTIONS OF THE KINGDOM

ALTHOUGH the actual term "Kingdom of God" is not found in the Old Testament, the idea itself runs through almost every part of it. Similarly, although outside of the Synoptic Gospels the expression is seldom used in the New Testament, Jesus' entire message focused upon the Kingdom of God (Mark 1:14–15),[1] and the idea itself is present under many different forms—as eternal life in the Fourth Gospel and as Christ mysticism in Paul, for example—throughout the whole of the New Testament. Indeed, so pervasive and central is the concept of the Kingdom of God in the thought of both the Old and the New Testaments that it constitutes one of the major unifying themes which bind the two together.[2]

In its origin, the idea of the divine kingship was closely related to the belief that Yahweh was the protector and ruler of Israel. From the beginning of Israel's worship of Yahweh, however, God was conceived of as a God of righteousness. Implicit in this faith was the recognition that Yahweh could not be concerned solely with the fate of Israel and that the enjoyment of His favor rested upon the condition that men and nations were faithful to the moral law. As we have seen, the conviction grew clearer among the prophets that the God of Israel was the Lord of the entire earth, and they foretold

[1] See Ernest F. Scott, *The Kingdom of God in the New Testament,* New York, The Macmillan Company, 1931, p. 54.
[2] John Bright, *The Kingdom of God,* New York, Abingdon-Cokesbury Press, 1953, pp. 10–11.

a day when all nations would acknowledge His sovereignty. The God of Israel was the Creator of "the ends of the earth"; He was the Judge of all the nations and all generations (Ps. 145:13); He was the Saviour who would redeem Israel and the nations and establish His righteous rule over all the earth (Isa. 45:22, 23; 49:6; 66:18–23). As yet, Yahweh was known only to Israel, but the prophets and the psalmists foretold the day when through Israel—either in the role of sovereign or in the role of the servant of Yahweh—He would establish His universal kingship.

Upon closer examination, we find that the kingship of God is conceived of in the Old Testament in three different ways.[3] In the first place, it is assumed that God is already King. He created the world and governs it with righteousness. He is the Lord of the nations and uses them, even though they do not know Him, as the instruments of His will. He is King eternally, although men are in rebellion against Him. He is sovereign even while men and nations bring judgment and disaster upon themselves by defying His righteous will. "The Lord sits enthroned as king forever" (Ps. 29:10), and amid the tumult of the fight against evil His servants can trust Him for even now He does "mighty acts": He creates and judges and redeems, and this same Lord "will reign for ever and ever" (Exod. 15:18; Ps. 99:1–4). In the second place, God's kingship is present in a special way in the lives of those who do His will. His rule is even now more fully manifest by the righteous man who obeys the law of God and thereby takes upon himself the yoke of the kingdom (Ps. 1:1–3; 74:12; cf. Ps. 23). In the third place, the kingship of God is pictured as a future reign in which His rule will be completely manifest over all the earth. This was the aspect of God's rule which found expression in the messianic hope. While this hope was expressed in a variety of ways in the Old Testament and later Judaism, it was essentially the anticipation of a new age when God would triumph over evil. In its earlier expression, it took the form of a political and national hope in which Israel would be victorious over her enemies and the former kingdom of Israel would be restored. As first it did not include the resurrection of the dead; hence, only the last generation would share in the blessing. But as the conception of evil broadened to include supernatural demonic forces as well as corrupt human powers, and as the understanding of God's justice

---

[3] C. T. Craig, *The Beginning of Christianity,* New York, Abingdon-Cokesbury Press, 1943, pp. 78–79.

and the importance of the individual deepened, the messianic hope took on the apocalyptic form and came to include belief in the resurrection. The contrast between the present age and the age to come was sharpened. The end of the present era would be presaged by persecution and dire calamities, and the coming victory of God would consist not simply in the conquest of Israel's national foes but of all of the supernatural powers of evil. The coming of the end of the present age would be accompanied by a general resurrection of the dead and a judgment in which the righteous would be separated from the wicked. Thus, according to this view, not only those living in the last days but the righteous of all times would participate in the age to come. Finally, along with the political hope and the spiritualized form of apocalyptic vision there developed in the post-Christian apocalypses and in the later rabbis a form of messianic expectation which combined elements of both of these in a "two-act drama," with a messianic kingdom on earth preceding the final eschatological consummation.[4] This combination became the most popular form of the messianic hope. The first act of the drama would take place in the present world order, and in general it corresponded to the hopes of the earlier Old Testament prophets. The Jewish exiles would be emancipated and return to Palestine, and the national kingdom would be restored and last for a period variously estimated at from forty to a thousand years. This era of national triumph would be followed by the institution of the new age in which all of the supernatural powers of evil would be overthrown and all things would be completely subjected to God's will.[5]

In summary, then, the idea of the Kingdom of God was familiar to Jesus' contemporaries. They thought of it in different ways, but essentially these ways supplemented rather than contradicted each other. Faith in the full manifestation of the Kingdom of God rested upon the knowledge of its partial manifestation within the historical order. Evidently Jesus believed in all three of the foregoing aspects of the reign of God, but he separated the concept from all that was nationalistic in it, especially in the traditional forms of the messianic hope. He transformed the concept by bringing it into relation with his own understanding of God and of the purpose of human life. He

[4] Millar Burrows, *An Outline of Biblical Theology,* Philadelphia, The Westminster Press, 1946, p. 201.
[5] For echoes of this third type of double hope in the New Testament see I Corinthians 15:22–28; Revelation 21:7–10.

emancipated the term and gave it a new and deeper meaning; but he did not need to define it, for it was the heritage of Israel and served as the focal point of his own message.[6]

THE KINGDOM OF GOD IN THE TEACHING OF JESUS

A short time before Jesus entered upon his public ministry, John the Baptist had appeared in the valley of the river Jordan proclaiming that a great crisis was at hand and summoning men to repentance. God was about to visit men in judgment, he declared: "Even now the ax is laid to the root of the trees; every tree therefore that does not bear good fruit is cut down and thrown into the fire" (Matt. 3:10). The winnowing fork was even then set to clear the threshing floor; the wheat would be gathered into the granery, and the chaff would be burned with unquenchable fire. In view of the impending judgment, the demand for repentance assumed a new urgency, for only repentance—not the fact that one was a descendant of Abraham—would suffice in the terrible day of the Lord.

Jesus was attracted to John by the latter's prophetic leadership and came to him for baptism. Indeed, Jesus looked upon himself as carrying on the work which his predecessor had begun. But while he joined in proclaiming a message which was similar in many ways to that of John, he was an independent teacher from the outset. Apparently he never became a disciple of the Baptist, for he did not practice the baptismal rite, and the manner of life and the method of teaching which he adopted were in sharp contrast to those of John.

Whereas John had pictured the coming consummation of the reign of God primarily as a terrible judgment upon sin, Jesus proclaimed it as *"good news."* John had sternly rebuked his generation, "You brood of vipers! Who warned you to flee from the wrath to

[6] Some writers—for example, Craig (*op. cit.,* p. 77), and Paul Ramsey (*Basic Christian Ethics,* New York, Charles Scribner's Sons, 1950, p. 2)—maintain that the teaching of Jesus revolves about two foci, the reign of God and the will of God, both of which he inherited through the Jewish faith. Others—for example, Scott (*op. cit.,* pp. 54, 194), and Bright (*op. cit.,* pp. 11–12)—speak of the Kingdom of God as the unifying concept. Craig and Ramsey recognize that the reign of God and the will of God are closely related, and Craig goes on to say that "God was the center which united them both." It seems unnecessary, however, to draw such a sharp dichotomy between the two terms as is suggested by "foci." When it is remembered that the Kingdom of God includes all three of the aspects outlined above, and when it is remembered that the Kingdom is *God's* Kingdom, the unity of the will and reign of God in the present and in the future becomes apparent.

come?" (Matt. 3:7); Jesus, on the other hand, represented God as desiring to give men the riches and joys of the Kingdom: "Fear not, little flock; it is your father's good pleasure to give you the kingdom" (Luke 12:32). Though the advent of the Kingdom was to be accompanied by judgment and though many would be excluded from it, it would bring the highest joy and blessedness to those who were gathered into it.

For Jesus, the Kingdom was of such great worth that a man should be willing to give all that he has in order to gain it. "The kingdom of heaven is like treasure hidden in a field, which a man found and covered up; then in his joy he goes and sells all that he has and buys that field. Again, the kingdom of heaven is like a merchant in search of fine pearls, who, on finding one pearl of great value, went and sold all that he had and bought it" (Matt. 13:44–45). The blessedness of life in the Kingdom is best described as *eternal life,* but this does not consist of endless survival; rather, it consists of a quality of life that is far superior to that of this age. Entrance into the Kingdom brings eternal life; and thus, insofar as the Kingdom is entered into now, eternal life becomes a present possession. Its fulfillment awaits the coming of the new age, however. Thus, Jesus tells his disciples that those who have left their possessions and loved ones will receive "a hundredfold now in this time" and "in the age to come eternal life" (Mark 10:29–30).

The first and most arresting proclamation that Jesus made about the Kingdom was that its consummation was *near.* While it is likely that the early Christians exaggerated the apocalyptic element in his teaching, it is impossible to understand either Jesus' career or his teaching unless we recognize that he thought of the Kingdom primarily as a future but imminent reign of God. This theme was the burden of his message when he began his public ministry in Galilee (Mark 1:14–15), and it was continually upon his lips until his last supper with the disciples when he promised reunion with them in the Kingdom of God.

Jesus' announcement of the nearness of the coming age was accompanied by a note of *extreme urgency.* Jesus had come to cast fire upon the earth and to set brother against brother. If one's hand or foot caused him to sin, he should cut it off; likewise if his eye caused him to sin, he should pluck it out, for it was better to enter the Kingdom of God maimed than with two eyes to be thrown into hell. The men of his generation were able to predict the morrow's weather, but they were unable to interpret the significance of the present times. If they had been able to do so, they would have repented at once. Just as it was prudent for the accused to attempt to settle the charge against him before he was hailed before a human magistrate, so it was the part of wisdom for men to make preparation for the divine judgment which was so close at hand (Luke 12:58–59). Let no one think that he was more righteous than the eighteen upon whom the tower of Siloam fell or the Galileans whose blood Pilate had mingled with their sacrifices! In the coming judgment all would likewise perish unless they repented (Luke 13:1–5). And the time for *repentance* was short: only one more chance was to be given. The Lord was like the owner of a barren fig tree who gave the tree one more year in which to bear fruit. If it was unfruitful then, it would be cut down.

While Jesus emphasized the nearness of the long-awaited reign of God, he refused to speculate as to the precise time of its coming. No one except God Himself knew the day or the hour of its appearing (Matt. 24:36). It was an evil and adulterous generation which sought after signs, and no sign would be given except the sign of the prophet Jonah (Matt. 12:39). As Jonah had summoned Ninevah to repent so Jesus was summoning his generation. This was the only warning of the impending crisis that would be given. If men did not heed this summons, their doom was at hand; for the coming of the Son of Man would be like a flash of lightning from heaven, and the Kingdom of God would appear suddenly in the midst of men (Luke 17:21, 24).[7]

While Jesus summoned men to prepare for the coming of the Kingdom by repentance and while he emphasized again and again that it should be the supreme object of man's striving, he never thought of it as something men might build or earn by any righteousness which they could achieve. For him the Kingdom was always in the final analysis *a gift of God*. This view is difficult for us moderns to grasp, for in the thought of the present day it has been largely replaced by the notion of a historical order which must be built by men of good will if it is ever to become a reality at all. Jesus said many things about the Kingdom: it may come; it may appear; it may be near at hand; it may be taken away; it may be given; it may be

[7] It is true that there are apocalyptic signs attributed to Jesus in the Gospels (Matt. 24, Mark 13, and Luke 23 in particular), but these are out of keeping with his customary refusal to give such signs, and they apparently represent later revisions of his original teaching.

locked up; it may be inherited; it may be expected; it may be preached; it may belong to somebody; or it may have violence done to it. People may seek it; they may go into it; or they may enter it. But in all of these relationships, it is dependent upon God. It is ultimately a gift, not something that men build.

The parables of the mustard seed and the leaven are frequently interpreted to imply a gradual evolutionary development of the Kingdom; but in view of the abundant evidence that Jesus believed that the coming age would break in upon men soon and suddenly, it is clear that the point of both parables is the contrast between the small beginnings in the tiny mustard seed and the little yeast on the one hand and the large endings in a great tree and three measures of leavened meal on the other. In either case these results are brought about, not by man's activity but by the power of God. Similarly, in the parable of the self-growing seed (Mark 4:26–29) Jesus likened the Kingdom to a situation in which a man planted seed in the ground. The seed mysteriously sprouted and grew until the harvest, and when the grain was ripe the farmer harvested the wheat. The point of the parable does not lie in tracing the successive steps of growth: the blade, the ear, and the full grain in the ear. Rather, it is that the Kingdom is just as dependent upon God as is every harvest of grain. The seed grew of itself, man knew not how; man's efforts did not make it grow—it grew night and day, while the sower of the seed slept as well as when he was awake. Similarly, the Kingdom rests upon God, not upon man's efforts, and He alone can send it.[8]

CONDITIONS FOR ENTERING THE KINGDOM

Since in the last analysis the Kingdom is sent by God, the most that man can do is to enter it. But, as we have seen, in order to be prepared to enter it, man must *repent*. For Jesus, as for the prophets of old and for John the Baptist, this meant something far more than a feeling of remorse for one's sins and one's worldly way of life. It meant an about-face on the part of the self, a change in the direction one was going, a turning away from one's sin and worldly way of life and a turning toward a new life. No man can serve both God and Mammon. Those who were serving Mammon needed first of all to repent. If they did not, this was a sign that they did not really

[8] Craig, *op. cit.*, pp. 88–89.

desire to enter the Kingdom. The choice was theirs, but God had sent a preacher of repentance to proclaim the good news of the Kingdom and call men to enter into its joys and blessedness.

Jesus' demand for repentance was similar to that of John the Baptist, as we have seen, but it was different in one important respect, for repentance had a deeper meaning for Jesus than for John. The Baptist's demand was for a change in man's outward behavior. Jesus, on the other hand, considered repentance worthless unless it signified a radical change of mind and will. Outward obedience to the will of God would not suffice. An inner transformation was needed so that men would freely and gladly submit themselves to the divine will.[9] So radical was the change which was required of man that the Fourth Gospel represents Jesus as saying that only those who have been born anew—born of the Spirit—can enter the Kingdom of God (John 3:3, 5).

Nowhere did Jesus seem more revolutionary to his hearers than in his description of those who stood in need of repentance before they could enter the Kingdom. It was easier for a camel to go through the eye of a needle than for the rich to enter the Kingdom, so far was Jesus from considering riches to be a sign of God's favor. The covetous and the proud would be rejected unless they experienced a transformation whereby the former desired to be servants of all and the latter were able to discern their need for repentance and healing. The scribes and the Pharisees—the wise men steeped in the knowledge of the Torah and the devout men who scrupulously tried to fulfill the detailed requirements of the law—needed to repent even more than the publicans and harlots who made no pretense of being righteous. Neither could the children of Israel rely on their religious heritage to guarantee them a place of special favor in the coming age. Indeed, many would come from the East and from the West and sit at the banquet table with Abraham, Isaac, and Jacob in the Kingdom, while the sons of the Kingdom would be thrown into the outer darkness (Matt. 8:11–12). Instead of promising the Kingdom to those who believed themselves to be secure in their own virtue and righteousness, Jesus pronounced its blessing upon the poor in spirit, upon those who hungered and thirsted after righteousness, upon the unpretentious, upon those who were as receptive as a little child, and upon those who lost their lives in unselfish service.

⁹ E. F. Scott, *The Kingdom and the Messiah*, Edinburgh, T. & T. Clark, 1911, pp. 118–119.

As we have seen, the call to repentance was urgent. It was also a present summons. Instead of giving men a series of signs which would serve as a warning as to when they should prepare for the Lord's coming, Jesus declared that they should be like faithful servants who were always ready for their master's return (Luke 12:35–40) or like wise maidens who had put oil in their lamps so that they would be ready to go in to the marriage feast whenever the bridegroom came (Matt. 25:1–13).

Jesus' demand for repentance was closely related to his demand for *faith,* and faith for him was much more than believing that God exists. It was putting one's trust in Him. This meant the grateful recognition of man's dependence upon God for the meeting of all of his daily needs both of body and of spirit. It meant having confidence that God loves all of His children and is seeking to save those who are lost. It meant believing that the God who is Creator and King is a heavenly Father who is willing to show compassion upon man and who is ever ready to give good gifts to those who ask Him. Only when one thus accepts his complete dependence upon God and entrusts himself to Him is he able to accept forgiveness and receive the Kingdom as a gift. Only then is he able to lose his life for Christ's sake and the Gospel's sake (Mark 8:35), for only then does he know that he can trust his own future to God.

A third and final condition which Jesus set forth for entrance into the Kingdom was *obedience.* As trees are known by their fruits, so men are known by their deeds. It is not those who say, "Lord, Lord" who shall enter the Kingdom but those who do the will of the Father who is in heaven (Matt. 7:21). The Kingdom is first of all, as we have seen, a gift, but it is also a demand. Men are free to accept or to reject the divine generosity; but if they accept it, both their deeds and their inmost being must be changed radically. The obedience which is required is not, however, something that men can perform of themselves by their own efforts. Rather, that which is demanded is also given before it is demanded and continually bestowed while it is demanded. Men are to forgive, but their ability to forgive is based upon the fact that they are themselves forgiven. Men are to show love, mercy, and kindness, but before these are required they are received as gifts from God who embodies these attributes. God has taken the initiative in offering the Kingdom, but man must still respond by repentance, by faith, and by obedience if he is to receive it. God will establish the Kingdom in His own good time, but men must decide here and now whether they will, with God's help, meet its conditions and reap its fruits.

We have said that Jesus assumed that man is free to accept or to reject the Kingdom. He did not mean that man could take it or leave it without reaping the consequences of his choice. Rather, man is free in the sense that the responsibility for his choice is his own. Jesus invited men to accept the Kingdom, but this very invitation confronted them with the necessity of making a decision either for it or against it. The decision which each makes in this crisis determines his eternal destiny. Those who reject the Kingdom will reap everlasting misery and death, for they have chosen to violate the inviolable law of God. Those who accept it will reap everlasting happiness and life, for they thereby become children of the heavenly Father. "Everyone then who hears these words of mine and does them will be like a wise man who built his house upon the rock; and the rain fell, and the floods came, and the winds blew and beat upon that house, but it did not fall, because it had been founded on the rock. And everyone who hears these words of mine and does not do them will be like a foolish man who built his house upon the sand; and the rain fell, and the floods came, and the winds blew and beat against that house, and it fell; and great was the fall of it" (Matt. 7:24–27).

THE RELATION OF JESUS TO THE KINGDOM

One of the most puzzling questions in the study of the Gospels has to do with Jesus' own conception of his relation to the Kingdom. The earliest tradition in the Gospels dealing with the messianic consciousness of Jesus is found in Mark. He assigns the incident to a time shortly after the conclusion of the Galilean period of Jesus' ministry and locates it in the region of Caesarea Philippi. Mark represents Jesus as inquiring of his disciples, "Who do men say that I am?" Up to this time the message of Jesus had dealt with the coming of the Kingdom of God and entrance into it. He had not previously spoken of his own relation to it. Now for the first time he raised the question privately with his closest followers. Judging from their replies, Jesus had been variously identified with John the Baptist, with Elijah, and with one of the prophets. But when he asked the disciples their opinion, Peter replied, "You are the Christ." Jesus then charged them to tell no one (Mark 8:27–30).[10] According to Mark, Jesus neither accepted nor denied Peter's confession but instead went on to tell of the suffering of the Son of Man and of his rejection by the elders and the chief priests and the scribes. His followers would likewise be called upon to suffer, but they would gain their lives in the new age when the Son of Man would come in his glory. For Mark, the messiahship of Jesus was a secret which he refused to divulge until the very end, and then only when asked directly by the high priest at the trial if he were the Christ (Mark 14:61–62).

Some New Testament scholars have explained Jesus' refusal publicly to proclaim his messiahship on the ground that such a claim would have been misunderstood because of the political and materialistic connotations of the title. Since he repudiated any conception of his mission in terms of the establishment of an earthly nationalistic kingdom, he refrained from claiming for himself a role to which the masses gave such a different interpretation from that which he himself held. He was convinced that his suffering, like that of the suffering servant of Second Isaiah, was somehow necessary for the salvation of the lost. After his death at the hands of the religious and political leaders, God would send the heavenly Son of Man in the clouds with great power and glory to gather the elect into the Kingdom and inaugurate the new age. According to this view, Jesus identified himself in some way with this apocalyptic heavenly being who would come in the future, but he interpreted his earthly mission in the light of the servant passages in the Second Isaiah. It is impossible for us to recover the psychological processes by which Jesus held these two roles together, but the evidence of the gospels is, according to this interpretation, that he thought of himself in both of these ways. "For the Son of man also came not to be served but to serve, and to give His life as a ransom for many" (Mark 10:45).

Other scholars take the position that belief in the messiahship of Jesus arose after his death. The messianic secret was, in this view, a device which the evangelists used for reading back into the life of Jesus the faith of the later church. Since for this reason the messiahship of Jesus could scarcely be assigned to his public preaching, it was presented as a secret during his lifetime. In support of this

[10] Matthew gives a later tradition according to which Jesus commended Peter's confession and declared it to be the foundation of the Church (Matt. 16:17–18).

view, it is argued that the account of the transfiguration of Jesus on a mountain in the presence of three of his closest disciples is a resurrection story dated back into the period of his earthly life. Moses and Elijah, it will be remembered, appeared with Jesus on the mountain. On the way down Jesus charged the disciples "to tell no one what they had seen, until the Son of Man should have risen from the dead" (Mark 9:2–9). Similarly, those who defend this interpretation assume that the charge against Jesus that he was "king of the Jews" amounted simply to the accusation that he was an insurrectionist and resulted from the indiscreet conduct of his disciples. During his lifetime no one, including himself, had looked to him as the Messiah. He had only preached the nearness of the Kingdom; it was the later church which, looking back from the vantage point of the resurrection appearances, affirmed that he was the long-expected Messiah.

While we shall probably never be able to know for a certainty whether Jesus thought of himself either as the Messiah or as the apocalyptic heavenly Son of Man, there can be little doubt that from the beginning of his public ministry he spoke with authority, offered men forgiveness of their sins, and assumed the right to admit men to the Kingdom. "Whoever receives one such child in my name receives me; and whoever receives me, receives not me but him who sent me" (Mark 9:37). He summoned men to follow him as a sign of their loyalty to the Kingdom. To give one's life for him was to give it for the Gospel. Whoever was ashamed of him and of his words would find that the Son of Man would likewise be ashamed of him when the new age was established. He believed the powers of this future Kingdom to be active in himself so that he could cast out demons and heal the sick. When he challenged the moneychangers in the Temple (Mark 11:15–18), the religious leaders in the parable of the vineyard (Mark 12:1–12), and the scribes as he taught in the Temple (Mark 12:38–40), he seemed convinced that his action and his words had behind them the authority of God and His Kingdom.

It is almost impossible plausibly to explain the relationship between Jesus' proclamation that the Kingdom was at hand and his journey to Jerusalem deliberately to permit himself to be put to death if one denies any messianic consciousness on the part of Jesus.[11] It is extremely difficult to escape the conclusion that he conceived it to be his mission to perform the decisive act through which God would inaugu-

[11] Reginald H. Fuller, *The Mission and Achievement of Jesus,* Chicago, Alec R. Allenson, 1954, pp. 54–55.

rate the coming reign of God which he proclaimed.[12] But it seems probable, however, as Manson declares, that Jesus only gradually and at a relatively late stage in his ministry reached the conviction that his mission was to perform the work of the Messiah, and that this work involved his own suffering and death. Nevertheless, this work appeared necessary before the Son of Man could be exalted, and it had redemptive significance.

Not only does it seem necessary to assume some messianic consciousness on the part of Jesus in order to understand his own action during the last weeks of his life, but this assumption is required in order to explain the rise of the faith of Christians that Jesus was the Messiah. If Jesus had not prepared his most intimate followers for the events which were to follow his journey up to Jerusalem by identifying himself with the Messiah and the Son of Man who would come in glory to bring the Kingdom, it is difficult to understand how the early Christians could have found in his death and resurrection the supreme assurance of forgiveness of their sins and the promise of salvation. That with the memory of his life and his death both fresh in their minds they affirmed that Jesus was indeed the Messiah is incontrovertible. That they saw in his life and death and resurrection the work of God reconciling the world unto Himself and triumphing over evil and that they saw in these beginning acts of salvation the pledge of an ultimate fulfillment in the new age which the vindicated Christ would usher in is the heart of the message which the evangelists proclaimed and which Christians continue to declare as the good news. The early Christians and the Church were able to proclaim that God had acted decisively in Jesus because he himself had declared within the circle of his disciples that He was about to act decisively in him.[13]

[12] Cf. Scott, *The Kingdom of God in the New Testament,* pp. 119–128; Bright, *op. cit.,* p. 198; Craig, *op. cit.,* pp. 122–123; William Manson, *Jesus the Messiah,* Philadelphia, the Westminster Press, 1946, pp. 34, 177, 197; Fuller, *op. cit.,* ch. III. Among those holding the view that Jesus made no messianic claims for himself are Rudolf Bultmann (*Theology of the New Testament,* I, trans. by Kendrick Grobel, New York, Charles Scribner's Sons, 1951, pp. 26–32) and Frederick C. Grant (*The Gospel of the Kingdom,* New York, The Macmillan Company, 1940, ch. 4).

[13] Cf. Fuller, *op. cit., pp.* 116–117; Craig, *op. cit.,* p. 123; Manson *op. cit.,* p. 177; Scott, *The Kingdom of God in the New Testament,* pp. 127–128.

THE APOCALYPTIC ELEMENT IN JESUS' TEACHING

In view of the fact that Jesus' expectation that the Kingdom of God would be consummated in the near future was not fulfilled, the question inevitably arises: What is the relation of his message as a whole to this expectation? While this issue confronted the early Christians of the New Testament period, it had a somewhat different implication for them than it has for us. Jesus' apocalyptic predictions had been general. He had refused to set a specific time for the coming of the new age, and his main concern had been to announce its coming and to call men to repentance in preparation for the judgment which would accompany its inauguration. Many of Jesus' followers made this generalized hope more specific by speculating on signs and setting up a more specific timetable. Paul was faced with this sort of problem, and with the inevitable disillusionment resulting from such speculation, in some of the churches which he founded. Indeed, Paul himself, when he wrote First Corinthians, had confidently expected the consummation of the Kingdom within his own lifetime, but he later recognized that he might have been mistaken. That the end was coming soon he continued to believe, but it might be delayed (II Thess. 2:3–12). Thus it was not so much a question of Jesus' misconception which perplexed Paul, for he had not set a particular year; rather, it was only a matter of the delay of the end.

The author of the Fourth Gospel, writing later than the authors of the Synoptic Gospels, also dealt with the implications of the apocalyptic elements in Jesus' teaching. For him, however, it was not so much a question of whether Jesus' views would be fulfilled as of how they were meant to be interpreted. For the most part this evangelist spiritualized those elements in Jesus' teaching. Eternal life was, for him, a present state of blessedness into which man might enter here and now by being born anew, and because of its quality it would endure forever. He who believes on Jesus has life eternal (John 6:47). The resurrection does not wait until "the last day," as Martha supposed, for Jesus declares, "I am the resurrection and the life; he who believes in me, though he die, yet shall he live, and whoever lives and believes in me shall never die" (John 11:25–26). Similarly, the divine judgment no longer appears primarily as an eschatological crisis but rather as a present reality (John 5:24). The judgment consists of the fact that the true light has come into the world and yet men choose the darkness rather than the light because their deeds are evil (John 3:19). Thus, while some references to a future judgment appear in the Fourth Gospel, these are of secondary importance, and the apocalyptic element in Jesus' teaching is clearly subordinated to the present transformation of life which is possible for the believer in this age.

Throughout most of the history of the Church it has been held that the end of the present order of history would be brought about by the catastrophic intervention of God through the agency of Christ who would come again in power and glory and establish the Kingdom. The return of Jesus might be delayed, but it was certain to come. Toward the end of the nineteenth century, however, this answer began to appear to be no longer acceptable to many biblical scholars. The reasons for this were rooted in part in the growth of evolutionary conceptions of the development of man and nature (God), the related ideas of inevitable and unlimited progress, and the impact of rationalism. Factors such as these contributed to the development of the so-called liberal movement in biblical scholarship. The latter, in turn, issued in an attempt to modernize Jesus and led some scholars to reject all of the eschatological references of Jesus in Mark as having been read back into the record by the later Church. Albert Schweitzer was alarmed by this, in his view, irresponsible treatment of the sources and this tendency to modernize Jesus and present him purely as a prophet. Thus he was led to challenge this liberal criticism. He defended the eschatological elements in the teaching of Jesus as authentic. Jesus cannot be properly understood, he believed, in the categories of modern man with his contemporary scientific and cosmological views; rather, he must be understood in terms of the categories and thought patterns of his own culture. Schweitzer's purpose was to vindicate the biblical records as reliable and to establish the true greatness of Jesus as over against the liberal school.[14]

Most New Testament scholars today accept Schweitzer's main contention: viz., that a whole flood of light is thrown upon Jesus and his teaching as well as upon that of the early Church if it is recognized that he expected the new age to come in his own generation. To make this assumption is, however, to raise the question as to whether Jesus' teaching as a whole is thereby discredited. The way in which we

[14] Amos Wilder, *Eschatology and Ethics in the Teaching of Jesus,* New York, Harper & Brothers, rev. ed., 1950, pp. 37–39.

answer this question will depend upon the way in which we view the relationship of his apocalyptic views to the rest of his teaching.

Schweitzer himself argued that since Jesus' eschatological views left no room for a continuing historical order, the sole aim of his ethical teaching was to provide an "interim ethic"—that is, an ethic that would be valid only during the short interval before the coming of the Kingdom. He held that Jesus conceived of the Kingdom entirely as a future reign of God and that the ethic which he taught was valid only because this reign was so imminent. Jesus' indifference to the family, to the state, and to property resulted from his belief that this historical order would shortly be brought to an end. Moreover, Jesus did not seek to describe how men would act in the coming age. His teaching was evidently intended for life in this world where there is need to turn the other cheek and to forgive seventy times seven rather than for life in the Kingdom where there will be no more evil. This teaching was intended only to show men how they should live in the brief span before the great crisis. Hence it is not applicable to our culture when these apocalytic views are no longer held, and it has no absolute validity.

While generally agreeing with Schweitzer that Jesus expected the new age to come soon, later biblical scholarship has concluded that Schweitzer's "interim ethic" must be rejected for three main reasons. In the first place, it overlooks the present character of the Kingdom in Jesus' teaching. That the age to come was already breaking in upon the present era was evidenced, Jesus believed, by his own ministry of exorcism, healing, and witnessing and by the response which his ministry awakened. Jesus' conception of the Kingdom was essentially eschatological in the sense that the meaning and purpose of history were to be revealed at the end of the present historical order when God would overthrow evil and establish His Kingdom wherein righteousness would dwell, but it was not an entirely future reign. The great redemptive work of God, to which Jesus witnessed and of which he felt himself to be a part, was under way and moving toward its climax.[15] The "eschaton"—i.e., the end—was arriving, and when it was fully come, the Kingdom of God would be present in power.

[15] *Ibid.*, pp. 50–51.
C. H. Dodd, *The Parables of the Kingdom*, New York, Charles Scribner's Sons, 1936, pp. 51 ff. Dodd advanced the thesis that Jesus taught that the Kingdom had already arrived and was implicit in his own work and death. The apocalyptic judgment and the establishment of the new age would follow immediately, but the essential meaning of Jesus' eschatological declarations

In the second place, even if all of Jesus' moral teaching is interpreted as the short term demands of such an "interim," it is difficult to escape the conclusion that there is something absolute about it—something that is valid for all time and relevant to life in the Kingdom. For example, his teachings about humility, about love, about integrity—these would seem to be normative for life in the Kingdom insofar as that is a moral order. And Schweitzer's own life bears eloquent testimony to his own personal conviction that Jesus' teachings have a profound relevance for the conduct of modern man, even when he no longer considers himself to be living in the "interim" for which they were formulated. Indeed, Schweitzer's own impressive words at the conclusion of his great work, *The Quest of the Historical Jesus,* indicate the permanent and existential significance of Jesus—who is in fact inseparable from his ethical teachings—for the moral life. One suspects, moreover, that Schweitzer's Master is hardly as "unknown" as he suggests: "He comes to us as One unknown, without a name, as of old, by the lakeside, He came to those who knew Him not. He speaks to us the same word: 'Follow thou me!' and sets us to the tasks which He has to fulfil for our time. He commands. And to those who obey Him, whether they be wise or simple, He will reveal Himself in the toils, the conflicts, the sufferings which they shall pass through in His fellowship. . . . ."[16]

A third reason why this view of an "interim ethic" is inadmissible is that it rests upon the erroneous assumption that Jesus' intention was to prescribe a set of rigid rules.[17] As we shall see in a later section of our study, Jesus set himself squarely against such an understanding of God's will in his criticism of pharisaic legalism.

THE SIGNIFICANCE OF ESCHATOLOGY
IN JESUS' ETHICAL TEACHING

We have concluded that Jesus *intended* that his moral teaching serve as a guide for his followers during his lifetime, and that he also

was already fulfilled in his own lifetime in the revelation of the reign of God in himself and in his ministry. Dodd's concept of "realized eschatology" is not, however, generally accepted by present-day New Testament scholars. The prevailing view today is that Jesus taught both the present and the future aspects of the Kingdom.

[16] Albert Schweitzer, *The Quest of the Historical Jesus,* New York, The Macmillan Company, 1955, p. 403.

[17] E. F. Scott, *The Ethical Teaching of Jesus,* New York, The Macmillan Company, 1924, p. 43.

viewed it as being relevant to life in the future Kingdom which was in some sense already present, but the question whether the authority of this ethic is undermined *for us* by the failure of his apocalyptic expectations must now be faced squarely. Jesus intended it to be binding in his generation, but should we consider it binding in our modern day? Would it be valid for us if we believed the end of the present age to be coming in our own lifetime in a way in which it is not valid for us today?

The key to the answer to this question is to be found in the nature of apocalypticism and eschatology. The essence of apocalypticism, as was suggested at the conclusion of the last chapter, consists in the affirmation that, no matter how evil the times may be, God is still Lord and His Kingdom will ultimately prevail. The same thing is true of eschatology, which may be more generalized and less detailed than apocalypticism generally, although the latter is itself a form of eschatology. Both are forms of myth which express in religious terms what faith believes the unknown future to hold in store. They are imaginative pictures of what is going to happen just as another type of myth—that of Genesis 1–3, for example—depicts the unknown origins of the race and sin. That they were meant to be taken symbolically and not literally is evidenced by the variety of apocalyptic pictures which were accepted in the orthodox circles of Jesus' day and by the inconsistent and bizarre character of many of the portrayals of the events which would precede the end of the present age. Extremely detailed and realistic imagery was employed to emphasize the genuineness of the author's religious experience; moreover, the foreshortening of the time before the end was an almost inevitable consequence of the vivid apprehension of the final outcome of the struggle against evil. Indeed, the imminence with which the coming of the end was viewed was directly proportionate to the intensity of the faith which gave rise to it.[18] The spiritual truth which was being declared was the important thing; the timing of faith's fulfillment was relatively incidental. The essence of the apocalyptic and eschatological hope in Judaism, as in the thought of Jesus, lay in the protest "of the ethical consciousness against things as they are, and the incontrovertible assurance of faith that God will act."[19]

Viewed in this light, it is clear that the fundamental message of Jesus does not depend upon the particular forms in which he ex-

[18] Wilder, *op. cit.,* p. 24.
[19] *Ibid.,* p. 36.

pressed it. Just as his words have been translated out of the Aramaic language in which they were uttered, so in a sense they can be detached from the apocalyptic expectations which had been given him along with his mother tongue.[20] By means of the conventional apocalyptic forms he taught a message of permanent value.

This does not mean, however, that the apocalyptic and eschatological elements in Jesus' teaching are merely incidental and have no importance in themselves as symbols or artistic expressions of such religious truth and faith. On the contrary, these forms have a more enduring value and appeal than do abstract, literalistic formulations of philosophical, metaphysical, and theological concepts. For this reason they give vivid and concrete expression both to the sanction and to the stimulus, or motivation, which underlie his ethic.[21] They point to the God who is behind, and guarantees, the apocalyptic Judgment and eschatological Kingdom, and they confront man concretely with the fact that he, whether he wills it so or not, stands judged by the perfect will of God. It is true that the eschatological sanction and motivation are formal and secondary, but they are natural appeals for a religious mind. The ultimate sanction for Jesus' ethic is the righteousness of God, and the fundamental motivation for doing God's will is the religious-prophetic motivation of gratitude, obedience, the discernment of moral truth, and the desire to act worthily of those who are the sons of the Heavenly Father.[22]

It follows, then, that Jesus' ethic is absolute in some sense. It represents the radical will of God which will ultimately be done when His Kingdom is fully come, but it also represents His will for men in this present historical order. Even the most difficult sayings of the Sermon on the Mount serve the important function of making men aware of the perfect will of God, whether they are able to do it in a sinful world or not. If they cannot perform the perfect divine will, they can nevertheless be transformed by it.[23] In this connection it must be remembered that for Jesus the standard for human conduct is the eternal will of God, not human ability (cf. Matt. 19:26). The ability to keep the ethic of Jesus is a power which is given by grace through faith; it is not an ability which is inherent in man inde-

---

[20] Scott, *The Kingdom of God in the New Testament*, p. 116.
[21] Martin Dibelius, *The Sermon on the Mount*, New York, Charles Scribner's Sons, 1940, pp. 97, 135; Wilder, *op. cit.*, pp. 187–188.
[22] Wilder, *op. cit.*, pp. 133, 140–141.
[23] Dibelius, *op. cit.*, pp. 135–136.

pendent of God. Where men through faith are able to, and do, fulfill the divine will, the Kingdom is come among them and their obedience shows them to be sons of the Kingdom; but wherever they do not fulfill the divine will there the Kingdom lies in the future, and there men are judged by it and by the ethic of Jesus. In a word, the Kingdom is both present and future, and it comes both with the promise of blessedness to those who receive it and with the pronouncement of judgment upon all who refuse to acknowledge its demands.[24]

The difficulties in the way of the application of this ethic in a sinful world, the issue of law and freedom, the relation of this ethic to the pressing social problems of our day—these are matters which will occupy our attention in subsequent sections of our study. Indeed, an examination of Christian ethics as understood by Paul, in addition to clarifying the content of Jesus' moral teaching, will offer much helpful guidance in the application of this teaching to problems and circumstances that are different from those to which Jesus directly addressed himself in many of his particular sayings.

---

[24] The problem with which we have dealt here in terms of the bearing of Jesus' apocalyptic opinions upon his ethics is fundamentally, of course, a christological problem. Christian ethics is clearly theologically rooted, as we have emphasized. Therefore, it may be helpful to suggest the general way in which the relation of Jesus' human nature and his divine nature is here conceived and also to suggest that, considered in this light, there has been an implied recognition of the limitation of Jesus' scientific and cosmological knowledge in classical, or orthodox, Christian theology from the beginning.

It is significant that Jesus viewed himself as speaking with the authority of God and the Kingdom and yet he confessed that he did not know the day and the hour wherein the Kingdom would come (Matt. 24:36). The author of Luke seems to have considered it most natural that the child Jesus should have grown in wisdom, for he wrote: "And the child grew and became strong, filled with wisdom" (Luke 2:40). In Greek this last phrase means "becoming full of wisdom."

The Church has from the beginning insisted that God became incarnate in the man Jesus of Nazareth. Jesus' human nature was declared to have been real just as surely as was his divine nature. God chose to reveal Himself in time—in a particular person who lived in a particular century in a particular culture. The purpose of the Incarnation was not to reveal to men scientific or historical truth but rather a knowledge of God, of man, and of God's will for man. Jesus simply accepted the world view of his contemporaries as the prophets before him had done in their day. Such limitation was the result of his human nature just as much as were the experiences of hungering, thirsting, growing weary, and suffering physical death. Jesus' teaching about God, man, and God's will were not dependent upon his apocalyptic views. Rather, they were derived from the religious heritage of Israel and his own religious consciousness. The apocalyptic views of his day served essentially as a framework for presenting his fundamental message.

RECOMMENDED READINGS

Bultmann, Rudolf, *Jesus and the Word,* New York, Charles Scribner's Sons, 1934, chs. II–III.

Craig, C. T., *The Beginning of Christianity,* New York, Abingdon-Cokesbury Press, 1943, chs. V–VII.

Dibelius, Martin, *Jesus,* Philadelphia, The Westminster Press, 1949, chs. V–X.

Dibelius, Martin, *The Sermon on the Mount,* New York, Charles Scribner's Sons, 1940.

Dodd, C. H., "The Ethics of the New Testament" in *Moral Principles of Action,* Ruth Nanda Anshen, ed., New York, Harper & Brothers, 1952.

Dodd, C. H., *Gospel and Law,* New York, Columbia University Press, 1951.

Dodd, C. H., *The Parables of the Kingdom,* New York, Charles Scribner's Sons, 1936, ch. II.

Manson, T. W., *The Teachings of Jesus,* Cambridge, Cambridge University Press, 2nd ed., 1951, chs. IV–IX.

Marshall, L. H., *The Challenge of New Testament Ethics,* New York, The Macmillan Company, 1947, chs. I–VI.

Ramsey, Paul, *Basic Christian Ethics,* New York, Charles Scribner's Sons, 1950, chs. I–II.

Scott, C. A. A., *New Testament Ethics,* London, Cambridge University Press, 1930, Lectures I–III.

Scott, E. F., *The Ethical Teaching of Jesus,* New York, The Macmillan Company, 1924.

Scott, E. F., *The Kingdom of God in the New Testament,* New York, The Macmillan Company, 1931, ch. II.

Wilder, Amos, *Eschatology and Ethics in the Teaching of Jesus,* New York, Harper & Brothers, rev. ed., 1950.

Windisch, Hans, *The Meaning of the Sermon on the Mount,* Philadelphia, The Westminster Press, 1951.

chapter 4

CHRISTIAN ETHICS IN PAUL

THE UNIVERSAL HUMAN SITUATION

THE person in the New Testament who, next to Jesus, has influenced the ethical thought of Christians most profoundly is Paul, and it is he, more than any other apostle, who helped to transform the new faith from a Jewish sect into a world faith. But Paul was able to interpret the mind of his Master so convincingly and to change the early Christian community into a church with a world-wide view only because he had himself passed through a correspondingly transforming and liberating experience in his conversion from Judaism to Christianity.

Paul tells us that prior to his conversion he had been a member of the strict Jewish party of the Pharisees. He had studied the ancestral law in the school of Gamaliel and had been extremely zealous in his effort to keep its requirements. And when the new sect of the followers of Jesus arose and proclaimed as the long-awaited Messiah an itinerant preacher from Galilee who had scandalized the religious leaders of the day by his highly critical attitude toward the Law and the Temple, Paul devoted himself zealously and effectively to the suppression of this heresy in and about Jerusalem. Eventually he was given the assignment to go to the local synagogue in Damascus to wipe out the blasphemous Galileans who were making inroads there. But on his way to Damascus something happened to Paul that caused him to make an about-face both in regard to the goal of his work and in regard to the method which he employed. Instead of carrying out his commission to stamp out the new faith, he gave himself completely to the preaching of the lordship of the lowly Nazarene whose followers he had so recently oppressed. But there was a difference between the method which he now used and that which he had formerly employed, for now he no longer attempted to win converts by threat of imprisonment and scourging and death; rather, he relied upon the power of the Gospel which he proclaimed to draw men to Christ.

What was the meaning of this shattering and transforming experience of Paul? How did he interpret his new faith? In what ways was it superior to that of Judaism? As we attempt to answer these questions, it will be helpful to bear in mind that the central and inclusive concept in Paul's understanding of Christianity is salvation.[1] The effort is sometimes made to explain Paul's interest in salvation by the influence of the mystery cults which were current in his day in the Hellenic world. Not only is it unnecessary, however, to look for such an explanation of his concern with salvation outside of Judaism, in view of the prominence of this theme in the Old Testament; but it is also abundantly clear that Paul's thought was much more closely akin to the Hebrew than to the Hellenistic conception of salvation. For one thing, whereas the Greek view was exclusively individualistic, Paul's concern was with a corporate experience made possible by the fact that God had dealt redemptively with humanity. In this respect it resembled the Jewish conceptions of the Kingdom of God rather than the mystery cults. Further, in the mystery religions far greater importance was attached to the performance of physical acts whereby certain spiritual effects could be attained.[2] Especially was this true of particular sacramental acts which united the religious devotee with his dying and rising savior-god. Sometimes this union was thought of as involving a substantive change in the worshipper in that through participation in the sacrament the believer acquired an immortal essence from the deity with which he was united. While Paul considered baptism a most suggestive analogy of the change wrought in the believer through faith, he insisted that outward baptism was of no value unless it was the symbol of a real inward experience of dying to sin and rising with Christ to a new life (Rom. 6:1–4; cf. Col. 2:12).

In order to understand Paul's conception of Christianity, we need to see why, in his view, man needs to be saved. As Paul analyzed the

[1] Cf. C. A. A. Scott, *Christianity According to St. Paul,* London, Cambridge University Press, 1932, p. 16.
[2] C. H. Dodd, *The Meaning of Paul for Today,* London, George Allen and Unwin, Ltd., 1949, pp. 118–119.

moral situation of man from his standpoint as a Christian, he saw
that all men are in bondage to forces of evil. Unlike Socrates, he
believed that man's great moral problem is not that of knowledge
but rather that of will. It is the dilemma of knowing the good but not
having the will to do it: "For I do not do the good I want, but the
evil I do not want is what I do" (Rom. 7:19). This, Paul declares,
is a universal problem. It is the dilemma of the Pharisees, the strict
sect to which he had formerly belonged and which Jesus had severely
criticized for their hypocrisy in practicing virtue in order to win the
praise of men and for binding heavy burdens on men's backs by
elaborating detailed requirements in regard to minor matters while
neglecting the "weightier matters of the law, justice and mercy and
faith." It is also the dilemma of the non-Jews who, apart from the
revelation of the Law in the Old Testament, know by reason what
is right and yet practice vice. All men acknowledge a moral law—
either revealed or natural—and all men are in revolt against the moral
law which they acknowledge. None is without excuse, and each man
will be judged by the law which he acknowledges. On this basis all
stand condemned.

The reason why mankind is caught in this moral dilemma, Paul
declares, is that all, both Jews and Greeks, are under the power of sin
(Rom. 3:9). Mankind is in bondage to an evil power which Paul
tends to personify because he conceives of it as external to man,
having an existence prior to and independent of his consent to it. In
this sense sin is objective in character, but Paul never conceives of it
as either an individual or a personal being.[3] Sin entered the world
through Adam, and sin has held all alike captive. Paul's point is not
that all of Adam's descendants have received a tainted inheritance
because he sinned; rather, his point is that the reign of sin is universal
and the proof of this judgment lies in the fact that "all have sinned"
(Rom. 3:23; cf. 5:12, 11:32). This is a fact both of experience and
of observation. Paul refers to Adam and his fall, not to prove this
fact but rather to explain it, for no further proof is needed. Along
with the fact that sin is universal Paul sees another universal
phenomenon, viz., all men die, and he believes that the second fact is
explained by the first: "Therefore as sin came into the world through
one man and death through sin, . . . so death spread to all men
because all men sinned" (Rom. 5:12). Death—whether physical or

[3] Scott, *op. cit.,* p. 47.

spiritual—is due to sin, and both sin and death entered the world through the transgression of Adam.

Neither of these concepts was entirely new with Paul. In the Old Testament the antediluvian generation had been condemned as wholly inclined to evil (Gen. 6:5), and apparently the same condition prevailed after the flood (Gen. 8:21) although Noah was approved as righteous (Gen. 6:9; 7:1). Psalm 14:1–3 declares that all men without exception are corrupt and go astray (cf. Ps. 53:1–3), and indeed Paul quotes from this and other Psalms to illustrate or confirm his observation that "all have sinned and fall short of the glory of God" (Rom. 3:23). Moreover, Jesus in many of his teachings assumed that all men are sinful and stand in need of repentance (cf. Mark 8:38; Luke 9:41; 13:1–5; Matt. 7:11).

While Paul's explanation of the origin of universal sinfulness is not found in the Old Testament, it had been current in Jewish circles for some generations. His reference to Adam as the source and cause of sin in his descendants does not rule out their personal responsibility for their sin; neither is Adam's sin adduced as proof of his descendants' sin. Furthermore, this relationship does not affect the substance of Paul's teaching on salvation and redemption; rather, he uses it primarily as an analogy to illustrate the universality of the need of salvation and the universality of the gift of life in Christ (Rom. 6:12–19). Adam is viewed as a type of the Christ. As sin entered the world through Adam's transgression, so the free gift of life entered the world through Christ's righteousness. But, just as sin became universal *because* all men sinned (although all men would not have sinned if the first man had not sinned), so righteousness is made available to all men because of the righteousness of God revealed in Christ, but it is actually imputed to men only through faith.

As the result of his slavery to sin, man is no longer free to follow his true nature and destiny, and his way of life is in contradiction to the nature of the moral universe in which he lives. That all men are thus in bondage to sin is evidenced by the prevalence of "all manner of wickedness," injustice, covetousness, malice, arrogance, and licentiousness among the Gentiles (Rom. 1:29); it is also evidenced by the universal moral struggle between men's desires and their consciences and by the impotence of moral requirements to induce obedience. This understanding of the universality and inescapability of sin provides the background for Paul's understanding of the need for salvation coming from outside of man and explains why he uses the concept of salvation as his central category to interpret the meaning of Christianity.

What we have been saying does not mean, as is often alleged, that Paul is fundamentally or ultimately a pessimist. It is frequently assumed that Jesus held an optimistic view of man whereas Paul held a pessimistic view. But, as we have seen, Jesus also believed that all men are sinful. Both Jesus and Paul were pessimistic about the possibilities of unredeemed man, but both were triumphantly optimistic about the possibilities of men who responded to the grace of God. "With God all things are possible," Jesus declared; and Paul was equally confident, "I can do all things in him who strengthens me" (Phili. 4:13). For Paul, human sinfulness is not the primary fact in terms of which the moral life must be understood; on the contrary, for him, as for Jesus and the Bible as a whole, the fundamental fact is the reign of God, or the Kingdom of God.

Sin is so tragic because it brings death to the potential sons of God. It is so heinous because it represents the defilement and corruption of men who know the moral law and whose true nature it is to keep it. It is because Paul has a high conception of the fundamental dignity and worth of man as he is intended to be that sin is presented in such awesome terms. It is a massive, terrible, God-defying force that holds man in bondage—not a small, weak power which men can overcome at will simply by "screwing their courage to the sticking point." But, if Paul's conception of sin is greater than most of our notions of moral evil, his conceptions of God's sovereignty and of His grace are likewise far greater than ours. God is quite enough in control so that the ultimate outcome of this spiritual warfare is certain, and His grace is sufficient for man's victory in the present age.

It should be remembered that in thinking of sin as rebellion against God, Paul and the prophets before him conceived of it as a revolt within the domain of God, not an attack by an alien power. When Paul speaks of sin as a power that is external to man, he personifies evil, but he does not mean thereby a force of evil which had its origin independent of God's creative power and will. As Professor H. Richard Niebuhr puts the matter, "Neither Paul nor any other theologian in the great line of Christian thinkers ever surrendered to a dualistic view, according to which the world is made up of two opposed realms, the kingdom of light and the kingdom of darkness, and according to which some things, such as the material world or the body, are inherently bad. Whatever evil powers are at work in the world, God is the author and ruler of all. The ethical thought of Paul rests on the double foundation of the convictions that God rules and that man is involved in a universal rebellion against that rule."[4]

Not only is man in bondage to sin, according to Paul, but before the coming of Christ man was in bondage to law—that is, to systems of morality that were essentially imperative in character. The coming of sin into the world had made such law necessary. Its purpose had been to lead men to life, but Paul sees that the moral law—whether of the Jews or of the Gentiles—has brought condemnation. The Jews had prided themselves on possessing the Mosaic Law, and they had looked upon this fact as giving them a certain superior merit in the sight of God over those peoples whose knowledge of God was limited to that which they could discern by their reason and through their consciences, but Paul argues that the Jews are not any better off in this regard than the Gentiles (Rom. 3:9), for each people is judged by its own law. Each has violated its own moral requirements, and no one is without excuse. Both the natural moral law of the Gentiles and the revealed moral law of the Jews have brought condemnation, for "through the law comes knowledge of sin" (Rom. 3:20). That is to say, the law reveals man's servitude to sin and his guilt, for it shows him wherein he has violated the will of God.

Not only does the moral law increase man's sense of guilt and consequently his fear of death, but this guilt and this fear bring further confusion and restrictions to his spirit so that he further transgresses the law. The law turns morality in upon itself so that instead of making men unselfish it leads them to even greater self-seeking in the name of doing God's will. Paul had begun to see this even before his conversion but in the light of his experience as a Christian the inadequacy of the law became painfully clear. He had once pinned his hopes on the law and surrendered himself to its authority, but now he was forced to recognize that the ax had been laid to the root of even that tree. He was understandably indignant and disillusioned at its failure. There is a kind of sting in his words: "That which the law could not do." But Paul was only echoing the thought of Jesus, except for the fact that Jesus had not himself been captive to the law and hence his criticism of it was singularly free of any note of personal frustration and disappointment. The heart of Jesus' criticism of the legalism of the Pharisees was his insistence that a corrupt tree cannot bring forth

[4] Waldo Beach and H. Richard Niebuhr, *Christian Ethics,* New York, The Ronald Press Company, 1955, p. 40.

good fruit and no amount of outward conduct can make men really good if their motives are wrong. The law is powerless to transform man at the core, and those who are in bondage to the law do not even know that such a transformation, or rebirth, is needed. Legal morality easily becomes defensive morality, and men seek to follow its requirements in order to avoid guilt which leads to the fear of death. The intent of the law is good, but the fruit of legalistic morality is Pharisaism with its smugness and self-righteousness and spiritual blindness. The law which was intended to bring life ends up bringing death.

Paul adds a final criticism which reflects the apparently universal experience of children as well as of adults when they are confronted by moral demands: their imperative form provides a further temptation to sin by arousing man's self-will and tempting him defiantly to transgress the law. "I should not have known what it is to covet if the law had not said, 'You shall not covet.' But sin, finding an opportunity in the commandment, wrought in me all kinds of covetousness" (Rom. 7:7–8).

This, then, as Paul sees it, is the human situation apart from the grace of God revealed in Christ. Man is sinful. He knows the will of God far better than he performs it. The presupposition of the moral law is a law of reward and punishment. Those who keep it will reap life and those who do not obey its precepts will reap some form of death even as it had been promised when the Hebrew law was promulgated: "Cursed be he who does not confirm the words of this law by doing them" (Deut. 27:26). But man by himself is unable to keep this law. Sin takes advantage of it, and death still rules over man despite the law. "Wretched man that I am! Who will deliver me from this body of death?" (Rom. 7:24).

PAUL'S EMANCIPATION FROM LAW, SIN, AND DEATH

Paul would indeed have been a pessimist had he believed that there was no answer to this poignant cry. But his answer is clear and triumphant: "Thanks be to God through Jesus Christ our Lord! . . . There is therefore now no condemnation for those who are in Christ Jesus. For the law of the Spirit of life in Christ Jesus has set me free from the law of sin and death" (Rom. 7:25–8:2). This in essence is the gospel according to Paul. What it meant in terms of his thought about God and the Christian life we have now to examine.

Fundamentally, what Jesus had done—through his life, death, and resurrection—was to reveal that life under the law had rested upon a false understanding of the nature of the moral and spiritual order in which we live. It had been based upon the assumption that this order is essentially retributive in character—"an eye for an eye," blindness at birth as a punishment for sin, death for the publicans and sinners who transgress the law. But Jesus had revealed that the moral order— the fundamental reality—is not like this. As Jesus had put it, it is the Father's "good pleasure" to give men the Kingdom. As Paul puts it, through Jesus, God has shown His love for man "in that while we were yet sinners Christ died for us" (Rom. 5:8). Henceforth, it is clear that salvation is through faith and by the grace of God rather than by the righteousness of men according to the law. God had always been love; He had always been righteous in the sense of being merciful as well as just; and man's justification before God had always rested upon faith, for no man is able to boast of and rely upon his works before God. Abraham's righteousness (justification) was by faith and rested upon his trust in God rather than upon the fact that he had been circumcised. In like manner the covenant which God made with Abraham rested upon the divine grace, and Abraham's true descendants are those men of faith who trust "him who justifies the ungodly" (Rom. 4:5; cf. John 8:37 ff.). The law had indeed been given to Israel as part of the divine plan of salvation, but because of man's sin it had become the occasion of further sin and brought condemnation. It had been given as a guide, not as a substitute for trust in God's goodness; but it was used by sinful men who did not really trust Him, to provide a basis for boasting and to enable them arrogantly to assert a claim upon God to justify them.[5] To be sure, Abraham and the prophets—indeed, the law itself, understood in terms of its intent—continued to bear witness to the righteousness of God; but now, in Jesus Christ, apart from the law, this righteousness of God has been made manifest in a way far superior to any of these foreshadowings of it. So much is this so that Paul, the former Pharisee, now declares that there are, so far as justification before God is concerned, no distinctions among men based upon the law, "since all have sinned and fall short of the glory of God" (Rom. 3:23). This

---

[5] Cf. Jesus' Parable of the Pharisee and the Publican (Luke 18:9–14). The Pharisee in this story is the classical example of those who make this claim, and the Publican of those who do not. When Jesus declared that the latter "went down to his house justified rather than the other," he taught the same truth which Paul expounded in his doctrine concerning the law and concerning "faith and works."

applies to Jew and Gentile, saint and sinner. But Jesus has revealed in a way in which the law was powerless to do that all men can nevertheless trust God and live in His grace and forgiveness. Thus the promise of the covenant which was given to Abraham has at last been fulfilled in the new covenant of grace, and faith in the Father of Jesus Christ makes the dispensation of the law irrelevant (Gal. 3:25–26).

Not only had Paul been freed from the law through his new faith, but he had also been liberated from bondage to sin, which was the more fundamental form of slavery. For it was sin which had brought about the need for the law and which, also, found in the law a temptation to further transgression. Sin, as we have seen, was for Paul a force external to man, and it was closely related to death. Death had indeed used sin as a means of gaining an entrance into human nature. Sin had come into the world, and death by sin (Rom. 5:12). Once sin had effected an entrance into the human race, it continued to dwell there, exercising a tyranny over man from which there was no escape until Christ came. It had corrupted the will, the intelligence, and the imagination of men. It caused man to use his flesh as an instrument of corruption. The true character and pervasiveness of sin, as we have seen, was first brought to light through the operation of the law although its true depth and power is fully revealed only in the light of Christ.

Christ's power to free men from this worst and most universal form of bondage arose, according to Paul, out of the fact that he had completely identified himself with humanity in his incarnation. He had felt the attack of sin in temptation; he had known its subtlety and danger. Yet he had been without sin, for he had not consented to it. In Christ, the dominion of sin both over himself and over mankind was broken because, while he "died to sin" (Rom. 6:10), death no longer held sway over him because he arose the victor over death. Thus both of man's ancient enemies, sin and death, were banished by Christ, and his victory over them is now possible for all those who by faith share in his dying unto sin and in his rising unto newness of life lived toward God rather than, as is the case with natural man, toward the self. Such a victory is possible only through faith which crucifies the self and enthrones Christ as the true center of life. Christ has revealed that life is more ultimate than death and that the righteousness of God is more powerful than sin. Those who respond to this revelation of the fundamental nature of the moral and spiritual reality in which we live are freed by grace through faith (trust) from sin. They are not only justified in the sense of having their sins—individual transgressions—no longer counted against them, but they are also reconciled unto God in that they are restored to fellowship with Him whereby they know Him to be their heavenly Father and themselves to be His children. Moreover, they are freed both from death, which is the wages of sin, and from the fear of death because their guilt is forgiven and death itself has been vanquished. Life eternal—to use the Johannine term—has begun for them here and now. Those who live by faith in Jesus Christ rest in the confidence that they will not be judged on the basis of their merit but rather that they will be justified by grace, and the presence and power of the living Lord who has triumphed over death persuades them that nothing will be able to separate them from the love of God which is in Christ Jesus—"neither death, nor life, nor angels, nor principalities, nor things present, nor things to come, nor powers, nor height, nor depth, nor anything else in all creation" (Rom. 8:38–39).[6]

AN ETHIC OF LIBERTY: THE INDWELLING SPIRIT

Theology, especially conservative theology, has frequently represented Paul as being supremely or even solely concerned in his thought about salvation with the sacrificial death of Christ on the cross and the atonement which he thereby effected. It has frequently represented Christ as fulfilling the demands of God's justice and reconciling God to man as well as man to God. But, as Professor Dodd points out, this is a rather "ironical fate for one who showed so clearly

[6] For a discussion of Paul's conception of salvation as also involving liberation from bondage to superhuman forces of evil which held the human race in captivity, see Scott, *op. cit.*, pp. 28 ff. The belief in the existence of such rebel forces against the will of God had been present in Judaic thought since the Babylonian exile in the sixth century, B.C. Paul seems to have conceived of these evil spirits as forming a hierarchy of powers, ranging from demons up through the intermediate forces—Principalities, Powers, Thrones, Dominions—to the Prince or Ruler of this Age, Satan. Man's real spiritual warfare is with these "spiritual hosts of wickedness in the heavenly places" (Eph. 6:12).

God in Christ has delivered men "from the dominion of darkness" and transferred them to the Kingdom of His Son (Col. 1:13). The spiritual warfare goes on, however; and, although the fatal blow against these spirit-forces has been dealt, Christ's triumph over them will not be completed until these "enemies" of God and man are put "under his feet," and the last of these enemies to be thus destroyed is death (I Cor. 15:25–56).

For non-Pauline but similar references in the New Testament see Acts 7:42; I John 5:19; John 12:31; Luke 11:21–22.

that his eyes were set upon the risen Christ."[7] As important and necessary as the death of Christ was in order to effect man's emancipation, the gospel of the risen Christ was an even greater thing for Paul: "But God shows his love for us in that while we were yet sinners Christ died for us. Since, therefore, we are now justified by his blood, *much more* shall we be saved by him from the wrath of God. For if while we were enemies we were reconciled to God by the death of his Son, *much more,* now that we are reconciled, *shall we be saved by his life"* (Rom. 5:8–10).

For Paul, the totality of Jesus' life, his teaching, his death, and his resurrection constituted the "event" through which God had made Himself known to men in such a way that a new relationship to Him was possible; and, most important of all, the advent of Jesus Christ had marked the beginning of a new era in human history, an era which is characterized by the presence of a new spirit, namely, "the spirit of sonship to God, of hopefulness and love."[8] The coming of Christ together with his fate was the one great act of God which made all other events in history intelligible and which constituted the decisive turning point in the relation of men to God and to one another. The risen Christ was understood in terms of the Christ who was "crucified, dead, and buried," and Christ both crucified and risen was understood in terms of an intimate knowledge of—although probably not a personal acquaintance with—the Jesus of history. Paul, like the author of the Fourth Gospel, was, however, more concerned to interpret the meaning of Jesus' life, death, and resurrection than to give a historical account of these events.

How was it possible that as the result of the coming of Christ a new age had dawned? In the first place, it needs to be said emphatically that God did not, according to Paul, need to be reconciled to man. God was not a God of vengeance who needed to have His demand for retributive justice satisfied before He would be willing to forgive men. Rather, "God was in Christ reconciling the world unto himself" (II Cor. 5:19). What was being revealed throughout the life and death of Jesus was the character of God and His attitude toward men, the attitude of a Father who "did not spare his own Son but gave him up for us all" (Rom. 8:32). In the death of the sinless Jesus on the cross two things were made plain: the depth of man's sin and his unworthiness of the divine love on the one hand, and, on the other,

---

[7] Dodd, *op. cit.,* p. 123.
[8] Beach and Niebuhr, *op. cit.,* p. 40.

the utter goodness and grace and love of God who showed His love for man "while we were yet sinners." In the cross, God made it plain that He had taken sin seriously. He had not overlooked it or "winked at" it; rather, He had shown man the "price" which He was willing to pay in order to reconcile man unto Himself. In the cross, quite "apart from law," was revealed the righteousness of God which freely forgives, which bears the "cost" of forgiveness[9] and takes the initiative in effecting man's restoration to fellowship with Himself. On the one hand, in the cross, God "pronounced the doom of sin": He revealed the depth of its hold upon man, its disastrous consequences, and its ultimate end. On the other hand, He revealed in the most unexpected but captivating way the love of the righteous and holy God of Israel for sinful men. The message of the cross is the message of forgiveness that is free and unconditional on God's side, though it can be accepted by man only on the condition of repentance. It is the promise of the forgiveness of sins, of not counting men's trespasses against them; but beyond this it is also the promise of reconciliation, of the restoration of fellowship between man and God.

It is the possession of the Spirit which makes it possible for the promise of the cross to be fulfilled in the present experience of life lived in the new age. The Spirit was, according to Paul, the gift of the glorified Lord, and he took it for granted that all who truly trusted in Christ had received this gift: "Any one who does not have the Spirit of Christ does not belong to him" (Rom. 8:9). For Paul the living Christ and the Spirit are so closely associated that he uses the two names almost interchangeably. Similarly, the Spirit of Christ and the Spirit of God are so intimately related that they, too, are practically identical. Thus Paul writes to the believers at Rome: "But you are not in the flesh, you are in the Spirit, if the Spirit of God really dwells in you. Any one who does not have the Spirit of Christ does not belong to him" (Rom. 8:9). But what is of most concern is that the Spirit is given by Christ to believers, and that the character of the Spirit has been revealed in Jesus Christ.

The term "mysticism" is frequently applied to Paul's conception of the indwelling Christ or Spirit, but it should be remembered that Paul's mysticism is always held in check by the memory of the historical Jesus—of his life, his teaching, and his death. Thus, unlike

---

[9] For an illuminating account of the "cost" of forgiveness in human relations as well as in the relationship between God and man, see Horace Bushnell, *Forgiveness and Law*, New York, Scribner, Armstrong & Co., 1874.

some other individualistic and untutored forms of mysticism, Paul's so-called "Christ-mysticism" is restrained and ethically serious. "If any one is in Christ, he is a new creation" (II Cor. 5:17). The believer has liberty, for "where the Spirit of the Lord is, there is freedom" (II Cor. 3:17). But the believer is free only if he lives in complete dependence upon, and in complete loyalty to, Jesus Christ.

The life of the believer is, then, characterized by his having the Spirit as a present possession. Paul sees in this gift the "first fruits" (what we might call the down payment) of salvation, and also the promise of its final consummation. It is the Spirit which is the creator of the new life.[10] The Spirit is also the author of the unity that binds Christians together into a common fellowship. It works in men to produce an ethical harvest of "love, joy, peace, patience, kindness, goodness, faithfulness, gentleness, (and) self-control" (Gal. 5:22–23). For Paul, as for the Fourth Evangelist, the Spirit is the instrument of revelation which will guide men into a deeper knowledge of God, and it is also the ever-present source of moral strength for the individual Christian. These and many other fruits of the Spirit point to the future completion of the work of salvation both in the individual believer and in the entire created order.

Although he assumes it to be almost axiomatic that the Spirit is given by Christ to the believer when one first puts his faith in Christ, Paul looks upon the realization of salvation as a progressive process. Salvation is present in principle the moment one comes to place his faith in Christ and the Spirit is bestowed upon him, but Paul sees quite clearly that man's passions and pride are not so suddenly subdued. The struggle against the "flesh," or wrong desires, continues within the believer's own spirit, but the very presence of the Spirit of Christ represents a guarantee that the flesh will be subdued and the Spirit will be triumphant if the believer remains faithful. Thus Paul is "sure that he who began a good work in (the Philippians) will bring it to completion at the day of Jesus Chirst," and he himself writes to them, not as one who has already gained Christ or attained perfection but rather as one who presses on to make this prize his own (Phili. 1:6; 3:12–13). Understood in religious terms of personal fellowship with Christ, salvation may be a present possession amid all of the trials as well as the joys of this life. Considered from the point of view of the fulfillment of this goal alone, it would be far

---

[10] See C. A. A. Scott, *St. Paul: The Man and the Teacher*, London, Cambridge University Press, 1936, pp. 115–116.

better to die and be with Christ (Phili. 1:23). Understood in moral terms as being "conformed to the image" of the Son of God (Rom. 8:29) and being made "holy and blameless and irreproachable" (Col. 1:22), salvation is a process whereby character is transformed. As such it has its beginnings here and now but awaits its fulfillment in the world to come.

We have seen that Paul looked upon the Christian as one who is no longer under the law. The question naturally arises as to whether he thought of the latter as having any value or validity for the believer in his effort to discover the will of God. Has the law been abolished, or has it been fulfilled? Is the final court of appeal the conscience of the individual believer? Or does the law perhaps have differing value for believers according to the extent to which they have been inwardly transformed? Paul recognized the danger that some might think he had identified the law with sin. He insisted, however, that his intention was quite to the contrary. One of the primary functions of the law was to bring to consciousness the presence of sin that was already in man; but, since human nature under sin is perverted, the very prohibition of covetousness has provoked man to covet. Paul may have been partly to blame for the misunderstanding on the part of his readers, for he probably exaggerated the universality of this human tendency to defy the moral law. But his main point is clear—each man is so entangled in the general "wrongness" of the human race that he has no power of himself to avoid committing acts which, whether he knows it or not, are evil.[11] The content of the law is good; its imperative form makes it weak. The law is powerless to effect compliance with the good which it commands, but Christ has freed men from sin and thus empowered those who live by his Spirit to fulfill all that the law stands for in the way of righteousness, holiness, and goodness.

Paul assumes that the Jewish moral law, with its prohibitions of idolatry, murder, theft, adultery, covetousness, and the like, continues to be valid. Not only so, but it serves as a kind of guide, or schoolmaster, to lead men unto Christ. If men cannot find Christian liberty on the plane of law, much less can they find it on the undisciplined plane of license. Since even Christians who are in the process of being saved are not activated solely by the Spirit, they need guidance in their effort to discover the will of God for their daily conduct. Hence the law remains as a guide although it is still true that those

[11] Dodd, *op. cit.,* p. 81.

who are led by the Spirit are not under the law in the sense that they do not feel its coercive character since they freely fulfill its intent.

While Paul does not give nearly as large a place to the category of law in his interpretation of Christian ethics as do some other writers in the New Testament, notably the author of Matthew, he nevertheless uses the concept to describe two fundamental aspects of the ethical life of the believer. In the first place, he uses it to refer to the accepted moral standards, whether of the Mosaic Law or of the natural law, which embody the ethical wisdom of different people and which offer practical moral guidance. It is true that these are not infallible formulations of the divine will for Paul, but they represent helpful guides or signposts amid the perplexities of life in a world where men are both finite and sinful. In a similar way he appeals, on occasion, to a remembered saying of Jesus and evidently attaches to it an absolute authority (I Cor. 7:10; 9:14). When his admonitions are questioned by persons who claim to be prophets or to have the Spirit, he argues that they should acknowledge that what he has written is "a command of the Lord." If anyone does not recognize this, he can be ignored (I Cor. 14:37–38). In one instance there is a definite note of regret on Paul's part that he has "no command of the Lord" and therefore must content himself with giving his own opinion (I Cor. 7:25). In addition to citing direct sayings of Jesus, Paul frequently echoes his Master's ethical teaching in such a way that it seems clear that he assigns to it a particular degree of authority. For example, his counsel to the Corinthians (I Cor. 6:7) concerning lawsuits and the advisability of suffering wrong or being defrauded rather than pressing one's personal claim is a striking reformulation of Jesus' familiar teaching about nonresistance (Matt. 5:39–40). Moreover, he also appeals to the example of the historical Jesus—to his humility and sacrificial love—as the norm of Christian conduct. Similarly, at times he also appeals to his converts to follow the example which he himself has set.

In the second place, Paul uses the category of law to refer to the moral will of God which man is free to make his own but which he cannot ignore except at his own peril and which he cannot change. Thus Paul speaks of his liberation in terms of his having been freed by "the law of the Spirit of life" (Rom. 8:2). Likewise, on another occasion he plainly points out that he is "under the law of Christ" (I Cor. 9:21). Again, he pleads with the Galatians "to bear one another's burdens, and so fulfill the law of Christ" (Gal. 6:2). Such expressions on Paul's part represent his recognition of the objective claims of the Kingdom of God or, in other words, of the sovereignty of God and His prerogatives as Creator and King. Paul's whole concern with ethics and morality and his complete repudiation of the antinomian tendencies of some of his followers at Galatia indicate the extent to which he recognized the objective structure of the moral order with which man must somehow come to terms if he is to achieve true freedom. Indeed, Paul does not hesitate to use the term *slave* to describe the absolute subjection of the self to Christ which is required of man before he can, paradoxically, find perfect freedom.

The terms "slave" and "law" reflect the fact that the Christian's action must conform to the nature of the moral order which God has created; the terms "son" and "freedom" reflect the way that the moral life looks from the inside to the man who has been transformed by Christ and has made the law of Christ his own. For those who walk by the Spirit, the intent of the codified law—not the letter of each injunction—is good and is to be fulfilled; but the imperative form of this law is no longer experienced as coercive, and it no longer defeats man. Under no circumstances, however, does the codified law offer adequate guidance for the Christian. In some instances it commands action which runs counter to the law of the Spirit—i.e., to the law of love—and in other instances no law has been formulated to deal with a particular situation in which one must act. The Christian is summoned to fulfill the law of Christ, but what this law requires can be finally comprehended only through the Spirit. The formulated law remains as a directive, pointing men toward the law of Christ; it points beyond itself to the law of love whereby it is fulfilled. But in fulfilling the traditional law, love shatters and transforms all such codes and remains finally obedient only to God. Moreover, if the content of the law of Christ cannot be discerned apart from faith and the Spirit, much less can it be fulfilled apart from grace which is mediated by the Spirit. Acceptance of the lordship of Christ means, therefore, the acceptance of a more demanding law, but it means, first and foremost, a transformation of the self so that the drive toward goodness no longer comes from the outside, but from within the heart of man.[12]

[12] Scott, *St. Paul: The Man and the Teacher*, p. 131.

AN ETHIC OF FAITH EXPRESSING ITSELF IN LOVE

THE RELATIONSHIP BETWEEN THE FIRST AND SECOND COMMANDMENTS

While it is clear that for Paul, as for Jesus, the essential intent of the legal codes of the Old Testament is to be fulfilled by the Christian, there is a striking difference between the ways in which they summarize the essence of this legislation. Jesus declared that the entire law as well as the prophets depend upon two commandments. The first and greatest of these is, "You shall love the Lord your God with all your heart, and with all your soul, and with all your mind." The second is like unto the first, "You shall love your neighbor as yourself" (Matt. 22:37–40). Paul, on the other hand, includes the entire law in the second of these requirements. "The commandments, 'You shall not commit adultery, You shall not kill, You shall not steal, You shall not covet,' and any other commandment, are summed up in this sentence, 'You shall love your neighbor as yourself' " (Rom. 13:9). Or again he writes, "For the whole law is fulfilled in one word, 'You shall love your neighbor as yourself' " (Gal. 5:14). It is sometimes argued that Paul, who as a devout Jew had repeated the *Shema*[13] several times daily, simply took the first commandment for granted and assumed that his hearers would do the same. Professor Ramsey seems to be on sounder ground, however, when he concludes that in the foregoing summaries Paul deliberately included the first commandment within the meaning of neighbor-love.[14]

Paul's formulation of the unity of Christian ethics in its orientation toward the neighbor seems at first glance identical with some secular humanitarian reductions of love-for-God to love-for-neighbor. But it must be clear from what we have already seen concerning Paul's understanding of salvation and the role of the Spirit in the life of the Christian that he is far from any merely humanistic version of Christianity according to which the Gospel is equated with loving one's neighbor in some fairly simple and obvious way. On the contrary, Paul insists that one cannot know what Christian love for one's

[13] Viz.: "Hear, O Israel: the Lord our God is one Lord; and you shall love the Lord your God with all your heart, and with all your soul, and with all your might" (Deut. 6:4–5).
[14] Paul Ramsey, *Basic Christian Ethics*, New York, Charles Scribner's Sons, 1950, p. 128.

neighbor means until he has first learned this from Christ, and much less can one actually love his neighbor with Christian love until he is freed and empowered by the Spirit so to love. Moreover, while Paul occasionally speaks of the single requirement of neighbor-love as including man's relationship to God, he usually uses other terms, especially "faith," to describe the latter. By "faith" Paul means a relationship of trust and complete self-surrender to God or Christ (I Thess. 1:8; Col. 2:5; Rom. 3:22; Gal. 3:22).[15] As Professor Niebuhr points out, according to the Synoptic Gospels Jesus "emphasized in conduct and in teaching the virtues of faith in God and humility before Him much more than love."[16] In this sense "faith" means the grateful, trustful response of man to God for what He has done in Christ and the commitment of one's fate to Him. It is an obedient response to God which accepts God's will as the law of the believer's own being. It is through faith that man has access to God's grace which freely justifies the unworthy. It is through faith that grace becomes operative in the believer and that the Spirit is received as the guide and renewer of the Christian. Climactically, such faith works—or expresses itself—"through love" (Gal. 5:6). Thus, it is clear that for Paul "faith" and "love" are really inseparable. Indeed, they are as closely related for him as are the two forms of love in the thought of Jesus, and they are related to each other in essentially the same way.

The distinction which Professor H. Richard Niebuhr makes between the love which is directed toward God and that which is directed toward the neighbor in the teaching of Jesus is particularly illuminating at this point.[17] Love for God and love for the neighbor, he writes, are "two distinct virtues" which have "no common quality but only a common source." Love for God is "adoration" of Him as the only true good; it is "gratitude" to Him as the giver of all good gifts; it is "joy" in His holiness and "consent to Being." Love for the neighbor, on the other hand, is "pitiful rather than adoring; it is giving and forgiving rather than grateful; it suffers for and in [men's] viciousness and profaneness; it does not consent to accept them as they are, but calls them to repentance."[18]

[15] Cf. Mark 11:22, where Jesus says, "Have faith in God."
[16] H. Richard Niebuhr, *Christ and Culture*, New York, Harper & Brothers, 1951, p. 16.
[17] *Ibid.*, p. 18.
[18] *Ibid.* Cf. Ramsey, *op. cit.*, p. 129. Professor Ramsey similarly maintains that it is "difficult if not impossible" to give precisely the same meaning to the

There is a similar distinction between faith and *agape* in the thought of Paul. Thus, according to Anders Nygren,[19] the Apostle's intent is not to eliminate the spiritual reality designated by the phrase "love towards God"; neither is it his intent to reduce this reality to love for the neighbor apart from God. Rather, his aim is to give it its proper name, which he believes to be "faith." As Nygren makes clear, faith is closely related to *agape,* but it differs from the latter. "Faith includes in itself the whole devotion of love" while at the same time the term itself emphasizes the responsive character of man's proper relationship to God. It stresses the primacy of God's action which makes it possible for man to trust Him and also makes it possible for one who trusts Him to love his neighbors with *agape.* Despite this difference in content as regards the meaning of the two concepts, however, it is clear that for Paul both *faith* and *agape* have their ultimate source in the redemptive action of God in Christ just as the two forms of love which Jesus commands have their common source in God. Although on occasion he spoke of the entire law as being included in the single requirement of neighbor-love, Paul, like Jesus, recognized that the possibility of man's loving his neighbor with *agape* depends upon man's proper response of trust in and devotion to God.

The question remains, however, as to whether the two commandments of Jesus can be adequately summarized in the second. In this connection there is point to Principal Lindsay Dewar's remark to the effect that in the final analysis Paul's omission of the First Commandment is "unfortunate," for it "lends support to the many who ignore the fact that though the chief requirements of ethical teaching can be summed up in two commandments, they cannot be summed up in one."[20] In our day, and without an English equivalent for Paul's term *agape,* to summarize the law in terms of neighbor-love tends to put the emphasis at the wrong place, viz., upon the neighbor rather than upon God.

---

term *love* in speaking of man's attitude toward God and toward his fellowmen, and he quite correctly suggests that the Pauline and Reformation categories—"faith," "obedience," "humility," "gratitude," "thankfulness," and the expression "to glorify"—are an accurate spelling out of the content of "love" in the relation of man to God.

[19] Anders Nygren, *Agape and Eros,* trans. by Philip S. Watson, London, Society for Promoting Christian Knowledge, 1953, p. 127.

[20] Lindsay Dewar, *An Outline of New Testament Ethics,* Philadelphia, The Westminster Press, 1949, pp. 129–130.

THE SOURCE AND NORM OF CHRISTIAN CONDUCT: *Agape*

When Paul speaks of love as the fulfillment of the law (Rom. 13:10), he uses the Greek word *agape* to designate the particular kind of love to which he refers. This noun is not found in classical Greek, but only in the Septuagint, the New Testament, and later Christian literature. It appears only twice in the Synoptic Gospels (Matt. 24:12 and Luke 11:42); it is not found in Acts; but it appears in the Fourth Gospel and all of the Epistles except that of James. It was the Christian literature which first gave this Hellenistic Greek noun real currency. Its meaning is radically different from, and even antithetical to, that of *eros,* another Greek word used to designate the kind of love which seeks to possess its object whereas *agape* was used by Christians to designate self-giving love which has its source in the redemptive goodness of God.[21] The word *eros* is found neither in the Septuagint nor in the New Testament. In addition to *agape* and *eros,* there was a third Greek word for love, *philia,* meaning primarily friendship which involves mutual consideration and affection; but this word is found only once (Jas. 4:4) in the New Testament although its verb form is found frequently. Whereas *eros* and *philia* were the common words for "love," Paul and the early Christians took the less familiar *agape,* and gave to it a distinctively Christian meaning. Unfortunately, this meaning is obscured in our English word *love,* which is used to translate all three Greek nouns.

Strictly speaking, *agape* cannot be defined; its meaning can only be made known in religious experience whereby men are made aware of the *agape* of God reaching out to meet them in their need, and it can become operative in men only as it is released in them in response to the outreaching *agape* of God. The purpose of the death of Christ had been to reveal the reality of God's love and to persuade sinful and unbelieving men to believe and to receive it. It was "out of the great love with which he loved us" that God had made those who had erstwhile been dead in sin alive with Christ (Eph. 2:4–5). "In this the love of God was made manifest among us, that God sent his only Son into the world, so that we might live through him. In this is love, not that we loved God but that he loved us" (I John 4:9–10). It is this *agape* of God which calls forth the response of faith in God and

[21] Scott, *Christianity According to St. Paul,* pp. 203–204.

agape toward the neighbor on the part of man. Thus, through faith *agape* comes to dwell in man as the compelling and controlling force in all of his ethical action, and the *agape* of God is the initiating and sustaining source both of man's faith and of his love.

It is not too much to say with Professor Dodd, then, that for Paul, love is "the supreme and all-inclusive gift of the Spirit."[22] And, just as the objects of man's love in the teaching of Jesus are both God and man, so the objects of the *agape* which dwells in man through faith are both God (Rom. 8:28; I Cor. 8:3; cf. I Cor. 2:9) and man (Rom. 13:8–9; Gal. 5:14; cf. I Thess. 4:9); but, as we have seen, Paul places the emphasis upon the latter, and customarily uses other terms to describe man's proper attitude toward God. Thus, *agape* directed toward the neighbor is, for Paul, the central ethical principle; and, indeed, without it no action—not even the most severe form of self-sacrifice—is fully ethical in quality (I Cor. 13:3). But it is impossible for man to manifest *agape* in relationship to his neighbor apart from faith in God and the experience of God's *agape* toward him.

PRIMARILY AN ETHIC FOR THE FELLOWSHIP

Although Paul occasionally speaks of God as one object of *agape,* he has little to say about the application of this love to God or Christ. He is concerned, rather, to describe the bearing of *agape* upon the practical relations of the Christian with his fellowmen, especially with his fellow believers. He rejoices to find it active among the Thessalonians (I Thess. 1:3), the Corinthians (II Cor. 8:7), the Ephesians (Eph. 1:15), and the Colossians (Col. 1:4), as well as in Philemon (Phile. 5). He exhorts the Romans (Rom. 13:8), the Galatians (Gal. 5:13), and the Philippians (Phili. 1:9) to "abound" in this quality. Paul's best-known description of *agape* is found in I Corinthians 13. "Love is patient and kind; love is not jealous or boastful; it is not arrogant or rude. Love does not insist on its own way; it is not irritable or resentful; it does not rejoice at wrong, but rejoices in the right. Love bears all things, believes all things, hopes all things, endures all things" (I Cor. 13:4–7).

Paul frequently spells out the meaning of *agape* even more concretely in terms of the mutual responsibility of all the members of the

[22] C. H. Dodd, "The Ethics of the Pauline Epistles" in *The Evolution of Ethics,* E. H. Sneath, ed., New Haven, Yale University Press, 1927, p. 311.

Christian fellowship for each other.[23] Those who are weak in faith are to be welcomed in order that they may be strengthened. One member is not to pass judgment upon another who differs from him concerning beliefs or ceremonial practices. Those who are strong in faith and love are warned against pride and boasting and vaunting their liberty before those who for reasons of conscience still observe certain ceremonial regulations which now seem useless to the former. The Christian will avail himself of his freedom to eat meat that has been offered to idols and to drink wine *only if* the eating of such meat and the drinking of wine does not cause his brother to stumble. "If your brother is being injured by what you eat, you are no longer walking in love" (Rom. 14:15). Those who are strong have a heavy responsibility for the moral upbuilding of the weak. The former are to respect the beliefs and practices of the latter, be patient with them, encourage them, and serve them. "For you were called to freedom, brethren; only do not use your freedom as an opportunity for the flesh, but through love be servants of one another" (Gal. 5:13). So great is this mutual responsibility within the fellowship that gross moral failure does not destroy it. "If a man is overtaken in any trespass," those "who are spiritual should restore him in a spirit of gentleness" (Gal. 6:1). The believers are admonished to "be kind to one another, tenderhearted, forgiving one another" as God in Christ has forgiven them (Eph. 4:32). Only scandalous and contemptuous defiance of the moral sense of the fellowship may lead to the exclusion of such an offender from the community, and even then he is to be looked upon not as an enemy but as a brother (II Thess. 3:14–15; I Cor. 5:9–11). The purpose of such discipline is "that his spirit may be saved in the day of the Lord Jesus" (I Cor. 5:5). And repentance is to be followed by the complete restoration of fellowship (II Cor. 2:6–8).

It is because Paul conceived of *agape* as providing both the spring and the controlling force for the moral conduct of Christians that he set it so sharply over against law and trusted those who are motivated by love freely to fulfill the law. The individual believer who lets the mind of Christ dominate him from day to day is morally autonomous. He is free from external coercion because he has his ethical standard within himself. Just as in the Gospels Jesus dealt with the law in a completely free and sovereign way because the Spirit of God who had

[23] See especially Romans 12:9–13, 15–16; 14:1—15:6; I Thessalonians 4:9–12; 5:13–14; and Galatians 6:1–5.

given the law was his Spirit, so Paul insists that he who has the Spirit judges all things and is to be judged by no one (cf. I Cor. 2:15). True moral autonomy could not be defended more vigorously. But the demand to let Christ's Spirit reign in one's life is far more searching than the demand of any code, while at the same time it carries with it the promise of indefinite growth and ethical spontaneity. Paul's emphasis upon the moral autonomy of the individual believer is checked, however, by his conception of the Body of Christ of which each believer is a member (I Cor. 12:27; Eph. 1:22 f.). The Spirit is a corporate possession as well as an individual one. Because perfect freedom still lies in the future for sinful men, because men are tempted to pride, and also because they are finite, Christians are to seek the guidance of the Spirit as it is revealed through the fellowship which is "rooted and grounded in love." This sacred community, which rests upon and is nourished by the *agape* of God in Christ, can be trusted to discover for itself what love requires in its own immediate life. All of its members are guided by the same Spirit, and all have need to share in the mutual upbuilding which life in this community makes possible.

The Ethic of *Agape* Beyond the Limits of the Christian Fellowship

Paul has much less to say about the relationships of Christians to non-Christians than about their relationships to each other. He recognizes that complete separation from pagan society is impossible (I Cor. 5:10). The moral standards of non-Christian neighbors are to be respected (Rom. 12:17; I Thess. 4:12; I Cor. 10:32; Col. 4:5). Moreover, there are certain moral standards common to both Christians and pagans (Rom. 2:14–15), and *agape* demands that the Christian make the most of such common convictions as a basis for harmonious relations. The Christian will strive to live peaceably with all men (Rom. 12:18). Not only will he refrain from offending his pagan neighbors, but he will seek to do them positive good. Beyond this, if one suffers injury, he is not to seek reprisal against his enemy. Rather, he is to bless those who persecute him. "If your enemy is hungry, feed him; if he is thirsty, give him drink" (Rom. 12:20). In short, Paul says, "Do not be overcome by evil, but overcome evil with good" (Rom. 12:21). This counsel is, as Professor Dodd observes, by far the most important guidance that Paul gives with regard to the wider application of *agape*.[24] Significantly, it constitutes an admirable summary of Jesus' teaching in the Sermon on the Mount about what is commonly called "nonresistance"; properly understood, it represents the most creative element in Christian ethics and is applicable both within the Christian fellowship and in relationship to those outside of it.

RECOMMENDED READINGS

Beach, Waldo, and Niebuhr, H. Richard, eds., *Christian Ethics,* New York, The Ronald Press Company, 1955, ch. I.

Bultmann, Rudolf, *Theology of the New Testament,* I, trans. by Kendrick Grobel, New York, Charles Scribner's Sons, 1951, pt. II: "The Theology of Paul."

Dodd, C. H. "The Ethics of the Pauline Epistles" in *The Evolution of Ethics,* E. H. Sneath, ed., New Haven, Yale University Press, 1927.

Dodd, C. H., *The Meaning of Paul for Today,* London, George Allen and Unwin, Ltd., 1949.

Enslin, Morton Scott, *The Ethics of Paul,* New York, Harper & Brothers, 1930, pt. II.

Marshall, L. H., *The Challenge of New Testament Ethics,* New York, The Macmillan Company, 1947, chs. VII–X.

Nygren, Anders, *Agape and Eros,* London, Society for Promoting Christian Knowledge, 1953, pt. I, ch. II.

Ramsey, Paul, *Basic Christian Ethics,* New York, Charles Scribner's Sons, 1950, ch. II.

Scott, C. A. A., *Christianity According to St. Paul,* London, Cambridge University Press, 1932.

Scott, C. A. A., "The Teaching of St. Paul," in *St. Paul: The Man and the Teacher,* London, Cambridge University Press, 1936.

[24] C. H. Dodd, "The Ethics of the Pauline Epistles," *op. cit.,* pp. 318–319.

PART III

GUIDING PRINCIPLES OF CHRISTIAN ETHICS

chapter 5

RADICAL MONOTHEISM:
GOD IS ACTIVE
IN ALL EVENTS

THE METHOD OF RESPONSE

WE have examined the biblical basis of Christian ethics—
the characteristic features of Hebrew morality, the development of
the major ethical emphases of the Old Testament, Jesus' criticism
of the legalistic morality of Judaism, his summary of the law in terms
of the two requirements of love for God and love for one's neighbor,
his teaching about the primacy of the Kingdom of God, and Paul's
interpretation of Christian ethics as "faith working through love."
There are, of course, many other aspects of biblical ethics that we
were unable to treat, many themes and motifs which would shed
light upon and provide a perspective for interpreting biblical morality
as a whole. The interested student, it is hoped, will already have
supplemented the foregoing analysis by reading in the biblical sources
and by reference to additional treatments of the ethics of both the
Old and the New Testaments; for, as we noted earlier, the Bible is
the fundamental source book for the study of Christian ethics. Without an understanding of biblical ethics it is impossible to understand
the meaning of Christian ethics for today, and without an understanding of biblical faith it is impossible to understand biblical ethics.

We have also seen that for Jesus, as for Paul and the prophets, law
in the sense of detailed prescriptions for conduct is grossly inadequate
in the guidance which it offers for moral conduct. For one thing, it
sets up the traditions of men in the place of the authority of God as

the final court of appeal. Further, it fails to take due account of the newness or uniqueness of each ethical situation. It also tends to attach the same importance to all of its requirements so that men often neglect the weightier matters in their preoccupation with regulations of minor importance. But, even more fundamentally, the law is overt and external in its emphasis; hence, it is powerless to reach the inward sources of man's action—his thoughts and motives—and transform these. It may bring about outward conformity, but it is powerless to make men pure in heart.

Since both Jesus and Paul rejected the method of legalism in their approaches to ethics, we did not focus our attention upon their detailed ethical admonitions in our analysis of their moral teaching. Rather, we sought to describe the method which they employed, a method that was similar in many ways to that of the prophets in the Old Testament. We were primarily concerned to examine the fundamental convictions out of which their specific ethical counsel stemmed. While their applied moral teachings help us to understand the nature and moral implications of their basic convictions about God and man, it is clear that the former are the fruit of the latter. Their fundamental convictions, like those of their biblical predecessors, are ultimately religious rather than moral and they have to do with the nature of God, the nature of man, and the character of the world in which we live.

In contrast to the method of legalism which the Pharisees employed and in which the central concept was that of duty to God, the method which Jesus used in arriving at the decisions which he made and which he also taught his followers to use is best characterized as that of *response to God*. It was a method which rested upon the faith that the same God who had in times past made His will known to men under particular circumstances continues to reveal His will to those who seek it. It was a method which rested upon the belief that while the contents of the legal codes of Judaism were essentially good and while these codes served as guides and directives pointing to the divine will, it was nevertheless idolatrous to make them blueprints of what God requires in the present. They constitute efforts by finite and sinful men to formulate the will of God which has been revealed to them, but these formulations cannot be absolutized both because of the inadequacy of man's apprehension of the perfect will of God and also because of the impossibility of reducing the latter to a set of laws. Hence man must go back of the law and seek to discover the divine intent which lies behind the law. This divine will, rather than a legalized formulation of it, is the standard by which man's conduct is to be judged.

For example, when the question whether it was lawful for a man to divorce his wife arose, Jesus asked, "What did Moses command you?" (Mark 10:2 ff.) Upon being told that Moses permitted a man to give his wife a certificate of divorce and put her away, Jesus replied that this law of Moses represented a concession to the hardness of men's hearts, and he proceeded to put the question in a more fundamental context by pointing to God's purpose in creation when He made male and female. Back of the specific Mosaic law lies a more fundamental conception of God's activity and God's purpose. This, rather than the Mosaic application of God's will in a sinful generation, is the final fact with which men must come to terms. This is the ultimate dimension in which they live. So it is also with oaths and Sabbath laws and tithes and man's relationship to his enemy. "What is the purpose of God which lies behind the Sabbath laws?" Jesus asks. Man was not made so that there would be someone to keep the Sabbath; rather, the Sabbath was made for man, and the question as to whether it is lawful to pluck grain or heal on the Sabbath can be answered properly only if one remembers the purpose of the Creator who always wills the doing of good. Similarly, when Jesus speaks of man's relationship to his enemies he rejects the conventional counsel that a person should love his neighbor and hate his enemy. Rather, he says, "Love your enemies and pray for those who persecute you, so that you may be sons of your Father who is in heaven; for he makes his sun rise on the evil and on the good, and sends rain on the just and on the unjust" (Matt. 5:44 f.). His final admonition is: "You must, therefore, be perfect, as your heavenly Father is perfect" (Matt. 5:48).

The method of response to God's action is clearly implied in Jesus' conception of man's moral life as an ethic of sonship, i.e., as the ethic of a child of God. It is intended primarily as an ethic for those who know themselves to be sons of their heavenly Father and who in their lives seek to do their Father's will. To say that Jesus' ethic is an ethic of sonship is to place the emphasis at quite a different point from a secular humanitarian interpretation of his ethic as one of brotherhood. In Jesus' teaching the central fact is God and His will. Because of their relationship to their common heavenly Father—not because of inherent similarities in terms of biology or reason—all

men are brothers and each is of value because of his relationship to
God, not because of something which he possesses in himself apart
from God. Therefore, the ethic of Jesus is an ethic of doing his
Father's will in relation to all men—to one's enemies as well as to
one's friends—not because they are members of the same species or
even because they are brothers, but because they are children of a
common Father who loves all and wills their good irrespective of
such accidental differences as race, nationality, intelligence, or social
status. God bestows His grace and bounty upon all irrespective of
their merit or their gratitude. He sends the rain on the unjust as well
as the just and causes the sun to shine upon the evil as upon the good.
He freely offers forgiveness to all who will put their trust in Him and
forgive their fellows. Indeed, His love is like that of a father who goes
out to meet his prodigal son and kills a fatted calf to celebrate his
return home (Luke 15:11–24). This is the kind of love which God
bestows upon the unworthy. This is the goodness with which God is
good. He is utter grace and steadfast love. Hence man can trust Him
to supply his deepest needs; and for this reason, too, those who are
aware of the grace and love of God out of gratitude seek to do their
Father's will. Because God is self-giving they will seek to be self-
giving, too. Because He loves all men, not because all men are lovable
or intrinsically valuable apart from God, they seek to love all men,
too. They love because God has first loved them and all of His other
children and wants all to become His sons in their own consciousness
of themselves and to receive and enter the Kingdom which He
bestows.

GOD IS ACTIVE IN ALL EVENTS

Since Jesus' ethic is best characterized as one of response to
God rather than, on the one hand, as an ethic of duty to obey some
revealed code of laws or some principle of reason, or, on the other
hand, as an ethic of aspiration after some value or good which reason
has judged to be the *summum bonum* of life (happiness or self-
realization, for example), it is essential to our understanding of his
moral decisions and teaching that we examine, first of all, the nature
of the divine activity with which men are confronted and to which
they are called to respond. To be sure, we cannot escape repeated
reference to principles of value and principles of duty for these are
also involved in Jesus' method. Men are admonished to *seek* the

Kingdom of God and His righteousness before all else (Matt. 6:33). They are commanded to love God with heart, mind, soul, and strength. But for Jesus, value and duty are grounded in God and His will. God is the primary reality with which man is confronted and with which man must deal, for He is the Creator and Sustainer and Judge of all. His will for men determines the conditions in accordance with which alone they can find fulfillment. They are free to seek the Kingdom or to reject it, but they are not free to find blessedness and fulfillment on any other terms. It is God, therefore, rather than duty or the good for man which is the focal point of Jesus' ethic.

For this reason we turn now to a consideration of Jesus' conception of the nature of the divine action to which he responded. Here Jesus stands in the stream of biblical religion as a whole, although in his life and teaching he revealed a uniquely close relationship to God and a peculiar consistency between his teaching and the practical decisions which he made. Morally and spiritually he and the Father were one (John 17:22). But in his conception of the God of Israel as the living Lord who is the Creator, the Judge, and the Redeemer of men, he represents a continuation of the faith of Israel, and in his life and teaching he represents the fulfillment of this faith by providing an even deeper revelation of the love of God for all men and of the possibilities of life lived in complete surrender to God's will than had been given prior to his coming.

When Jesus, like the later prophets, assumed that God is active in all events, he was simply taking the monotheism of Judaism seriously and radically. As we have noted, the monotheism of earlier Judaism was practical rather than theoretical. Much of the monotheism of our modern day, however, is intellectual rather than practical; hence, we are likely to miss the impact of this fundamental conviction of Christian faith. We are tempted to think of God's will and action as limited to certain spheres, to religious actions, to miracles, to revelations in Scripture, or perhaps to personal virtues rather than as including the demand for justice in the social order. Amos, on the other hand, had seen God's will related to the fate of those who bore the brunt of an unjust social order, and he had seen that this will could not be ignored with impunity. Second Isaiah and Job had recognized that in the midst of extreme suffering on the part of the innocent, God is working out His purposes. By the stripes which the innocent servant of the Lord bore without bitterness or complaint, many transgressors were healed (Isa. 53:5, 12). Through his suffering Job had been enabled to see the greatness and majesty of God whose ways and thoughts were beyond the comprehension of finite man. Similarly, Jesus saw God as the One who gives men their daily bread, who cares for the lilies of the field, who marks the sparrow's fall, by whose power he casts out demons, who forgives sin, and whose will is being accomplished even through his own death on the cross. For the Christian there is no situation so dark or desperate that God is not there and that His will is indifferent to the outcome of the battle being waged there. In the words of Paul, the Christian knows by faith "that in everything God works for good with those who love him" (Rom. 8:28). God is present in every event, and in each He works His will.

This does not mean, of course, that God causes evil; neither does it represent a denial of man's freedom. God does not cause all action, but He is active in all events—sustaining them, ordering them, providing resources of grace for meeting them. God did not betray Jesus. This was the traitorous act of Judas, but God was present in or throughout the betrayal, the trial, and Jesus' agony upon the cross; and Jesus responded to the saving intent of God whose will he sought to fulfill. God is good; hence, He cannot be the author of evil. But He is present amid evil deeds by intention—not as the doer of evil but as the One who in the midst of, and in spite of, evil is working out His purposes and His will. Evil results from rebellion against God, but no one can escape from God and from His will, neither the perpetrator of evil nor the innocent who suffer because of evil.

That God is present in any event—peace or war, a happy marriage or a divorce, a true community where fellowship enriches the life of all or one torn by racial strife, the incarnation or the cross—can be seen only by faith. Given the assumption of a thoroughgoing monotheism, the faith that God is good, and the conviction that men are free, the question for faith is, what meaning do these events have and how shall I respond to them? Jesus made these assumptions, and he acted in complete consistency with them. Other men may act on the basis of a different faith, but ultimately all of our actions rest upon some kind of faith—that there is some meaning or no meaning present, that there is a divine intent which is good or a grand indifference or an evil power which intends evil for man. The faith of Jesus is that back of every event is the intention of an infinite, all-good Being who is at the same time the Creator and Sovereign of all and who wills and seeks the salvation of all. It is the will of this God which Jesus seeks to discover and to which he responds.

GOD IS ACTIVE AS CREATOR

The fundamental conviction of Jesus and the fundamental affirmation of Christian faith is that God is the Creator. He is the ground of all temporal existence. Everything that is outside of Him has been created and established by Him. As the Fourth Gospel declares, "In the beginning was the Word, and the Word was with God, and the Word was God. He was in the beginning with God; all things were made through him, and without him was not anything made that was made" (John 1:1–3; cf. Col. 1:15–16; Rev. 4:11). Similarly, the purpose of the creation myth in the first chapter of Genesis is to assert that everything is dependent for its existence and meaning upon the will and power of the transcendent and sovereign God: "In the beginning God created the heavens and the earth" (Gen. 1:1).

The biblical doctrine of creation affirms not only that God is the source of all created being, but also that it is He who sustains all in being. He upholds the universe by His power (Heb. 1:3). All things have their unity in God who has made them for His purpose (cf. Col. 1:17). He is the source of the order which characterizes the universe and keeps it from being a chaos.

It is important to note, in this connection, that the biblical conception of creation is not a theory of the manner in which the world came into existence. This is especially clear in the New Testament references to God as Creator, but it is also implicit in the creation myths found in Genesis.[1] The main point of both the Genesis narratives and the New Testament passages to which we have referred is that the whole of nature, including man, is absolutely dependent upon God while He is dependent upon nothing outside of Himself. Scientific accounts of the origin of the world and of life upon the earth are only remotely and indirectly related to this biblical idea of divine creation. There can be no antagonism between science and religion at this point when the two approaches to the world are rightly understood. Conflict arises, however, when the biblical idea of creation, which in actuality "describes the limits of the world's rationality and the inadequacy of any 'natural' cause as a sufficient explanation

---

[1] A myth is a "pictorial way of representing ideas which lie at the limits of human understanding." (Alan Richardson, *The Gospel and Modern Thought,* London, Oxford University Press, 1950, p. 152.) To take it literally is to destroy its meaning altogether.

for the irrational givenness of things," is corrupted into a theory of secondary causation and thereby comes into conflict with a valid scientific account of causation at the natural level.[2] And conflict also arises when scientific theories of natural causation are posited as adequate explanations of ultimate causation and coherence. Yet, when they are rightly understood, these two views supplement each other.

Not only does the biblical account of creation differ from a scientific account of secondary causation within a system of nature that is "given," but the method whereby men in Scripture are brought to acknowledge God as Creator differs from the method whereby speculative reason is led to posit God as the First Cause. In the Bible, God is known first as the sovereign Lord of men and nations, of history and nature; He is known secondly as the Creator who, because He is sovereign over all, is also Creator of all. Israel encountered God first as Lord over herself and also over the nations before she came to know Him as the Creator of the heavens and the earth. The starting point of the biblical understanding of God is man's personal encounter with God who confronts him first as Lord and secondly, but in a sense more ultimately, as his Creator, or the ground of his being and value. The starting point of the philosophical quest for an explanation of the origin of the world and for its ultimate principle of coherence is man's reason. The starting point of the biblical quest for an answer to these questions is "faith"—not some theory which man is led to accept as a reasonable explanation for that which reason has observed, but a conviction, or "ultimate concern," by which he has been grasped and which in turn illuminates all the rest of his experience. It is by faith, therefore, that the Bible declares that the world was created by the Word of God (Heb. 11:3). Moreover, the Bible does not attempt to prove this conviction; rather, it describes the way the world and life look from the standpoint of this insight. It witnesses to the meaning of life and death, of the "whence" and the "whither" of existence, of good and evil, as seen from the standpoint of this faith by which it has been grasped.

The traditional formula for expressing the Christian doctrine of creation is *creatio ex nihilo,* i.e., creation out of nothing.[3] This phrase

[2] Reinhold Niebuhr, *Faith and History,* New York, Charles Scribner's Sons, 1949, p. 33.

[3] As Professor Irwin points out, the Old Testament does not explicitly affirm the doctrine of "creation out of nothing." Indeed, Genesis 1:1 may even imply the reverse so that matter was assumed to be preëxistent although there is certainly no suggestion that it was therefore considered evil (W. A. Irwin,

represents an explicit rejection of any ultimate dualism.[4] God did not create the world out of something that was "given" to Him and which influenced Him in His creativity and resisted His creative purpose. All that existed "before" the creative work of God was God. The created order had its foundation and its origin in Him alone. It exists solely because He chose to call it into being: "Thou didst create all things and by thy will they existed and were created" (Rev. 4:11). God was under no external compulsion to make a world; He did so only because it seemed good to Him so to do.

In addition to providing a rejection of every form of ultimate dualism the doctrine of "creation out of nothing" represents the strongest possible affirmation of the goodness of creation. Each created thing is called into being by the divine Word and in accordance with the divine will. Each created thing is finite—it has a beginning in time, but each is good.[5] Evil and sin and the tragic, therefore, are not ultimate; they do not belong to the essential nature of things. This view is incompatible, moreover, with any form of asceticism which seeks to escape from the world of nature and finiteness because it is evil.

A classical expression of this faith in the goodness of creation is found in the *Confessions of St. Augustine*. This concept signifies primarily two things for Augustine. In the first place, it means that all things are good for God who is the source and center of all being and value, and in the second place it means that each thing is good in its order, manifesting the goodness of beauty and contributing to the

---

The Old Testament: Keystone of Human Culture, New York, Henry Schuman, 1952, pp. 69–70). With the possible exception of Hebrews 11:3—"What is seen was made out of things which do not appear"—the doctrine itself does not appear in the Bible. Rather, it represents an effort to state in theological and philosophical terms what is implied by the biblical concept of creation—its ultimate mystery and the absolute dependence of all created things upon the will and power of a transcendent Being who creates by fiat, i.e., by His Word. By contrast, the Bible expresses its faith in God as Creator thusly: "And God said, 'Let there be light'; and there was light" (Gen. 1:3). Or, again, it declares: "For he spoke, and it (the earth) came to be; he commanded, and it stood forth" (Ps. 33:9). Similarly, the Fourth Gospel asserts: "In the beginning was the Word. . . . all things were made through him" (John 1:1–3). In this connection see also Emil Brunner, *The Christian Doctrine of Creation and Redemption, II: Dogmatics,* London, Lutterworth Press, 1952, pp. 9–12.

[4] Cf. Paul Tillich, *Systematic Theology,* I, Chicago, University of Chicago Press, 1951, p. 253. See also Emil Brunner, *loc. cit.*

[5] Cf. Genesis 1:31: "And God saw everything that he had made, and behold, it was very good."

perfection of the order as a whole.[6] "Whatsoever in any degree is, is good," Augustine declares, for if things were deprived of all of their goodness they would cease to be.[7] Insofar as they retain the nature with which they were created all things are good, but insofar as their nature has been corrupted they are evil. However, no being is absolutely evil, for in the process of becoming so it would cease to be. "Hence not even the nature of the devil himself is evil, in so far as it is nature, but it was made evil by being perverted."[8]

In pointing to the absolute dependence of the world upon God while at the same time affirming the absolute independence of God as Creator, the biblical doctrine of creation makes clear the infinite gap between the two. "The greatest dissimilarity between two things which we can express at all," writes Brunner, "is that between the Creator and that which is created."[9] All created things, whatever differences may distinguish them from each other, have one thing in common which distinguishes them from God: they are created and finite; He is uncreated and infinite. They are dependent upon, or conditioned by, His originating and sustaining will; He is dependent upon, or conditioned by, nothing outside of Himself.

It is true, of course, that man has a certain power to create, but this power is very limited. Unlike God, man cannot create absolutely. He must be given materials with which to work and the power to work.[10] He must submit, moreover, to the nature of the materials as these are given to him. The sculptor must be given stone, the painter pigments, the physicist atoms; and each is limited by the qualities inherent in these substances. God, however, is not thus dependent upon, or limited by, a reality independent of Himself to which He must submit. The biblical doctrine of creation therefore recognizes the ultimate mystery of the divine creation, for we have no parallel to it in our experience. God's ways are not man's ways, and His thoughts are not man's thoughts. He is transcendent, "wholly-other"; yet through His creation He has given man a clue to His ways and purposes. He has manifest His moral will in the moral order which He

[6] St. Augustine, *The Confessions of St. Augustine,* New York, E. P. Dutton & Co. (Everyman's Library), 1950, XIII, xxvii, 43. See also H. Richard Niebuhr, *Christ and Culture,* New York, Harper & Brothers, 1951, pp. 210 ff.

[7] St. Augustine, *op. cit.,* XIII, xxxi, 46.

[8] St. Augustine, *The City of God,* New York, Random House (Modern Library), 1950, XIX, 13.

[9] Emil Brunner, *Man in Revolt,* trans. by Olive Wyon, Philadelphia, The Westminster Press, 1947, p. 90.

[10] Cf. Deuteronomy 8:18: "You shall remember the Lord your God, for it is he who gives you power to get wealth."

has established. He has declared His will and His purpose in history. He has revealed Himself as Creator, as Sovereign, and as the Savior of men. Such an understanding of God is possible for man only because He has created man in His own image with the capacity to respond to His self-disclosure in creation, in history, and in the personal experience of God's presence.

God's originating work of creation and His continuous creativity in the preservation of the structure of reality provide the ground for the biblical conception of God's sovereignty and His providence. Out of eternity, Augustine declared, He creates things and time together.[11] "In the beginning"—that is, at the beginning of the temporal order—God called the temporal order into being. He continually sustains it, and He will bring it to fulfillment. This fulfillment is only partially accomplished within history, however, and its completion lies at the end of the historical or temporal order. This is the meaning of the eschatological expectations of the prophets and of Jesus. In a sense the Kingdom of God is present in history, but its final establishment lies beyond history after the purpose of creation has been fulfilled. The temporal order will pass away, but God is eternal. He and His Kingdom remain. God is both "before" the temporal order was called into being and "after" it shall have been fulfilled and passed away.

This faith in God as Creator and Ruler of the universe, then, is the foundation of all Christian thought about the world and man's place in it. In the first instance, it calls our attention to the fact that God, not man, is the center of the world in which we live. His will and purpose are primary, and ultimately He will not be defeated for He is sovereign in history because He is the ground of history. This faith reminds us, in the second place, that man and the entire created order belong to God. "The earth is the Lord's and the fulness thereof, the world and those who dwell therein" (Ps. 24:1). All human ownership is relative, for God is the ultimate owner of all. Man is therefore not free to use anything—his neighbor, himself, the dumb animals, the resources of nature—as he will to serve only his own selfish ends. Finally, since man is a creature whose nature and destiny are determined by the Creator, it follows that his existence has meaning only in relation to the intention or purpose of his Maker. His fulfillment, the realization of his true self, is possible only if man fulfills the will of his Creator which is the law of his being. In the language of the Reformation, each person is "called" to fulfill the creative purpose of

[11] *The City of God,* XI, 6.

God, and the acceptance of this summons is what gives meaning to human life.

GOD IS ACTIVE AS JUDGE

Not only does the Bible speak of God as the One whom men meet in all events as the ground of being—the source and sustaining power of the world and all that is in it—but it also speaks of Him as the One whom men encounter at every turn as their Judge. The Genesis accounts of Creation are followed immediately by the story of the Fall and the "curse" which God placed upon man for his disobedience. To Eve God said, "I will greatly multiply your pain in childbearing; in pain you shall bring forth children; yet your desire shall be for your husband, and he shall rule over you" (Gen. 3:16). And to Adam God said, "Because you have listened to the voice of your wife, and have eaten of the tree of which I commanded you, 'You shall not eat of it,' cursed is the ground because of you; in toil you shall eat of it all the days of your life . . ." (Gen. 3:17). And the Lord drove Adam and Eve forth from the Garden of Eden. Taken together, the myths of Creation and the myth of the Fall assert that man's Creator is also his Judge, and while it is possible for man to live without God's blessing, it is impossible for him to live without His judgment.[12]

The recognition of the judgments of God in the national crises and catastrophes of Israel was the unique contribution of the prophets to the development of biblical faith. Long before the appearance of the great prophets of the eighth to the sixth centuries, Israel had acknowledged Yahweh as her jealous Lord. From its beginning the concept of a covenant relationship between God and Israel had represented a recognition of the latter's obligation to serve not her own purpose but the will of God. By the time of Amos, however, the covenant had become widely misunderstood as a promise of Israel's ultimate vindication over all of her foes. Israel had come to identify her own will and national interests with the divine will of which she was in actuality only the instrument. Hence she was unable to understand her crises and the calamities which had befallen her. Amos saw clearly, however, that Yahweh was righteous and because He was righteous and sovereign He must execute judgment in history. There-

[12] John Baillie, *Our Knowledge of God*, New York, Charles Scribner's Sons, 1939, p. 3.

fore, he argued, catastrophe is what Israel should expect from God in view of her rebellion against Him. Evil doesn't just happen to a community, and Israel cannot hope to escape because she is Yahweh's elect. "Does evil befall a city, unless the Lord has done it?" (Amos 3:6). Woe to those who desire the day of the Lord, for "it is darkness, and not light" (Amos 5:18). Not only Israel but all the nations stand under God's judgment. He is sovereign over all, for He is the Creator of all. He who made the Pleiades and Orion, who formed the mountains and creates the wind, is also the One who established the moral order and maintains it by His judgments. In a similar manner, Jeremiah represented God as declaring, "The Lord will roar from on high, and from his holy habitation utter his voice. . . . The clamor will resound to the ends of the earth, for the Lord has an indictment against the nations; he is entering into judgment with all flesh, and the wicked he will put to the sword" (Jer. 25:30–31). Likewise, the Second Isaiah prophesied against Babylon, "You felt secure in your wickedness, you said, 'No one sees me' . . . But evil shall come upon you for which you cannot atone; disaster shall fall upon you, which you will not be able to expiate; and ruin shall come on you suddenly, of which you know nothing" (Isa. 47:10–11).

The judgments which the prophets saw God as meting out in the catastrophes of history were in the main judgments against human pride and man's effort to put himself in the place of God. The calamities followed "naturally" and inevitably from man's refusal to acknowledge the dependent character of his existence and the moral nature of the world in which he lived. Hence, far from proving the indifference or weakness of God, they confirmed the prophets' faith that He is righteous and sovereign. These events revealed Him as "the structure, the law, the essential character of reality, as the source and center of the created world against which the pride of man destroys itself in vain rebellion."[13]

The prophets, it should be remembered, were not led to their faith in God as righteous and sovereign *by* the course of historical events any more than a modern historian or observer of the events leading to the destruction of Mussolini and Hitler and the rise and spread of Communism is led thereby to such a belief in our own day. Rather, what the prophets observed in the course of history confirmed the faith which they already had, just as an analysis of events in recent

[13] Reinhold Niebuhr, *The Nature and Destiny of Man,* I: *Human Nature,* New York, Charles Scribner's Sons, 1943, p. 141.

European history confirms the faith of some contemporary historians such as Herbert Butterfield. That some form of judgment takes place in history, it is difficult to deny, Professor Butterfield writes, "but those who do not believe in Christianity will hardly admit that it is there by any providential and purposeful ordination."[14] Nevertheless, since it is impossible to interpret history at all without some principle of interpretation which history as such does not yield, it is significant that history confirms the prophetic interpretation.

It would be a misunderstanding of the prophets and of the Bible as a whole, however, if we were to assume that they saw in history a simple correlation between judgment and sin so that one could say that only the wicked suffer and that their suffering is strictly proportionate to the evil which they have done. Job protested strongly against such a view, and Second Isaiah recognized that Israel had received double for her sins while her wicked oppressors had gone unpunished. Jesus strongly rebuked his disciples for assuming that it was either because of his own sins or those of his parents that a certain man was born blind: "It was not that this man sinned, or his parents, but that the works of God might be made manifest in him" (John 9:3). The Bible does not give a speculative answer to the problem of the suffering of the innocent; rather, it is concerned to show men how they may come to grips with evil and overcome it by drawing upon the resources of faith. Moreover, it strongly warns men and nations against the proud assumption that their prosperity and temporary security are proof of their virtue. God uses the nations as His instruments to execute judgment even though they themselves may be intent only upon fulfilling their own proud ambitions and even though they in turn may also be brought low. The defeat of Italy and Japan in World War II, for example, does not mean that the Allies were righteous and the defeated nations were necessarily more wicked than the victors, nor does it imply that the latter will not also be judged for their pride and idolatry.

There is a sense in which, as Professor Butterfield points out, the recognition of judgment in history is valid only in its application as self-judgment—as a matter between the person or nation which is being judged and God; and third parties, or outsiders, are not entitled to presume upon the observable fact of suffering or defeat.[15] Thus

[14] Herbert Butterfield, *Christianity and History,* New York, Charles Scribner's Sons, 1950, p. 57.
[15] *Ibid.,* pp. 62–63.

Jesus warned his followers: "Judge not, that you be not judged. For with the judgment you pronounce you will be judged" (Matt. 7:1 f.). Or concerning "those eighteen upon whom the tower of Siloam fell and killed them," he asked, "do you think that they were worse offenders than all the others who dwelt in Jerusalem? I tell you, No; but unless you repent you will all likewise perish" (Luke 13:4–5). God's judgments in history are thus first of all a summons to repentance. All men stand under the judgment of God's holiness and righteousness. Viewed in this perspective, the differences between the saints and sinners provide no ground for boasting; rather, the similarities between them provide a common ground for repentance, for all have come short of the glory of God.

Since the judgment that is being passed upon men and nations in history is rough and incomplete, the Bible looks for a last judgment in which the justice of God will be fully vindicated. In later Judaism and in Christianity the picture of this final judgment is accompanied by the resurrection of the dead so that all people—not just those living in a historical messianic age—will participate in it. Again and again Jesus spoke of an eschatological reckoning and of the consequences which it holds in store for men. Such a judgment is the corollary of faith in the sovereignty and righteousness of God. In essence, it is a judgment which men have passed upon themselves by the lives which they have lived. God did not send His Son into the world to condemn the world (John 3:17), but this revelation of His love inevitably implied a judgment which men brought upon themselves. "This is the judgment, that the light has come into the world, and men loved the darkness rather than light, because their deeds were evil" (John 3:19). The "last" judgment is in reality a symbol for the final work of love which rejects and leaves to self-destruction those who ultimately resist the divine love and do not permit themselves to be subdued and ruled by it.

Like Amos' contemporaries, we moderns are reluctant to recognize in the events of history the judgments of God upon ourselves. We are even inclined to dismiss such notions as the "anger" and "wrath" of God as anthropomorphic relics of a primitive conception of religion, and there is a tendency in popular religious thought to distinguish sharply between the God of the Old Testament as a God of wrath and the God of the New Testament as a God of love. This reluctance to take seriously the biblical testimony about God as Judge represents a gross misunderstanding of the nature of the moral and spiritual life.

It reflects a highly sentimental conception of the nature of goodness and love as well as a serious misapprehension of the purpose of God in executing judgment.

Thus far we have spoken primarily of the divine judgments which are represented in the crises and catastrophes of history, and we have seen the relevance of such an understanding of history in our own day. But men encounter the judgment of God in many forms whether or not they are aware that a divine "No" is being pronounced against their egotism, their idolatry, and their efforts to be a law unto themselves. They encounter the "wrath" of God when they are convicted by their consciences and also when they become insensitive to the good through their persistence in evil. Sometimes this judgment takes the form of "the Hound of Heaven" which pursues them relentlessly "down the days and down the years"; again, it takes the form of a hardening of men's hearts and a dulling of their powers of moral and spiritual awareness so that they become dehumanized (cf. Rom. 1:23). "The wrath of God," writes Paul, "is revealed from heaven against all ungodliness and wickedness of men who by their wickedness suppress the truth" (Rom. 1:18). It is revealed in the distortion of men's thinking, in the darkening of their minds, in the corruption of the image of God wherein they were created, in their lustings and degenerate sexual practices, and in their envy, murder, strife, faithlessness, heartlessness, and ruthlessness (Rom. 1:21–31).

In *Killers of the Dream,* Lillian Smith gives a striking portrayal of the way in which the judgment of God is being meted out in similar fashion upon those in our day who because of racial pride arrogantly shut off members of other racial groups from any genuine fellowship with themselves. She writes of her early life in the South:

I began to understand so slowly at first but more and more clearly as the years passed, that the warped, distorted frame we have put around every Negro child from birth is around every white child also. . . . And I knew that what cruelly shapes and cripples the personality of one is as cruelly shaping and crippling the personality of the other. I began to see that though we may . . . gain the strength to tear the frame from us, yet we are stunted and warped and in our lifetime cannot grow straight again any more than can a tree, put in a steel-like twisting frame when young, grow tall and straight when the frame is torn away at maturity.[16]

---

[16] Lillian Smith, *Killers of the Dream,* New York, W. W. Norton & Company, 1949, pp. 30–31.

Or, again, men experience the divine judgment in the daily round of work. When the entire range of technical, social, and normative relationships that are involved in a typical human task is taken into account, writes Professor Calhoun, "there is perhaps no more inescapable and convincing judgment upon human inadequacy than can be found in the refusal of a working situation to tolerate careless or dishonest response."[17] God's "word of judgment is spoken silently . . . . in every sequence of work and in every human career." Sometimes it "crashes like thunder when a cumulative mass of human failure brings down in ruin . . . . a bridge or a dam, a business or a government, an empire or a civilization." Such calamities do not come about for any mysterious reason, rather they befall men because they fail to meet "the requirements that God lays down."[18]

In all of these ways, then, men encounter God as Judge, and they find themselves experiencing His wrath. They find themselves confronting the one God who is at the same time their Creator and also their Judge. Hence it is no accident that the Bible speaks of man's experience of the wrath of God as one of the fundamental ways in which man is related to Him. This aspect of man's relationship to deity cannot be lost sight of without making God something less than the God of the Bible.

It should be clear from what has already been said that the concept of divine wrath does not mean that God acts out of anger after the fashion of our purely natural impulses. But on account of the widespread misunderstanding of the motivation which lies behind the divine judgment, this fact needs to be emphasized. Unless it is recognized, it is impossible to understand the suffering and calamities of history in a Christian way. The "wrath" of God is a symbolic way of describing the self-destructive character of evil which is self-destructive precisely because God established the kind of moral order with which man is confronted. It is a metaphorical way of describing the fact that evil men reap the fruits of evil in this kind of moral order. It describes sinful man's experience of estrangement from the ground of his being, his experience of life when it is organized around a false center. Sinful men experience the divine judgment as wrath, but the purpose or intent of God in visiting such judgments upon them is disciplinary and ultimately redemptive rather than vindictive.

---

[17] Robert L. Calhoun, "Work as Christian Vocation Today" in John Oliver Nelson, ed., *Work and Vocation,* New York, Harper and Brothers, 1954, p. 179.
  [18] *Ibid.,* pp. 179–180.

Punishment and judgment, as Luther saw, are the "strange" work of divine love.[19] The former are not in conflict with, but rather a part of, the continuing *agape* of God. "The Lord reproves him whom he loves, as a father the son in whom he delights" (Prov. 3:12).

GOD IS ACTIVE AS REDEEMER

The final word of Christian faith about God is not that He is Judge but rather that He is Redeemer. As we have seen, this is the testimony of the prophets in the Old Testament as well as the witness of Jesus and the New Testament. Although the God of the Old Testament is frequently pictured in present-day popular thought as a God of wrath, the prophets of Israel saw, as we have noted, that the primary relation of God to Israel was not that of wrath but that of love. Not only was His love manifest in creation, but it was manifest in a special way in the history of Israel—in the revelation of Himself to Abram and in the covenant which He made with him, in the Exodus from Egypt, and in the giving of the Ten Commandments and the renewal of the covenant through Moses. All of these were blessings which did not rest primarily upon Israel's merit but rather upon God's grace and love. Their meaning was that Yahweh, Israel's sovereign Lord, was also her Redeemer. He had taken the initiative in bringing about her salvation. And as the knowledge of God deepened and monotheism became explicit, Second Isaiah declared that the salvation of Him who had created all would extend to the ends of the earth.

In biblical thought, the work of the Redeemer is inseparable from His work as Creator. As Canon Richardson has observed, "There is . . . no meaning in the word 'salvation' unless God is the one who saves."[20] Amos had seen that it was "He who made the Pleiades and Orion" who used the nations to execute judgment upon the earth, and he had glimpsed the possibility that the Creator-Judge might yet spare a remnant, but it was Hosea and Second Isaiah who saw most clearly that the intent of the Creator—who, as Judge, executed judgment— was ultimately most profoundly understood as love rather than as wrath. The history of biblical revelation is the history of the revelation of the nature and will and purposes of the Creator; it is the history

---

[19] Cf. Gustaf Aulén, *The Faith of the Christian Church*, trans. from the fourth Swedish edition by Eric H. Wahlstrom and G. Everett Arden, Philadelphia, The Muhlenberg Press, 1948, pp. 169 ff.

[20] Alan Richardson, *op. cit.*, p. 152.

of the unfolding of God's love which has been regnant from eternity, not the history of the transformation of His wrath into love. The history of redemption is the history of the work of the One God who has revealed Himself in many ways and in many events, not the history of the work of a Redeemer God opposing another God who is viewed as man's Creator and Judge. "Thus says the Lord, your Redeemer, who formed you from the womb: 'I am the Lord, who made all things, who stretched out the heavens alone, who spread out the earth" (Isa. 44:24). Similarly, for Jesus the Creator of nature is the One who wills the salvation of all. Thus he admonishes his followers not to be anxious about their lives but, rather, to trust God to supply their deepest needs. "Look at the birds of the air: they neither sow nor reap nor gather into barns, and yet your heavenly Father feeds them. . . . Consider the lilies of the field, how they grow; they neither toil nor spin . . . . But if God so clothes the grass of the field, which today is alive and tomorrow is thrown into the oven, will he not much more clothe you, O men of little faith?" (Matt. 6:26–30). God is like a good shepherd who goes out into the night to seek his lost sheep, or He is like a devoted father who runs out to meet his prodigal son. The Creator and the Judge is most adequately understood as man's heavenly Father who loves even the least and most unworthy of His children and who freely offers forgiveness and life to all who trust in Him. Christians from the beginning have seen in the coming, the life, the death, and the resurrection of Jesus, the fullest revelation of the redemptive purpose of God. The purpose of his coming, they believe, was not to condemn the world but that through him men might have life. Moreover, it was the Word of God through which all things were made which became manifest in the flesh and dwelt among men in the person of Jesus of Nazareth (John 1:1–2, 14).

The fact that it is the Creator who saves men gives to salvation an ultimate meaning. The redemptive work of God is a revelation of the ultimate or essential nature of that which is fundamentally real in the universe. In the language of the Fourth Gospel, "The only Son, who is in the bosom of the Father, he has made him known" (John 1:18). Thus the biblical conception of redemption is monotheistic through and through. "There is no other god besides me, a righteous God and a Savior" (Isa. 45:21). It is also filled with positive content. Salvation is not understood primarily in negative terms as being saved from evil to something neutral or from death to meaningless, purposeless existence. Rather, it is being brought into participation in the will and purposes of God. It is redemption from sin to righteousness, from death to life. It is being delivered from the dominion of darkness and transferred to the kingdom of Christ (Col. 1:13). Thus, in this sense, as Brunner points out, it is inaccurate "to say that it is the idea of Redemption and not that of Creation which is the standard and distinctive feature of the Christian Faith."[21] The idea of redemption exists outside of biblical faith, but where it is divorced from the idea of Creation it is "disintegrating in its effects" and issues in an ethic of world-abandonment or asceticism.[22]

But not only is the work of God the Redeemer inseparable from His work as Creator; it is also inseparable from His work as Judge. Just as the concept of Redemption becomes disintegrative apart from the idea of Creation so it becomes sentimental apart from the idea of judgment or discipline. The prophets, as we have observed, saw that God's judgment was not merely punitive; rather, its ultimate purpose was to make redemption possible. Even Amos, who perhaps of all the prophets stresses most exclusively the retributive character of Israel's punishment, held out the possibility at least that if she would only repent and be faithful to Yahweh He might yet be gracious to a remnant (Amos 5:14–15). Isaiah represented God as saying to Israel, "I will turn my hand against you and will smelt away your dross as with lye and remove all your alloy. . . . Afterward you shall be called the city of righteousness, the faithful city" (Isa. 1:25–26). And Hosea saw in Israel's suffering the means whereby Yahweh would woo His unfaithful bride back unto Himself: "I will betroth you to me forever; I will betroth you to me in righteousness and in justice, in steadfast love, and in mercy. I will betroth you to me in faithfulness" (Hos. 2:19–20). Beyond the manifestation of God's wrath there would be a new disclosure of His mercy and forgiveness. Just as He had watched over Israel and Judah "to pluck up and break down, to overthrow, destroy, and bring evil, so I will watch over them to build and to plant, says the Lord" (Jer. 31:28). Beyond the day of punishment will come the day when God will make a new covenant with Israel and Judah. The covenant will become an inward bond uniting them to Him, and it will reveal to them the deepest dimension of God's love: His forgiveness. "But this is the covenant which I will make with the house of Israel after those days, says the

---

[21] Emil Brunner, *The Divine Imperative,* trans. by Olive Wyon, New York, The Macmillan Company, 1942, p. 127.
[22] *Ibid.*

Lord: I will put my law within them, and I will write it upon their hearts, and I will be their God, and they shall be my people. . . . I will forgive their iniquity, and I will remember their sin no more" (Jer. 31:33–34).

We have said that redemption becomes sentimental if it is separated from judgment. This does not mean, however, that it is always the guilty who must suffer or be punished before they can be healed. What it does mean essentially is that evil brings suffering and that redemption is costly. Evil cannot be sown in a moral universe without the fruits of evil being reaped. The earlier prophets had seen Israel's punishment and suffering primarily as chastisement for her own unfaithfulness and as a means for her salvation. Second Isaiah, on the other hand, saw that while the disaster that had befallen her was in part a sign of God's punishment of a sinful people it had a far deeper significance, for it represented the high destiny for which she had been chosen—she who had received double for all her sins—viz., the summons to be God's agent in bringing blessing and salvation to the ends of the earth. Israel had been chosen to be obedient even unto suffering and death that, by her witness to God's redemptive activity in history, she might be the means of bringing salvation to the Gentiles. Thus the nations are pictured as confessing that the tiny nation which they had previously held in contempt had actually been suffering all the while in their stead:

> Surely he has borne our griefs
>   and carried our sorrows;
> yet we esteemed him stricken,
>   smitten by God, and afflicted.
> But he was wounded for our transgressions,
>   he was bruised for our iniquities;
> upon him was the chastisement that made us whole,
>   and with his stripes we are healed.   (Isa. 53:4–5)

Evil and sin bring suffering. In part it falls upon the guilty, but in a moral universe where men are free the wicked sometimes flourish while the innocent are cut off. This does not mean that God is not just. On the contrary, this is what is to be expected on occasion if man's freedom is to be preserved. But if God is really the Lord of history, His purposes will not ultimately be defeated. Indeed, He is rather working out His purposes in and through the order which He has established and which permits the wicked to prosper at the expense of the righteous although He certainly does not will that they should do so. But since God is the one who has revealed Himself as the Creator who is righteous and who is also love, the Jewish exiles in Babylon have nothing to fear. They have seen God's grace and His purpose manifest in their history since the time of Abraham. They have found that despite their own unfaithfulness God has been faithful to His covenant with Israel. Seen from the perspective of the purpose of God as it has been disclosed to Israel, her chastisement is only partially judgment; it is also a summons to her to witness to the redemptive love of God and share in the richness of that love which bears the "cost" of forgiveness and reconciliation. This "cost" is the pain and suffering which vicarious love takes upon itself in the offender's stead in order to effect the renewal of fellowship between those who are estranged. It is the "price"—not in terms of sacrifices of fruit or lambs or humans which must be offered to settle an account or preserve someone's honor, but in terms of love which takes upon itself the consequences of wrong and makes overtures of forgiveness to the offender in order that a bond of love may reunite those who are alienated from each other by guilt and pride.

Nowhere in the Old Testament is there a deeper understanding of the meaning of Israel's suffering and the depth of God's love than in Second Isaiah's description of the suffering servant. Centuries later Jesus pointed to his own mission as the fulfillment of this prophetic vision (Luke 4:17–21), and the Christian Church has from the beginning found in Isaiah 53 one of the most nearly adequate interpretations of the meaning of Jesus' death upon the cross. Speaking of his own work, Jesus declared, "The Son of man came to seek and to save that which was lost" (Luke 19:10). He "came not to be served but to serve, and to give his life as a ransom for many" (Matt. 20:28). He told his disciples that in the fulfillment of his special vocation he would have to "suffer many things, and be rejected by the elders and chief priests and scribes, and be killed" (Luke 9:22). Jesus forgave men their sins in the name of the Father, and he described God's seeking love in terms of the parables of the Prodigal Son, the Good Shepherd, and the Lost Coin. "There is joy before the angels of God over one sinner who repents" (Luke 15:10). The early followers of Jesus, looking back upon his death in the light of his teaching about the love of God and his own vocation, saw in it the fullest disclosure of God's redemptive love. "God shows his love for us in that while we were yet sinners Christ died for us" (Rom. 5:8). "God so loved the world that he gave his only Son, that whoever believes in him should not perish but have eternal life. For God sent the Son into the world, not to condemn the world, but that the world might be saved through him" (John 3:16–17).

Redemption is costly in terms of God's reconciling men and the world unto Himself, just as it is costly in terms of the reconciliation of children who have gone astray to their parents or of the restoration of true oneness in a marriage relationship which has been broken by unfaithfulness, pride, and self-centeredness. However this is precisely that which constitutes the Gospel: viz., the message that God—the Creator and the Judge—is also the Redeemer who takes the consequences of man's sins upon Himself and freely offers him forgiveness, the possibility of a new beginning, and the promise of renewed strength and fulfillment. Instead of the wrath which men deserve they are made aware of a love which accepts and forgives and sustains them.

When God's relation to men is seen to be redemptive in purpose rather than punitive or indifferent, the whole of life and history becomes a drama of reconciliation and liberation. The arena of history is a place where God is doing a new thing, bringing into actuality "a new creation" (Gal. 6:15),[23] calling into being a community of those who have been redeemed and who in turn manifest the reality of His redeeming love by being themselves instruments of redemption. What this means we shall endeavor to see more in detail in the remainder of our study, but here it is important to notice the scope and relevance of the salvation to which the Bible as a whole and the New Testament in particular witness; for this is the heart of the Gospel and at the same time that part of the Christian faith which seems most incredible to modern man—incredible in large part because it so frequently becomes an empty theological symbol, an abstract formula rather than a concept which points to a living reality in the common life of the community of faith.

In seeking to rediscover the meaning and the relevance of salvation it is instructive to note that the biblical writers use a variety of symbols to describe what the term signifies to them. For Paul, salvation is primarily *liberation* from sin, from legalistic morality, from death, from the fear of death, and from superpersonal powers of evil. Elsewhere he speaks of it as the *reconciliation* of man with God

[23] Cf. Paul Tillich, *The New Being*, New York, Charles Scribner's Sons, 1955.

which makes possible the reconciliation of man with himself and with his fellowmen. Redemption takes place wherever men know themselves forgiven by God and their fellows and where they are able to accept themselves and achieve a new level of integration. God is at work amid all of these experiences, for the fundamental reconciliation which is basic to its other forms is the restoration of fellowship with God. The metaphor of *healing* is frequently used by others to suggest the meaning of salvation in terms of the restoration of sinful men to wholeness. Thus the psalmist blesses God "who forgives all your iniquity, who heals all your diseases" (Ps. 103:3). Similarly, Jeremiah speaks of God as healing Israel's unfaithfulness (Jer. 3:22), and Second Isaiah looks forward to the time when the Gentiles will be healed by the stripes which the Servant of the Lord bears in their behalf (Isa. 53:5). Jesus likewise speaks of the publicans and sinners as being in need of a physician (Matt. 9:11–12), and in the Gospels he is frequently pictured as healing those who are vexed with unclean spirits. Still another symbol that is often used to describe the meaning of redemption is *justification*. By itself, however, this term connotes a courthouse view of redemption that is far too juridical to do justice to the love of God; moreover, it is frequently interpreted by Fundamentalists in a way that does violence to His moral nature. Rightly understood, however, this concept points to the basic conviction of Christianity that it is God who freely justifies man rather than man who saves himself by his own works. Yet another metaphor that is used in the New Testament is *regeneration,* or being born again (John 3:3, 5, 7; I Pet. 1:23). This is closely related to Paul's concept of a *"new creation"* and to the Johannine understanding of *resurrection* as a radical transformation that takes place here and now. "I am the resurrection and the life; he who believes in me, though he die, yet shall he live, and whoever lives and believes in me shall never die" (John 11:25–26).

As Professor Daniel D. Williams points out in *God's Grace and Man's Hope,* there has been a widespread tendency in much recent and contemporary theology to neglect the meaning and relevance of the Christian understanding of salvation as a present deliverance and transformation of life.[24] Not only is this true of "liberal" theologians who have frequently seen little need for man's redemption because they have believed that he could save himself, but it is also true of

[24] Daniel D. Williams, *God's Grace and Man's Hope,* New York, Harper & Brothers, 1949, pp. 27–32.

"neo-orthodox" theologians, many of whom have tended to limit sal-vation almost exclusively to a realm which lies "beyond history." We have already stressed both the fact that the Bible assumes that man needs a savior and also the fact that it affirms that God is actively engaged in man's redemption. Our concern here is to inquire to what extent salvation is, according to Christian faith, a present possibility and a present reality in human life.

Although the eschatological motif is strong in the New Testament teaching about salvation, it is clear that a new principle of life has been introduced into history and that it has become a reality in the lives of those who are presently in Christ, for they are now new crea-tions (II Cor. 5:17). As Professor H. Richard Niebuhr, writing of Paul's view of the redemptive work of God, declares, "It would seem false to interpret all this in eschatological terms. . . . The new life, moreover, was not simply a promise and a hope but a present reality, evident in the ability of men to call upon God as their Father and to bring forth fruits of the spirit of Christ within them and their com-munity. The great revolution in human existence was not past; neither was it still to come: it was now going on."[25] For Paul, salvation was a process which begins when faith becomes vital but which remains incomplete on this side of the grave. Thus, "The word of the cross is folly to those who are perishing, but to us who *are being saved* it is the power of God" (I Cor. 1:18).[26]

In his interpretation of the new life of the Christian as a present reality, Paul was true to the mood of the gospel proclaimed by Jesus. For not only did Jesus summon men to repent, but he offered them the blessings of life in the Kingdom which was present although it was also yet to come in its fullness. Those who had faith were ex-pected to show the fruits of faith and obedience in this life; and in this life they would be freed from anxiety, fear, alienation from God, self-centeredness, pride, impure motives, and the worship of mammon. "Today," Jesus said to Zacchaeus, "salvation has come to this house" (Luke 19:9). In this, as in many other connections, the Fourth Evan-

[25] H. Richard Niebuhr, *op. cit.*, pp. 162–163.
[26] Cf. Millar Burrows, *An Outline of Biblical Theology*, Philadelphia, The Westminster Press, 1946, p. 185: "Thus salvation for Paul is threefold: past, present, and future. The believer *is* already saved; he has been forgiven, justi-fied, adopted, reconciled, delivered from the fear of judgment. He *will* be saved; in the life to come he will be free altogether from the power of sin in the flesh. Meanwhile he is *being* saved; in Christ he is overcoming the power of sin in himself."

gelist expressed the testimony of Christian faith when he represented Jesus as saying to his disciples, "As the Father has loved me, so have I loved you; abide in my love. If you keep my commandments, you will abide in my love, just as I have kept my Father's commandments and abide in his love. These things have I spoken to you that my joy may be in you, and that your joy may be full" (John 15:9–11). To abide thus in the Father's love is eternal life. It is, moreover, a present possibility for man in this life. That this is so is the meaning also of the author of the First Letter of John when he declares, "Beloved, we are God's children now" (I John 3:2).

This New Testament understanding of redemption is in keeping with the Old Testament testimony of the prophets and the psalmists. We have noted the manner in which the former saw God as doing a saving work in history. They saw God's judgment upon their sin as the means whereby He was bringing men to a knowledge of the depth of their sin and thus to repentance and the restoration of a right relationship with Himself. Sin might yet have its harvest, but the promise of redemption was for them the promise of forgiveness and of the possibility of a present renewal.[27] The psalmists speak eloquently of the way in which they have experienced God's redemptive grace and love as present realities.

> The Lord is my shepherd, I shall not want;
>   he makes me lie down in green pastures.
> He leads me beside still waters;
>   he restores my soul.   (Ps. 23:1–2)

> O give thanks to the Lord, for he is good;
>   for his steadfast love endures for ever!
> Let the redeemed of the Lord say so,
>   whom he has redeemed from trouble. . . .

> Some were sick through their sinful ways,
>   and because of their iniquities suffered affliction;
> they loathed any kind of food,
>   and they drew near to the gates of death.
> Then they cried to the Lord in their trouble,
>   and he delivered them from their distress;

---

[27] Speaking of the prophets, Professor Snaith says that their concept of holiness "should be regarded as involving Salvation to at least an equal extent as Righteousness. God is Saviour at least as surely as He is Judge." (Norman H. Snaith, *The Distinctive Ideas of the Old Testament,* London, The Epworth Press, 1944, p. 79.)

he sent forth his word, and healed them,
and delivered them from destruction.   (Ps. 107:1–20)

That this conviction that the saving work of God constitutes a present transformation of life has been part of "the great central tradition" of the Christian Church is clearly shown by Professor H. Richard Niebuhr's analysis of the "conversionist" type of theological ethics. The belief which most strikingly characterizes the conversionists' understanding of the moral life is their conviction that a process of transformation of men and culture is being effected by Christ in the here and now. In this group Niebuhr places such men as Augustine, Calvin, John Wesley, Jonathan Edwards, and F. D. Maurice. It is also apparent that he himself belongs to this group, which lives "somewhat less 'between the times' and somewhat more in the divine 'Now' " than do the new law and dualist groups.[28]

In many ways Augustine is the outstanding representative of the "conversionists," and his understanding of the transformation which Christ makes possible is typical of the group as a whole. Far from being an abstract and academic concept, salvation involves a vital and existential transformation of all of man's capacities, all of his loyalties, and all of his virtues. Interpreting Augustine, Niebuhr writes:

By humbling human pride and detaching man from himself on the one hand, by revealing God's love and attaching man to his one good, Christ restores what has been corrupted and redirects what has been perverted. He transforms the emotions of men, not by substituting reason for emotion, but by attaching fear, desire, grief, and joy to their right object. . . . The moral virtues men develop in their perverse cultures are not supplanted by new graces, but are converted by love. . . . The life of reason above all, that wisdom of man which the wisdom of God reveals to be full of folly, is reoriented and redirected by being given a new first principle. Instead of beginning with faith in itself and with love of its own order, the reasoning of redeemed man begins with faith in God and love of the order which He has put into all His creation; therefore it is free to trace out His designs and humbly follow His ways.[29]

Although Augustine's understanding of salvation is profound and comprehensive, it does not itself describe adequately the meanings which this transformation has even for his fellow conversionists—much

---

[28] H. Richard Niebuhr, *op. cit.*, p. 195. For an illuminating discussion of the conversionists' position, see the whole of ch. 6.
[29] *Ibid.*, pp. 214–215.

less for those believers who understand the relationship of Christ to culture in other terms—any more than one biblical symbol of salvation is adequate to suggest the meanings of this experience for the biblical writers as a whole. God as Redeemer meets men in their individual as well as in their universal needs, and the transformation which He effects is relevant to the uniqueness of each person's sin and bondage, as well as to the bondage which they share in common. Moreover, the interpretations which Christians give to the inner meaning of salvation differ widely according as their thought patterns, their diagnoses of the fundamental human predicament, and their conceptions of God differ. Thus Calvin, for example, with his emphasis upon the actuality of God's sovereignty, his dynamic conception of men's vocations, and the close relationship which he saw between church and state, represents the conversionist emphasis upon the divine possibility that human nature and culture may be transformed into a kingdom of God. John Wesley, on the other hand, while maintaining a dynamic conception of God's redemptive work, speaks less of the present transformation of earthly society into a kingdom of God and emphasizes instead the idea of perfection. For him God's redemptive work is epitomized in the present possibility of deliverance from sin which He offers and the perfection in love which He makes possible in the here and now. But Wesley interprets this transformation largely in individualistic terms and tends to neglect the biblical concern for the transformation of society which is implicit in the ideas of the Kingdom of God and the Lordship of Christ.

A suggestive summary of the meaning of faith in God as Redeemer is found in Professor Robert L. Calhoun's *God and the Common Life*. Professor Calhoun is one of the leading "realistic" theologians of our day. His description of the saving action of God is striking both for its concreteness and for the clarity with which it relates the work of the Redeemer to that of the Creator and Judge:

Man in waywardness and folly is able . . . to act in conflict rather than in harmony with God's will. . . . He may act thus in ignorance of God and of his own obliquity; or he may act thus in deliberate rebellion. In either event God is with him—"the Hound of Heaven"—patiently, silently turning him back from satisfaction craved but wrongly sought; silently urging upon him, by signs within and without, the need to repent, to orient himself anew. By the suffering he brings upon others and upon himself; by the failures and the unnourishing successes he achieves; by the love of those who love him, and the pain of those he may love;

by the inward gnawings of whatever repugnance he may have for cowardice, cruelty, sham, and by the outward and upward pull of whatever may be his measure of response to beauty, truth, and right: *by all these ways, epitomized in confrontation with Christ crucified, God works with him to his own salvation.* Silently: yet speaking. For *these are ways . . . through (which) God persuades man of His presence, power, and love.* "All things betray thee, who betrayest me," He says: and when man hears and begins to respond, his salvation is begun.[30]

RECOMMENDED READINGS

Baillie, John, *Our Knowledge of God,* New York, Charles Scribner's Sons, 1939.

Barry, F. R., *Recovery of Man,* New York, Charles Scribner's Sons, 1949, chs. III–VI.

Barth, Karl, *The Knowledge of God and the Service of God,* New York, Charles Scribner's Sons, 1939, chs. II–III, VI–IX.

Brunner, Emil, *The Christian Doctrine of Creation and Redemption,* II: *Dogmatics,* London, Lutterworth Press, 1952.

Brunner, Emil, *The Divine Imperative,* trans. by Olive Wyon, New York, The Macmillan Company, 1942, chs. XI–XIII, XXI.

Butterfield, Herbert, *Christianity and History,* New York, Charles Scribner's Sons, 1950, chs. III–V.

Calhoun, Robert L., *God and the Common Life,* New York, Charles Scribner's Sons, 1935, ch. IV, sec. III; ch. V, pp. 240–249.

Farmer, H. H., *God and Men,* New York, Abingdon-Cokesbury Press, 1947, chs. IV–VI.

Gogarten, Friedrich, *The Reality of Faith,* Philadelphia, The Westminster Press, 1959.

Niebuhr, H. Richard, *Christ and Culture,* New York; Harper & Brothers, 1951, ch. VI.

Niebuhr, H. Richard, *The Meaning of Revelation,* New York, The Macmillan Company, 1941.

Niebuhr, Reinhold, *Faith and History,* New York, Charles Scribner's Sons, 1949, chs. VII–X.

Niebuhr, Reinhold, *The Nature and Destiny of Man,* 2 vols., New York, Charles Scribner's Sons, 1943.

St. Augustine, *The City of God,* New York, Random House (The Modern Library), 1950, bks. XI; XIX, 13.

St. Augustine, *The Confessions of St. Augustine,* New York, E. P. Dutton & Co. (Everyman's Library), 1950, bks. XI–XIII.

[30] Robert L. Calhoun, *God and the Common Life,* New York, Charles Scribner's Sons, 1935, p. 248. Italics added.

Tillich, Paul, *Biblical Religion and the Search for Ultimate Reality,* Chicago, The University of Chicago Press, 1955.

Tillich, Paul, *Systematic Theology,* 2 vols. available, Chicago, The University of Chicago Press, 1951–57. See esp. pt. II, ch. II, and pt. III, ch. II.

Williams, Daniel D., *God's Grace and Man's Hope,* New York, Harper & Brothers, 1949, chs. I–II.

chapter 6

THE NATURE OF MAN

THROUGHOUT the centuries Christians have differed widely in their conceptions of the nature of man. One of the major reasons why this is so is to be found in the fact that the Bible is not primarily concerned with man as such but rather with man in relation to God and with man's response to God's action upon him. It is primarily an account of the divine initiative in creation, in judgment, and in redemption. From beginning to end it is theocentric rather than anthropocentric. Nevertheless the Bible cannot escape the question of man's nature and destiny, for its understanding of God is the result of God's confrontation of man with Himself. In contrast to the speculative and rationalistic reflection of the Greeks upon the nature of God and man, the Hebrew understanding of both is existential in the sense that it comes out of man's effort to understand his existence in relationship to God—a relationship which is inescapable and in which God is the primary agent. The major concern of the Bible is with the will and purpose of God, but consideration of the will and purpose of God involves the question of the nature and destiny of man whom He has placed in relationship to Himself.

Just as the Bible is more concerned with God's acts than with speculation about His metaphysical nature, so in its thought about man it is more concerned with the relationships and responses of the self than with speculation about the metaphysical nature of the soul. As we shall see, it gives us many profound insights into man's nature and conduct, but it nowhere gives us a systematic and comprehensive description of his nature and destiny. Although the different writers vary in the depth of their insights into the various facets of human nature, the biblical view of man as a whole witnesses both to his grandeur and to his misery, both to his possibilities and to the contradiction of his actual existence to the high estate for which he was made. Further, it witnesses to the renewal which is possible for man through his response to the saving action of God. The Bible as a whole recognizes the enigma of human freedom and the ultimate irrationality of human evil; it recognizes the transitoriness of man's life and the ultimate dependence of man's destiny upon the will and purpose of God. In increasing measure it recognizes the dignity which the love of God for sinful man confers upon him and the unlimited possibilities for growth in liberty and love and blessedness which are open to man through faith.

If we are to begin to understand biblical ethics, it is obviously essential that we have some understanding of the biblical view of the nature and destiny of man. Only against the background of this estimate of man is it possible to appraise the relevance and validity of biblical morality. Moreover, the attempt to gain such an understanding of man as well as of the biblical ethic acquires added importance and urgency from the twin facts that this view has greatly influenced the development of our whole Western civilization and culture—its science, its economic institutions, its political systems, its family life, as well as its religious life—and the fact that this view of man is so widely challenged in our own day. For all of these reasons it is necessary for us at this point in our study to try to summarize the biblical-Christian insights into the nature and destiny of man and, by implication at least, set them over against the other major views that are clamoring for dominance in our world today.[1] For convenience these insights may be grouped under three main headings: (1) man as created, (2) man as sinner, and (3) man as redeemed.

MAN AS CREATED

MAN AS CREATURE

The first affirmation that the Bible makes about man is that he is a creature. "So God created man. . . . male and female he created

---

[1] For fuller comparisons of the Christian and non-Christian appraisals of man the reader is referred to the following works: Reinhold Niebuhr, *The Nature and Destiny of Man*, 2 vols., New York, Charles Scribner's Sons, 1943; Emil Brunner, *Man in Revolt*, trans. by Olive Wyon, Philadelphia, The Westminster Press, 1947; John A. Hutchison and James Alfred Martin, *Ways of Faith: An Introduction to Religion*, New York, The Ronald Press Company, 1953; John C. Bennett, *Christianity and Communism*, New York, Association Press, 1951.

them" (Gen. 1:27). To be sure, He created man with special powers which make him preëminent among the creatures, and He gave man authority to rule over them; but like all other creatures, man is a created being. As Brunner declares, this is "the first and the fundamental thing which can be said about man."[2] It points to the great gulf which exists between man and God, between the creature and the Creator. The doctrine of man as creature represents in the strongest possible terms the fact that it is God who is the center of reality and all efforts of creatures to make themselves the center are idolatrous and doomed to failure. The doctrine of creation is at the same time a protest against an extreme form of immanence which issues ultimately in pantheism and says that human nature is divine, thus making it impossible to take evil seriously without attributing it to God.

Not only has God called man into being but man, like all other creatures, is constantly dependent upon Him for his continued existence—for what he is and also for what he may become. Man is dependent upon God for his capacities and powers, for the resources of the earth, and for his fellows whose existence and labor are essential to his existence and well-being. "Beware lest you say in your heart, 'My power and the might of my hand have gotten me this wealth. You shall remember the Lord your God, for it is he who gives you power to get wealth" (Deut. 8:17–18). Man is dependent upon the orderly processes of nature, which in turn are dependent upon the Creator of nature. It is God who "makes his sun rise on the evil and on the good, and sends rain on the just and on the unjust" (Matt. 5:45).

Because the Bible is primarily concerned about the proper relationship of man to God, is emphasizes again and again the fact that man as creature is not only a dependent being despite his efforts to be independent and sufficient unto himself, but also that he is finite and limited. He is most obviously and dramatically limited by death. His days are numbered, and death is inevitable. His mental powers are also limited, and in the face of God's perfect knowledge he knows that his thoughts are not God's thoughts just as his ways are not God's ways. Indeed the thoughts of God are as far above man's thoughts as the heavens are above the earth (Isa. 55:8–9).[3] Face to face with God's holiness man recognizes that he is unclean and

[2] Brunner, *op. cit.,* p. 90.
[3] Cf. God's answer to Job out of the whirlwind (Job 38:1–42:6).

dwells in the midst of an unclean people (Isa. 6:4). "No one is good but God alone" (Mark 10:18). Finally, the strength and physical power of even the strongest and mightiest of men is weak and fleeting when compared to the creative and sovereign power of God.

Thus, when the psalmist considers man in relation to God who has fashioned the heavens with the moon and the stars as their majestic ornaments, he is moved to ask, "What is man that thou art mindful of him, and the son of man that thou dost care for him?" (Ps. 8:4). Compared with the agelessness of the earth and the eternity of God, man is fleeting and frail:

> Before the mountains were brought forth,
>   or ever thou hadst formed the earth and the world
>   from everlasting to everlasting thou art God. . . .

> For a thousand years in thy sight
>   are but as yesterday when it is past,
>   or as a watch in the night.   (Ps. 90:2–4)

But as for man,

> Thou dost sweep men away; they are like a dream,
>   like grass which is renewed in the morning:
> in the morning it flourishes and is renewed;
>   in the evening it fades and withers. . . .

> The years of our life are threescore and ten,
>   or even by reason of strength fourscore;
> yet their span is but toil and trouble;
>   they are soon gone, and we fly away.   (Ps. 90:5–10)

Or, again, compared with the power and strength of God, "Man is like a breath, his days are a passing shadow" (Ps. 144:4).

In a word, over against the majesty and power of God as exemplified in the splendour and immensity of the physical universe which He has created, man seems transient and insignificant and unworthy of God's care and love. So far the Bible seems to agree with the cynic in its estimate of man.[4] The agreement is only apparent, however, for the biblical appraisal of man's nature can be properly understood only

---

[4] The author of Ecclesiastes is a thoroughgoing cynic and pessimist in his view of man, but the very terms which he uses "reveal that the consensus of Hebrew thought was against him. He is clearly at pains to criticize and repudiate an accepted belief" (W. A. Irwin, *The Old Testament: Keystone of Human Culture,* New York, Henry Schuman, 1952, pp. 65–66).

when it is viewed in the light of the Bible's high conception of God who is the ground of all good and value and who is perfect goodness and power. Between the Creator and the creature man, just as between the Creator and all other created beings, there is an abyss which separates absolutely the finite from the infinite, the conditioned from the unconditioned. Man's great temptation is to forget the fact of his creaturehood and attempt to play God. Hence the Bible emphasizes man's dependence, his finitude, and the limited character of his existence; but—unlike the cynic again—it does not consider his insufficiency, his finiteness, and his dependence to be evil. Quite to the contrary, the Bible declares that these characteristics of human life belong to God's plan of creation and are to be accepted as good: "And God saw everything that he had made and behold, it was very good" (Gen. 1:31). It is not man's dependence but his effort to be independent, not his insufficiency but his lack of trust, not his finitude but his effort to gain infinitude, not his sexuality but his sensuality, not even death so much as the fear of death which are evil.[5] Therefore, these facts concerning man's mortal life are to be accepted with reverence and humility, with gratitude and trust. Since man is completely dependent upon God, he has no ground for boasting in himself. His proper attitude is rather that of reverence for Him upon whom he depends, and humility concerning his own importance. Since he has received all that he has from God, his proper response is one of gratitude to Him who is the source of every good gift and every perfect gift. Since man has experienced the goodness of God in the gift of life, in the preservation of life, and in the meeting of his deepest needs, his proper response is that of trust. "But if God so clothes the grass of the field, which today is alive and tomorrow is thrown into the oven, will he not much more clothe you, O men of little faith? Therefore do not be anxious, saying, 'What shall we eat?' or 'What shall we drink?' or 'What shall we wear?' . . . your heavenly Father knows that you need them all. But seek first his kingdom and his righteousness, and all these things shall be yours as well" (Matt. 6:30–33).

MAN AS IMAGE OF GOD

The Bible also makes a second affirmation about man in relationship to the Creator. Not only is there an absolute separation between

[5] Reinhold Niebuhr, *op. cit.,* I, pp. 173–176.

him, as between all other created beings, and God, but man differs from all other creatures in that he alone is made "in the image of God" (Gen. 1:27), and as the result of his special relationship to God he is given authority over the other living things. "Be fruitful and multiply, and fill the earth and subdue it; and have dominion over the fish of the sea and over the birds of the air and over every living thing that moves upon the earth" (Gen. 1:28).

This concept of "the image of God" is found side by side with the concept of man as creature in the Genesis myth of creation. Man is created in the image of God; he does not fashion himself into it. He is a creature, but God has bestowed upon him a dignity and a worth that is far greater than that of other living things. Similarly, though the psalmist is led by the contemplation of the heavens to wonder why God should care for puny man, he nevertheless recognizes that God *does* care for him:

> Yet thou hast made him little less than God,
>   and dost crown him with glory and honor.
> Thou hast given him dominion over the work of
>   thy hands;
>   thou hast put all things under his feet,
> all sheep and oxen,
>   and also the beasts of the field,
> the birds of the air, and the fish of the sea,
>   whatever passes along the paths of the sea.   (Ps. 8:5–8)[6]

While the full meaning of the image of God has not been spelled out very precisely either in the Bible or in traditional theology, it is clear that the central meaning of this formula, as far as the Bible is concerned, is that man exists in a special relationship to God which sets him apart from other living things. It is this relationship rather than his biological or his rational nature which most adequately describes his essence. It is this which constitutes his *human* nature as distinguished from his animal nature.

Included in the image of God is man's rational capacity. Reason is necessary in order that man may understand the relationship in which he exists and in order that he may be able to respond in his freedom to God's will. The image of God includes, therefore, man's rational capacity for self-transcendence, for self-knowledge, and for introspec-

---

[6] Cf. Matthew 6:26: "Are you not of more value than they?" (i.e., the birds of the air).

tion.[7] But, following Augustine, classical Christian theology has maintained that man's powers of reason and self-transcendence, as well as his capacity for self-determination, point beyond man to God; and it has affirmed that these capacities can be completed only in the light of revelation which is accepted through faith, only as man recognizes the limits to his capacities and is apprehended by a more adequate disclosure of truth about himself and reality than he is able to discover by his unaided reason. Human life points beyond itself to the completion of its powers, and man can understand the total dimension in which he stands only by making faith the presupposition of his understanding: "For although, unless he understands somewhat, no man can believe in God, nevertheless by the very faith whereby he believes, he is helped to the understanding of greater things. For there are some things which we do not believe unless we understand them; and there are other things which we do not understand unless we believe them."[8]

The proper place of reason in the image of God is suggested by the description of man as a spiritual being. While the Bible does not define the term *spiritual* in a precise sense, it is clear that man's spirit refers primarily to his "capacity for and affinity with the divine."[9] As Reinhold Niebuhr points out, "What is ordinarily meant by 'reason' does not imply 'spirit', but 'spirit' does imply 'reason.' "[10] The concept of the divine image includes the rational faculties of man, but it also includes the capacity to know God by faith and to achieve blessedness by subjecting man's life to the Creator.

In more concrete terms, the meaning of the doctrine that man is made in the image of God points to the personal relationship which exists between man and his Creator. That which constitutes him *man* is the fact that "he stands first, last, and all the time in relation to the eternal Person, to God."[11] This is a relationship which exists whether a man is aware of it or not; it is a relationship which is inescapable. By the very act by which God creates man He creates that relationship, and if (as is impossible) that relationship were to cease he would cease to be man. Man is inescapably related to God; this

[7] Reinhold Niebuhr, *op. cit.*, I, pp. 150–166.
[8] St. Augustine, Psalm 118, Sermon xviii, 3, in Secundo Editio Veneta, vol. VI, 1761. Translation found in Reinhold Niebuhr, *op. cit.*, p. 158.
[9] Reinhold Niebuhr, *op. cit.*, p. 152.
[10] *Ibid.*, p. 162, fn.
[11] Herbert H. Farmer, *God and Men*, New York, Abingdon-Cokesbury Press, 1947, p. 79. Cf. Brunner, *op. cit.*, pp. 102–105.

is his fate. To say that this relationship is personal is to recognize that it involves freedom both on the part of God and on the part of man, but it is important to notice carefully wherein the freedom lies. God as the primary Person freely creates man to be related to Himself through the exercise of the freedom with which He endows man. Man is created in relationship to God—with the claim of the Creator upon him for "complete obedience in complete trust."[12] Man is not free to escape from God (Ps. 139:7–10); he is free, however, to accept or to reject His claim upon him.

Not only does the biblical understanding of man's personal relationship to God point to the high estimate which the Bible has of man's worth and to the importance which it attaches to the individual person and the decisions which he alone can make concerning his own individual relationship to God, but it also points to the social character of his being as an individual who is related to other individuals within the community of which he is a part. These relationships are given to man, and they also place claims upon him. The individual is nurtured in these relationships, and his responsibility to God includes his responsibility for these other individuals whom God has created, each with his own uniqueness but all alike in their creaturehood and divine image as well as in their mutual dependence upon each other. On the one hand, it is true that, as Brunner declares, "God the Creator does not create humanity, but He creates each human being separately, He has 'called thee by name,' He knows you 'personally,' 'specially.' Hence you are not an example but a person, a self which cannot be exchanged for any other."[13] But, on the other hand, it is also true that God creates individuals for life in community. It is impossible for an individual self to exist in complete isolation from other selves. The purpose of God in the creation of man, therefore, is seen to be the creation of individual persons who mutually nourish and complete each other in the manifold relationships of life in community. Responsibility to God on the part of the single individual involves responsibility for the members of the community of which one is a part, and in biblical thought this community becomes increasingly the universal community symbolized by the Kingdom of God. Each man exists alone as an individual before God, but it is equally true that each man is his brother's keeper (Gen. 4:9). On the one hand, the biblical view of man represents the strong-

[12] Farmer, *op. cit.,* p. 80.
[13] Brunner, *op. cit.,* p. 322.

est possible protest against the submergence of the individual in any form of collectivism or totalitarianism, and on the other hand it represents an equally strong warning against an atomistic conception of man as an individual who is sufficient unto himself and responsible only for himself.[14]

It should not be forgotten that while the Bible identifies man's spiritual nature as his distinctive endowment, it nevertheless maintains a strong sense of the unity of body and spirit in a total personality. All of man's capacities and relationships taken together comprise his total endowment as a human being. While it is the divine image which differentiates man most significantly from other creatures and gives him his highest worth, the Bible as a whole avoids a dualistic conception of man's nature whereby his spirit alone is considered good and his body evil. It is man with his total endowment who stands in relationship to God, but it is his spiritual nature which makes it possible for him to be aware of this relationship and makes him responsible before God. Man as a whole—with his body, his desires, his appetites, his reason, his individuality, and his relationships to God and his neighbors—is created good, and the self is responsible for the use which it makes of this total endowment.

In view of the widespread albeit heretical tendency within the Christian tradition to look upon the body and the natural vitalities with which the self is endowed as evil, there is great need to consider more carefully the implications of the Christian understanding of God as Creator and man as a creature made in the image of God for psychotherapy and the whole field of mental health. As an affirmation of man's capacity and striving for wholeness and for harmony with nature, with his fellows, and with God, these biblical concepts imply that the struggle for such wholeness and harmony is an integral part of the cosmic creativity. They imply, further, that man can be harmoniously related to himself, to nature, and to his fellows only as he is harmoniously related to God. The buried resources for his struggle against psychic and spiritual illness are "there" so that they can be drawn upon in psychotherapy only because they have been implanted there by the Creator; moreover, they can be properly used

---

[14] Reinhold Niebuhr has developed the content of the "image of God" metaphor in very perceptive fashion in terms of the three dialogues of the self—with itself, with its various neighbors, and with God. (Reinhold Niebuhr, *The Self and the Dramas of History,* New York, Charles Scribner's Sons, 1955. See, e.g., pp. 4–5.)

only when man becomes harmoniously related to God. As David E. Roberts puts it,

> The resources he draws upon, in seeking to become at one with himself, are not merely "his"; they are rooted in the whole creation, which is grounded in God. Therefore man can become at one with himself only by finding his place in a harmony much wider than himself; but this harmony is not "pre-established"; he has a share in winning, in actualizing, it. He cannot fulfill his own nature unless his capacities gain free expression; but neither can he fulfill his own nature unless his freedom is brought into right relationship with God.[15]

Although Christian faith rejects any form of vitalism as grossly inadequate in its view of man and although it insists upon the need for discipline and restraint in the exercise of man's biological drives, it does not consider these drives to be evil *per se*. Although it condemns egocentricity, it does not condemn the desire to be a self. Although it condemns pride in the sense of trusting in one's own works, it does not regard man's longing to exercise his creative powers as a necessary indication of pride. Although it condemns an inordinate grasping at power, it does not condemn the desire and effort to continue in existence as a responsible self or center of action.

MAN AS SINNER

Thus far we have been considering the nature of man as God created him. Man was created finite—a child of nature and as such involved in the necessities of the natural order like other created things. But man was also created a spiritual being existing in personal relationship with God—a free, rational creature with the capacity to have knowledge of, and fellowship with, God. In this respect he was created different from other living things and preëminent among them. But these same capacities and endowments which are the marks of man's grandeur are also the marks of his misery. It is man alone who can become a sinner. It is man alone who "falls" from the state of innocence in which he is created, just as it is man alone who can become a saint.

Christianity affirms that there is a vast difference between man as he was created and man as he actually it. Something has gone wrong with man which affects him to the very center of his being. Not only are all of his actions distorted and corrupted, but his fundamental

[15] David E. Roberts, *Psychotherapy and a Christian View of Man*, New York, Charles Scribner's Sons, 1950, p. 93.

relationship to God has become perverted. Consequently he is out of harmony with himself, with his fellows, and with God. Viewing man, on the one hand, in the light of the high estimate which is given him as the "image of God" and viewing him also realistically as he has become through sin, Reinhold Niebuhr declares that "Christianity measures the stature of man more highly and his virtue more severely than any alternative view."[16]

It is essential to understand both estimates which Christianity makes of man. Together they appear paradoxical, but the seeming contradiction is resolved if the biblical estimate of man's sinfulness is rightly understand. "The greatness of man is so evident," writes Pascal, "that it is even proved by his wretchedness. For what in animals is nature we call in man wretchedness; by which we recognize that, his nature being now like that of animals, he has fallen from a better nature which once was his."[17] "The greatness of man is great in that he knows himself to be miserable."[18] Similarly, Augustine declares that "the very sensibility to pain is evidence of the good which has been taken away and the good which has been left (even in the devil). For, were nothing good left, there could be no pain on account of the good which had been lost."[19]

Thus the biblical concept of man as sinner witnesses in a negative way to man's greatness and God-likeness. The biblical view of sin is serious because man is conceived of in such high terms as a spiritual being fashioned in the image of his Creator. The affirmation that man is a sinner points to the contradiction between man's actual existence and his true nature and destiny as a spiritual being. All men—regardless of their physical and mental capacities, regardless of their moral goodness or badness—are destined by creation for communion with God, and the fulfillment of this destiny is the goal which God the Creator and Redeemer undertakes to effect. The biblical concept of man as sinner does not mean that man is bad in the sense that it would be better if he did not exist. Rather, he is a sinner, unable to save himself, but accounted worthy of God's love and initiative in reconciling him unto Himself. And, what is more, there remains in man some affinity for his high destiny so that he is able to respond to God's forgiveness and summons. In confused and distorted ways

---

[16] Reinhold Niebuhr, *The Nature and Destiny of Man,* I, p. 161.

[17] Blaise Pascal, *Pensées,* New York, Random House (The Modern Library), 1941, par. 409.

[18] *Ibid.,* par. 397.

[19] St. Augustine, *The City of God,* New York, Random House (The Modern Library), 1950, XIX, 13.

man still seeks the fulfillment of his true destiny, for such is his nature that he is unable to be permanently satisfied with lesser goods and idolatries which, he is aware, contradict his true nature and his true good. "Thou madest us for Thyself, and our heart is restless, until it repose in Thee."[20]

The significance of the biblical understanding of man as sinner has been obscured in much recent and contemporary theological discussion. On the one hand, liberal Protestantism has frequently overlooked the seriousness and depth of sin, and it has tended to agree with secular Humanism and Idealism that evil will be eliminated through the natural process of evolutionary development and by intelligent human effort. Thus Professor A. C. Garnett writes: "Human nature is on the side of human progress. The problem is to set aside the *damnosa hereditas* of prejudice, false tradition, superstition, fear, hatred, that survives from the childhood of the race, and to develop institutions adequate to its maturity. There is in the human heart enough of natural good will. It remains for intelligence to enable it to find its way."[21] Similarly, Professor Harrison S. Elliott, in his *Can Religious Education Be Christian?*, sets forth the view that selfhood is a social product and that human evil therefore has its origin in corrupt social institutions. Personality can be so modified in the future, he maintains, that there is hope that sin may be abolished.[22] Such estimates of man's moral and rational capacities, however, ignore the biblical warning that it is precisely when man begins to put his trust in these capacities as the mediators of uncorrupted goodness and truth that he falls into the most disastrous forms of pride and commits his greatest sin.

On the other hand, some neoörthodox writers have reacted so strongly against the illusions of liberal Protestantism and secular Humanism that they have tended to speak of the image of God in "natural" man as having been completely lost. Human nature, they have sometimes declared, has become so totally corrupted by sin that there is no remaining "point of contact" between the Word of God and sinful man. Karl Barth, who is widely considered the most outstanding

[20] St. Augustine, *The Confessions of St. Augustine,* New York, E. P. Dutton & Co. (Everyman's Library), 1950, I i, 1.

[21] A. C. Garnett, *A Realistic Philosophy of Religion,* Chicago, Willett, Clark & Co., 1942, p. 176. Cf. Shirley Jackson Case, *The Christian Philosophy of History,* Chicago, The University of Chicago Press, 1943, p. 213.

[22] Harrison S. Elliott, *Can Religious Education Be Christian?,* New York, The Macmillan Company, 1940, pp. 191 ff.

theologian in contemporary Protestantism, at one time held this view. Although he even then acknowledged that "man is man and not a cat," he insisted that man was no more able than a cat to receive divine revelation unless the image of God was recreated in him.[23] D. R. Davies has similarly interpreted the Christian view of man's sinfulness in a one-sided way which fails to do justice to the higher capacities and goodness of human nature. "Evil in man is fundamental," he writes. "That famous rock-bottom ego is devil, not angel."[24] But if evil is fundamental in man, how can his struggle to attain the morally good be explained, and how can the response of the sinner to the Gospel be understood? If man were fundamentally evil, he would not feel that his choice of evil is in contradiction to his own nature; and if the image of God were completely destroyed, man could not be blamed for continuing to reject the Word of God since he could neither understand it nor see its relevance to his own condition. As Paul Tillich puts the matter, "The demand (*i.e.*, for the fulfillment of his true origin) which man receives is unconditioned, but it is not strange to him. If it were strange to his nature, it would not concern him; he could not perceive it as a demand on him. It strikes him only because it places before him, in the form of a demand, his own essence."[25]

On the one hand, man is declared to be "fundamentally good";[26] on the other hand, evil is said to be fundamental in man. Upon closer examination it will be seen that both of these appraisals of human nature fail to do justice to the biblical understanding of man, although each represents a valid protest against the opposite position. But the genius of the Christian insight into the nature of man can best be made clear to modern man if our approach is existential rather than polemical. What is needed is an analysis of the facts of our own moral experience and that of our fellowmen as these are made known to us through introspection, anthropology, and psychoanalysis and as

[23] Karl Barth, "No!" trans. by Peter Fraenkel, in *Natural Theology*, London, The Centenary Press, 1946, p. 88. His later views are developed most fully in the third volume of his *Dogmatik* where he maintains that this image is not lost, for man's existence as man involves his continued existence in the image of God (*Die Kirchliche Dogmatik*, Zurich, 1947, III, 1, p. 207). For a summary of Barth's teaching concerning the image of God, see David Cairns, *The Image of God in Man*, New York, Philosophical Library, 1953, pp. 164 ff.

[24] D. R. Davies, *Secular Illusion or Christian Realism?*, New York, The Macmillan Company, 1949, p. xi.

[25] Paul Tillich, *The Interpretation of History*, trans. by N. A. Rasetzki and Elsa L. Talmey, New York, Charles Scribner's Sons, 1936, p. 208.

[26] Cf. F. R. Barry, *The Recovery of Man*, New York, Charles Scribner's Sons, 1949, p. 62.

this experience is illuminated by the biblical witness concerning man. The biblical writers are not, after all, primarily concerned either to attack or to defend man, but rather to witness to the various aspects of his paradoxical nature as one who is made in the image of God but as one also who knows himself to be a sinner before God. They are concerned to help man understand himself so that he may fulfill the destiny for which he was created, and in the light of their own moral experience and that of the race they are led to conclude that man cannot reach this fulfillment unless God Himself becomes his Savior.

But God cannot save man unless man wills to be saved. And, unless man knows that he is in such need of salvation that he cannot save himself, he will not turn to God for his redemption. Moreover, unless man is aware of the greatness of his sin, he cannot be aware of the richness of God's grace and love. If he believes that the sin which God has forgiven him is little and inconsequential, then his understanding of God's love will be small and his gratitude will be little. But if he is aware that he has been forgiven much (as is actually the case), his gratitude will be great and he will love much in return.[27] Only as he rightly understands the depth of his own unworthiness can man begin to fathom the depth of God's love and thus enter into the full richness and joy of fellowship with God, and only if he rightly understands the *agape* of God will he be able to know how he ought to love his neighbors. In a word, the Bible is not primarily interested in sin but rather in redemption, and yet it sees that redemption can be adequately understood only if sin is adequately understood; and it also sees that sin can be adequately understood only in the light of God's redeeming grace, especially as that grace is revealed ultimately in the cross.

We turn therefore to an analysis of the Christian understanding of man as sinner:

ALL MEN ARE SINNERS

In the first place, the Bible asserts that all men are sinners. While there are some exceptions to this view, especially in the Old Testament, Psalm 14 clearly asserts the universality of sin:

> The Lord looks down from heaven upon the children
> of men,

[27] Cf. Luke 7:47: "He who is forgiven little, loves little."

to see if there are any that act wisely
that seek after God.
They have all gone astray, they are all alike corrupt;
there is none that does good,
no, not one.   (Ps. 14:2–3)

Jesus calls the men of his generation evil and adulterous (Mark 8:38; Matt. 16:4; 17:17). He assumes that all men stand in need of repentance (Luke 13:1–5). While he recognizes the best possibilities in all individuals and regards none as hopeless except the self-righteous and the insincere, his conception of the perfect divine love as the norm by which human love is to be measured makes all men sinners (Matt. 5:48).[28] Whereas Jesus seems to assume the universality of human sinfulness, Paul emphatically states this view (Rom. 3:9–20; Gal. 3:22). Christ alone is without sin (II Cor. 5:21). Because all men are sinners, they stand under God's judgment and are summoned to repentance. Paul does not deduce universal sinfulness from the corruption of human nature through Adam, however; rather, it is for him an observed and incontrovertible fact of human experience that "all have sinned" (Rom. 3:23).

It will be impossible for us to understand the biblical conception of human sinfulnesss unless we bear in mind that *sin* is a religious rather than simply a moral term. Immorality is included within the meaning of sin and constitutes its primary outward manifestation, but immorality cannot be equated with sin. On the contrary, the primary reference of sin is to

. . . that which lies *purely* within the realm of *religious* relationships: it is primarily the failure, inhibition, or atrophy of the purely religious spiritual functions themselves, of reverence and awe towards God, of trust, fear, love for God; of the life hidden with Christ in God, of immediate dependence upon and frank communion with God; it is the obstruction of the workings of his word and spirit, or in short, as Luther would say, disobedience to the first commandment. Such sin is . . . made up . . . of godlessness. In this respect . . . it is entirely *sui generis,* and not reducible to the merely moral order.[29]

Moral wrong-doing is recognized to be *sin* when it is viewed as the violation of the divine will, as when the prodigal son confesses,

[28] Millar Burrows, *An Outline of Biblical Theology,* Philadelphia, The Westminster Press, 1946, pp. 164–171.
[29] Rudolf Otto, *Religious Essays: A Supplement to 'The Idea of the Holy,'* trans. by Brian Lunn, London, Oxford University Press, 1931, p. 6.

"Father I have sinned against heaven and before you" (Luke 15:21). Sin is not merely transgression of known moral laws; it is the violation of God's will. Viewed in the light of God's perfect will as this has been revealed especially in the life, teachings, and death of Jesus, it is evident to Christian faith that "all have sinned and fall short of the glory of God."

By pointing men to the absolute standard of God's perfection, the Christian conception of the universal sinfulness of mankind provides the strongest possible safeguard against human pride; for face to face with God's goodness, when this is profoundly apprehended, men invariably condemn rather than praise themselves. The saint knows far better than others how much his own self-centeredness keeps him from loving God with *all* his heart, mind, soul, and strength. While it is true that such a person is a far better man than others, he still sees himself as a sinner and knows how far short of God's goodness he yet remains. Seen in this light, it is apparent how superficial is the charge that the concept that all men are sinners is psychologically unhealthy in that it makes men feel inadequate and inferior and induces abnormal feelings of guilt. While it cannot be denied that the doctrine of sin has frequently been interpreted in such a way as to justify this charge, it must be recognized that the religious affirmation of man's sinfulness *before God's goodness* is but a sober and realistic appraisal of his own moral goodness which he can ignore only at the peril of himself and his fellows or which he can accept as a sober diagnosis of his spiritual health and as a basis for renewal and further growth and maturing in goodness. When men become content with making comparisons with other sinful human beings and when they judge themselves on the basis of their own external conduct, which may be prompted by fear of public opinion or of the penalty of the law or even of the divine judgment, they are in danger of falling into pride and complacency about their own goodness; they are also in danger of using their false estimates of their own merit as a rationalization for imposing their will upon others, whether the latter be individuals, or nations, or races, or religious groups.[30] It is only when men recognize the claim of God's perfect goodness upon them

[30] It is one of the major contributions of Reinhold Niebuhr that he has brilliantly and probingly exposed the moral pretensions of complacently religious and smugly moral men by pointing out the manifold ways in which the self uses such pretensions to advance the claims of the self. See especially *The Nature and Destiny of Man,* I, chs. VII–VIII; and compare *The Irony of American History,* New York, Charles Scribner's Sons, 1952.

that they are able to see, both in regard to themselves and their heroes, that "No one is good but God alone" (Mark 10:18).

Sin Is Love of Self in the Place of God

We have already noted that sin is a religious rather than a moral term. It has to do not so much with individual acts which have an immoral quality as with a relationship between man and God which has been perverted. Back of the particular acts of wrongdoing is the *status* or condition of the sinner which on occasion breaks out in more or less isolated sins or transgressions. It is this condition of the sinner—a corrupt state of will—which prompts him to commit sins. As Augustine observed, the transgression of eating the forbidden fruit in the Garden of Eden was committed by persons who were already wicked, and their wickedness consisted in their being turned away from God toward themselves.[31]

It is true that the Old Testament and the teaching of Jesus in the Synoptic Gospels characteristically speak of *sins* in the sense of acts rather than *sin* in the sense of a state of being, but it is evident that Jesus in particular is interested not just in the external acts alone but far more in the purpose and spirit behind these outward acts. "For out of the heart come evil thoughts, murder, adultery, fornication, theft, false witness, slander" (Matt. 15:19). (See also, Matt. 5:22, 28). Moreover, numerous references in both the Old and the New Testaments to sin as disease and to God's redemptive work as that of "healing" (Ps. 103:3; 41:4; Isa. 53:5; Jer. 3:22; Hos. 14:4; Mal. 4:2; Matt. 9:11–12; I Pet. 2:24; Rev. 22:2; cf. Matt. 4:24; Luke 4:33–41; 6:17–19) imply that the fundamental reason why men commit evil deeds is that they stand in need of being made whole again.

Thus, it is not just isolated sinful acts with which the Bible is concerned, although it is characteristic of biblical religion as a whole to think of man's relationship to God in terms of dynamic acts of the will—either acts of loyalty to, or rebellion against, God—rather than in terms of static states of being. While Paul on occasion also speaks of sin in terms of specific acts, he represents a departure from the general biblical usage in this regard in his characteristic tendency to speak of sin in the abstract as an alien power which dominates man (Rom. 5:12–8:10). The Fourth Gospel similarly speaks of sin in the

[31] *The City of God*, XIV, 13.

abstract as the condition of those who walk in darkness (John 3:19). But in view of the concern of the Old Testament, particularly the prophets and the psalmists, with man's inward relationship with God, and especially in view of the emphasis which Jesus places upon purity of heart and the wholeheartedness of love, it is doubtful that much significance should be attached to the fact that the word *sin* is so seldom found in the singular form in the Old Testament or in the Synoptic Gospels.[32] Regardless of the words which they employ, there is implicit in both the Old Testament and the Synoptic Gospels, as well as in the writings of Paul and the Fourth Gospel, the notion that sin is a condition or state of being which erupts now and again in sinful acts which are the symptoms of a deep-lying illness or "contradiction" within the soul of man. But the idea of a sinful state of being, whether this appears implicitly or explicitly as in the writings of Paul and in the Fourth Gospel, can be rightly understood only if it is borne in mind that in biblical thought sin is always an act in the sense that it is a personal decision which involves the being of the person as a whole. It is not a static relationship so much as it is a relationship of personal rebellion against God.[33] One is not in a state of sin in the same way that one is in the condition of having blue eyes; rather, the state of sin involves a continuous act of the will. It is not a state for which man is no longer responsible; rather, a dynamic personal relationship is involved. It is not a metaphysical attribute which man inherits; rather, it is a decision which he continually reaffirms so long as he loves himself in the place of God and refuses to repent.

The biblical view of sin, then, includes both *acts* and a *state of being* (disease, darkness) from which man himself needs to be delivered. In the most fundamental sense, it recognizes that all particular sins are manifestations of a sinful state or condition which is prior to the evil act and that what man needs is not simply the forgiveness of his guilt but a changed state of being. He needs to become a new being, not in the sense of having his old self replaced by a different self but in the sense of having the old, corrupted self transformed into a new creature (John 3:3; Gal. 6:15).[34] He needs to be

---

[32] Millar Burrows, however, seems to attach considerable importance to this fact (*op. cit.,* pp. 167–168). See also Brunner, *op. cit.,* pp. 116–117, fn.

[33] Cf. Brunner, *op. cit.,* pp. 116–117, fn.; p. 148. See also Cairns, *op. cit.,* pp. 189–190.

[34] Cf. Paul Tillich, *The New Being,* New York, Charles Scribner's Sons, 1955, ch. 2.

restored to a condition of living in trust and dependence upon God, of experiencing the divine love and righteousness and drawing upon the divine power. In essence, then, the biblical view of sin is that it is alienation from God, or—in words which mean the same thing— love of the self in the place of God. It is quite proper to define it as "the condition of the self when it has turned away from God and become estranged from Him,"[35] provided it is recognized that this alienation is self-alienation and not an alienation which is the result of man's being created finite or being endowed with a body. Man is responsible for this alienation, for it rests in an *act* of decision on his part; and he constantly reaffirms and deepens this alienation by his continual effort to live independently of God.

To define the essence of sin in terms of love of self in contempt of God is to state in positive terms what the concept of alienation from God defines in negative terms as turning away from God. This under- standing of sin also makes more apparent what we have said about the character of sin as act even while it is also a *status*. Love involves a dynamic relationship of the self to the object to which it is attached. When man becomes alienated from God, he is not without loyalty to, or faith in, or love for, some other object. In turning away from God, man turns essentially toward the self. Viewed in relation to this new, albeit false, center of his life, it is out of this love of self in the place of God that all particular sins issue. The great difference be- tween the City of God and the City of the World, Augustine declared, is that the former is guided and fashioned by love of God, the latter by love of self.[36] That this insight is true to the biblical understanding

[35] George F. Thomas, *Christian Ethics and Moral Philosophy*, New York, Charles Scribner's Sons, 1955, p. 175.

[36] *The City of God*, XIV, 13. Augustinian theology has generally equated self-love with pride in defining the essence of sin. Thus Augustine writes: "And what is the origin of our evil will but pride? For 'pride is the beginning of sin.' And what is pride but the craving for undue exaltation? And this is undue exaltation, when the soul abandons Him to whom it ought to cleave as its end, and becomes a kind of end to itself. This happens when it becomes its own satisfaction. And it does so when it falls away from that unchangeable good which ought to satisfy it more than itself" (*loc. cit.*). Luther uses pride and self-love synonymously, and the great danger which he attaches to pride is made clear in his emphasis upon justification "by faith alone" (*Works of Martin Luther*, vol. V, Philadelphia, A. J. Holman Company, 1931, pp. 20–21). Similarly, Calvin maintains that pride rather than ignorance is the ultimate root of man's sin: "Whence it follows, that their folly is inexcusable, which originates not only in a vain curiosity, but in false confidence, and an immoderate desire to exceed the limits of human knowledge" (*Institutes of the Christian*

of the nature of sin is indicated by the Old Testament characterization of sin as disobedience, rebellion against God, and the attempt to use God in the service of the self. It is indicated also by such words of Jesus as: "No one can serve two masters; for either he will hate the one and love the other, or he will be devoted to the one and despise the other. You cannot serve God and mammon" (Matt. 6:24; cf. Matt. 6:19–22, 33; 7:21). Similarly, for Paul, as we have seen, man's basic sin consists in his persistent tendency to make the self rather than God the center of his moral life.

MAN'S WILL IS IN BONDAGE TO SIN, BUT MAN IS
RESPONSIBLE FOR HIS SIN

We have already noted that, according to the biblical view of man, all men are sinners. We have seen, further, that the essence of sin is love of self in the place of God. If sin represents a revolt of man against the destiny for which he was created and therefore a denial of his own true good, the question inevitably arises as to why men sin. Here we come to the heart of the problem of moral evil. Throughout the history of Christian thought since the time of Augustine this has been one of the most hotly debated questions to have occupied the minds of theologians. It is a leading issue in contemporary discussions between liberal and neoörthodox writers. The lines are drawn even more sharply between those humanists who believe that man is essentially good and free to choose the good so that he can save himself from evil and those Christians who believe that man is in such bondage to evil that he is unable to save himself. The issue is crucial for Christianity, for the Gospel is addressed to men who are in need of deliverance and healing. The question is also of central importance for every man—for the philosopher seeking to understand evil, for the psychotherapist seeking to free man from evil forces, for the statesman insofar as he is concerned with the possibilities of legislation, for the parent seeking to rear his children. Of course the question is most often raised in terms which the moralist uses, Why do men choose that which is morally evil rather than that which is good? The theologian, on the other hand, asks, Why do men sin? As we have seen,

---

Religion, Philadelphia, Presbyterian Board of Education, 1936, bk. I, ch. 4). Reinhold Niebuhr in *The Nature and Destiny of Man* (I, chs. 7–8) has analyzed the nature of sin as pride more thoroughly than any other contemporary theologian.

the theologian's question is concerned with the more ultimate relationship, and includes the question raised by the moralist.

The most impressive answer to the question of why men sin is that associated with the name of Augustine. In a word, this answer is that men sin because their wills are in bondage to evil. This reply did not originate with Augustine; it is also found in Paul's analysis of man's fundamental moral problem. But the formulation which Augustine gave to this idea was so profound that it has influenced all subsequent Christian thought. In the language which he used, before the Fall Adam had the "ability to sin or not to sin," *"posse peccare aut non peccare."* Since the Fall, however, neither Adam nor any of his descendants has had the "ability not to sin," *"non posse non peccare."* On the contrary, as the result of the Fall, both Adam and all of his posterity have had only the "ability to sin," *"posse peccare."* Following Augustine, Luther spoke of "the bondage of the will" to sin, and in our own time Reinhold Niebuhr has spoken of a "bias toward evil" which makes it "inevitable" though "not necessary" that man sin. Neibuhr has never been willing to say that sin is "necessary" because this would imply a lack of responsibility and freedom on the part of man; and in fairness to Niebuhr it should be pointed out that he has more recently acknowledged that the phrase "inevitable but not necessary" may not be adequate to safeguard both insights of man's bondage and his freedom. In view of the widespread tendency in many quarters to dismiss the Augustinian concept of man's "bondage to sin," it is impressive to note the manner in which the validity of this conception is being confirmed by findings in the field of psychotherapy. Thus, Professor David E. Roberts, surveying this concept in the light of psychotherapy, writes, "Indeed the theologian has not invented the doctrine at all. It has grown up because it has described accurately the situation in which spiritually sensitive men have found themselves; and the more insight they possessed, the more inescapable have such descriptions of their plight become. They 'know' the good, in the sense that they are adequately aware of what their motives and actions should be; and yet something stronger than their own wills prevents them from having such motives and from carrying out such actions."[37]

Modern Augustinians such as Reinhold Niebuhr and Emil Brunner reject a literalistic-historical account of the fall of Adam from a state

[37] Roberts, *op. cit.,* pp. 107–108.

of holiness into a state of sin and guilt through the act of eating the forbidden fruit of a certain tree. They reject the notions of an hereditary corruption of human nature and the biological transmission of guilt because these notions undermine man's responsibility. Insofar as they speak of a corruption that is inherited, they speak of it as being inherited historically and socially in terms of personal relationships that have been distorted rather than in terms of a biological substance that has become tainted.[38] Yet they see in the Augustinian analysis of the problem of sin and evil a profundity that is lacking in the Humanist-Liberal, Protestant-Pelagian assertion that man is able of himself both to will and to do the good. They recognize the limitations of the Augustinian and Reformation categories as symbols for expressing the biblical insights into the nature of man as being in bondage and yet being responsible for his bondage, and they recognize the failure of their own efforts adequately to describe this paradox.[39] Nevertheless, they believe that in the main the Augustinian conception of man's predicament rings true to our human experience and is confirmed by modern discoveries in the fields of psychology, sociology, and anthropology.

It would be fruitless to try to revive the traditional formulae in which these insights have been expressed. The primary purpose which such concepts as "original sin" and "total depravity" were designed to serve has generally been lost sight of, and the terms themselves have been almost hopelessly perverted in meaning by a rigidly literalistic orthodoxy. In reaction against such literalism, Liberals have frequently been equally doctrinaire, and as a result they have discarded the valid insights contained in these formulae along with the formulae themselves. Hence we shall try to state as specifically as possible what classical Christianity has generally affirmed about the origin and effects of sin.

SIN IS A FREE ACT OF THE WILL.   This is true of the first sin, and it is also true (although within much narrower limits) of all sins. "Man's nature, indeed, was created at first faultless and without any sin," wrote Augustine; "but that nature of man in which every one is

[38] Reinhold Niebuhr, *The Nature and Destiny of Man*, I, p. 261; Brunner, *op. cit.,* pp. 121–123.
[39] Cf. Reinhold Niebuhr's "Reply to Interpretation and Criticism" in Charles W. Kegley and Robert W. Bretall, eds., *Reinhold Niebuhr: His Religious, Social, and Political Thought,* New York, The Macmillan Company, 1956, p. 437; Brunner, *op. cit.,* p. 277.

born from Adam, now wants the Physician, because it is not sound. All good qualities, no doubt, which it still possesses. . . . it has of the most High God, its Creator and Maker. But the flaw, which darkens and weakens all those natural goods so that it has need of illumination and healing, it has not contracted from its blameless Creator—but from that original sin which it committed *by free will*."[40] No cause in the sense of an antecedent factor or event which would provide a necessary and sufficient ground for the occurrence of sin can be given. Not only is this true as regards man's first sin, but despite the example and effects of that first sin upon the first man and all of his descendants, Adam retained enough freedom to be responsible for his subsequent sins and his posterity similarly has not been so devoid of freedom of the will that each man has not been partly responsible for the evil which he has done.

Although the first man's position was singular in that there was no prior example of evil, each man in a sense becomes his own Adam when he falls from a state of innocence into sin. Statistically, such a fall seems inevitable; logically, it is not necessary. But to deny that each man is responsible for his own fall is to deprive him of his true dignity as a free moral agent. As long as man is man, he retains the capacity to discern, however faintly, the good and to repent and live again by God's grace in dependence upon, and trust in, God. "Ever since the creation of the world his invisible nature, namely his eternal power and deity, has been clearly perceived in the things that have been made. So they are without excuse," writes Paul, "for although they knew God they did not honor him as God" (Rom. 1:20–21).

MAN BY HIMSELF IS NO LONGER FREE NOT TO SIN. Once man has fallen into self-centeredness and out of his proper fundamental relationship to God, he is no longer free in the same sense in which he was free before he fell. So long as he continues to center his life about himself he sins inevitably.[41] This indeed constitutes his basic sin, by definition. Man is still free, however, in the sense that his actions are his own; they constitute a reaffirmation of his self-love for which he is responsible. Moreover, although he cannot take the initiative in returning to his proper state of humility and trust, he can respond

---

[40] "Treatise on Nature and Grace," ch. III, in *Basic Writings of Saint Augustine*, I, edited with an Introduction and Notes by Whitney J. Oates, New York, Random House, p. 523. Cf. *The City of God*, XIV, 13.

[41] Brunner, *op. cit.*, p. 274.

to the initiative which God has already taken and is continuously taking to redeem man.

It should be clearly noted that the assertion that sinful man is no longer "able not to sin" does not mean that he can do nothing that is morally good.[42] It does not imply that there is no love or justice anywhere. Rather, it affirms that there is no love or justice which is not tainted with egoism.[43] Insofar as self-love remains the motive for the pursuit of justice, the pursuit of justice is sinful although it is certainly morally good. Insofar as the motive in ministering to the neighbor's needs is to promote the power and interests of the self, this service is sinful although it is certainly good and right and God's will that the neighbor's needs be met. As Brunner pointedly puts the matter, "When God commands; 'thou shalt not commit adultery,' He actually wills that adultery should not be committed, in the solid everyday sense in which the term is used by everyone."[44] But, of course, He also wills that man will refrain from adultery not because of fear but because of love (*agape*).

There is a close parallel between the Christian conception of man's bondage to sin and the psychoanalytic conception of neurosis, as has been frequently pointed out. Both recognize the extent to which the power of the will itself to choose good may become limited. The psychotherapist knows, for example, how futile it is to exhort the neurotic to cease feeling inferior without at the same time helping him to want to accept himself without undue self-effacement—i.e., without helping him change his will, which is precisely what he cannot do. An effort of the will is not enough; the will itself must undergo a change. Similarly, the psychotherapist knows how futile it is to exhort a prejudiced person to love his fellowmen by merely calling upon him to change his attitude. This is precisely what he needs help in doing— in overcoming his inner conflicts, his hostility and his envy, even when he knows that these conditions are wrong and that his prejudice is wrong. Thus, from this point of view psychotherapy may be regarded as "documenting to the full, and widening our awareness of what the

[42] Cf. Matthew 7:11: "If you then, who are evil, know how to give good gifts to your children, how much more will your Father who is in heaven give good things to those who ask him?"

[43] Brunner, *op. cit.,* pp. 138, 154–155. Even Calvin recognized that natural man could perform some good (*op. cit.,* bk. II, ch. II, par. 15). See also Reinhold Niebuhr's "Reply" (in Kegley and Bretall, *op. cit.,* p. 437), where he explicitly rejects the phrase which he used in his Gifford Lectures, "equality of sin and inequality of guilt."

[44] Brunner, *op. cit.,* p. 155.

human race is up against in attempting to reach inner freedom and social security."[45]

THE *whole* SELF IS IN BONDAGE AND THE COMMUNITY ITSELF IS CORRUPTED BY SIN.   Not only does the classical Christian doctrine of sin declare that all men are sinners in the sense that some of each person's acts are sinful and tainted with self-love but it also affirms that all of man's capacities and faculties—his conscience, his reason, his emotions—have become affected by his self-love so that no one of these faculties can be relied upon to lead him to impartial truth and completely unselfish acts of goodness. It is not just one of man's faculties that has become perverted by being directed toward a wrong ultimate goal; rather, it is the *self,* the center of all of man's faculties or capacities, which has become dominated by self-love.

Theologians have frequently used the formula "total depravity" to describe this perversion of the whole self, but this term has often been assumed to imply that man is totally bad. The latter view, as we have seen, has been rejected by the main stream of Christianity, including Calvin, with whose name the term itself is generally associated. The concept of "total depravity" does not mean that human nature is "bad"; rather, it is "warped, twisted, and misdirected."[46] Man's capacity to reason is good, but apart from faith he uses his reason in the service of the self. The conscience of natural man—his capacity to discern duty—is good, but apart from the dominance of love for God the conscience is inclined to see duty through the tainted glass of self-interest. Natural man's capacity to love is good, but his love for others is perverted by an inordinate love of the self so that it becomes possessive and seeks to dominate its object. Only when the self is freed from anxiety concerning itself through being made aware that it is sustained by the love of God, only then is it free to love unselfishly as God loves.

Human nature under sin, then, is perverted or distorted. The ultimate harmony of man with God and his fellows is broken in all of its aspects. Man himself—not just his reason or his physical nature or some one relationship—is affected at his very core. Moreover, since man is so inescapably social in nature, not only is the whole self (*ego totus*) affected by sin but the entire community of men (*nos toti*) is

[45] Roberts, *op. cit.,* p. 110.
[46] H. Richard Niebuhr, *Christ and Culture,* New York, Harper & Brothers, 1951, p. 194.

thrown out of harmony and runs counter to its true good. One of the enduring insights in the Augustinian concept of the fall of the entire human race in Adam is this insight into the communal nature of man. It is the fate of man to live in a community of men whose destinies are bound up together. No man sinneth unto himself alone, and no man doeth good unto himself alone. God has created each man, but He has created each for community with others, and this means with responsibilities for others. Whether he wills it or not, each man is his brother's keeper, and each shares the responsibility for the sin of the group.

While the Christian understanding of man as an individual-who-exists-in-community recognizes that the freedom of the individual is greatly restricted by a corrupt community just as it may be greatly enlarged by a community that is morally healthy, it also recognizes that the basic problem for man is not evil institutions (the state, capitalism, communism, segregation) but man himself whose corruption has produced these evil institutions. Rousseau and Marx were unable to explain why these institutions, which stem out of the social nature of man, first became corrupt; and they, like their followers, naively supposed that if the state and private property were to be abolished all men would be good. Evil and sin are more deeply rooted in the human spirit than such an analysis supposes. Corrupt institutions, in short, are built by corrupt men. It is true, however, that corrupt institutions do tend in turn to corrupt those who are affected by them. This was the primary meaning which Walter Rauschenbusch found in the traditional doctrine of original sin. The individual is so closely bound together with society that the evil which has become entrenched in social patterns and institutions tends to foster and strengthen evil in individuals, and so closely is the present linked to the past that the evil of the latter tends to perpetuate itself in the present.[47]

THE ORIGIN OF SIN IS ULTIMATELY A MYSTERY. We have seen that, although man is in bondage to sin, this bondage is of his own making and he is still responsible for his sin in the sense that he is not altogether the victim of circumstances over which he has no control. We have noted that there are many pressures operating to pull him in the direction of sin, but these pressures can be resisted. In traditional language these pressures or forces have been referred to

[47] Walter Rauschenbusch, *A Theology For the Social Gospel*, New York, The Macmillan Company, 1919, chs. VII, IX.

as temptations, but in modern terminology they are frequently referred to as "occasions of sin." They are not sin in themselves, but they serve as stimuli or incitements to sin. In themselves they do not necessarily lead to sin, but the self which is already corrupted by self-love finds in them an opportunity to serve the aims of the self. Hence, it is tempted to sin. Among these occasions of sin three are particularly outstanding: the natural desires and appetites, social institutions and patterns of conduct, and anxiety stemming out of man's dual nature as a being who is involved in both freedom and necessity. We have already commented upon the fact that man's natural desires and appetites cannot be the cause of sin without relieving man of the responsibility which he feels for his sin by placing the responsibility upon the Creator. As created, man's natural endowment is good; it is only when the desires and appetites are perverted by self-love, thereby gaining the consent of the self to be used for selfish purposes, that sin ensues. We have also noted that social evil does not cause the self to sin; rather, it, too, is an occasion—almost an insurmountable one oftentimes—of sin. Moreover, back of the corrupt institutions and social patterns are individuals, the self included, and groups, including the groups to which the self belongs, who sustain these institutions and participate in their corporate actions. These institutions can be changed—slowly, imperceptibly, perhaps, but man still retains some freedom in regard to his relationships to them. The third occasion of sin—anxiety, in the sense of man's insecurity as a finite, spiritual being who is aware both of his finitude and of his freedom—is a necessary characteristic of human existence. In itself it is not sin. Rather, it is the "precondition of sin"; but it is also the basis of all human creativity as well.[48] Anxiety does not lead to sin except when man abandons faith in God's love as his ultimate and sufficient security and seeks to provide his own security in abortive ways. Hence, it is not the cause of sin, but it becomes a temptation to sin once man's relationship to God in faith has been broken.[49]

The final word about the origin of man's sin, therefore, must be

---

[48] Reinhold Niebuhr, *The Nature and Destiny of Man*, I, p. 183.

[49] The most thorough and profound analysis of the relationship of anxiety to sin that is available is found in Soren Kierkegaard, *The Concept of Dread*, trans., with an Introduction and Notes, by Walter Lowrie, Princeton, Princeton University Press, 1946. Kierkegaard declares, "Dread (i.e., anxiety) is the psychological state which precedes sin, comes as near as possible to it, and is as provocative as possible of dread, but without explaining sin, which breaks forth first in the qualitative leap" (p. 82).

that it is a mystery. "Sin . . . is the one great negative mystery of our existence, of which we know only one thing, that we are responsible for it, without the possibility of pushing the responsibility on to anything outside ourselves."[50] The possibility of sin lies in man's existence in the image of God; it lies in his nature as a spiritual being, i.e., as a personal being with the power to make significant moral decisions and respond to God's action and will.[51]

MAN AS REDEEMED

There is the danger that some will conclude from what we have said about man as sinner that the Christian view of man is low and mean. Those who think of man as essentially a moral rather than a spiritual being will almost inevitably conclude that the Christian conception of man is pessimistic and even cynical. Those who seek to understand man solely from the standpoint of psychology may conclude that the Christian doctrine of sin is essentially masochistic or sadistic; or they may regard it as a convenient rationalization for continuing in sin "that grace may abound." Both the moralist and the psychologist are likely to regard it as an effort to "force men into a specious situation of hopeless guilt for the sake of forcing them to accept a specious means of rescue."[52]

It must be granted that theologians have been partly responsible for such distortions of the biblical doctrine of man. Not only have they sometimes seemed to blame man for having a body, for being finite, and for having any self-interest at all; but they have also talked about his sin in purely moral rather than religious terms. They have likewise talked about sin in terms of inherited guilt and about salvation in terms of "decrees" and "irresistible grace" as if man had no freedom left him in determining whether or not he would be saved. And in our own day some neoörthodox writers, reacting against the illusions of liberal Protestantism and secular Humanism alike, have frequently emphasized the sinfulness of man in such a way that they

---

[50] Brunner, *op. cit.*, p. 132. "Only he who understands that sin is inexplicable knows what it is" (*ibid.*).

[51] Similarly, Immanual Kant in his *Religion Within the Limits of Reason Alone* comes to the conclusion (bk. I, sec. IV) that the origin of moral evil lies beyond the limits of rational categories and for this reason it remains inscrutable. This treatise is available in *The Philosophy of Kant,* Carl J. Friedrich, ed., New York, Random House (The Modern Library), 1949.

[52] Roberts, *op. cit.*, p. 111.

have seemed to imply a low view of man's nature and of his possibilities. This impression, it is true, has frequently been exaggerated by popular journalistic efforts to dramatize the thought of some of the most influential of these theologians such as Karl Barth and Reinhold Niebuhr in a few slogans and clichés drawn from isolated portions of their theologies; but it has stemmed in part out of the failure of these theologians themselves to give adequate attention to the context in which they have set forth their doctrines of sin. Undoubtedly, the self-righteous of all ages need to be reminded of the new temptations to sin which arise at each level of moral and spiritual life (as the saint is most keenly aware); but exclusive emphasis upon sin and human shortcomings may drive men into "paralyzed hopelessness," into hostility against themselves as well as their fellows, into fantasy, or into further acts of rebellion and defiance in an effort to find meaning and fulfillment on their own terms.

At any rate, at a time when the illusions of man about himself have been widely shattered by world events and when man's inadequacy to meet the problems and crises of history creatively is widely decried in secular circles, it seems imperative that the doctrine of sin be restored to its proper context so that the Christian estimate of man's dignity and possibilities shall be made clear. "Today," writes John Bennett, "the primary danger is that man . . . will see himself as a biological creature and little more, that he will pity himself as a helpless victim of historical forces over which he has no control, that he will regard himself and his neighbors as candidates for nuclear extermination or for the role of nuclear exterminators. So he will become hopeless about winning or preserving spiritual freedom over against the surrounding culture which so oppressively controls the choices, the habits, even the expressions of opinion and the appearances of feeling among us."[53]

THE CONTEXT OF THE DOCTRINE OF SIN

The doctrine of sin can be rightly understood only when it is viewed in the light of two other biblical insights into human nature. That man is a sinner is neither the first nor the last but rather the middle word which Christian faith has to say about man. The first word is that man is made in the image of God. As we have seen, this

[53] John C. Bennett, "Toward a Christian Humanism," *The Christian Century,* LXXIV, no. 10 (March 6, 1957), p. 292.

insight has come to symbolize his responsibility to God, his capacity for rationality, his freedom, and his capacity for self-transcendence. This image remains in man, not in its pristine purity but in a distorted form, so long as man remains human. In periods in which war and the threat of war, crime, juvenile delinquency, racial tension, and dishonesty in government are widely prevalent and monopolize the news, it is easy to overlook the genuine goodness that is often found even in the most unsuspected places; and it is easy to forget that man still retains the divine image and that he still has a latent affinity for the good to which appeal may be made if some way is found of breaking through his defense mechanisms and overcoming his hostilities and anxiety.

Speaking of her experiences in the Nazi concentration camps, Mme. Olga Lengyel writes: "Yet I saw many internees cling to their human dignity to the very end. The Nazis could debase them physically but they could not degrade them morally. Because of them I have not entirely lost my faith in mankind. If even in the hell of Birkenau there were those who were not necessarily inhuman to their fellow men, then there is still hope. It is that hope which keeps me alive."[54] The data provided by psychiatric and psychoanalytic case studies of the mentally ill reveal the extent to which the human spirit remains human and capable of responding creatively to moral claims once a relationship of acceptance has been established. And each of us, like Jesus, has doubtless been surprised at the goodness—the trust, the love, the compassion—that we have seen break forth in the most unpretentious, in the "publicans and harlots," and in those who make no claims to respectability and no profession of belief in God.

The second or middle word which Christianity has to say about man is that he is a sinner. But this word can be rightly understood only in the light of the first affirmation about human nature. Indeed, when it is rightly understood, the assertion that man is a sinner points to his essential dignity as a child of God. As we have seen, this doctrine does not affirm the universal badness of the race—that indeed would be blasphemous! Rather, it declares that man throws his whole

[54] Olga Lengyel, *Five Chimneys*, Chicago, Ziff-Davis Publishing Company, 1947, p. 212. Quoted by Daniel D. Williams, *God's Grace and Man's Hope*, New York, Harper & Brothers, 1949, pp. 184–185. Cf. Helmut Gollwitzer, *Unwilling Journey*, Philadelphia, The Muhlenberg Press, 1954. This book, which is an account of Gollwitzer's experiences in Russian prisoner of war camps, shows how the humanity of man persists even under the most difficult circumstances.

being out of harmony with reality when he forgets his limitations and when he refuses to recognize that all that is great and good in him is a gift. The concept of man as sinner thus presupposes the concept of man as made in the divine image, and it points to the contradiction in man between that image in which he was made and the perversion of that image in his actual existence.

The purpose behind the classical Christian emphasis upon man's sinfulness, therefore, has not been to drive men to a sense of despair and insufficiency "just because one enjoys seeing men wriggle in agony."[55] Rather, it has been to help them reach a full awareness of the depth of the human problem in order that they might be healed. So long as men think they are whole, they do not feel themselves to be in need of a physician. But the biblical affirmation is, on the one hand, that man is not whole and, on the other hand, that he can be made whole.

Moreover, as we have seen, Christianity does not argue that man is sinful just because the Bible says he is sinful; rather, it affirms that this biblical insight is true because in human experience it is found to be true. By the same token, it does not argue that man can be made whole just because the Bible announces that God is man's Saviour; rather, it bears witness to the saving work of God throughout history in the lives of countless men and women who have experienced this salvation as a gift from God in their own lives. But man has first to be brought to a recognition of his need for salvation. Then he will be in a position where he can at least see the relevance of the message about "a balm in Gilead" that heals the sin-sick soul and a sin-sick people. Christian faith recognizes that healing does not necessarily follow the awareness of man's illness. Recognition of man's illness may lead, on the one hand, to the despair of hopelessness or defiance; or, it may lead, on the other hand, to contrition, repentance, and trust in God whereby man is freed from the false assumption that he can and must first heal himself before he can find forgiveness and reconciliation with God.

Recognition that man is a sinner is, then, the first step toward salvation. Seen in the light of the image of God alone, however, the concept of sin issues in despair, in self-accusation, in hopelessnes, or in defiance. But seen in the light of the love and forgiveness of God, it leads to trust and gratitude, to cleansing and healing and renewal.

[55] Roberts, *op. cit.*, p. 108.

Moreover, this is the only light in which the full meaning of man's sin can be brought home to him. The fuller the comprehension of His love, the deeper does man's understanding of his own sinfulness become.

THE FINAL WORTH OF MAN SEEN IN CHRIST

In order to round out the Christian concept of man, we need, therefore, to view him in the light of the possibilities which are open to him through the grace of God as this has been mediated through Christ.[56] If some may be tempted to suppose that the concept of universal human sinfulness implies a great leveling down of all men, the concept of man as redeemed and liberated from bondage implies a great leveling up of all men because God has undertaken to save man by becoming incarnate in Christ. Despite man's sin and rebellion, God has undertaken to reconcile the world unto Himself. That means all men—and all men as sinners, no matter how deep their bondage or how hardened their hearts may have become. This is the supreme evidence of man's worth to God—that "while we were yet sinners Christ died for us" (Rom. 5:8). For Jesus, the men of an evil and adulterous generation were of much more value than the lilies of the field and the birds of the air although these, too, were of value to God; and he pictured again and again the great joy of God over the salvation of those who are lost.[57]

A second implication of the Christian conception of salvation is that *our human nature* can be redeemed through the removal of the causes of sin and guilt and through the restoration of our selves to wholeness and the opening of our lives to the creative and redemptive power of God. Christianity speaks of the redeemed man as being a "new creation" (II Cor. 5:17; Gal. 6:15; cf. John 3:3), but this does not mean that a new creature simply takes the place of the old, sinful self; rather, the old self which has been corrupted and distorted by sin is renewed and transformed into a new being. Man is not saved through the eradication or annihilation of the old self and the substitution of Christ in its place. Rather, he is saved through being enabled

---

[56] It should perhaps be noted that the main body of Christian thought has never restricted the saving work of Christ to the churches or to those who call themselves Christians.

[57] See The Parable of the Lost Sheep, The Parable of the Lost Coin, and The Parable of the Prodigal Son in the fifteenth chapter of Luke.

to bring the only self which he has, with its limitations and its possibilities, into participation in the redemptive power which Christ incarnates. Through this experience the self is made aware that the divine love is the inescapable law of the moral order, and it is led to the acceptance of this love as the only hope for salvation.

The Christian solution to the problem of sin and guilt, therefore, is the entrusting of one's self with one's objective guilt to the love and grace of God who does not desire that any man will be defeated by sin but that all shall find fulfillment. God does not need to be reconciled to man; man, however, does need to be reconciled to God. God is not hostile to man, but man is hostile to God. Man is alienated from God because he is sinful and knows himself to be guilty. Hence, he feels rejected by God. And since he feels rejected by God, he in turn is hostile toward God; for man is always hostile, consciously or unconsciously, toward those by whom he feels rejected.[58] Thus the first thing that man must do, according to Christianity, is to entrust himself as he is to God's love and redemptive power. Of course, this is not something that he can do completely once and for all; rather, he must entrust himself again and again to God even as he must be forgiven again and again by his neighbor. When this relationship of trust is restored, self-love and pride are overcome (although temptations to fall into both reappear in still more subtle forms at the higher levels of moral and spiritual development and growth), and man finds his true security in the loving purpose of God. When this happens, one is able to accept oneself with its limitations and guilt, precisely as one is, because he is aware that God accepts him thus and that he is now open to His redemptive power. To continue to reject oneself and even to hate oneself would be ungrateful. Rather, one is called upon to accept oneself as one is to God—"eternally important, eternally loved, eternally accepted."

Similarly, when man is freed through faith from the tyrannical love of self he then is able to love the neighbor without regard for what the neighbor can do to enhance the importance and power and security of the self. When God is restored to the center of life and the doing of His will becomes man's primary concern, then man is able to love those whom God loves, and he is able to love them because of their worth to God. This means loving one's enemies as well as one's friends; it means loving those against whom one harbors racial or

---

[58] Tillich, *The New Being*, p. 20.

religious prejudice as well as the members of one's own race and those who adhere to one's own faith; it means loving the outcast as well as those who are considered respectable.[59]

Finally, it needs to be noted that the Christian understanding of man's possibilities of renewal implies that salvation is a *dynamic process* rather than a *static condition.* Man's proper relationship to God and his proper relationship to his fellowmen are restored, but they need to be continually restored, for these relationships are dynamic and man is never fully freed from sin in this life. Selfishness and pride and lack of faith linger on, and they must continually be overcome and rooted out. But that they can to a vastly significant degree—even largely—be effectively overcome in this life by God's grace is the message of Christianity to all men. That they can be overcome in fact as well as "in principle" is the testimony of myriads of men and women who have experienced this liberation and reconciliation through faith. Whether man responds to the divine love or not, God is continually working for man's salvation and continually undergirding man's efforts to find wholeness and harmony with God, with himself, and with his fellowmen.[60]

The Christian estimate of man is fully seen only in the light of Christ's revelation of perfect manhood. This is the final measure of man's possibilities—of the way in which his love can be transformed and his "natural" self renewed when it is opened to the divine love and power. This is the life of spontaneous goodness to which man is called—a goodness that is not enforced by law or rewards or threats but a goodness that is based upon gratitude and love. This is the life of freedom to which man is summoned—a freedom which he can enter into only as he freely surrenders his will to the divine will so that the more captive he becomes to the divine will the freer he finds himself to be. The man who has thus dedicated himself with purity

[59] Cf. Brunner, *The Divine Imperative,* trans. by Olive Wyon, New York, The Macmillan Company, 1942, p. 129: "To *love* a human being means to accept his existence, as it is given to me by God, and thus to love him *as he is.* For only if I love him thus, that is, as this particular sinful person, do I love *him.* For this is what he really is. Otherwise I love an idea—and in the last resort this means that I am merely loving myself."

[60] That man's salvation is by grace is presented freshly and delightfully in *Grab and Grace,* a modern morality play written by Charles Williams. Gabriel is made to remind Man, who has been tempted to complain about how difficult it is to lead the Christian life: "Sir, . . . you have been constantly helped. This boy Grace does most of the work." Quoted in *The Christian Century,* LXXIV, no. 10 (March 6, 1957), p. 298.

of heart to God and has disciplined himself thoroughly in the doing of God's will is free to do as he pleases because he pleases to live in harmony with his essential nature. Whereas man before the Fall was, in the language of Augustine, free either to sin or not to sin, *posse peccare aut non peccare;* moreover, whereas fallen man by himself is able only to sin, *posse peccare,* the fully redeemed man is able only not to sin, *posse non peccare.* This is the kind of freedom which God enjoys, and to the extent that man is redeemed from bondage to sin to the service of God, to this extent he obeys the law of his being and finds therein his perfect freedom and fulfillment.

RECOMMENDED READINGS

Barry, F. R., *Recovery of Man,* New York, Charles Scribner's Sons, 1949, chs. III–V.

Barth, Karl, *Die Kirchliche Dogmatik,* Zurich, 1948, III, pt. II.

Barth, Karl, "No!" trans. by Peter Fraenkel, in *Natural Theology,* London, Geoffrey Bles, 1946.

Beach, Waldo, and Niebuhr, H. Richard, eds., *Christian Ethics,* New York, The Ronald Press, 1955. See especially the selections from St. Augustine, John Calvin, and John Wesley.

Berdyaev, Nicolas, *The Destiny of Man,* London, Geoffrey Bles, 2nd ed., 1945, pt. I, chs. II–III.

Brunner, Emil, *Man in Revolt,* Philadelphia, The Westminster Press, 1947, chs. V–VII and "Epilogue."

Brunner, Emil, "Nature and Grace," in *Natural Theology,* London, Geoffrey Bles, 1946.

Bultmann, Rudolf, *Essays Philosophical and Theological,* London, Student Christian Movement Press, Ltd., 1955, chs. IV–VI, VIII–IX.

Cairns, David, *The Image of God in Man,* New York, The Philosophical Library, 1953.

Calhoun, Robert L., "The Dilemma of Humanitarian Modernism," in T. E. Jessop *et al., The Christian Understanding of Man,* London, George Allen and Unwin, Ltd., 1938.

Calvin, John, *Institutes of the Christian Religion,* 2 vols., Philadelphia, Presbyterian Board of Education, 1936, bk. I, ch. XV; bk. II, chs. I–III.

Eichrodt, Walther, *Man in the Old Testament,* London, Student Christian Movement Press, Ltd., 1951.

Farmer, Herbert H., *God and Men,* New York, Abingdon-Cokesbury Press, 1947, ch. III.

Kierkegaard, Soren, *The Concept of Dread,* trans. by Walter Lowrie, Princeton, Princeton University Press, 1944.

Kierkegaard, Soren, *The Sickness Unto Death,* trans. by Walter Lowrie, Princeton, Princeton University Press, 1941.

Maritain, Jacques, *True Humanism,* London, Geoffrey Bles, 1946, chs. I–II.

Niebuhr, Reinhold, *The Nature and Destiny of Man,* I: *Human Nature,* New York, Charles Scribner's Sons, 1943, chs. I, VI–IX.

Roberts, David E., *Psychotherapy and a Christian View of Man,* New York, Charles Scribner's Sons, 1950, chs. V–IX.

St. Augustine, *The City of God,* New York, Random House (The Modern Library), 1950, bks. XII, XIV, XXII.

St. Augustine, "On the Morals of the Catholic Church," in Whitney J. Oates, ed., *Basic Writings of Saint Augustine,* I, New York, Random House, 1948.

Thelen, Mary Frances, *Man as Sinner in Contemporary American Realistic Theology,* New York, King's Crown Press, 1946.

chapter 7

CHRISTIAN ETHICS
AS RESPONSIVE LOVE
TO GOD

THE CHRISTIAN LIFE AS RESPONSE TO GOD'S ACTIVITY

BEFORE undertaking to describe the Christian's response to the action of God in more specific terms, it will be helpful to summarize the ground which we have covered up to now insofar as this relates to the distinctive concern of the present chapter, viz., a more detailed analysis both of the nature of this response and of the method itself.

We have already seen that there is both an element of aspiration after the good and an element of law or duty involved in all efforts to understand ethics. This is true of Christian ethics as well as of philosophical ethics, and at various times and among various groups both the method of aspiration and the method of duty have been held up as representing *the* Christian approach to ethics. On the one hand, Christians have sought after the vision of God, immortality and eternal life, the brotherhood of man upon earth, or perfection. On the other hand, they have sought to obey the commandments of God as these have been mediated through the Decalogue, or the Sermon on the Mount, or the Roman Catholic Church, or various Protestant traditions. The first of these approaches, however, is essentially man-centered. Primarily, it seeks something for the self even though this be the vision of God or eternal life or the brotherhood of man or the perfection of the self. Doubtless each of these represents a good for the self, but to seek them because they are goods for the self cannot be made the central principle of Christian ethics because the latter makes God the center of man's life and demands that man show his love to God through service to his fellowmen. Neither can the second approach—viz., that of duty or law—be made the primary method of Christian ethics, for law is too inflexible to interpret love adequately and it ignores the fact that man by himself is unable to keep the law, especially the law of love. Hence, while Christian ethics recognizes a legitimate place for aspiration after the good and for law as a guide to the discovery of God's will, its method is best understood as that of man's response to the activity of God. It is man's response to what God reveals His will and His purposes to be—through history, through Scripture, through the present social upheavals, and through the experience of the Christian community all brought to focus upon the concrete ethical decision. This response is one which each individual must make in each new situation which he faces. It is an existential decision which must be made "on the spot" although not without guidance.

This understanding of Christian ethics as response to the divine activity, we have observed, is in keeping with the method used by the prophets of the Old Testament, by Jesus, and by the writers of the New Testament in general. The prophets seek to understand the meaning of the events connected with Israel's past history and also those that are taking place in their own lifetimes. God has made His will and purposes known through the call of Abraham, through the liberation of the Israelites from bondage, and through the establishment of the Covenant with Israel; and He continues to reveal His will and purposes through the use of the nations to execute judgment, through the suffering of the innocent servant of Yahweh in exile in Babylon, and through His faithfulness to those who trust in Him. Amos, for example, sees in the doom which threatens Israel the judgment of Yahweh upon her unfaithfulness and her injustice, and the divine judgment constitutes a call to Israel to repent and reform. Isaiah similarly sees God rather than Assyria or Egypt as the primary agent in history to whom Israel should turn for guidance and deliverance:

> Woe to those who go down to Egypt for help
>   and rely on horses,
> who trust in chariots because they are many
>   and in horsemen because they are very strong,

> but do not look to the Holy One of Israel
> or consult the Lord!   (Isa. 31:1)

It is not Assyria but the power beyond Assyria with which Israel must ultimately reckon and whose will provides the ultimate meaning of the historical crisis.

In like manner, Jesus seeks to respond to God's will as this is revealed not just in a set of laws but in the divine action in his own experience: in his own life and vocation, in the power which has been given him to cast out demons and heal the sick, in his own confrontation of human need on the Sabbath, and in the summons to go to Jerusalem and suffer death upon a cross. In all of these events he sees the action of God and seeks to make His will done upon earth in his own life rather than to conform to the traditions of men or seek some good for himself. And the New Testament as a whole witnesses to the faith that God was active in the person of Christ, and it summons men to respond to this action with which they are confronted. Not only has God acted redemptively in Christ—in his life and death and resurrection, but He continues to confront men in Christ as their Risen Lord and in the Spirit which is ever active in their midst.

We have likewise examined the three-fold way in which Christianity sees God as active in all events—creating and sustaining, ordering, and redeeming them. We have also seen that in the biblical view man is essentially a spiritual being, made in the image of God and existing in personal relationship with his Creator. God is the true center of existence, and man's true good lies in the acceptance of the divine will as the law of his being. This is the starting point of man's moral and religious life. If God's will, then, can be most adequately understood in terms of His creative, ordering, and redeeming purposes, there is need now to examine in more detail what response man should make to each of these forms of divine action upon him.[1]

[1] For many of the insights in the following interpretation of the Christian ethic as an ethic of response to God's three-fold activity as Creator, Judge, and Redeemer, I am greatly indebted to Professor H. Richard Niebuhr. Other particularly helpful statements of this view of Christian ethics, to which I am also indebted, are found in Emil Brunner, *The Divine Imperative* (although Brunner speaks only of a two-fold response to the Creator and the Redeemer) and in an article by Professor Rachel Henderlite entitled, "The Christian Way in Race Relations," which appeared in *Theology Today,* XIV, no. 2 (July, 1957), pp. 195–211.

In *Faith and Community: A Christian Existential Approach* (New York, Harper & Brothers, 1959), which appeared after the writing of these pages,

THE RESPONSE TO THE CREATOR: GRATITUDE AND LOVE

In the first place, the action of God as Creator calls for the response of *praise and gratitude to the Creator and love and reverence for the creation.* In all of our conduct we meet God as the One who has called us into being at a particular time and under a particular set of circumstances. Our existence has ultimate meaning only in relation to His will and purposes, and the part of history into which we are placed also has meaning only in this relationship. Neither can be viewed as the result of mere "accident" or fate if the work of the Creator is taken seriously. The particular "I" is something that is given, and the particular time and place in which I exist are also given to me; and it is in this particular "here" and "now" that I meet my Creator who is also the Creator of all other agents and all other times and places. This is implicit in the biblical view of God as the sovereign Lord of history. This is the point at which God's will is relevant for me if it is relevant at all, and here I must seek to discover what He as the providential Creator is sustaining and maintaining in being amid all of its corruption by sin and also what He is calling into being through His creative and providential action in the here and now.

From this point of view it may seem that Christianity should be fundamentally a conservative religion in the sense that it would endorse the *status quo* as being good since it is a part of history viewed as providential and since God makes it possible for this *status quo* to continue in existence through His sustaining power. But to draw such a conclusion would be to ignore the other two aspects of God's activity as Judge and as Redeemer. The *status quo* has some good in it, and the origin of this good is in God. Moreover, God's will for this particular situation and those who are in it is good. Both the persons and the good in the conditions and circumstances in which they live are to be affirmed, for this is what God wills; and, if I am a faithful child of God, His will becomes my will.

God wills, for example, that man shall live in community and not

---

Professor Clyde A. Holbrook has provided a profound and richly rewarding interpretation of Christian ethics in terms of a theological analysis of the nature of community as this is understood in Christian faith. "In its most general form," he writes, "the term 'community' designates the reality which faith holds to be the will of God. Community signifies His way of creating, sustaining, judging, and redeeming His creation" (p. 112).

as an asocial being. Certain institutions are essential to the on-going life of the community, and these are frequently referred to as the "orders of creation," for they stem out of the social nature of man as he was created. Among these institutions are the family, the economic order, and the state. It is God's will as manifest in the creation of man as a social being that these orders should come into existence and be maintained for the purpose of meeting man's needs (cf. Mark 10:2–9; 2:27). This does not mean, however, that any existing order as it is now manifest represents the complete embodiment of God's will for that order. All existing orders are corrupted by sin and stand under God's judgment, but in all existing orders man confronts God the Creator who summons him to fulfill the divine will for these orders. In view of their actual corruption, however, it would be as justifiable to claim that the Christian ethic is revolutionary as to claim that it is conservative, and indeed both tendencies are amply illustrated by the history of the social teachings of the Christian churches.

The response of those who by faith know that God is the Creator of all and that He wills only the good for man[2] is that of *praise and gratitude* to Him for life itself, for the good gifts which He has bestowed upon them, for the possibilities which are open to them, and for the knowledge that in all things God works for their good. Praise and gratitude to the Creator are not, however, simply feelings; rather, they are to be understood in terms of the personal encounter of man with God in specific moments of decision in which by one's deeds one either shows praise and gratitude or one dishonors God and unthankfully rejects His creative intent. In the former case man responds in trust and obedience; in the latter he responds in distrust and disobedience. The gift of the Creator is at the same time a demand that man accept the will of the Giver of all good as his own will. This means, more specifically, that he will accept himself with his talents and capacities; that he will accept his fellowmen with their particular endowments as good—regardless of their social respectabil-

---

[2] In *The Republic*, bk. II, pp. 379–380, Plato similarly maintains that God is good and the author only of good to men. Cf. Robert L. Calhoun: "This [belief in the goodness of God] is, so far as I can judge, the very crux of religious faith. The world is great: that needs no proof. In it the sovereign power is good: this admits no proof. But to affirm it with all one's heart and mind is to believe in God, great beyond all conceiving, yet not too great to be good" (*God and the Common Life*, New York, Charles Scribner's Sons, 1935, pp. 190–191).

ity or IQ or race or nationality or religion; and that he will affirm each person in his need, seeking to fulfill the creative intent of God for each.

Viewed thus, from the standpoint of his relationship to God whom he confronts as Creator, man's response is praise and gratitude. Viewed from the standpoint of man's relation to his fellows and to the rest of the created order, his response is *love and reverence*. This double relationship is inescapable for man since he is a free, self-transcendent being placed in relationship with his fellow creatures and with his Creator. The unifying relationship amid all of these relations of the self to others is its relationship to God who is the Creator of all and in whose will the harmony of the good of all is finally found. As an expression of his praise and gratitude to God man is summoned to love his fellowman—enemy as well as friend—and to show respect and reverence to all of His creation. Christianity does not teach as its ultimate principle of conduct reverence for life in all of its forms—as Jainism, for example, does—without the recognition of any principle of discrimination among the competing forms of life and the different values which are attached to different forms of life. It does teach that in relation to all created things— not just animate beings—man is called upon to show respect and reverence for each in its order of being and in accordance with the purpose of the Creator. In relationship to the created order man's grateful response to God demands that he seek to fulfill the divine will; hence, he is not free to start with himself and use anything whatsoever with regard *only* to the desires of the self.

In a word, the first and basic response to God's action as Creator is that of accepting and affirming that which He has created. It is saying "Yea" to God's "Yea." The negative response of self-denial can be properly understood only in the light of this positive attitude toward life and the world. These are good insofar as they are the creation of God. That they contain evil insofar as the good intent of the Creator has been distorted and twisted is obvious to the Christian, but that they are good by creation is the fundamental thing to be said about them; and everything else that is said about them must be understood in the light of this basic conviction. Similarly, man's response to the other phases of the divine action must be interpreted in the light of his primary duty of affirming God's creative will.

THE RESPONSE TO THE JUDGE: REPENTANCE,
SELF-DENIAL, AND RESTRAINT OF EVIL

We have seen, however, that man is confronted not only with the creative intent of God, whether in himself or in his fellowmen or in the family or in the economic and political and religious orders, but also with the divine judgment upon all of these insofar as they are distorted and misdirected by sin. The response which man is summoned to make to this form of divine action is *repentance and self-denial*. Man is summoned to accept the divine judgment upon himself and his works and the restraint upon the self which such judgment embodies, and he is called to coöperate with God in denying the self in order that God's positive, creative will may be done.

It is because of the seriousness which the Bible ascribes to sin in that it distorts and twists the work of the Creator that the Scriptures place so much emphasis upon the urgency of man's repenting. This does not mean that man is summoned simply to have feelings of remorse but rather that he is called to turn around, to make an about-face, and to "return unto the Lord." This is the meaning of the divine judgment which the prophets see in history. It is the meaning of God's judgment that is being passed upon evil in Jesus' own ministry, and it is the purpose of the proclamation of the final judgment at the end of history. In these and many other ways man confronts the Creator who is also the Judge and who does not permit evil to triumph over the purpose which He had in creation. Face to face with this "No!" which God says to man's evil, man is summoned to confess his wrongdoing and his sin, to desist from his evil ways, and to begin to do good.

Since man's basic sin consists of his love of self in the place of God, the divine judgment is understood by faith to be judgment upon the self—its inordinate love of itself, its pride, its will to exploit others, and its attempt to make itself the center of its own life. This self-love, as we have seen, masquerades in many forms, both individual and collective. Similarly, the divine judgment is encountered in many forms. It is met, for example, in the high infant mortality and crime rates that are found in our slums; in divorce which results from the failure to achieve God's will in marriage; in the low educational level and the high educational costs that are prevalent in the South; in the racial tension and strife that exist in both the North and the

South; in corruption and decay in government; and in armament races and wars between nations.

Since the judgment which is being passed upon man is directed primarily against his self-love and pride, it is of course far easier to recognize it as being directed toward others than toward oneself; and it is easier, by the same token, to recognize it in the past than in the present. It is easier to recognize the judgments of the Lord upon Israel or upon Nazism or upon Russian Communism than upon our own country and culture, or upon our own class and community, or especially upon ourselves. But the biblical witness to the universality of human sinfulness coupled with its thoroughgoing monotheism which sees the divine judgment as being equally universal constitutes a summons to man to humility and self-examination. Moreover, man is reminded again and again that his greatest danger lies in the temptation to vindicate his own righteousness and assume that he is himself without sin. This is true of groups as well as of individuals; and the more moral and spiritual the individual and the group pretend to be, the greater is the danger that they will fall into pride, and the more destructive and tyrannical this pride is likely to be.

In a word, the first response to the action of God as Judge is humility and repentance; it is the acceptance of the divine judgment upon ourselves and coöperation with the intent of God that the self shall be held in restraint in order that the will of God for the whole community of men shall not be defeated. Although it is a negative principle, the truth of which can be seen only in its relation to the positive will of God in creation and in redemption, self-denial is, nevertheless, an essential element in man's proper relationship to God and to his neighbors. The importance which is attached to self-denial by Christianity stems out of the recognition that man's greatest temptation is to self-love. Self-denial points to the radical redirection of his basic loyalty which is required of man before he can do the divine will.

But obviously man does not confront God's judgment upon himself alone, for judgment is being passed in greater or lesser measure upon all men and upon all human institutions. Each person is faced, therefore, with the summons not only to affirm the creative intent of God for his fellows but also to seek to discover and affirm the will of God the Judge who seeks to restrain the neighbor as well as the self and who is passing judgment upon the various socio-cultural institutions in which the neighbor participates along with the self. Oftentimes the neighbor does not recognize the need of restraint upon his will and actions, whether he be a husband, a patriot, a member of the dominant racial group, or an ecclesiastical potentate. Similarly, I am oftentimes unaware of my need to be restrained, and my neighbor is frequently confronted by my pride and self-love even when I profess to have subdued my pride and denied myself. God's creative will is that I affirm my neighbor and that my neighbor affirm my existence; but, since both my neighbor and I together with all our mutual neighbors are sinful, we must also coöperate with God's will to *restrain sin and evil*. We are forbidden to judge in holier-than-thou fashion; but we cannot remain neutral amid the many social struggles of which we are inevitably a part by the very fact of our creation as social beings; and we cannot remain indifferent to the suffering and injustice of man against his fellowman without thereby contributing to the defeat of God's creative and redemptive will. Love of the neighbor implies that I will seek his good even if it means restraining him out of love or restraining his oppressors for the same reason.

This restraint of the neighbor must always be under restraint, for the Christian knows that he is constantly in danger of seeking to hold others in check out of self-love rather than out of neighbor-love. He knows, also, that no individual and no group with which he may side in the struggle against injustice is entirely just and sufficiently righteous to go unchecked. Moreover, he is aware that he must continually choose between causes which represent different degrees of justice, not between absolute justice and complete injustice; he is also aware that he cannot remain neutral. He must act purposefully or he will act by default. Hence, the Christian is summoned to align himself with what he believes to be the righteous will of God in the particular conflict between good and evil, and in so doing he must not only minister to the positive needs of his neighbor but he must also restrain his neighbor from injustice and evil. Not to coöperate with God in the restraint of evil, whether this is manifest in economic groups or hate organizations or imperialistic powers, is to reject the divine will. This does not mean, of course, that all are called to exercise such restraint in the same way or that the same kind of restraint is to be used against all forms of evil. There are many forms of restraint—passive resistance, physical force, the ballot, economic pressure, the use of the courts, the written and spoken word. Though devoted Christians will differ as to which groups most need to be checked and what methods should be employed to this end, each is summoned to seek to discover the will of God amid the dynamic tensions and the possibilities that are presented to him; and each is called to affirm the divine will in trust in God and out of love for the neighbor.

It is in its response to the judgment of God, therefore, that Christian ethics becomes an ethic of reform. Emphasis upon the preservation of creation alone leads to an unqualified support of the *status quo* in any area, for this is idolatrously equated with God's will. Emphasis upon the restraint of evil alone leads to the destruction of the good along with the evil, of the order along with the disorder. This is why Christians have generally rejected insurrection and rebellion as methods of dealing with injustice in the political sphere; for the overthrow of an evil government by violence results in the overthrow of whatever order even the evil government maintains, unless another government is able to assume authority at once. The Christian, it must be emphasized, is not summoned to respond alternately to the Judge and to the Creator. Rather, he must respond to the will of the Judge who is at the same time confronting him as the Creator. The unifying characteristic of both forms of the divine action is love, and love is the motive which prompts the Christian to coöperate with the will of God both in creation and in judgment.[3]

THE RESPONSE TO THE REDEEMER: FORGIVENESS AND FREEDOM

Since God also confronts man as his Redeemer, man is called to respond to the divine action upon him in *forgiveness and freedom*. This means, in the first place, that man is called to accept forgiveness in humility. It means that since God accepts him as he is—that is, as a sinner—and freely forgives him, he is to accept this forgiveness gratefully as a gift. Man is summoned to cease being anxious about his own merit, about his own righteousness, and about his own salvation,

[3] Although Brunner speaks of the Christian response to God's action as a two-fold response to the Creator and the Redeemer, he does not overlook the work of God as Judge but includes this under the work of the Redeemer. He writes: "It is legalistic, abstract, Utopian idealism to leave out this concrete situation; it means giving no heed to the command of the Creator. But on the other hand, it is lazy worldliness to do merely what is required by the claims of our order, without trying to attack all that is contrary to God within this situation with the whole energy of love" (Emil Brunner, *The Divine Imperative*, trans. by Olive Wyon, New York, The Macmillan Company, 1942, p. 130).

for the message of the Redeemer is that man does not have to earn any merit in order to get God to love him and accept him and forgive his sin. God already loves him and accepts him exactly as he is—in his weakness and bondage and state of rebellion. All that man must do in order to be forgiven is to trust God, repent, and forgive those who have trespassed against him.

The divine forgiveness can be accepted only in humility and with repentance. Man must be willing to acknowledge that he is in the wrong before God and that nothing that he can do can put him in the right. His proper relationship to God is one of trust and response. It is a relationship of dependence upon the sovereign will of God. But man has broken this proper relationship, and the only way in which the harmony of his "original" existence can be restored is for him freely to confess his sin and accept the divine love which seeks to restore man rather than to condemn him. If this desire to accept the divine forgiveness for oneself be genuine, it must also manifest itself in offering forgiveness to the neighbor whom God also accepts and to whom He also offers forgiveness. Otherwise, the willingness to accept the divine forgiveness for oneself reflects an essentially selfish desire rather than a readiness to accept the total will of God, the universal Redeemer, who seeks the reconciliation of all men with each other and with Himself. Such forgiveness of one's neighbors, however, does not merit forgiveness of oneself on the part of God. The divine forgiveness is freely offered, and it stems solely out of God's love and grace.[4]

But the divine forgiveness means not only that the believer is freed from his preoccupation with himself—with his own salvation and purity—but also that he is now able to begin to act toward the neighbor with primary regard to God's will for the neighbor. Since God freely forgives those who trust in Him, the believer is now free to forget about himself and center his concern upon the neighbor under God. Hence, he is freed from bondage to the law and from the paralyzing fear that in the service of the neighbor the self may become polluted by involvement in the evils of politics and the economic life and racial prejudice. The believer is freed from the legalism of Sabbath laws, the tyranny of the absolute prohibition of divorce, and bondage to such moral rules as the requirement to tell the truth

---

[4] Cf. The Parable of the Pharisee and the Publican (Luke 18:9–14), The Parable of the Unforgiving Servant (Matt. 18:23–35), and The Parable of the Prodigal Son (Luke 15:11–32).

understood in a narrowly literalistic sense; for he knows that if he wholeheartedly seeks to do God's will, God will still accept him with whatever uncleanness he incurs in the effort to serve the neighbor. The Christian is now free and commanded to do everything that love for his neighbor requires,[5] for he knows that this is God's ultimate will and he knows that the grace of God is sufficient to forgive him the guilt which he incurs out of love. He sees quite clearly that the effort to escape involvement in the world of economic and political and ecclesiastical life out of the motive of seeking one's own purity and salvation is, in actuality, a subtle form of self-love and represents a lack of trust in the grace and love of God. The Christian is summoned to coöperate with God in the task of redemption; and he is called to do this within the sphere of creation, not by withdrawal from the world.

This response of the Christian to the redemptive action and purpose of God is implied in the Reformation formula, "salvation by faith alone," although this formula has frequently been interpreted in terms that are far too passive and socially conservative to do justice to the dynamic character of Christian love.[6] Luther saw clearly that salvation is a free gift of God and that man can never earn it by his own works, no matter how moral he may be. But Luther to a certain extent, and many of his followers to a far greater degree, failed to do justice to the positive works of love which the Christian is freed through faith by grace to do—indeed, is commanded to do—by way of serving the neighbor through social action. Such works of love are not a substitute for faith; they earn man no saving merit; but they are the fruit of faith. They represent the effort to be obedient to the will of the Creator and Judge and Redeemer and thus to respond to the whole will of God.

Not only is the Christian called to forgive and to act in freedom toward his fellow-believers, but he is also called to imitate the love of God for those who do not yet know themselves to be His children. Thus the believer is summoned to proclaim to all, by deed as well as by word, the meaning of God's redemptive love. It is not sufficient simply to forgive those who ask to be forgiven, but the imitation of

---

[5] Cf. Paul Ramsey, *Basic Christian Ethics,* New York, Charles Scribner's Sons, 1950, p. 89.

[6] The phrase "salvation by faith alone" is a somewhat misleading way of stating the Pauline doctrine of "salvation by grace through faith." Salvation is freely offered by the grace of God; it is appropriated, but not actually merited, by faith.

God's *agape* means that the believer will take the first step and bear the "cost" involved in leading the unbeliever toward a goal which he has not yet seen and accepted. It means taking the initiative in effecting reconciliation and brotherhood even when one has been wronged. It means bearing one another's burdens. It means bearing a cross, not in the Stoic sense of something one cannot escape but in the spirit of Christ who out of love for sinful men vicariously bore the "cost" of reconciling them to their heavenly Father. It means seeking to make God's will done upon earth as it is in heaven and in the "orders of creation" as well as in the inward personal life of the believer.

While, in a sense, the response to the Creator is the fundamental response which the Christian makes in that he thereby affirms the goodness of the created order as the appointed sphere in which he is to serve God, it is nevertheless true that the summons of the Creator can be properly understood only in the light of the summons of the Redeemer. In the act of His Creation and in His continuous sustaining and nurturing of that which He has created, God reveals the value of the created order, including men; but it is only in the light of His persistent efforts to save those who have rebelled against Him that men are able to see how deep is His love for them—a love which never lets them go, a love which never turns ultimately against them, but a love which is patient and long-suffering, which loves without regard to the inherent worth of its object and without counting the cost, and which seeks even through its own rejection to save them. It is only in the light of the action of the Redeemer that the final significance of man's creation in the image of God can be seen and that his true dignity and worth can be ascertained.

Unless the summons of the Judge is similarly understood in the light of the purpose of the Redeemer, the judgments which men render easily become destructive and vindictive. Unless those who exercise judgment and restraint do so as men who are aware of the forgiveness which they have received and continually stand in need of no matter how righteous the cause which they happen to be championing may be, they are tempted to forget the will of the Creator and the Redeemer and assume that they are the instruments of God's judgment alone. Out of love for the neighbor, Christians are called upon to pass judgment on issues and causes; but they are called to do so in humility, recognizing that the causes which they themselves espouse are also the instruments of some evil and that they therefore have no right to assume that they are righteous and their opponents are unrighteous. All are unrighteous, and God wills the transformation and salvation of all. In response to the Redeemer the Christian is summoned to participate in the restraint of others only insofar as such restraint may be a work of love. Vengeance and self-righteousness and willful destruction are forbidden by the Creator and Redeemer.

And, finally, the summons of the Redeemer must likewise be understood in the light of the command of the Creator and the Judge. When the nature of the divine will is clearly perceived, the purpose of the Redeemer is seen to include that of the Creator and the Judge. Obedience to the Creator gives ultimate direction and purpose to life and history, but this direction and purpose are clarified by the work of the Redeemer who is bringing into being a new creation, a new community where the divine will is being done and will be done completely when the Kingdom of God is fully come. Thus the response to the Redeemer includes the response to the Creator, and the former represents the fulfillment of the latter. But the response to the Redeemer must also be made in the light of the summons of the Judge. Otherwise Christian love easily degenerates into sentimentality and neglects the neighbor's need for restraint and discipline. When the response to the Redeemer includes the restraint which love requires, it represents the fulfillment of the will of the Judge. Hence, although the meaning of the response to the redemptive action of God cannot be understood without reference to His creative and judging action, the Christian ethic may be briefly characterized as an ethic of response to the redemptive action and will of God, or more simply as *responsive love to God.*[7]

AGAPE, SELF-LOVE, MUTUAL LOVE, AND SACRIFICIAL LOVE

The Christian ethic is generally interpreted as essentially an ethic of love, and it is commonly assumed that this love has two objects: God and the neighbor. There have been many attempts to reduce the two commandments of Jesus to a single requirement of love for God or love for the neighbor. But, in the main, traditional Christianity has recognized that every such attempt inevitably misrepresents the essential nature of Christian love. In the first place, such attempts

[7] Cf. I John 4:11: "Beloved, if God so loved us, we also ought to love one another."

ignore the fact that in the teaching of Jesus Christian love is specifically directed toward *two* objects, not just toward one. And, in the second place, it is generally recognized that there are important differerences between man's love for God and his love for his neighbor. As we have seen (see above, Chapter 4, pp. 84–86), love for God means trusting and adoring Him; it means showing gratitude and rendering obedience to Him; it means walking in humility before Him. Love for the neighbor, on the other hand, means forgiveness and compassion; it means ministering unto the needs of all of one's neighbors without regard to their merit and without thought of recompense for oneself.

In speaking of the Christian ethic as response to the divine action we have endeavored to suggest in more concrete terms what love for God and love for the neighbor mean. But in view of the widespread debate within Christian circles concerning the relations of self-love, mutual love, and sacrificial love to *agape,* which is the distinctive Greek word for "love" in the New Testament, it will be helpful to examine the fundamental issues raised in this debate in the light of the foregoing analysis of the Christian ethic as man's response to the three-fold action of God. We have suggested that the distinctive character of the Christian ethic is most effectively safeguarded against sentimental and humanistic distortions when it is understood as an ethic of sonship rather than simply as an ethic of love. It was not love of love as a cosmic principle or force but love of God which motivated Jesus' conduct both in relationship to God and in relationship to his neighbors. Jesus' ethic was theocentric through and through, and the meaning of Christian love can be made clear only when God rather than love is made central.[8]

The Christian ethic rests upon the fact that God has taken the initiative in revealing His love to man. The divine love (*agape*) for man is, as Nygren points out, spontaneous and unmotivated in the sense that it has no motive apart from its own nature. It is not evoked by some merit in man; rather, it seeks "sinners" just as much as the "righteous," those who do not deserve it and can lay no claim upon it just as much as the saints. In this sense it is indifferent to value. But it is also creative of value in that it imparts value to its object through the forgiveness of sin and the impartation of new worth. Finally, it is the initiator of fellowship with God. Man is unable to

[8] Cf. H. Richard Niebuhr, *Christ and Culture,* New York, Harper & Brothers, 1951, p. 19: "It was not love but God that filled [Jesus'] soul."

bring such fellowship into existence either by his meritorious conduct or by repentance; it is possible only because God's *agape* reaches out to draw man into fellowship with Him.[9]

God's love for man is free, spontaneous, and unmerited; but as the sovereign Lord God claims man for Himself, for a life of love. God demands the response of the whole self: "You shall love the Lord your God with all your heart, and with all your soul, and with all your mind, and with all your strength" (Mark 12:30). Moreover, God does not confront a single individual in isolation from his fellows; rather, He confronts him as a social being set in relationship to many other persons upon whom He also bestows His *agape* in equal measure as upon the self. For this reason, in the very act whereby He reveals His love to man, He also confronts man with a second commandment: "You shall love your neighbor as yourself" (Mark 12:31). The two commandments are inseparable, but they remain two. The person who is aware of the depth and inclusiveness of God's *agape* recognizes that it is the divine will both that man shall trust and adore Him and that man shall love his neighbors as God in actuality does already love them. Love for God seeks to express itself both in trust in God and in love for one's fellowmen. Man cannot, however, love his fellowmen in a Christian way unless he also loves God with all of his heart, soul, mind, and strength; for, apart from trust in God and ultimate loyalty to Him, man's love for his fellows is either selfish or idolatrous or both. Only when man entrusts his whole self to God in the present and for the future, only then is he free to love his neighbors with Christian love. Only when he is freed through faith from anxiety concerning the self, only then does it become possible for man to love his neighbors as God does rather than as the self by nature is inevitably inclined to love them.

Viewed in the light of God's *agape,* which is the source of man's love both for God and for the neighbor, the Second Commandment clearly means that the follower of Christ is summoned to love all men and not just those who belong to the Christian fellowship or to one's own racial or national group. God's love for man is universal; therefore, man's love for his fellowmen ought to be universal, too. Christian neighbor-love is not elicited by the value of the neighbor to the self but rather by his value to God. Christian faith declares that all men are of equal worth to God and that all share equally in His love;

[9] Anders Nygren, *Agape and Eros,* trans. by Philip S. Watson, London, Society for Promoting Christian Knowledge, 1953, pp. 75–80.

hence, the Christian is summoned to imitate the universality as well as the spontaneity and unselfishness of the divine love.[10]

But what about love for oneself? When Jesus says, "You shall love your neighbor as yourself," does he imply a third commandment, "You shall love yourself"? It scarcely needs to be said that he nowhere speaks explicitly of such a commandment, and no writer of the New Testament interprets him as requiring self-love. Rather, self-love is simply presupposed by Jesus as the attitude of natural man toward himself. Jesus merely recognizes its existence as a natural fact and requires that each man love his neighbor as by nature he loves himself. Seen in this light, the Second Commandment focuses attention upon the fact that self-love is both man's natural condition and the reason for the perversity of his will.[11] Since this is so, what is required is that man's love be given a new direction; i.e., toward the neighbor instead of the self. In the process whereby this change is effected, the perversion of man's will is overcome and the circle of self-centeredness is broken.

If we look at the divine love for man, we see why Jesus did not include a commandment of self-love. The divine love is outgoing; it is directed toward man rather than toward some good which God may derive from loving man. It is manifest most clearly in His generosity in creation and in the forgiveness which He offers to sinful men. "He makes his sun rise on the evil and on the good, and sends rain on the just and on the unjust" (Matt. 5:45). God is like a shepherd who goes out to seek the lost sheep (Luke 15:3–7). "There will be more joy in heaven over one sinner who repents than over ninety-nine righteous persons who need no repentance" (Luke 15:7). Or again, God is like a father who runs forth to meet his prodigal son (Luke 15:11–24). In view of the other-directed character of the divine love, one cannot really emulate God's *agape* in relation to oneself but only in the relation which one bears to his neighbors.

It must be remembered, moreover, that Jesus does not require neighbor-love in isolation from the First Commandment which describes man's primary requirement to love God. It is true that in setting forth the demand for neighbor-love Jesus quotes a summary of the law found in Leviticus 19:18, but it is clear that he goes far

[10] Cf. The Parable of the Good Samaritan (Luke 10:29–37) and Jesus' requirement that his followers love their enemies (Matt. 5:44) as well as his own example in seeking out the "lost sheep," the "publicans," and the "sinners" that he might minister especially to them in view of their special needs.

[11] Nygren, *op. cit.,* p. 101.

beyond the mere "as yourself" formula in the love which he shows toward men and in the demands which he places upon his followers. Like the Golden Rule, the Second Commandment with its "as yourself" measure points to man's fundamental moral problem, viz., his self-centeredness. Yet it is impossible to fulfill this commandment without going far beyond what it literally prescribes and losing the self in the service of the neighbor under God. Love that seeks merely to pursue the claims of the neighbor and the self impartially out of a sense of obligation to do so ends up being calculating and prudential; it remains essentially self-centered still. Hence, the only genuine answer to the perversion of man's natural will is to be found by first loving God with heart, soul, mind, and strength and by discovering in that act how God loves the neighbor. For those who would be sons of God the divine *agape* becomes the norm of man's love for his fellowmen. Thus Professor H. Richard Niebuhr writes: "The virtue of neighbor-love in Jesus' conduct and teaching can never be adequately described if it is in any way abstracted from the primary love of God. Christ loves his neighbor not as he loves himself, but as God loves him. Hence the Fourth Gospel, discerning that the Jewish statement, 'Love thy neighbor as thyself' fitted adequately neither Jesus' actions nor his requirements, changed the commandment to read, 'Love one another as I have loved you.' "[12] We have already seen how Paul similarly makes the *agape* of God as manifest in Christ rather than man's natural self-love the standard of neighbor-love. And the author of the First Letter of John likewise points to the revelation of love in Christ rather than to the fact of natural love of oneself as the test of Christian love.

When the requirement of neighbor-love is thus viewed in relation to God's love, the reason why Jesus does not also require self-love—that is, a love that is directed primarily toward the self—is clear. It is also clear why Christian love for the neighbor excludes and overcomes self-love. In summary, neighbor-love is modeled after the divine *agape*. Its nature is to affirm the neighbor rather than the self, and this is possible only in so far as one's action is directed toward the claims of the neighbor rather than toward those of the self.

This does not mean, however, that the Christian is unmindful of his true nature and his worth to God. It does not mean that he should have a mean and low view of himself. On the contrary, one who is

[12] H. Richard Niebuhr, *op. cit.,* p. 18.

aware of the divine forgiveness and love for himself should "accept" himself and gratefully acknowledge the worth which God has bestowed upon him through creating him and in redeeming him through Christ.[13] He should "respect" himself as a child of God upon whom the Father has graciously bestowed His love and whom the Father wills to draw into fellowship with Himself. This does not mean, of course, that he is to look upon his own life as having value in itself as an independent center of existence; its dignity lies, rather, in the fact that man is the recipient of the divine love and is capable of freely becoming an instrument of that love in doing the Father's will. Moreover, the Christian who is aware that he is the recipient of this divine *agape* knows that the summons to love one's neighbor heedless of the interests of the self represents the paradoxical way in which the self finds fulfillment. "Whoever would save his life will lose it, and whoever loses his life for my sake will find it" (Matt. 16:25). This is so because, as we have seen, man's basic sin is love of the self in the place of God (i.e., self-centeredness). His true good lies in restoring God to the center of his life. God becomes this center when man in his freedom and in his response to the love of God ceases to center his concern upon himself and centers it instead upon God and His Kingdom. When this happens, he aspires first and foremost after the Kingdom of God and the divine righteousness, not for the sake of the satisfaction of himself but out of love for the good and God.

If, then, self-love is incompatible with neighbor-love, is it also incompatible with man's proper love for God? If so, does this imply that every form of self-concern is thereby forbidden to the Christian? These questions can best be answered by referring again to Nygren's monumental study of *Agape and Eros*. Nygren defines *eros* as being essentially self-love, but he interprets the latter in such a way as to include every form of concern for the self. He then goes on to maintain that there is absolutely no place for *eros* in *agape,* whether this be directed toward the neighbor or toward God.[14] Nygren is surely right in his contention that man's proper love for God excludes self-love in the sense of an egocentric desire to possess God because of some reward or value which He may bestow upon the self, but recognition of this fact does not justify the conclusion that there is absolutely no place for *eros* in the Christian's love for God. Nygren's fundamental error in this regard lies in his failure to differentiate

[13] Brunner, *op. cit.,* p. 171.
[14] Nygren, *op. cit.,* pp. 216–219.

clearly between *love of the self,* which is egocentric and obviously selfish, and *love of the good,* which is essentially unselfish; between *desire for the satisfaction of the self,* which is essentially selfish, and *desire for participation in the highest good* because of the values which the good embodies, which may be quite unselfish.[15] Love of the self and of the good, desire for the satisfaction of the self and for participation in the highest good, are included in *eros;* and Nygren believes that both are essentially selfish. Moreover, this is the only kind of love that natural man is able to have, no matter how much he may "love" his fellowmen and no matter how much he may "love" God; for the latter forms of love are inevitably dominated by concern for the self. For this reason Nygren hesitates to speak of love for God as something that is demanded of the Christian. It is true, he recognizes, that Jesus requires love toward God and that the love which he requires is *agape.* But Nygren maintains that the new meaning which Jesus gave to the First Commandment strained it "almost to (the) breaking-point."[16] Man can have *agape* toward God only if he, like Jesus, is so completely possessed by God that he belongs absolutely to Him and cannot any longer be said to have "anything he can call his own in relation to God."[17] But since other men are not so completely possessed by God, their response must be that of faith rather than love for God. Thus the requirement of love for God is replaced by the requirement of faith because the former is believed to be an impossibility since man's love can never be spontaneous and unmotivated in relation to God.[18] When *agape* for God is realized in human life, its "subject is no longer the man himself, but God, Christ, God's *agape,* God's Spirit."[19]

The full implication of this effort to replace *eros* with *agape* can be grasped, however, only when it is recognized that on occasion Nygren reaches a similar conclusion with regard to the possibility of Christian neighbor-love. *Agape* toward the neighbor is possible, he believes, only because the "acting subject is not man himself . . . (but) God, the Spirit of God, the Spirit of Christ, the *Agape* of Christ."[20] Or, again, Nygren declares that the love which the Christian

[15] Cf. George F. Thomas, *Christian Ethics and Moral Philosophy,* New York, Charles Scribner's Sons, 1955, p. 57.

[16] Nygren, *op. cit.,* p. 93.

[17] *Ibid.,* p. 94.

[18] *Ibid.,* p. 213.

[19] *Ibid.,* p. 133.

[20] *Ibid.,* p. 129.

"shows to his neighbor is the love which God has infused into him."[21]

The result of Nygren's effort to separate *agape* and *eros* so sharply and to exclude the latter absolutely from Christian love appears to be that man ceases to be the moral agent in relation to his fellowmen and also that love for God is replaced by faith in God and obedience to Him. In the former case man no longer retains his moral responsibility and freedom. In the latter case the content of the First Commandment is drastically changed. Both of these results are avoided, however, while at the same time the radical and theocentric character of Christian love is maintained when the Christian's love is understood primarily as man's response to God's *agape*.

Man is so created that he inevitably desires what he conceives to be his true good. This desire is given to him with life itself. The revelation of God's *agape* makes it clear that man's good is to be found in God. It is to be found in making God rather than the self the center of man's existence and in accepting the divine will as the law of human life. In this way man's true good is affirmed while his self-centeredness is shattered. God's *agape* does not replace human *eros* in relation to God; rather, the former redirects and transforms the latter. Sinful man's love for God is *eros* that is possessive and acquisitive and egocentric; redeemed man's love for God is also *eros,* but it is *eros* that is God-centered rather than self-centered and seeks first the Kingdom of God. Love for God clearly excludes self-love in the sense of the desire to draw all things into oneself, but it does not, therefore, exclude *eros*. On the contrary, according to its biblical usage, the notion of love for God presupposes and requires *eros* in that it includes the desire to have fellowship with God.

When *eros* is completely rejected, the concept of love toward God becomes a meaningless term. But the concept itself is not meaningless, as its biblical usage, the history of Christianity, and an ontological analysis of the qualities of love all make abundantly clear. However, it is precisely because Nygren conceives the concept to be essentially meaningless as an expression of man's relationship to God that he prefers to use the term "faith" in this connection. This, he declares, "denotes a receptive attitude";[22] it is the free "surrender of the heart to God"; or, in more activistic terms, it is "obedience to God, without any thought of reward."[23] But love is not the same thing as passive

---

[21] *Ibid.*
[22] *Ibid.*, p. 130.
[23] *Ibid.*, pp. 94–95; cf. *ibid.*, p. 148.

surrender and active obedience taken together. It may indeed be quite the opposite of both surrender and obedience.[24] Love for God expresses itself in joyful acceptance of the divine sovereignty, not in passive surrender; it does not obey God reluctantly but delights in obedience to Him. Above all, it seeks to be reunited in fellowship with God.[25]

When love for the neighbor is similarly understood first of all in terms of man's response to God, it is made clear that the subject of this love is man himself, although its ultimate source is God. God's *agape* is recognized to be the norm for human conduct because it is seen to be the way in which God loves all men. Such love becomes a possibility for the Christian because he knows himself to be sustained by the divine *agape* which frees him from his self-centeredness and anxiety about himself. In this way, and for the first time, he is made free to love his fellowmen as God loves them—i.e., without thought of reward or benefit to the self. One who knows himself to be the recipient of this love recognizes that this gift also places a demand upon him to become an agent of this love. But man is not simply a passive instrument of God's *agape*. The love which he shows to the neighbor is not God's *agape* which has been "infused' or poured into man and which is then poured out again upon the neighbor; rather, it is *agape* which is called forth responsively in man by the divine *agape* which has been revealed to man and which, he now knows, already sustains him. It is finite, sinful man who is called to accept the divine love, to repent, and to manifest *agape* toward his fellowmen; but the possibility of his doing so is given even before the demand is made, and the motive of gratitude is evoked through the bestowal of the gift.

Professor Tillich's examination of the ontology of love not only confirms the validity of the foregoing analysis of the relationship of *agape* to *eros* in man's proper love to God, but it also sheds a great deal of light upon the place of *agape* in man's proper relationship to his fellowmen and to himself. Love, he declares, is essentially one

[24] Cf. Paul Tillich, *Love, Power, and Justice*, New York, Oxford University Press, 1954, p. 31.

[25] Cf. H. Richard Niebuhr, *op. cit.*, pp. 18–19. Speaking of Jesus' love for God and love for his neighbor, Niebuhr writes: "The love of God is non-possessive *Eros;* the love of man pure *Agape;* the love of God is passion; the love of man compassion." And Niebuhr goes on to say that Jesus "loves God as man should love Him, and loves man as only God can." See, further, Thomas, *op. cit.*, pp. 55–58; and Daniel D. Williams, *God's Grace and Man's Hope*, New York, Harper & Brothers, 1949, pp. 67 ff.

although it has many qualities. Understood in ontological terms, it is "the drive towards the unity of the separated."[26] The latter is true both of *agape* and of *eros;* it is also true of love when it takes the form of *libido* as well as that of *philia*. Tillich defines libido as the "normal drive towards vital self-fulfilment" rather than as the pursuit of the pain-pleasure principle,[27] and he cites the testimony of depth psychology to the effect that every being desires to fulfill itself through union with other beings. Thus, there is, he declares, an element of libido even in the most spiritual friendship and the communion of the saint. Such libido cannot properly be equated with self-love; for it may be other-centered as well as self-centered. There are also qualities of *eros* and *philia* in all human love. *Agape* does not destroy or cast out the other qualities of love; rather, it enters into the whole of life and "transforms life and love" in much the same way that revelation cuts into the life of reason and transforms it. *Agape* elevates the other forms of love above the self-centeredness to which they are bound by sin. It frees libido, which belongs to man's created goodness, from the tyranny of the pleasure principle; it frees *eros* from its sexual distortion and possessiveness; it purifies *philia* and elevates it into universal love. *Agape* sees the other person as God sees him and affirms each self as a person in the same way that God accepts each and affirms each as a person. *Agape* seeks to unite those who are separated into a holy community of persons who know themselves to be loved by God and who are therefore free to love their fellowmen without anxiety for themselves.

Sometimes an effort is made to provide a place for a carefully restricted self-love in Christian ethics by interpreting the latter in terms of mutual love. An outstanding example of this is found in Daniel D. Williams' Rauschenbusch Lectures, *God's Grace and Man's Hope*. Professor Williams describes the love that is revealed in Christ as "a love which seeks the fulfillment of all things in such a relationship to one another that what flows from the life of each enriches the life of all, and each participant in the whole life finds his own good realized through the giving of self to the life of the whole."[28] Christian love "intends the mutuality of the Kingdom," he declares, and for that very reason it must become sacrificial under the present conditions of history because of the opposition of evil to the Kingdom. But, as

[26] Tillich, *op. cit.*, p. 25.
[27] *Ibid.*, p. 30.
[28] Williams, *op. cit.*, p. 78.

Professor Paul Ramsey points out, according to this view, "mutuality is the very substance of love, while sacrifice is—in the philosophic sense of the word—only an 'accidental' part either of the intention or of the behavior of love."[29] Williams is right in seeing that Christian love represents the path to self-fulfillment, but he fails to do justice to the paradox of the Gospel insight that the pursuit of the self's good for the sake of the self is self-defeating and that it is only in the surrender of the self to the Kingdom of God without thought of reward that one really finds oneself and that one is genuinely freed for unrestricted love of God and the neighbor. To seek the Kingdom for the sake of mutual fulfillment may actually be only enlightened self-love. Such love is possible apart from the awareness of God's *agape*. But Christian love understood as *agape* becomes possible for man only when he is certain that he is loved already in such a way that his anxiety about himself is overcome (justification by grace through faith).

Reinhold Niebuhr, on the other hand, has interpreted Christian love as sacrificial love.[30] Mutual love, he declares, cannot really be mutual so long as it is concerned about being loved in return. *Agape,* or sacrificial love, is needed to complete mutual love and to keep it from degenerating into prudential calculations of probable reciprocity. In those areas of history where new achievements of mutual love, or brotherhood, have been possible, the consequence of mutuality has been "the unintended rather than purposed consequence of the action."[31] Reinhold Niebuhr believes, however, that Nygren has made the contrast between *agape* and *eros* too absolute, and he rightly points out that, according to the ethic of Jesus, the motive for Christian love in relation to the neighbor is always the emulation of God ("that ye may be sons of your Father who is in heaven") or gratitude to God for His *agape*.[32] Yet, in his effort to combat all forms of sentimentalism which look upon Christian love as a simple possibility in history, Niebuhr emphasizes in almost as absolute a manner as Ny-

[29] Paul Ramsey, "Love and Law" in Charles W. Kegley and Robert W. Bretall, eds., *Reinhold Niebuhr: His Religious, Social, and Political Thought,* New York, The Macmillan Company, 1956, p. 106.

[30] Reinhold Niebuhr, *The Nature and Destiny of Man,* II: *Human Destiny,* New York, Charles Scribner's Sons, 1943, ch. III. See, especially, pp. 82 ff. See also Reinhold Niebuhr, *Faith and History,* New York, Charles Scribner's Sons, 1949, pp. 184–185.

[31] *The Nature and Destiny of Man,* II, p. 84.

[32] *Ibid.,* pp. 84, 88.

gren the uniqueness of *agape* and the impossibility of man's making it an effective reconciling force among men.[33] *Agape* in its pure form stands at the edge of history, Niebuhr declares. If it becomes fully incarnate in a human life, it ends inevitably upon a cross. It is history's "impossible possibility"[34] and "it is not even right to insist that every action of the Christian must conform to *agape*, rather than to the norms of relative justice and mutual love by which life is maintained and conflicting interests are arbitrated in history."[35] Such a conception of Christian love seems, however, to separate it too sharply from the present will of God in relation to the existing sinful order and to one's neighbors in this order. The Christian is commanded to love his neighbor without exception and in all places, and it is confusing to be told that most of the time this means exhibiting sacrificial love but sometimes it means exhibiting mutual love toward the neighbor.

When love for the neighbor is understood in terms of affirming God's threefold (creating, ordering, redeeming) will for the neighbor, the real meaning of neighbor-love becomes clearer. It means the affirmation of the neighbor's true good. Moreover, in motive and in intent it seems to be a possible possibility for the man of faith who is sustained by the *agape* of God. *Agape* is concerned far more with the intention or motive of the agent than with the "accidental" character of the overt act. It is "mainly intent on the good of another."[36] A more adequate recognition of this fact would do greater justice to the total will of the Creator and the Judge who calls man to act in love toward the neighbor in the concrete realities of history and to the intent of the Redeemer who is at work in history redeeming men from their isolation, from fear, and from bondage to evil in many forms.

Niebuhr's frequent usage of such terms as "suffering" and "sacrificial" in speaking of Christian love causes him to run the risk of stressing this aspect of *agape* at the expense of losing sight of the primary intent of love. As a corrective against the tendency to equate *agape*

---

[33] Speaking of Nygren's concept of *agape*, Niebuhr says, for example, that it "is really a complete impossibility and irrelevance for man" (*Faith and History*, p. 178). But while Niebuhr does speak of the partial realizations of faith and *agape* in history he also refers to them as "impossible possibilities" (*Ibid.*, p. 176).

[34] *The Nature and Destiny of Man*, II, p. 76.

[35] *Ibid.*, p. 88.

[36] Ramsey, "Love and Law," *op. cit.*, p. 109.

with mutual love and as a reminder both of the radical character of the former and of the consequences which it frequently incurs in history, Niebuhr's emphasis is needed; for certainly the Gospel does not promise "success" in terms of economic rewards and prestige and peace to those who practice *agape*. But it also needs to be remembered that Christianity makes no virtue out of asceticism and self-denial *per se* or out of the choosing of the most difficult or painful path simply because it is difficult or painful. Love is not intent upon the sacrifice of the self any more than it is intent upon mutuality or the good of the self. Rather, it is intent solely upon affirming the neighbor as God affirms the neighbor in *agape*.[37]

THE ROLE OF LAW AND MORAL PRINCIPLES IN CHRISTIAN ETHICS

In the foregoing interpretation of the Christian ethic the inadequacy of legalism has been emphasized. It may even seem to some that moral laws and principles—both those found in the Bible and those of philosophical ethics such as Aristotle's concept of the "golden mean" or the Stoics' concept of natural law—have been rejected entirely. Such a conclusion, however, would represent a gross misunderstanding of our aim. Indeed, in our view, the rejection of all such rules and principles (antinomianism) represents equally as serious a misunderstanding of the Christian ethic as does legalism. What we have sought to make clear is the fact that the Christian ethic subordinates all other norms to the final norm of *agape*.

But in view of the widespread reaction against law and moral principles in many contemporary discussions of Christian social ethics, it is necessary to inquire what function these serve and to see whether they are in any sense necessary for the implementation of Christian love in a finite and sinful world. The relevance of, and the demand for, such a reëxamination of the role of moral laws and principles is indicated by the growing number of interpretations of Christian ethics as essentially a contextual ethic and the frequent failure to assign moral rules and imperatives any significant place. A justifiable anti-legalism frequently results in an unjustifiable antinomianism. Emphasis is frequently centered so exclusively upon the uniqueness of each ethical situation that an effort is made to approach it *de novo* with

[37] Cf. *ibid.*, pp. 103 ff. I am indebted to Professor Ramsey for his comparison and critique of the positions held by Daniel D. Williams and Reinhold Niebuhr.

insufficient attention being given to the universal character of the relationships involved.[38]

This tendency to reject all moral laws and principles is, of course,
not a new one. Some of Paul's followers interpreted his attack upon
legalism as a rejection of the moral tradition of Judaism. If men are
justified by faith instead of by works, they argued, then works are not
essential and men are free to do as they desire. But this clearly was
not Paul's intent any more than it had been Jesus' intent in his criticism of the legalism of the Pharisees. For just as Jesus had declared
that he had not come to "abolish" but "to fulfill" the law and the
prophets and that "till heaven and earth pass away, not an iota, not
a dot, will pass from the law until all is accomplished" (Matt. 5:17–
18), so Paul declared that the moral law of Judaism was summed up
in the one requirement of neighbor love and that "love is the fulfilling
of the law" (Rom. 13:8–10). Paul's point was that Christians possess
the Spirit and therefore do willingly from love that which men had
previously felt constrained to do out of fear.

Similarly, many of Luther's followers have been so strongly influenced by his emphasis upon "the liberty of the Christian man" that
they have either minimized or ignored the importance which he attached to the moral laws of Scripture. Luther believed, for example,
that the Law of the Old Testament, especially the Ten Commandments,
was good and necessary in that it taught men what they ought to do
and thus helped them recognize their own inability to do good.[39]
Only when men are thus brought to despair of their own ability to do
the good through the preaching of the Law are they in a position to
hear and receive the word of grace proclaimed in the Gospel. Once
men respond to this word with faith in the righteousness and goodness
of God they receive the ability to keep the commandments, and they
keep them henceforth out of gratitude and love.[40] But Luther's emphasis upon justification by "faith alone, without works," encouraged
many of his followers to falsify the freedom of the Christian man both

---

[38] Since formulations of moral laws and principles which are based upon
biblical faith are of most obvious and general interest to Christians, we shall
be primarily concerned in the present discussion with an examination of the
role of these in relating Christian faith to practice. For a discussion of the
relation of moral philosophy generally to Christian ethics, see Chapter 1,
pp. 10–15.

[39] *Works of Martin Luther,* vol. II, Philadelphia, A. J. Holman Company,
1915, p. 317.

[40] *Ibid.,* p. 319.

by neglecting the place of law in the continual instructing of the believer, who is at the same time "justified and sinful," and by neglecting the demand for works as an expression of faith that is vital.

There is a similar reaction against law and moral principles in many contemporary discussions of the nature of Christian ethics. Professor Paul L. Lehmann, for example, defines Christian ethics as "koinonia ethics."[41] By this he means that it is "from and in the *koinonia*," or Christian fellowship of the Church, that the will of God is recognized as the norm of Christian behavior and also that one gets a clue as to what the will of God is. The Christian ethic is "always concrete and contextual," beginning with the concrete facts involved in a specific "ethical situation" rather than with "absolute" moral laws or principles. Similarly, Christian ethics is "indicative" rather than "imperative"; it gives "primary attention to what is" rather than to what ought to be.

In seeking to answer the question of what the will of God is in a specific situation, Christian ethics "has tended to fall between two stools," Lehmann declares. Viewing love either on the one hand as a statement, a precept, or a law, or on the other hand as an attitude of benevolence, sympathy, or mutuality, it has wound up making practical decisions either on a purely pragmatic basis or on the basis of "some value system in which Christian love has a difficult time eking out a discrete existence."[42] *Koinonia* ethics, however, is able to avoid both of these pitfalls "by spelling out the meaning of love in terms of what God is doing and has done in the world." Within the *koinonia* love is seen to be "God's concrete action in Christ establishing a bridgehead of forgiveness in the world," and the aim of the Christian is to extend this bridgehead until all that is opposed to the divine will is "brought into the orbit of God's reconciling action in Jesus Christ."[43] Thus, a *koinonia* ethic speaks of the will of God as "forgiveness and justice and reconciliation, rather than as love," for these represent "the concrete reality of love in the *koinonia* in the world."

As a protest against legalism and as a reminder that Christian love gets its meaning from the *agape* of God revealed most fully in Christ, Lehmann's emphasis upon the contextual character of Christian ethics

[41] Paul L. Lehmann, "The Foundation and Pattern of Christian Behavior" in *Christian Faith and Social Action,* John A. Hutchison, ed., New York, Charles Scribner's Sons, 1953, p. 102.

[42] *Ibid.,* p. 111.

[43] *Ibid.,* p. 112.

is a valid one. But Professor Lehmann fails to do justice to the normative character of the love commandments. It is true that the Christian's understanding of *agape* is based primarily upon the action of God in Christ and in the *koinonia,* but it is also true that the divine indicative of God's action constitutes a "divine imperative" for man, showing him how he ought to respond to God's activity. Recognition of this fact is implied in the acknowledgment that Christ is Lord. Through His *agape* for man God claims man for His love—i.e., for participation in the Kingdom of God in which love is universal and unlimited. In the words of Brunner, "The revelation which makes it plain that the will of God is lavish in giving *to* man makes it equally clear that His will makes a demand *on* man. His will *for* us also means that He wants something *from* us. He claims us for His love. This is His Command . . . it is the command of One who gives before He demands, and who only demands something from us in the act of giving Himself to us."[44]

Lehmann also limits God's activity far too exclusively to His redemptive work of forgiveness and reconciliation. He fails to do justice to the revelation of God's love in Creation and in Judgment—in the orders of creation and in the judgments of God in history. To be sure, he speaks of "justice" as the crucial problem of Christian behavior, but he defines justice almost exclusively in negative terms. Justice involves the breaking down of the existent patterns of social organization and the building up of new patterns. "God's justice (righteousness) is being concretely applied in the world in which God's will is being done, whenever and wherever the exalted are brought low, and those of low degree are exalted."[45] But surely there is some justice in the world, and simply to break down and overthrow existing structures of power and existing cultural and social patterns would bring injustice as well as invite chaos. Doubtless some structures are so evil that they should be overthrown radically, but in other cases the cause of justice would be best served by the transformation or conversion of the existing structures so that the good in them would be preserved while the evil is being purged away.

Finally, Lehmann limits the revelation of God's will too sharply to the Christian fellowship, and for this reason his ethic, like Paul's, is largely an ethic for the fellowship. Hence it fails to provide adequately for the coöperation of Christians with non-Christians in meeting the

[44] Brunner, *op. cit.,* p. 116.
[45] Lehmann, *op. cit.,* p. 113.

problems and issues which confront all men in common. Far more attention needs to be given to an analysis of the nature of man as a moral being and to the significance of natural revelation. The final norm for the Christian is the *agape* of God in Christ. But the *agape* of God in Christ is fully disclosed only in the context of the more general revelation of God's will in Scripture, in sacred and in "secular" history, and in other faiths. Ultimately, of course, each individual must make the final decision as to what God's will for him in a specific ethical situation is, no matter how much guidance he may get from the *koinonia;* and it is worth noting in passing that, although one may not begin with precepts and laws, one can really be aided by the *koinonia* in his effort to discover God's will for himself only insofar as the experience and witness of the *koinonia* are generalized in terms of precepts or principles which can be applied to new situations. Such formulations of the demands of love are indeed "abstract," and they fail to do justice to the diversity and complexity of particular concrete situations; but they are useful in much the same way that any other kind of generalization is useful.

Another representative of the contextual, or situational, approach to Christian ethics is Professor Albert T. Rasmussen. In his *Christian Social Ethics,* he relies heavily upon the analysis of Professor Lehmann.[46] Following the latter, Rasmussen characterizes the Christian ethic as "contextual and concrete," and he likewise contends that it is "indicative rather than imperative." But Rasmussen also draws upon the insights of a number of other contemporary interpreters of Christian ethics whose views cannot be so precisely equated with Lehmann's and his own. Specifically, he identifies his own interpretation with the positions of Paul Lehmann, Alexander Miller, Daniel D. Williams, James Gustafson, and H. Richard Niebuhr.[47] In actuality, however, Rasmussen modifies and supplements Lehmann's position by drawing upon Miller's concepts of "covenant ethics," "a community of loyalty," and "the mores of the Kingdom of God."[48] He em-

---

[46] Albert T. Rasmussen, *Christian Social Ethics,* Englewood Cliffs, New Jersey, Prentice-Hall, 1956.

[47] Alexander Miller has developed his view in *The Renewal of Man,* Garden City, New York, Doubleday & Company, 1956. Daniel D. Williams has developed his in *God's Grace and Man's Hope.* H. Richard Niebuhr has indicated important aspects of his position in *Christ and Culture* and in his essay on "The Center of Value" in *Moral Principles of Action,* Ruth Nanda Anshen, ed., New York, Harper and Brothers, 1952. He has not as yet, however, stated his position in print in a comprehensive and systematic form.

[48] Miller, *op. cit.,* pp. 88–90.

phasizes more strongly than Lehmann the fact that love is "rigorous and demanding in its ethical requirements"[49] and also the fact that the Christian ethic is absolute in character. In both of these emphases as well as in his concern with the existential character of this ethic as a *commitment* in faith Rasmussen shows the influence of H. Richard Niebuhr. The resulting interpretation thus differs in several important respects from Paul Lehmann's, as it does also from the positions of Daniel D. Williams, James Gustafson, and H. Richard Niebuhr.

In dividing contemporary discussions of Christian social ethics into two groups, Rasmussen distorts the current reaction against law.[50] The implication is that every Christian ethicist is either a contextualist or a legalist. Moreover, by his failure to deal seriously with the group which begins the ethical inquiry upon the basis of laws or principles rather than upon the basis of an analysis of the concrete ethical situation he leaves the impression that there is little strength or value in the former position, which, incidentally, he associates only with John Bennett.

Professor James Gustafson has outlined his position in the form of an essay entitled "Christian Ethics and Social Policy," appearing in *Faith and Ethics*.[51] Gustafson seeks to interpret Christian social ethics in the light of the basic motifs of Niebuhr's thought. There are, he believes, four such motifs which are fundamental: the relativism of life in faith, existentialist personalism, response, and the sense of flux and process in experience. The first of these, Gustafson suggests, is perhaps the central one, and the other three are derivative from it. The relativism of faith means that God alone is absolute and all other things are relative to Him and derive their value from their relationship to Him. It is this "relativism," or "relationalism," which provides the basis of the Christian's freedom in responding to the one God who is active in all events.[52]

Employing these motifs in his analysis of ethics from a theological perspective, Gustafson develops the view that Christian social ethics

---

[49] Rasmussen, *op. cit.*, p. 167.

[50] *Ibid.*, p. 192.

[51] Paul Ramsey, ed., *Faith and Ethics: The Theology of H. Richard Niebuhr*, New York, Harper & Brothers, 1957, ch. 4.

[52] As Paul Ramsey points out, Niebuhr uses the term "objective relativism" to make clear that values are objectively related to structures and organic needs instead of being abstract essences which have an autonomous existence. This expression seems, however, to entail an unintentional prejudice against their objectivity. Hence, Ramsey suggests the term "relational objectivism" as a more adequate designation of Niebuhr's position (*ibid.*, pp. 142, 152).

is analytical instead of prescriptive, relational rather than abstract, and contextual rather than deductive. While he holds that "the 'indicative' takes priority over the 'imperative,' " he does not make the dichotomy between these two as sharp as does Rasmussen. And, significantly, he speaks of values as being "relational" rather than "objectively relative." Like Rasmussen, Gustafson recognizes the "significant effect of values and principles" in the analysis of the concrete situation.[53] Both see that the moral agent inevitably comes to each particular situation with some abstract understanding of values and principles. It is quite true, as Gustafson points out, that the opposing parties in a labor dispute, for example, do not first of all agree on a definition of justice, or the good society, and then deliberate about the implications of these definitions in the current dispute. But it is also true, as Gustafson acknowledges, that conceptions of justice and the good society are involved in such discussions. Clearly, these concepts must be related dynamically to each particular situation, but they are nonetheless indispensable as guides in any effort to resolve the conflicts of interest involved in such disputes. Indeed, some recognition of their validity is presupposed in all efforts to resolve such conflicts on any basis other than self-interest or power. This fact is recognized by both Rasmussen and Gustafson, but its significance is obscured by their emphasis upon the uniqueness of each situation and their failure to consider the ontological meaning of justice.

Finally, one misses in Professor Gustafson's analysis of Christian social ethics any reference to the importance of the specific ethical teachings of Jesus such as those recorded in the Sermon on the Mount. These particular sayings provide part of the data for any theological understanding of Christian ethics; and, while they are not to be applied as new laws, they cannot be ignored any more than they can be dismissed simply as hyperboles or as an "interim ethic." They provide an important part of the context in which Christians seek to discover the divine will today just as they have always formed an inescapable part of this context throughout Christian history.[54]

One of the primary values of this widespread reaction against law

---

[53] *Ibid.,* p. 127; cf. Rasmussen, *op. cit.,* p. 170.

[54] Professor Georgia Harkness makes a similar criticism of Emil Brunner in her *Christian Ethics* (New York, Abingdon Press, 1957, p. 29). Miss Harkness defines Christian ethics primarily in terms of the effort to apply the ethical insights of Jesus to the problems and decisions of men in the present day. While this method is inadequate for the reasons which we have already indicated, it provides an important corrective to Brunner's silence in this regard.

is that it warns Christians against the dangers of ethical legalism. Among these dangers are the negative and restrictive character of legalistic morality, the fact that it stifles individuality and creativity, its tendency to fall into externalism, and its inability to secure obedience.[55] Moreover, the contextual ethicists to whom we have referred[56] have performed an important service in emphasizing the close relationship between faith and ethics, in calling attention to the complexity of the moral situation and the moral aspects of economic, political, and social relationships, and in emphasizing the dynamic character of human relationships and human needs. None of these insights, however, necessitates the denial of an important place for laws and moral principles in the ethical life.

Notwithstanding the values implicit in the contemporary reaction against moral laws and principles, its dangers must not be obscured. Among these are its tendency to lead to an excessive individualism; its tendency to ignore the need which all men, including Christians, have—because of their finiteness and their sinfulness—for the guidance which is provided by moral laws and rational ethical principles; and its tendency to restrict the contribution of Christian faith in the area of social ethics to the provision of a disposition of responsible concern for the neighbor. A right "disposition" is essential, but it is not enough to assure ethical responsibility. Some conception of the essential nature of man as well as some guidance in the form of general patterns for dealing with particular kinds of historical and cultural situations is also needed. That the fundamental elements in an

[55] Cf. Thomas, *op. cit.,* pp. 128–129.

[56] Another extremely suggestive presentation of the general contextualist interpretation of Christian ethics is found in Dietrich Bonhoeffer's *Ethics* (Eberhard Bethge, ed., London, Student Christian Movement Press, Ltd., 1955). Because of his martyrdom at the hand of the Nazis, the *Ethics,* which was published posthumously, is incomplete and fragmentary. Although Bonhoeffer's discussion of particular ethical problems does not succeed in being as concrete and contextualistic as he implies at the outset, his emphasis upon concreteness, the particular situation, the recovery of the importance of the "natural" in Protestant ethics, and the totality of the Christian's responsibility before God represent important contributions to the understanding of Christian ethics in our day. Bonhoeffer's concern with the Christian's responsibility in culture is particularly striking and instructive because of the circumstances under which he developed this theme and the fate which he suffered.

In the present discussion, however, Bonhoeffer has not been singled out for special treatment as a representative of the contextualist interpretation of Christian ethics because the group of Americans whom we have considered have raised most of the problems presented by his *Ethics,* and they have developed their positions largely independently of the latter.

CONCORDIA COLLEGE LIBRARY
2811 N. E. HOLMAN ST.
PORTLAND, OREGON 97211

adequate understanding of the essential nature and true end of man are given in Christian faith is implicit in the historical and revelatory character of the Christian religion. The content and implications for the present of the revelation which has taken place in the past needs to be made clear. Similarly the revelation which continues to take place in our day needs to be identified, interpreted, and made available to those individuals who are being urged to act responsibly in the situations in which they are involved.

In their reaction against legalism, contextual ethicists generally make the dichotomy between love and law too sharp. The Christian who is wholeheartedly intent upon doing the divine will needs guidance in discovering what *agape* demands in a particular situation where he is faced with a whole series of obligations and with the necessity of deciding which values ought to be sacrificed in the effort to realize other values. While each person is different from all other persons and while the uniqueness of each is cherished in Christianity as being grounded in the creative will of God, it is also true that the "nature of man is universal and permanent in its primary characteristics."[57] By creation, every normal person has certain needs and capacities; and these in turn constitute the basis of his claims upon his fellows. Moreover, man is social by nature, and he has many relationships to other individuals and to groups with whom he exists in community. These relationships in turn are the basis of his obligations or duties to his fellowmen. It is because of the similarities in the needs of all men and in the relationships which exist among men that moral laws and ethical principles have arisen to crystallize the wisdom gleaned from the experience of the race as to how these needs can best be fulfilled and what the duties implied in these relationships are. The knowledge of such rules plays an essential role in the moral training of children and in the deepening of the ethical understanding and discipline of adults. This is true both in the case of Christian moral training and discipline and also in the case of the ethical training and discipline that seeks to give practical expression to every other religion and every secular faith.

Since our primary concern in the present discussion is with the reaction against law in Christian ethics, let us examine more closely the function of the moral laws of the Bible in relation to Christian faith and practice. According to Brunner, the biblical commandments

[57] Thomas, *op. cit.*, p. 130.

such as those contained in the Decalogue and the Sermon on the Mount serve a threefold function. In the first place, they serve a disciplinary function, regulating human life in accordance with certain minimal standards. This is especially true of the Decalogue as compared with the Sermon on the Mount, for example, for the former provides an order of community life in a way in which the latter does not. In the second place (and this applies even more strikingly to the Sermon on the Mount than it does to the commandments of the Old Testament) the law has a judgmental value, leading men to repentance and humility by revealing to them the depth of their sin. And, in the third place, it provides guidance in the effort to discover the will of God.

To take an example which Brunner uses, the Seventh Commandment—"You shall not commit adultery"—performs a disciplinary function by prescribing an order of life for the community.[58] Such discipline is necessary for the believer as well as for the nonbeliever, for "even the believer is always also an unbeliever." Moreover, this commandment also leads men to repentance when its meaning is taken radically as Jesus took it when he applied it to a lustful glance. Thus the believer is forced to recognize that even in the honorable civil state of marriage, with the blessings of the Church, he stands before God as an adulterer and that he, too, like the less respectable people of ill repute must rely ultimately upon the forgiveness of God. Finally, the Seventh Commandment, interpreted in this radical way, becomes an instruction to the believer as to how he ought to live if he would be truly a child of his Heavenly Father. When recognition of the value of moral laws is coupled with recognition of their limitations, it becomes clear that any interpretation of Christian ethics is inadequate unless it provides a place for laws and principles as well as a standard by which these can be judged and a more adequate motivation for fulfilling them. Viewed in this light, the relation of moral laws to the command to love the neighbor is best understood as a *dialectical* one.

Neither the law of the Bible—whether of the Old Testament or of the New—nor that of those systems of ethics which are based upon the biblical law is in its literal form the will of God. Such laws do not constitute the "divine imperative," or the "divine command," but they point men to the present will of God. "Without the Law, in this radical

[58] Brunner, *op. cit.*, p. 150.

and at the same time dialectical sense it is impossible to hear the real command of God."[59] But, no matter how necessary the law may be as an instrument to aid men in hearing the divine command, the divine command itself is heard only in faith—when the law is transcended and the will of God is freshly discerned in a particular situation. From this vantage point alone—that is, from the vantage point of faith when the intent of the law has been recognized and "fulfilled," when the law has itself become internalized and when its fragmentary character has been overcome by being related to whole persons in whole situations—does the inadequacy of the law as a legalism become fully apparent. The divine command is addressed to a whole person who stands in a whole cluster of relationships and in a situation that is unique. Not just one law but many laws give direction, but only love understood as the will of God to create, govern, and redeem man can integrate these fragmentary laws and be truly responsible before God for the neighbor. The Christian uses many laws and principles in his effort to discover God's will in a concrete situation, but he can never be content to treat any neighbor simply as another "case," and he can never assume that he can tell in advance precisely what love will require when the next *similar* situation arises. Love remains sovereign over all other moral rules and laws, but love uses these freely as directives or guides.

Implicit in the place which we have given to laws and principles in Christian ethics is the recognition of the obligation of Christians to formulate what they have learned in their wrestling with new problems or with old problems in new settings in terms of guiding principles or general rules which they can apply themselves and which they can recommend to others who are in earnest about relating their faith to daily life. There is a great need that the gap between theory and practice should be bridged, and one of the essential steps in this process seems to be the disciplined, patient, and realistic wrestling with the practical implications of faith and love for specific areas of human relationships and for ways of meeting the specific needs of our neighbors under specific types of circumstances. For example, what guidance can Christians offer the lawmaker or the doctor or the teacher or the engineer or the lawyer or the businessman or the nurse or the housewife that will help each better to understand what love demands in the pursuit of one's daily activities in each of

---

[59] *Ibid.*, p. 147.

these occupations in mid-twentieth-century America? Or what guidance can dedicated Christians, sharing their moral insights and
technical skills, offer to each other with regard to what love demands
in the facing of problems of segregation and integration, or economic
exploitation, or the need to bring about political reform?

One of the major contributions of Professor John C. Bennett to contemporary Christian social ethics has been his insistence upon the need
for such an application of Christian ethics to social policy through
the formulation of a series of moral judgments which become increasingly tentative but which offer increasingly immediate guidance
for action.[60] Thus, there is need in the first place for the formulation
of "guiding principles" about which there is no disagreement (e.g.,
the equal dignity of all men before God). Beyond these there is need
for "middle axioms" (e.g., the removal of all segregation within the
churches). Finally, Christians need to seek mutual guidance concerning the next specific steps which should be taken in a particular
situation (e.g., steps leading to the abolition of segregation in a
particular denomination or the overcoming of racial exclusiveness in
local congregations). The demand for such specific guidance in the
effort to apply Christian love to concrete situations is daily becoming
more and more urgent as the need for specialized technical knowledge
in many fields becomes increasingly intensified and as the fact that our
social problems have an ethical and theological dimension becomes
more generally recognized.

As the result of the foregoing analysis of the place of law and
principles in Christian ethics, we are led to conclude, in the first
place, that *love (agape) is itself both a law and a gift.* It partakes
of the character of law in that it places an unconditional demand
upon man, but it also partakes of the character of a gift in that man
knows that he is loved before it is required of him that he shall love
and also in that he must know himself to be loved with *agape* before
he is able to love his neighbor with *agape* rather than with *eros*.
Love may thus be spoken of as a law or a command although it is
above all other moral laws. It is unconditional or absolute in the
sense that there are no exceptions to it, and hence it is unlike all
other "absolute" laws and principles. It is related to the needs of the
neighbor in every specific situation, but it is not therefore relativistic.
As Paul Tillich writes:

[60] John C. Bennett, *Christian Ethics and Social Policy*, New York, Charles
Scribner's Sons, 1946, ch. IV.

You *can* express it as a law, you can say as Jesus and the apostles did: "Thou shalt love"; but in doing so you know that it is a paradoxical way of speaking, indicating that the ultimate principle of ethics, which, on the one hand, is an unconditional command, is, on the other hand, the power breaking through all commands. . . . Love alone can transform itself according to the concrete demands of every individual and social situation without losing its eternity and dignity and unconditional validity. Love can adapt itself to every phase of a changing world.[61]

And, in the second place, we are led to conclude that while sets of moral laws such as those found in the Ten Commandments or the Sermon on the Mount or the disciplines of churches or statements of policy adopted by groups of devoted Christians cannot tell one ahead of time and without question what he ought to do, they do point one in the "general direction" which he ought to go, and in this sense they *offer indispensable guidance for conduct.* They are of the highest significance in the effort to discover what the will of God is, but they are nevertheless subordinate to love.

Finally, *moral laws and traditions undergo a profound change when they are used in faith in the service of love.*[62] The believer no longer follows them out of fear. Instead of being burdensome requirements upon man, they become cherished guides to joyful obedience to God whose will the man of faith wants to do out of love. As H. Richard Niebuhr, true to the insight of Paul, declares, the recognition on man's part of the omnipotence and goodness of God "changes the bondage to men and their traditions into a bondage to God."[63] With this change there comes "a great *conversion* of the power, spirit and content of the law."[64] Men know it to be God's requirement which is based upon His goodness and mercy and sovereignty. Man's relationship to God rather than to the law becomes the primary relationship. The law itself takes on the character of "counsel," and bondage to the law is transformed into the freedom of sonship. The isolated demands of manifold laws and principles are brought to-

---

[61] Paul Tillich, *The Protestant Era,* Chicago, The University of Chicago Press, 1948, p. 155.

[62] Cf. Brunner, *op. cit.,* pp. 149–150. Compare, also, Paul Ramsey's essay on "The Transformation of Ethics" in *Faith and Ethics;* but contrast the chapter in his earlier *Basic Christian Ethics,* "Christian Liberty: An Ethic Without Rules."

[63] H. Richard Niebuhr, "Evangelical and Protestant Ethics," in Elmer J. F. Arndt, ed., *The Heritage of the Reformation,* New York, Richard R. Smith, 1950, p. 226.

[64] *Ibid.* Italics added.

gether and harmonized by love which relates them dynamically to each new ethical situation and "fulfills" their intent by creatively ministering to the neighbor's need as this is freshly discerned in its individual as well as in its universal aspects.

THE PROBLEM OF COMPROMISE

In view of the secondary place which moral laws and principles have in the interpretation of Christian ethics as man's response to the divine action upon him, it becomes clear why we have thus far intentionally avoided the use of the concept of *compromise*. This concept implies a frame of reference that is primarily legalistic. It suggests that the norm or standard to which one owes his primary allegiance is inapplicable without some concession. The will of God as it is related to the particular moment of decision does not admit of compromise but only of acceptance or betrayal.[65] It does not—like some rule of reason or some static principle—demand absolute obedience to a precisely defined rule or principle which may be in conflict with other precise rules or principles. Rather, it unconditionally demands one thing, and one thing only, namely, that man love his neighbor as God loves him. As Brunner reminds us, God does not command "something in general."[66] His commands are always personal and concrete. They are addressed to individual persons, and they tell "me, or us, or you, as definite persons to do some definite thing."[67]

This does not mean, of course, that the Christian is free from the "conflict of duties" which torments the consciences of other morally sensitive men. It does mean, however, that the divine will is not really known and accepted as long as a person is torn between "conflicting duties." There is a profound difference between knowing what Christian love requires and accepting that requirement as the thing which one will do. One who knows what love of the neighbor demands in a particular situation is no longer faced with the problem of deciding what he *ought* to do; he very likely may still be faced with the problem of deciding what he *will* do. To faith, the divine will in relation

[65] Cf. H. Richard Niebuhr, *Christ and Culture*, p. 241: ". . . an absolute standard cannot be compromised—it can only be broken. . . . We cannot excuse ourselves by saying that we have made the best compromises possible. We shall try to recognize our faithlessness, and in faith rely on the grace that will change our minds. . . ."

[66] Brunner, *op. cit.*, p. 198.

[67] *Ibid.*

to the particular neighbor becomes one's duty; and it cannot meaningfully be said that one has a "conflicting duty" to disobey God. To obey God may be painful; it may involve sacrifice and bearing one's cross. But one who follows the claims of one's race or one's nation or one's family at the expense of disobeying the divine summons to love the neighbor in the particular situation according to the demands of *agape* does not simply compromise the concrete demand of God; he rejects it. God's will for man in relation to his neighbor does not change merely because a person decides that he cannot live up to that will.

The Christian conception of the universality of human sinfulness constitutes a recognition of the fact that man's actions always fall short of *agape,* but this does not imply either that the measure of man's sin is an "impossible possibility" or that *agape* is irrelevant to the complex demands of life in the here and now. What it does imply is that man always falls short of being as loving as he can be when the conflicting demands of the many neighbors whose claims impinge upon him are harmonized by relating them all to the will of God—the Creator, the Judge, and the Redeemer. It implies also that all men are sinful insofar as they have contributed to the evil in society and have helped make it impossible to achieve a fuller realization of the ultimate will of God for a community of brotherhood and justice here and now.

Obviously, the Christian must be very wary of claiming that he knows precisely what God's will is. In a sense, he is never free from "conflicting duties," for he must constantly seek to harmonize all lesser loyalties with his final loyalty to God. But when the Christian knows what his final loyalty requires, he is fortified by faith to do his duty and he is "justified by grace" which frees him from paralyzing anxiety and fear of guilt for doing that which must be done out of *agape* toward the neighbor under God. The Christian is summoned to act in love, but he ought to act in humility because he knows that all of his actions also stand under the judgment of God's perfect will and that he himself is in part responsible for the evil in society which frequently limits his choice to the selection of the lesser of two evils or the least of many evils.[68]

[68] Cf. F. R. Barry, *The Recovery of Man,* New York, Charles Scribner's Sons, 1949, p. 50: "The Christian must seek to discover the will of God not away from these limitations but inside them. And, as sin is a part of our environment, it may often be that the only choice open is not that between good and evil, but that between a greater evil and a lesser. Where this is so, the 'lesser of two evils' is not only the morally right choice, but in a relative

While the term "compromise" is misleading when it is applied to the ultimate norm of Christian love, there is a secondary sense in which it is the duty of a Christian to compromise. Insofar as the Christian uses moral laws and principles—the Ten Commandments or the injunctions of the Sermon on the Mount, for example—as in aid in discovering the will of God in difficult situations, he must compromise in the sense of attempting to reach the best possible adjustment of the competing claims upon him. But this is not to compromise love; it is to compromise rules and abstract principles and use them in the service of love.

In an effort to clarify the proper place which compromise has in Protestant ethics, Professor Edward Le Roy Long, Jr., has sought to revive the term "casuistry" and use it to designate the process of applying the demands of the Christian faith to the perplexing dilemmas of daily life. This term, he insists, must be purged, however, of any implication of the idea that handbooks and guides can ever become the final norm for Christian conduct.[69] Compromise in this sense is necessary in the same way that laws and rules are necessary; but, as Professor Long points out, such casuistry always contradicts the ultimate norm of love even while it partially embodies love. It is necessary in order to relate Christianity to life in the world, but each decision that is reached on the basis of casuistry alone must be reëxamined in the light of the demands of Christian love.[70]

It is perhaps unimportant whether one uses the term "casuistry" or the term "compromise" to describe the process whereby the effort is made to relate faith to the concrete demands of daily life. It is of the utmost importance, however, according to Protestantism, that the secondary place which this process has in Christian ethics be made clear and also that there should be no mistaking the fact that the norm by which all casuistry and all compromises are tested is love.

---

and sinful world it is our Christian duty before God." Cf. also Nels F. S. Ferré, *Christianity and Society*, New York, Harper & Brothers, 1950, p. 139: "The use of the best available means in history is not to compromise, but to do God's actual will."

[69] Edward Le Roy Long, Jr., *Conscience and Compromise: An Approach to Protestant Casuistry*, Philadelphia, The Westminster Press, 1954, p. 10.

[70] *Ibid.*, pp. 142, 146. Cf. W. Norman Pittenger, *The Historic Faith and a Changing World*, New York, Oxford University Press, 1950, pp. 171 ff.

RECOMMENDED READINGS

Barth, Karl, *The Knowledge of God and the Service of God,* New York, Charles Scribner's Sons, 1939, pt. II.
Beach, Waldo, and Niebuhr, H. Richard, eds., *Christian Ethics,* New York, The Ronald Press Company, 1955.
Bennett, John C., *Christian Ethics and Social Policy,* New York, Charles Scribner's Sons, 1946, chs. IV–V.
Berdyaev, Nicolas, *The Destiny of Man,* London, Geoffrey Bles, 1937, pts. II–III.
Bonhoeffer, Dietrich, *Ethics,* London, Student Christian Movement Press, Ltd., 1955.
Brunner, Emil, *The Divine Imperative,* trans. by Olive Wyon, New York, The Macmillan Company, 1942, bk. II.
Bultmann, Rudolf, *Essays Philosophical and Theological,* London, Student Christian Movement Press, Ltd., 1955, ch. III.
Calvin, John, *Institutes of the Christian Religion,* 2 vols., Philadelphia, Presbyterian Board of Education, 1936, bk. II, ch. VII; bk. III, chs. VI–X, XIX.
Gogarten, Friedrich, *The Reality of Faith,* Philadelphia, The Westminster Press, 1959, chs. 5, 8, 9, 12.
Holbrook, Clyde A., *Faith and Community,* New York, Harper & Brothers, 1959, ch. 6.
Kierkegaard, Soren, *Works of Love,* Princeton, Princeton University Press, 1946.
Lehmann, Paul L., "The Foundation and Pattern of Christian Behavior," in *Christian Faith and Social Action,* John A. Hutchison, ed., New York, Charles Scribner's Sons, 1953.
Luther Martin, "Treatise on Christian Liberty," in *Works of Martin Luther,* vol. II, Philadelphia, A. J. Holman Company, 1915.
Maritain, Jacques, *True Humanism,* London, Geoffrey Bles, 1938, ch. III.
Niebuhr, H. Richard, *Christ and Culture,* New York, Harper & Brothers, 1951.
Niebuhr, H. Richard, "Evangelical and Protestant Ethics," in *The Heritage of the Reformation,* Elmer J. F. Arndt, ed., New York, Richard R. Smith, 1950.
Niebuhr, H. Richard, "The Center of Value," in *Moral Principles of Action,* Ruth Nanda Anshen, ed., New York, Harper & Brothers, 1952.
Niebuhr, Reinhold, *An Interpretation of Christian Ethics,* New York, Harper & Brothers, 1935, ch. IV.
Niebuhr, Reinhold, *The Nature and Destiny of Man,* II: *Human Destiny,* New York, Charles Scribner's Sons, 1943, chs. III, IX.

Nygren, Anders, *Agape and Eros,* London, Society for Promoting Christian Knowledge, 1953, pt. I, ch. I, sec. I; pt. I, ch. III, secs. II–IV.

Ramsey, Paul, *Basic Christian Ethics,* New York, Charles Scribner's Sons, 1950, chs. III–VII.

Ramsey, Paul, ed., *Faith and Ethics,* New York, Harper & Brothers, 1957, chs. IV–V.

St. Augustine, *The City of God,* New York, Random House (The Modern Library), 1950, bks. V, XIV, XIX.

St. Augustine, "On the Morals of the Catholic Church," in *Basic Writings of Saint Augustine,* 2 vols., Whitney J. Oates, ed., New York, Random House, 1948, vol. I.

Temple, William, *Christianity and Social Order,* London, Student Christian Movement Press, Ltd., 1950, chs. IV–VI.

Thomas, George F., *Christian Ethics and Moral Philosophy,* New York, Charles Scribner's Sons, 1955, chs. 3–4, 5, 9, 22.

PART IV

CHRISTIAN ETHICS AND SOCIETY

chapter 8

SEX AND MARRIAGE

We turn now to an application of the theological principles which we have been examining to the major problems of society. The term which is frequently used in Neo-Protestant circles to designate the general areas with which the Christian ethic is concerned in its social aspects is "the orders of creation." Following Luther, Brunner uses this term to designate those institutions or forms of community which arise out of the nature of man as he is by creation: marriage, the economic order, the state, the community of culture, and the church.[1] The divine will for man is that his life shall find expression in, and be ordered in accordance with the requirements of, these social structures understood as general ordinances and not, of course, as particular, existing, concrete institutions. The purpose of these orders is to make possible life in community as opposed to isolated existence. The Christian, therefore, should look upon these social structures both as divine creations and as divine gifts. As such they are not meaningless facts, for they reflect the purpose of God in the creation of man as a social being for life-in-community. They represent specific areas in which God calls men to work and they offer guidance as to the forms of work which the Creator wills to be done.

But Brunner makes it quite clear that all particular institutions or orders that are found in society have been corrupted by sin; hence, they cannot be identified with God's will. For this reason the Christian is summoned to seek to bring about the transformation of the existing social structures so that they will more faithfully serve the intent of

[1] Emil Brunner, *The Divine Imperative,* trans. by Olive Wyon, New York, The Macmillan Company, 1942, pp. 333 ff.

the Creator. Thus, while he is called to remain *in* the world, he is also forbidden to be conformed to the world.

THE FAMILY AS A BASIC SOCIAL INSTITUTION

The first of the orders of creation to which we direct our attention is marriage. There is general agreement among sociologists and psychologists as well as among moralists and theologians that the family is one of the most basic of all social institutions. It is found in every known society, and its roots "go deeper into the biological nature of man than do those of any other institution except perhaps the economic organization, which rests principally upon the hunger drive."[2] Indeed, until modern times the family itself discharged the economic activities which were essential to satisfy the hunger drive, and the economic ties of the family provided one of the major stabilizing forces which held the family together. The family continues to be *a* basic, if not *the* basic, institution in the sense that in the earliest and most formative years of life it exercises almost "a monopolistic influence on the child."[3] This is true of the child's physical endowment and nurture, of its emotional development, of its growth in social awareness, and of its moral and religious development. The family is, in the words of Nimkoff, "the nursery of human nature."[4]

Psychiatrists emphasize the lack of genuine affection and security in childhood as one of the major causes of mental illness. Similarly, there is wide agreement among criminologists that one of the most important factors in the etiology of juvenile delinquency is to be found in the emotional rejection of children by their parents. In fact, so important are the relationships within the home for the development of character and social responsibility that Paul Tappan, speaking of steps which need to be taken in the prevention of juvenile delinquency, writes, "If there is to be any really effective curtailment of law violation in the society, it can come only through the medium of the family."[5] The effectiveness of other social institutions in curtailing and preventing delinquency, he holds, is mainly dependent

[2] Meyer F. Nimkoff, *Marriage and the Family*, Boston, Houghton Mifflin Company, 1947, pp. 22–23.
[3] Robert F. Winch, *The Modern Family*, New York, Henry Holt and Company, 1952, p. vii.
[4] Nimkoff, *op. cit.*, p. 337.
[5] Paul Tappan, *Juvenile Delinquency*, New York, McGraw-Hill Book Company, 1949, p. 496.

upon their efforts and influence being channeled through the family. The noted psychoanalyst Abram Kardiner similarly refers to the family as "the place where we can exert the greatest influence" on all forms of morality.[6] Indeed, there is much evidence to indicate that the influence of the family in the development of the moral ideals of children is far greater than the combined influence of the school and church.[7]

The primary importance of the family in the moral and religious development of children has been recognized in Judaism and Christianity from their very beginnings, and the sanctity of this institution has been zealously safeguarded. In both the Old and the New Testaments the relationships of God to man are described in terms of imagery drawn from the family, for this is considered to be the natural human institution that most fully embodies the ideal of true community among men and most fully symbolizes the relationship between believers and God in the community of faith. The high place which the rite of marriage has been accorded in all branches of the Christian Church and the responsibility for moral and religious training which is placed upon parents by all of these groups is ample evidence of the importance which is attached to the family in Christianity.

THE CRISIS IN THE FAMILY AND IN SEX

Not only is there a general consensus among sociologists, psychologists, and theologians concerning the fundamental importance of the family; there is also general agreement that the modern family is faced with a serious crisis of far-reaching consequences. There is further agreement, moreover, that the crisis in the family is closely related to an even more fundamental crisis in modern sexual behavior in general.

Of course, the feeling that both of these relationships are in a critical state is not a new phenomenon in itself, but the present crisis differs from preceding ones in certain important respects, due to the impact of a number of powerful and relatively new social changes in our Western Civilization. These changes have been so deep-rooted and far-reaching in their influence that they have made it impossible

[6] Abram Kardiner, *Sex and Morality*, New York, The Bobbs-Merrill Company, 1954, p. 263.
[7] Cf. Hugh Hartshorne and Mark A. May, "Testing the Knowledge of Right and Wrong," *Religious Education*, XXI, no. 5 (October, 1926), pp. 539–554.

to return to the old patterns of family life and to reliance upon authoritarian codes of sexual morality. The family, for example, is no longer bound together as strongly as it once was by economic ties, for women have gained a large measure of economic independence. That the patriarchal type of family organization is no longer taken for granted is due in part to the economic liberation of women and also in part to their political emancipation. Along with this weakening of certain traditional family ties, there has been a widespread revolt against Puritanism and legalism in the whole area of sex relationships. This revolt has been strengthened by many forces including the spread of certain forms of Freudian psychology, the widespread use of contraceptives, the discovery of means of controlling venereal disease, the breaking of family ties by war and periods of military training, and the impersonalization of life in modern industry and in large cities.

The present crisis in the family and sexual behavior differs from preceding ones, moreover, both in its scope and in its depth. It is not concerned simply with divorce or birth control or premarital sexual relations but with the place of marriage itself and with the whole question of the meaning of sex. According to Elton and Pauline Trueblood, the family in America is "withering away" through neglect of its members to face up seriously to the question of what a family ought to be.[8] For great numbers of people, they point out, traditional sexual morality has become "quaint and meaningless," and marriage has lost its sanctity so that it is now generally considered to be merely a private contract without public significance. Such a breakdown in sex morality and the family represents a genuine threat to the moral health of the entire nation, for it affects not only the well-being of adults but also the emotional and spiritual health of children; it affects not only the family but also all the other institutions of social control.

This crisis has been dramatized and called to the attention of the general public in more specific terms by the startling statistics on the increase of divorce, by the reports of Alfred C. Kinsey and his colleagues on American sexual behavior, and by the general increase in juvenile delinquency.[9] Statistics on the divorce rate in the United

---

[8] Elton Trueblood and Pauline Trueblood, *The Recovery of Family Life,* New York, Harper & Brothers, 1953, ch. I.

[9] See Alfred C. Kinsey, Wardell B. Pomeroy, and Clyde E. Martin, *Sexual Behavior in the Human Male,* Philadelphia, W. B. Saunders Company, 1948; and Alfred C. Kinsey *et al., Sexual Behavior in the Human Female,* Philadelphia, W. B. Saunders Company, 1953.

States reveal, for example, that in the year 1948 one out of four marriages ended in divorce whereas in 1910 only one out of ten marriages ended in this manner.[10] Regardless of the critical questions which must be raised about the methods which Kinsey and his associates used in their studies,[11] their reports concerning the frequency of premarital intercourse were shocking to many readers. Still others were surprised, not so much by the statistical results of these studies, as by the almost complete absence from most of the nominal Christians who were interviewed of any "genuine Christian understanding of the meaning of human sexuality."[12] Almost equally dramatic have been the statistics on the rise of juvenile delinquency in this country. During World War II there was a sharp rise in the incidence of juvenile delinquency which hit a peak in 1945. Following the war there was a general decline in delinquency, but in 1950 it began to rise again. The number of police arrests of persons under eighteen years of age reported to the FBI increased 55 percent between 1952 and 1957 although the population in this age group for the country as a whole increased only 22 percent during the same period.[13] Assuming that the cities reporting the number of police arrests to the FBI experienced a population growth similar to that which characterized the country as a whole, arrests of young people increased two and one-half times faster than the population in this age group. In 1957, persons under eighteen accounted for 53.1 percent of all arrests for major crimes against property and 10.3 percent of all arrests for major crimes against the person.[14]

Reactions to the different facets of the present disorder have been

[10] These estimates are based upon Figure 7 entitled "Trends in Divorce Rates in Specific Countries, 1910–1948," appearing in Winch, *op. cit.*, p. 482. The precise reference of this Figure is to the "Ratio per 100 of Divorces in Each Year to Average Annual Number of Marriages in Preceding Decade."

[11] Kinsey and his associates, for example, assume a completely biological definition of sex and therefore fail to take into account its *human* meaning. Moreover, their methods of sampling and interviewing are open to serious question. For an appraisal of the methodology employed in these reports, see *An Analysis of the Kinsey Reports on Sexual Behavior in the Human Male and Female,* Donald Porter Geddes, ed., New York, E. P. Dutton & Co., 1954; and Edmund Bergler and William S. Kroger, *Kinsey's Myth of Female Sexuality,* New York, Grune & Stratton, 1954.

[12] Cf. W. Norman Pittenger, *The Christian View of Sexual Behavior,* Greenwich, Connecticut, The Seabury Press, 1954, p. 17.

[13] *Uniform Crime Reports For the United States,* Issued by the FBI, XXVIII, no. 2 (Annual Bulletin, 1957), p. 112.

[14] *Ibid.,* p. 113.

varied, ranging all the way from a desire to return to the conditions which prevailed before the present critical state of affairs emerged to the desire to abandon the old restraints and live simply "according to nature." On the one hand, suppression of the sex drive, stricter divorce laws, and more rigid discipline for children are advocated. On the other hand, sexual liberty, a relaxation in the requirements of present divorce laws, and an emphasis upon love without discipline in parent-child relationships are recommended as the paths to emotional health and happiness. Or, analyzing the crisis in the family in somewhat different terms, Winch speaks alternately of the "institutionalists" who emphasize the value of conformity to certain traditional patterns of family life and of the "individualists" who emphasize the primary importance of personal happiness in whatever form this can best be provided. Neither the institutionalists nor the individualists, however, believe that all is well with the family, although the two groups use different value systems and different criteria in appraising it, and therefore draw different conclusions concerning its future. "Looking back toward the old rural family," Professor Winch writes, "the institutionalists fear that the family is getting worse. Looking forward to what they know not, the individualists hope it is getting better. The institutionalists appear to be trying to recreate the old rural family by exhortation in the modern urban-industrial social order. The individualists appear to say that they cannot clearly envisage the emerging family form, but that it is futile to seek a reversion under modern conditions."[15]

It is useless to urge a return to the old traditional patterns of family life which prevailed before the present crisis emerged. Such an attempt overlooks the fact that institutions are basically designed to meet human needs and that these needs can be met only if the institutions themselves are adapted to the social forces which provide the context in which these needs arise. As these forces change, institutions themselves must change; otherwise they lose their vitality and power and inner reason for being. "The sabbath was made for man, not man for the sabbath" (Mark 2:27). To this extent the "individualists" are right as over against the "institutionalists," no matter how true it may be that it was easier to preserve the family as a social unit when it was bound together by economic necessity. It is not held together in this manner to a marked degree now, and for this reason

---

[15] Winch, *op. cit.,* pp. 488–489.

some other basis must be found for its unity if the latter is to be preserved. The "individualists" are also doubtless right as over against the "institutionalists" in seeing some of these changes as representing a great gain, potentially at least, in freeing the members of the family to devote more of their time to the pursuit of non-economic interests and in liberating women in particular from economic and political peonage. But the modern "individualists" are inclined to overlook the basic similarity in the needs of men and the social consequences of the satisfaction of these needs. Moreover, their motivation is largely negative in that it is primarily characterized by reaction against the traditional institutional forms rather than by positive proposals of alternative ways of meeting carefully defined human needs.

In view of all of the confusion that has arisen in the wake of the contemporary breakdown in marriage and sex relationships, it seems clear that neither a dogmatic traditionalism nor an unchastened individualism is adequate to point the way either to a recovery of the integrity of the family or to a consistent understanding of the meaning and depth of human sexuality. Judged in the light of the fundamental crisis in the meaning of sex, it is useless to attempt to deal with the problem of divorce or premarital or extramarital sexual intercourse upon a purely legalistic or moralistic basis. Even if such a method could bring about conformity to the external pattern of monogamy as an inviolate life-long union between one man and one woman, it would not in itself be able to make monogamy a spiritually rich and satisfying experience, and it would not necessarily result in a wholesome environment for the rearing of children. The only adequate way to deal with the moral breakdown in the areas of family life and sex relationships generally, therefore, is to begin by inquiring into the meaning of the family and of sex. These are ultimately theological questions, and the necessity for raising them is implicit in the method of Christian ethics which we have already examined. In keeping with this method we need to ask what, from the standpoint of Christian faith, is the purpose of God in ordaining marriage and in creating man a sexual being. What human needs are fulfilled in and through the institution of the family? In view of the appropriateness of marriage for meeting these needs, can it be adequately understood merely as a human convention, or does it point to the will of the Creator? And, more ultimately, we also need to examine the meaning of human sexuality when this is understood in terms of the creative, ordering, and redeeming will of God. Is human sexuality merely a physiological characteristic of human existence, or is man's spiritual nature also involved in and affected by his sexual relationships?

THE CHRISTIAN INTERPRETATION OF SEX

Because it is the more fundamental of the two questions which we have raised, we turn first to that of the meaning of sex according to Christian faith. In seeking to answer this question, we must begin with the basic conviction of Christian faith that back of the whole multiplicity of things which confront us in the created order there is a fundamental oneness, a harmony, a purpose which binds the whole together, and that this purpose is revealed—albeit incompletely to men's finite minds—in the action of the Purposer (the Logos) in creating, ordering, and renewing that which it pleased Him to create. This is the beginning point in the Christian interpretation of all reality, including sex. Seen in this light, sex cannot be an "accidental" fact with no meaning, for it is part of the plan of the Creator. Neither can its meaning be adequately discerned if man begins with his selfish desire for pleasure, for this is to make man rather than God the center of this sphere of life and also to ignore the fact that since man is essentially a moral and spiritual being, he cannot find genuine happiness on this basis. According to biblical faith the meaning of sex cannot be adequately understood unless the latter is seen in relationship to God's purpose in the creation of man as a unity of body and spirit.

Viewing it then as the work of the Creator, the first thing that Christian faith says about sex is that *it is good*. "So God created man in his own image, in the image of God he created him; male and female he created them. . . . And God saw everything that he had made, and behold, it was very good" (Gen. 1:27, 31). According to the Bible sex is sacred, and it is to be accepted in gratitude and not in fear. Man is a unity of flesh and spirit, and each is to be accepted as good in its order. As flesh, man's desires for food, for water, for rest, and for sexual relationships all belong to normal human existence; and as such they are grounded in the will of the Creator. Of course, each of these desires is subject to abuse because of man's freedom, but none of them is for this reason to be considered evil.

The significance of the Christian view of sex can best be seen by contrasting it with two other views which have confronted it with a serious challenge. The first of these is asceticism, which has at times exercised a strong influence in some branches of the Church. No trace of sexual asceticism is to be found in the Old Testament. There sex is regarded as good, and marriage is considered the normal state for men and women. Indeed, procreation is viewed as one of God's commandments: "Be fruitful and multiply, and fill the earth" (Gen. 1:28). Promiscuity, however, is never condoned, and those cults which engaged in sexual orgies in connection with their religious rites are strongly condemned.

In general, the conception of sex which is characteristic of the Old Testament underlies New Testament thought upon the subject. To be sure, Jesus did not marry, and he spoke of the need to be willing to forsake those to whom one is bound by domestic ties for the sake of the Kingdom (Luke 14:26). But he clearly implied that marriage was ordained of God when he declared, "What therefore God has joined together, let not man put asunder" (Matt. 19:6). Paul also was unmarried. He believed that the celibate state was preferable for those who were able to remain continent (I Cor. 7:8–9, 32–35), but his preference for celibacy was due mainly to eschatological considerations. "In view of the impending distress," he wrote to the unmarried as well as to the married Christians at Corinth, "it is well for a person to remain as he is" (I Cor. 7:26). It is not a sin to marry, he insisted, but the cares of family life would be a source of anxiety to the married and would serve to distract them from preparing themselves for the imminent return of the Lord. Thus, neither Jesus nor Paul required celibacy or even favored it for all Christians.

In the early centuries of Christian history, however, sexual asceticism did make inroads into the teachings of the Church. Due in part to the impact of Greek and Oriental views of matter as evil, in part to a growing tendency to regard all forms of self-denial as meritorious, and in part to a desire of early Christian monks to withdraw from society as a whole—from men as well as from women— marriage came to be subordinated to celibacy in the teachings of many of the Fathers of the Church such as St. Jerome, Tertullian, St. Ambrose, and St. Augustine.[16] Yet not even the most extreme of the Christian ascetics wholly condemned marriage for others. St. Jerome, who took one of the most austere views in this regard, rated

[16] See Roland H. Bainton, *What Christianity Says About Sex, Love and Marriage,* New York, Association Press, 1957, pp. 25 ff.

marriage sixty-fold as compared with virginity which he reckoned at one hundred, and he saw one good in the former, namely, that it produced virgins.[17]

While St. Augustine upheld the superior worth of celibacy, he took a more moderate view than St. Jerome. St. Augustine's position is of particular importance, however, because in general it represents the position which the Roman Catholic Church has taken right on down to the present. Celibacy, he believed, was superior to marriage; nevertheless, the sexual act as such cannot be wrong because procreation thereby has been divinely ordained. However, the sexual act is always accompanied by concupiscence, which is sinful. But, since marriage is a sacrament, according to St. Augustine, for the Christian the sexual act involved in procreation within marriage involves only a venial sin. Relationships within the marriage bond for satisfaction rather than for procreation are likewise accompanied by passion, and hence they also involve sin; but this sin is similarly covered by the sacrament of marriage. Thus, for St. Augustine, while celibacy is preferable to marriage, the latter is permissible; and, while it is best to remain celibate even within marriage, it is permissible to have sexual intercourse within the confines of this union for the sake of procreation and as a remedy for sin.[18] Marriage would be an uncorrupted good if man had not sinned, but in man's present sinful state it has two provisional goods: procreation (to fill up the number of the elect) and companionship. St. Augustine's views on sex gradually became dominant in the Medieval Church, and they were in the main taken over by St. Thomas Aquinas in the thirteenth century. In this manner they became authoritative for later Roman Catholicism, as witnessed by the Council of Trent and the pronouncements of recent Popes. Thus the Council of Trent anathematized those who said "that the conjugal state is to be preferred before that of virginity or celibacy and that it is not better and more blessed to remain in virginity or in celibacy than to be joined in matrimony."[19]

The leaders of the Protestant Reformation rejected this disparagement of marriage. Wedlock was for them of equal worth with celibacy, and indeed Luther on occasion exalted it above virginity, which he looked upon as an evasion of social responsibility. However, in

---

[17] *Ibid.*, p. 30.

[18] "The Good of Marriage," in Roy J. Deferrari, ed., *Writings of Saint Augustine*, XV, New York, The Fathers of the Church, Inc., 1955.

[19] The Canons and Decrees of the Council of Trent, Session XXIV, Canon X.

actuality a negative attitude toward sex has persisted in various segments of Protestantism, and it is still frequently evidenced in the
fear and apprehension which many Protestants feel in entering into
sexual relationships within marriage and also in interpreting sex to
their children. It is also abundantly evidenced in the clinical data
of psychotherapy as well as in the general tendency of theologians
to discuss sex in the context of sin rather than of salvation.[20] The
latter fact does not imply, however, that theologians generally regard
sex as intrinsically sinful but, rather, that they give relatively little
attention to the positive contribution which sex can make to "the
good life" as compared with its tendency to get spoiled by human
sinfulness.

The biblical view of sex also differs sharply from a purely physiological conception of human sexuality such as that evidenced by
Kinsey and his associates. According to the latter, man is essentially
an animal, although a complex and highly developed one, and sex
represents simply a biological desire, like hunger or thirst. Man's
physical well-being demands that it be satisfied regularly. Hence, it is
considered harmful to refrain from sexual intercourse until marriage;
moreover, it is alleged that some such experience prior to marriage
helps make adjustment within wedlock more successful.

According to this view, love is merely a matter of sexual attraction.
Men and women marry primarily for the sexual satisfaction which
they can give each other. Of course they are generally drawn together
also by other common interests. If the marriage is a happy one, they
will no longer need to seek sexual satisfaction outside of their marriage, and their companionship will deepen as their common interests
grow. However, if one ceases to find sexual satisfaction within wedlock, one is free either to seek it outside of marriage or to seek a
divorce and marry again. There may be recognition of a husband's
obligation to provide for his wife and children, but there is no recognition of any permanent bond which binds husband and wife together once sexual attraction vanishes.

The most spectacular attempt to apply this biological-hedonistic
conception of sex to a society as a whole on an individualistic basis
took place in Russia during the early years of the Bolshevik revolution. Following the lead of Marx, who had condemned the monogamous family as an institution based upon the property interests of

[20] Cf. David E. Roberts, *Psychotherapy and A Christian View of Man,*
New York, Charles Scribner's Sons, 1950, p. 136.

the capitalist class, the leaders of the revolution deliberately undertook to destroy marriage and the family. They glorified free love in the official "glass of water" theory of sex. Just as it is immaterial what glass a thirsty person uses when satisfying his thirst, so it was considered unimportant how one satisfied his sexual desire. The only important thing in either case is the pleasureful emotion accompanying satisfaction of the desire. Hence the Communists abolished the legal distinction between casual sexual relations and marriage; they permitted divorce and remarriage at will; they praised premarital relations and considered extramarital relations normal. After a few years, however, the social results of this policy were seen to be so appalling that the government was forced to reverse it. The "glass of water" theory of sex was declared counter-revolutionary, and was replaced by an official glorification of premarital chastity and the sanctity of marriage. Abortion, which had been encouraged in the earlier period, was prohibited except under unusual and critical conditions; and divorce was greatly restricted.[21]

It should not be assumed that the reversal of Soviet policy with regard to sex and marriage implied a rejection of the essentially biological-hedonistic conception of sex. It did, however, constitute a rejection of a completely individualistic interpretation of sex and marriage which overlooks the stake society has in both of these matters. The Soviet authorities have undertaken to restrict individual men and women in their pursuit of sexual pleasure at the point where this pursuit interferes with the aims and purposes of the collectivist state, especially with its needs for more offspring and for far greater stability on the part of its workers in the factories. But the underlying conception of sex remains essentially a materialistic one, as does the whole concept of man of which it is an integral part. In order properly to evaluate the adequacy, from a Christian point of view, of this underlying conception of sex and human nature we shall have to consider it in the light of the Christian conception of man which we examined in a previous chapter.

Viewed in the light of the biblical understanding of man as a spiritual being endowed with freedom and the capacity for self-transcendence, any purely physiological understanding of sex is inadequate. Man's true dignity consists in the fact that he stands in personal relationship to God and to his fellowmen. Moreover, man stands in this personal relationship with God and with his neighbors in the totality

[21] Pitirim A. Sorokin, *The American Sex Revolution,* Boston, Porter Sargent, 1956, pp. 113–115.

of his being as body and spirit. Body and spirit are so closely joined together that what affects one affects the other. As a result of this fundamental unity of man, it is not possible to treat sex as if it were simply a physiological thing, for one is always dealing with other selves who are far more than biological beings with sexual attractiveness and sexual desires of their own. In sexual relationships, one is always dealing primarily with persons rather than with things. In fact, from the standpoint of the Bible, it is in the experience of human love expressed in the intimacy of sexual union and in becoming "one flesh" that the personal character of man and woman is most fully revealed to each other.

Thus the Old Testament generally uses the term "to know" in describing the act of sexual intercourse, and it uses it interchangeably of the man and of the woman. In view of the customary frankness of the Bible in speaking about sex, it is difficult to believe that this term is merely an euphemism.[22] The use of this term implies, rather, that, although two persons may be drawn together by sexual desire, the act of intercourse involves the whole person, the entire *ego* or self, in each case; and it implies, further, that when the inner meaning of this act is properly understood, it becomes the means whereby there is disclosed more fully than is possible in any other relationship between two people what it means to be a person and what it means to be a man and a woman. The meaning of human sexuality is fully revealed only in this context of the meeting of two persons, of an "I" and a "Thou," to use Martin Buber's terminology. This is not simply an act whereby a "human male" and a "human female" satisfy a biological drive. On the contrary, one self meets another self, and in this coming together of two persons there is disclosed to each something of the mystery of human existence—the complementary character of the sexes, the dependence of the self upon other selves, the freedom of the self to give its whole self to another, the mystery of creation, and the fulfillment of the self which comes from the transformation of *eros* and *philia* by *agape*.[23]

---

[22] Otto A. Piper, *The Christian Interpretation of Sex,* New York, Charles Scribner's Sons, 1941, p. 52.

[23] Cf. Peter A. Bertocci, *The Human Venture in Sex, Love and Marriage,* New York, Association Press, 1949, pp. 47–48: "Sex is an increasing source of personal enrichment when dedicated to objectives other than mere self-satisfaction. The fact of human experience seems to be that persons enjoy deeper, more lasting, and more profound satisfaction when the normal experience of sex lust is not primarily an end in itself but a symbolic expression of other values."

The sex relationship and the family which stems out of it provide the basis for the fullest fellowship of one person with another, a fellowship that is based upon the recognition of the essential worth of each person and in which there is the fullest possible opportunity to understand and serve each other's needs. Many of these needs cannot, of course, be recognized as such if one's partner is viewed merely as an animal and if sex is interpreted accordingly in purely physiological terms. If, however, man is more than an animal and in particular if he is recognized as a spiritual being, sex becomes sacred and the sexual experience opens up in the most personal way possible the mystery of human existence. Beyond the "I" and the "Thou" united in this union, the sex relationship points to the Author of life, who has created man as a spiritual and personal being and endowed him with the blessings of sex, including the joys of creativity and companionship which accompany the expression of it when its inner meaning is properly safeguarded.

When the full meaning of the personal character of the sex relationship is recognized, it is easy to understand why the writers of the Bible, unlike many later ascetics, did not think it necessary to justify sexual relations on the basis of procreation. The dignity of sex is to be found in its capacity to serve as an instrument of fellowship between two persons just as much as in its ability to be the instrument of procreation. Indeed, according to one account of Creation in Genesis, woman was made because God saw that it was "not good that the man should be alone" (Gen. 2:18). "Therefore a man leaves his father and his mother and cleaves to his wife, and they become one flesh" (Gen. 2:24). Passages such as these seem to imply that children are an additional blessing added to the sex experience by the Creator, whereas the primary value of sex is fellowship.[24] This view does not mean, of course, that the function of procreation is an additional blessing in the sense that it was bestowed at a later point in time; rather, it constitutes a recognition of the fact that in human experience sex does actually fill a much larger role than providing offspring. Indeed, in ordinary experience sex is not even primarily connected with the desire to have offspring but rather with the desire for union with another person and hence for fulfillment of the self by union with another who can to this extent complete one's isolated and fragmentary existence. In the light of the need each person has for the fulfillment of the self in such fellowship, Berdyaev seems to be right when he declares that a marital union for the sole purpose of

[24] Piper, *op. cit.*, pp. 47–50.

procreation must be judged to be immoral. "As a matter of fact," he writes, "no one ever married for that purpose, though he may have hypocritically said so for the sake of public opinion. People marry because of an irresistible desire, because they love and are in love, because they want to be united to the loved one, and sometimes through interest. No one longs for physical sexual union because he wants to beget children. It is an invention of the conscious mind."[25]

It turns out, therefore, that the biblical understanding of sex is more "natural" in the sense that it is more in keeping with the total needs and psychological facts of man's sexual life than is the physio-logical-hedonistic view of sex which prides itself on being completely in accordance with nature; for the latter sees only the biological drive and the psychological desire for pleasure to be gained through the satisfaction of the biological drive. Not only is this biological-hedonis-tic view inaccurate insofar as it commits the hedonistic fallacy of sup-posing that pleasure rather than the fulfillment of the self is the object of desire, whether in animals or in man, but it also completely over-looks the *human* significance of sex. In man, sex is so interwoven with his entire psychological being that, once allowance is made for certain physiological similarities between sex in man and sex in animals, the contrasts between the two are more illuminating than the likenesses.[26] Why this is so is made strikingly clear by the analysis which Hubert Benoit makes of the psychological consequences of a purely biolog-ical view of sex in *The Many Faces of Love*. Benoit shows why it is impossible to escape the psychological and moral consequences of engaging in the act of sexual intercourse.

The complications of erotic love, of self-love, and of attachment, are hard to neutralize. There are people who do dismiss these, and engage in the sexual act apparently with the same ease as animals, but then the complications are internal; there is a sense of degradation, of culpability, or an inner compulsion to continual repetition without real organic desire, or there are sexual obsessions; so that the act of this kind—'easy come and easy go'—does not let the actors depart in peace to their occupa-tions. The animal in you may deplore this state of things, but your in-telligence is bound to admit that you are no ordinary animal, that you are under obligation to the nobility of your virtually timeless being.[27]

[25] Nicolas Berdyaev, *The Destiny of Man*, London, Geoffrey Bles, 2nd ed., 1945, p. 240.
[26] Cf. Bertocci, *op. cit.*, p. 48.
[27] Hubert Benoit, *The Many Faces of Love: The Psychology of the Emo-tional and Sexual Life*, trans. by Philip Mairet, New York, Pantheon Books, 1955, pp. 246–247.

That the Bible does not view the sex relationship as intended only for procreation is indicated, as we have seen, by the fact that Adam was given a female rather than a male companion to save him from being alone. More significantly from the Christian standpoint at least, since Judaism has been far freer of a negative attitude toward sexual intercourse within marriage than has Christianity, the New Testament always bases this act upon the natural impulse rather than upon procreation. Thus Paul, whose views concerning sex are considered by many to be the prototype of Christian asceticism in this regard, does not deal with the subject from the standpoint of reproduction but rather from that of a mutual obligation (I Cor. 7:3–5). According to Paul, the limits of sexual intercourse are set, not by the intent to procreate, but by the desire temporarily to devote oneself wholeheartedly to prayer. After such a limited period of prayer, however, a husband and wife are counseled to resume their normal conjugal relationships (I Cor. 7:5; cf. I Peter 3:7). Moreover, in view of the realism of the Bible as a whole in regard to these matters, the fact that it nowhere prohibits intercourse because propagation is impossible or unintended confirms the general biblical understanding of the double purpose of this relationship as it was intended by the Creator. This conception of sex was taken over by Luther and Calvin, but some branches of Protestantism broke away from the position taken by these leaders of the Reformation and espoused the semiascetic views of Roman Catholicism. The repression which results from this semiasceticism not only prevents the natural deepening of the "one flesh" union through the mutual expression of love in intercourse, but it is emotionally and spiritually harmful insofar as it results in lasciviousness, fantasy, abnormal feelings of guilt, and self-abuse which, from the standpoint of the New Testament, are just as evil as overt immoral relations because the former also stem out of lust.

Today it is generally agreed in Protestant circles that birth control has a rightful place within marriage. As a matter of fact, it is not something new; it has been practiced by Christians from the beginning —long before contraceptives were invented. However, the urgency of the need for limiting the number of children in a family has been greatly increased by the growth in national and world populations, by the costliness of life in cities, by the great decrease in infant mortality, and by the tremendous increase in the life expectancy of those who survive infancy. While the Roman Catholic Church does not permit the use of contraceptives, it does permit the limitation of the size of families not only by abstinence when both parties consent but also, since the issuance of the papal encyclical *Casti Connubii* in 1930, by the restriction of intercourse to those periods when conception is least likely to occur. The latter concession by the Catholic Church represents a break in principle with its former position according to which only intercourse for the sake of procreation was sanctioned. Now the major difference between the position of the Catholic Church and that of Protestantism concerns the method to be employed in the control of conception.

The argument that the Catholic Church advances against birth control by artificial means is that it is "against nature" and, therefore, against the divine will. If this argument were used consistently, it would seem to prohibit interference with any of the ordinary processes of nature. Yet, it is not so employed in regard to the use of medicine to combat disease, in regard to the wearing of clothing, or in regard to engineering feats whereby rivers are diverted, swamps are drained, and desert places are made habitable. Moreover, natural limitations of space and food themselves require limitation of the population despite the fact that the sex drive continues to draw persons together without regard to the density of population.

Not only is the control of conception—a much more precise term for what is involved than "birth control"—permissible in the Protestant view, but it would seem to be a positive duty in view of the emotional needs of children and the depletion of a mother's physical strength if children follow one another in too rapid succession. Other considerations are involved, of course, such as the limited family resources for meeting the physical and educational needs of each child as well as needs of the parents and sometimes of other dependents. Attention also needs to be given to the proper spacing of children. All of these factors combine to make the control of conception a Christian duty incumbent upon all parents, and the use of artificial means of preventing conception is no less a worthy way of achieving this end than is abstinence in periods that are assumed to be "safe." Indeed, in view of the importance of what is at stake, especially as regards the consequences for an unwanted child, and in view of the anxiety of parents, the use of artificial means of preventing conception would seem to be the more responsible way. While even this does not absolutely guarantee the prevention of pregnancy, it is far more effective than the practice of rhythm and it reduces the element of chance to a minimum.

What has been said about birth control does not minimize the two-fold function of sex as a means of procreation and as a means of fellowship. Neither does it lend endorsement to the hedonistic desire of many couples to be free from the responsibilities connected with childbirth and the rearing of children. On the contrary, it implies that the responsibility of rearing children is taken with genuine seriousness. It must not be forgotten that a marriage—a "one flesh" union—is in a real sense incomplete so long as children have not come to bless it; for in procreation husband and wife share in the creative purpose of God, which is a deeply significant part of the meaning of sex, and their union is also enriched by the hopes, the joys, and the heartaches which are attendant upon the rearing of children.

While Christianity, insofar as it is true to the biblical view of man, gives a very high place to sex as one of the greatest blessings of man's earthly existence, it nowhere assigns to it the highest value or meaning in life. Sex is confined to the present temporal order which will pass away. "In the resurrection they neither marry nor are given in marriage, but are like angels in heaven" (Matt. 22:30). And while traditional Christianity has defined sin primarily in terms of pride and self-love, it has also recognized that, partly because they involve the whole ego in such large measure and partly because of their intensity, the sexual desires and appetites provide particularly strong occasions for sin. Although sex is not in any sense evil in itself, in sinful man it easily becomes an instrument of self-assertion and self-deification, on the one hand, and, on the other hand, the means whereby the self seeks to escape from itself. In the former instance it represents the final form of self-love; in the latter instance it may either take the form of the deification of another person or, as the expression of an uneasy conscience and a lack of faith, it may take the form of a flight into unconsciousness or nothingness.[28]

In the Christian view, therefore, sex never represents life's highest good. Unless it is seen within the context of man's total nature, its inner meaning is perverted and every effort to seek the fulfillment of the sexual desire ends in disappointment and frustration of the self at some level of its need and longing. From the standpoint of Christian faith, such perversion and frustration represent the divine judgment upon man's sinfulness. This judgment falls, moreover, not only upon the libertine but also upon all those who, while preserving an

[28] Cf. Reinhold Niebuhr, *The Nature and Destiny of Man,* I, *Human Nature,* New York, Charles Scribner's Sons, 1943, pp. 236–237.

external fidelity, nevertheless use their mates as instruments for the gratification of their own passions and upon those ascetics who seek to ignore their sexuality either by taking flight into the monastery or by refusing to recognize their own sexual needs as well as the needs of their partners within marriage. In a word, God's judgment falls upon man's sexual life in his emotional impoverishment, in the isolation of the self, and in the fear and anxiety which stem out of the repressed but unsublimated sexual desires of the ascetic as well as in the moral degeneration of the profligate.

THE CHRISTIAN VIEW OF MARRIAGE

The Christian view of marriage is closely related to the Christian interpretation of sex. Indeed, the former is based upon the latter. This does not mean, however, that in Christianity marriage is based upon sexual attraction or sexual compatibility. If this were its basis, it would be dissolved when such attraction disappeared or when psychological or physiological obstacles to sexual harmony appeared. According to the Christian view, marriage is much more stable and permanent than such a physiological-hedonistic conception implies, and it is more stable and permanent precisely because of the profundity of the biblical view of sex. As we have already observed, the Bible always sees man's sex relationships in the context of his total nature viewed as a unity of body and spirit and in the context of his personal relationship to his neighbor and to God. Sex is a gift of the Creator for man's use and enjoyment, but this gift implies a responsibility for its use. To reject it as evil is to be ungrateful and unfaithful. To use it promiscuously is to be irresponsible to God and to one's partners in the sexual act.

Viewed in the light of this understanding of sex, two forms of sex life have been considered responsible throughout Christian history: celibacy and monogamy. Polygamy was recognized in the Old Testament, but before the beginning of the Christian era monogamy had become the established form of marriage in Judaism. Both the Old and the New Testaments condemn the expression of the sexual impulse in premarital and extramarital intercourse. Normally it is expected that men and women will enter into marriage. The Bible does not place any special premium upon remaining celibate. By the same token it attaches no special merit to marriage as over against celibacy. Just as sex, although good by creation, must be subjected to the claims of the neighbor under God, so the question of whether one will remain celibate or marry is to be decided in terms of man's primary responsibility to God. The answer to this question lies in one's vocation, understood as the summons to a life of faith and service. Neither celibacy nor marriage has virtue in itself but only in relationship to one's total calling. Moreover, as Paul recognizes, both celibacy and marriage are gifts, and some should not try to be celibate just as some should not marry (I Cor. 7:7). Roman Catholicism as well as Protestantism recognizes the validity of the latter insight although Catholicism, unlike Protestantism, attaches superior merit to celibacy as a "counsel of perfection."

From the standpoint of Protestantism, the ideal of celibacy in itself is a negative one, and as such it is basically egocentric. Insofar as it stems out of the desire to gain some merit for the self by remaining aloof from the world, it is an expression of ingratitude and lack of trust in God; moreover, it is not responsible to the Creator who has made man a sexual being and placed him in relation to other sexual beings. The Bible agrees at this point with those psychiatrists who insist upon the unhealthiness of the *repression* of sexual desire, although it strongly rejects the view of many of the same psychiatrists who do not see that it is possible to sublimate the sexual impulses and integrate these energies into the larger pattern of a disciplined life of devotion to some end or goal accepted and cherished by the total self.[29] Celibacy is desirable and becomes possible when devotion to something else demands it, but the primary loyalty is to that for the sake of which one is celibate—e.g., to a life of study, to certain types of ministry, or to nursing under particular circumstances—not to celibacy *per se*.

The second form of sex life which is considered responsible in Christianity is, as we have already noted, monogamous marriage. This concept implies that sexual relations are to be strictly limited to one's married partner. Moreover, in the Christian view, such marriage

---

[29] In this connection it is interesting to note that, although Kinsey considers sublimation to be only "an academic possibility," the statistics he cites concerning the restraint of the sexual impulse among American males who attend college as compared with the relatively freer expression of this impulse in intercourse among males with a lower educational level, and the evidence which he offers to the effect that in any age and educational group the males who are "most actively connected with church activities are . . . the least active sexually" are strong indications of the actual success of sublimation in the lives of many people. See Kinsey *et al.*, *Sexual Behavior in the Human Male*, pp. 213, 347–351, 467–472.

should be a permanent, life-long union. According to Brunner, monogamy—not just marriage—is an order of creation. That it is the will of God is evidenced, he believes, by three main facts of experience: the irrevocable community created by the father-mother-child relationship, the long dependency of the child upon its parents for nurture and guidance, and the essentially monistic character of genuine natural love which resents "the intrusion of a third person" into the love relationship.[30] It is perhaps more accurate, however, to say that monogamy is an outgrowth of the deepening biblical conception of the dignity of woman and of her fundamental equality with man than to say that it is an order of creation in the sense of a natural law implicit in the created order and discernible by reason alone. Polygamy was, as George Thomas points out, "the institutional expression of the inequality of men and women, enabling a man to dispose of the lives of an indefinite number of women to suit his own pleasure or convenience."[31] Monogamy, on the other hand, is more in keeping with the Christian estimate of women; it is also better adapted than polygamy to meet the emotional needs of children.

Polygamy, however, is not a live alternative to monogamy in our society today. Therefore, our main concern is to examine the reasons why biblical faith condemns premarital and extramarital sexual intercourse and why it insists that marriage ought to be a life-long union. Few men in our society want two wives, and few women want two husbands at the same time, but a great many men and women reject the demands of genuine monogamy. Not only are both the norm of restricting sexual relations to one's married partner and the norm of permanency violated on a large scale in actual practice, but the validity of the norms themselves is frequently called into question on anthropological, sociological, and psychological grounds. Marriage ideals, it is argued, are the product of a particular culture; hence, they are relative to the culture which produces them. Due to the many and profound changes that have taken place in Western civilization in the last two hundred years, it is argued, the attempt to preserve the ideal of a permanent monogamous family, which arose in an agrarian society more than two thousand years ago, is futile. Moreover, such an attempt is said to be harmful because it demands restraint of the sexual impulse, and such restraint is considered psychologically unhealthy.

[30] Brunner, *op. cit.*, pp. 344–349.
[31] George F. Thomas, *Christian Ethics and Moral Philosophy*, New York, Charles Scribner's Sons, 1955, pp. 233–234.

In view of this fundamental challenge to the Christian concept of marriage, what can be said concerning the validity of this concept in our own day? Is it useless to try to preserve this institution? Is there some other form of relationship between the sexes that would offer a better possibility for the fulfillment of the meaning of sex? These are some of the questions which we must seek to answer. It will be futile to do so by citing isolated passages of Scripture in a legalistic way. Rather, we must, on the one hand, seek to understand the fundamental questions that are being raised in our own day concerning the validity of the Christian concept; and we must, on the other hand, seek to understand the inner meaning of the Christian concept as it is related to the universal and enduring character of human nature, including human sexuality. Unless there is a genuine recovery of this inner meaning of marriage, it is useless to expect the Christian ideal to capture the allegiance of the masses of young people in our own day; moreover, it will clearly be impossible for the richness of the ideal to be realized in actual marriages if its inner meaning is not understood. If there were to be a revival of authoritarian religion, there might be a recovery of the outward form of this ideal; but this in itself would fall far short of a realization of the positive meaning of marriage which is implicit in the Christian view and which is the basic reason for the existence of the institution of monogamy. It should be remembered that Christian faith protests as strongly as do anthropologists and sociologists against empty outward forms. Also, it protests as strongly against repression for repression's sake as do modern psychiatrists even of the Freudian school. But at the same time it insists that such is the nature of man and of the reality in which he lives that his true fulfillment can be found only in the recognition and acceptance of his nature as it is given to him and of the moral order in which he is placed.

In trying to discover the inner meaning of marriage one of the most important questions which we need to ask is, What is the basis of marriage as it is understood in Christianity? Is it love? Is it the vows of fidelity which the partners make to each other? Is it the common interests which a couple share and which enrich their companionship? If it is love, what is the meaning of this love? If it is fidelity, is this a conditional sort of thing so that one is bound to be faithful to the other only as long as the other remains faithful? If it is love or common interests, what happens when these no longer exist?

In his very incisive and illuminating discussion of marriage in *The Divine Imperative,* Brunner declares that "while marriage springs from love . . . its stability is based not on love but on fidelity."[32] Natural love is "an essential part of the order of marriage," and it is not right to marry without this kind of love. But a union which is based solely upon this subjective emotional feeling between two people does not constitute a true marriage. In addition to love there is an objective element in marriage which is even more essential to it, notwithstanding the fact that such a union is incomplete without both. "Marriage is not a natural occurrence, but a moral act based upon the foundation of a natural occurrence. Marriage does not consist in the mere fact that two persons feel that they are bound to each other in love, marriage only exists where the divine order of marriage is recognized as binding in itself, and when two people know that they are bound by it."[33] Marriage is recognized as a divine order because it is seen to be the institutional structure in which the sexual relationships between men and women can best be fulfilled. As a structure which is so peculiarly adapted to meet the sexual needs of human beings who were created with these needs, marriage is an "order of creation"; it represents the intent of the Creator.

To recognize marriage as a sacred institution that is ordained of God and designates an objective structure of existence is to recognize that the act of entering into matrimony places a great responsibility upon one. It is to recognize that far more is involved in the relationship that is to be established than the subjective individual feelings of two people. Hence, the partners to a marriage join in making vows of fidelity to each other; and it is the mutually and publicly recognized obligation to be faithful to each other that provides the basis, according to Brunner, for permanency and stability in marriage. A union that is based upon natural love alone is, as it were, built upon sand; fidelity "enhances natural love" and makes it an act of the personal will. Unless there is recognition of such an obligation to be faithful to one's partner, sexual union—whether in marriage or outside of it— simply means that one person "makes use" of the other, even though this use may be mutual and willed by both parties. Under such circumstances the sex relationship "remains subpersonal, the enjoyment of the other, not identification with the other. It is not the *eros,* but

---

[32] Brunner, *op. cit.,* p. 357.
[33] *Ibid.*

solely the responsibility of fidelity, which creates that bond which means that one is bound to the other person."[34]

Without the mutual recognition by the partners in marriage of their responsibility to and for each other, there is no adequate basis for the total commitment of one to the other such as is implied in the Christian understanding of sex. Without fidelity, there is no adequate basis for entering wholeheartedly into the building of a life-long companionship which so deeply affects the whole self as does the sexual relationship when it is fully understood; for, although natural love may "intend" to be permanent, there is always the danger that it may not be so. Hence, a marriage that is based solely upon romantic love is inevitably accompanied by the fear that such love may fade and that the marriage itself may be dissolved. Moreover, entering into marriage upon the basis of natural love alone frequently makes it impossible for such a union to be a genuine one because either one or both of the partners may be entering it on the provisional basis that if it should prove unsatisfactory he can dissolve it and contract another "trial" marriage. Such relationships have little chance of proving "satisfactory" because they lack the most essential element in marriage, namely, recognition of the obligation to be faithful.

While Brunner on occasion seems to read too much specific content into the "orders of creation" with the result that he sometimes confuses the word of man (or culture) with the Word of God, he nevertheless has probed deeply into the meaning of human sexuality. He has demonstrated the inadequacy of legalism and authoritarianism in dealing with sex and marriage, and he has set the problems pertaining to these relationships in the context of a dynamic understanding of man's encounter with the living will of the Creator and Redeemer who constantly confronts man in all of his sexual and marital relationships. Brunner's contention that monogamy is itself an order of creation and that "normally the external guidance of family life belongs to the husband"[35] may be open to the charges of ethnocentrism and male pride; but his emphases upon the importance of fidelity, upon the personal character of the sexual relationship, and upon the concern of the community with and for marriage stem out of a profound insight into the nature of man and the inner meaning of human sexuality in particular.

Although Brunner is correct in emphasizing fidelity as the stabiliz-

[34] *Ibid.,* p. 348.
[35] *Ibid.,* p. 380.

ing element in marriage, he makes the dichotomy between love and fidelity too sharp. As D. S. Bailey points out,[36] Brunner is unable to keep these concepts nearly as distinct as he implies that they are. Without defining what he means by "love," he uses the term to refer primarily to a subjective feeling of attraction of a man for a woman and of a woman for a man. In view of the personal character of human sexual relationships it seems doubtful, however, that *genuine* natural love is ever completely limited to this bond between two people; for the sexual relationship involves whole persons who, although they may not be fully aware of their grandeur and their misery, are nevertheless aware that more than their bodies are being joined together in the sex act. The biological relationship is accompanied, however disproportionate the role assigned to it, by other relationships which are interwoven with it. Hence, genuine natural love demands for its fulfillment some fidelity or faithfulness.

Bailey speaks of three kinds of love that are found in the total love-relationship: *eros, philia,* and *agape.* These three kinds of love correspond to three different relations that are involved in every such relationship, and all three are always found together. Sometimes one and sometimes another is dominant, but the three are indistinguishably intermingled. All genuine sexual love—as distinguished from passion—contains an element of *eros,* or the desire to possess the beloved because of his or her objective value.[37] True natural *eros* is not limited exclusively to the sexual life, and it does not diminish with the passing of the sexual impulse; rather, it is directed to the whole person of the beloved and desires "above all the establishment of a permanent and meaningful union" with the beloved. Similarly, in all genuine love there is an element of *philia,* or the love of mutual friendship. Such love stems, most obviously, out of common interests or common concerns which form the basis of such friendship. Finally, there is in all genuine love an element of *agape,* or altruistic self-giving, which places the good of the beloved first in the relationship. *Eros* and *philia* are not replaced by *agape;* rather, the former are "controlled and enriched" by the latter, which permeates every aspect of the total relationship.[38]

[36] Cf. D. S. Bailey, *The Mystery of Love and Marriage,* New York, Harper & Brothers, 1952, p. 21.

[37] *Ibid.,* pp. 25–26.

[38] *Ibid.,* p. 27. Cf. Paul Tillich, *Love, Power, and Justice,* New York, Oxford University Press, 1954, p. 33.

Summarizing the complementary character of these qualities of all genuine love between persons of the opposite sexes, Bailey writes:

> None of the three kinds of love just described is confined solely to one aspect of the love relation; *eros* cannot be limited to the sphere of sexual activity and the physical relation; for although it is certainly felt very strongly as sexual desire, yet it may also seek mental and spiritual satisfaction from the beloved; *philia* must find, among others, both sexual and religious expression; and *agape* pervades the relation as a whole. Each has its contribution to make to the fulness of love. But balance and proportion between the different constituents of love is not automatic, and is usually attained only with that persistent effort which is one of the joys and responsibilities which lovers share. It is the purpose of *agape* to secure and preserve a due balance by establishing a true objectivity. *Eros* can never be disinterested, and even *philia* by a subtle transformation may become *eros* rationalized or disguised. Without *agape* as the controlling, conditioning, and directing factor, sexual love would be in danger of lapsing into anarchy, and would cease to be a true mode of personal relation.[39]

One may speak of one or the other of these three kinds of love as having an ethically or spiritually higher value than another, but this does not mean that one kind is more important than the other. Each "is itself a distinct mode of relation making its own unique and necessary contribution to the total experience, and, without all there in due balance, the relation is defective."[40]

If love is thus understood in terms of the different kinds of *personal* relationships that are involved in it, one may say with Berdyaev that "love is the ontological basis of the marriage union."[41] This does not necessarily conflict with Brunner's contention that fidelity rather than romantic love is the basis of its stability; rather, it constitutes a recognition of the fact that genuine, human love—that is, love between *persons* who are aware of their nature and destiny as personal, spiritual beings—implies the claim of fidelity. This is not a claim that is added when a couple make a pledge to each other that they will be mutually faithful. Indeed, genuine love implies fidelity in premarital relationships as well as in marital ones. The love-experience is a continuous one, and marriage is only the continuation and development

[39] Bailey, *op. cit.*, p. 28.
[40] *Ibid.*, p. 30. Cf. Tillich *op. cit.*, pp. 27 ff.
[41] Berdyaev, *op. cit.*, p. 239.

of a relationship that was begun earlier when two lovers were drawn to each other and accepted their "vocation" to become united in a growing and deepening union of their selves one with the other.[42]

To refer to the purpose which they see in their mutual attraction as a "vocation" does not mean that one lover was created for the other and can truly love only that one person; rather, it means that through the God-given sexual attraction they are drawn to each other, and it means also that they recognize that as persons they are responsible to God for each other and for whatever union they establish. They see in their spontaneous, unwilled attraction for each other a God-given opportunity for the establishment of a sacred union, and they accept—by an act of the will—responsibility for this union. But only if sexual attraction is accompanied by a vision of the "potential perfection" of the beloved—a vision of what the beloved by God's grace may become as he or she grows and finds the fulfillment of his or her God-given capacities and endowments—only then do two persons have a right to consent to the sexual impulse in intercourse which affects both at such a deep and irretrievable level. "Where the vision is wanting there is no true love and therefore no inwardly valid 'one flesh' union."[43]

The term "one flesh" or *henosis,* is the expression which is generally used in the Bible to designate the union which is instituted by sexual intercourse. The creation of this union, it is recognized, is a sacred summons or vocation. "Therefore a man leaves his father and mother and cleaves to his wife, and they become one flesh" (Gen. 2:24). In his teaching on divorce Jesus refers to this purpose of God for man and woman as evidenced in the creation of man as a sexual being, and he makes this the basis of the permanency of the marriage relationship. " 'And the two shall become one.' So they are no longer two but one. What therefore God has joined together, let not man put asunder" (Mark 10:6–9). Paul implies that any act of sexual intercourse results in a "one flesh" union: "Do you not know that he who joins himself to a prostitute becomes one body with her?" (I Cor. 6:16). Piper and Bailey follow this interpretation. Piper declares, for example, that "every coition institutes an indissoluble unity between two persons."[44]

While Bailey concedes that "sexual intercourse always establishes

---

[42] Bailey, *op. cit.,* p. 37.
[43] *Ibid.,* p. 19.
[44] Piper, *op. cit.,* p. 138.

a 'one flesh' union", he recognizes that all such unions do not have the same meaning. Hence he distinguishes between three forms of "one flesh" relationships.[45] In the first place, there is the "true, authentic *henosis*" which is instituted by intercourse which follows consent of both partners and which is based upon responsible love and has the approval of the community. In the second place, there is the "false, invalid" *henosis* which is effected by prostitution or adultery. And, finally, there are what Bailey refers to as "defective" unions which have no foundation in love or which, because of some psychical maladjustment, represent a level of personal relation that "falls considerably below the ideal implied by 'one flesh.' " Bailey recognizes that there are cases such as the seduction of the young or the feeble-minded and rape where Paul's principle was not meant to be applied and where it is inapplicable, for the "mere occurrence of the sexual act without consent, desire or understanding" cannot make two persons "one body." But, whenever a man and a woman enter freely into the sexual relation, "their intercourse always makes them in some sense 'one flesh.' "[46]

Sexual love seeks its fulfillment in the "one flesh" union which is instituted by sexual intercourse. Genuine love finds its highest and most significant expression in this *henosis*. Love is the basis of this union, and as such it is also the ontological basis of marriage. A genuine "one flesh" union is impossible without love (*eros, philia,* and *agape*), and a marriage is not a real marriage unless there is a genuine "oneness." Where the vocation to become "one flesh" is accepted, there true marriage exists in principle;[47] and it ought to be possible for those who are of age and have accepted such a vocation to marry and fulfill their purpose of "becoming one" by expressing their union more fully. It must be recognized, however, that social and economic considerations frequently make this impossible under the present circumstances of our society; and lovers who are aware of the seriousness and reseponsibility of the sex relationship, including the extent of their involvement in the life of the community and the claim which the latter makes upon them, ought to postpone such completion of the

---

[45] Bailey, *op. cit.,* p. 52

[46] *Ibid.,* p. 53.

[47] As Brunner points out, law and custom do not create a marriage, and even Christian marriage is independent of the blessing of the church. The consent of the state and the blessing of the church make a marriage more complete, but they do not make it more real. Brunner, *op. cit.,* p. 359. Cf. Piper, *op. cit.,* p. 168.

"one flesh" union until marriage becomes possible. It is encouraging to note that in some respects the social and economic pattern of our society is undergoing improvement at this point. It is much easier now than formerly, for example, for young people who genuinely desire to marry to find ways of meeting the economic needs attendant upon the establishment of a marriage and the completion of the college and professional training of the husband; moreover, our society no longer frowns upon the practice of both husband and wife being gainfully employed to meet the family needs, particularly in the first years of marriage.

In view of the widespread attack upon the Christian condemnation of premarital intercourse as arbitrary, "unnatural," and even harmful, it is important to make as clear as possible the reasons why Christianity condemns this form of sexual relationship as irresponsible. The validity of this position is not essentially affected by the lessening of the dangers of disease or by the increased effectiveness of contraceptives, although, in the past, major stress has often been laid upon the dangers of venereal disease and pregnancy. Even more basic reasons, however, are implicit in what has been said about the Christian interpretation of sex and marriage, for the latter constitute the theological basis for premarital sexual continence. The basic arguments for such continence are rooted in the effects of indulgence upon the persons involved. Taken together, the consequences of premarital sexual intercourse show that it is inconsistent with genuine love and that it endangers the true fulfillment of such love in marriage.

In the first place, premarital intercourse results in the habit of exploiting others for one's own pleasure, and as a result it "hardens the arteries of tender feeling." The person who decides "to get all he can out of sex . . . is driven into an almost endless progression" of searching for new conquests and forms of sexual experience because each proves unsatisfying. Such a person loses the sympathy and tender feelings which are essential accompaniments of genuine love and without which sexual relations are meaningless.[48]

In the second place, premarital intercourse makes the attainment of a harmonious and happy sexual adjustment within marriage more difficult. A person who is accustomed to thinking of his sexual partner primarily as a means for his own enjoyment will have a difficult time "meeting a new situation in which his highest nature wants expression

---

[48] Thomas, *op. cit.,* pp. 240–241; Bertocci, *op. cit.,* p. 47. Cf. Bergler and Kroger, *op. cit.,* pp. 25, 43–44.

for the sake of his beloved."[49] Moreover, past associations and images, previous adjustment to certain modes of response, and feelings of guilt and insecurity, all of which a person with such experience brings to a marriage, make it more difficult to build a genuine oneness out of the relationship of two persons each of whom is psychologically and emotionally unique. Indeed, for these reasons, premarital sexual intercourse, instead of making a harmonious sexual adjustment within marriage easier, "is itself frequently a cause of breaking up."[50]

In the third place, the practice of premarital intercourse makes it more difficult to maintain fidelity within marriage. A person who has not disciplined himself to practice continence prior to marriage will find it difficult to practice sexual restraint at those times when it may be necessary within marriage on account of illness or enforced separation. Moreover, one who has not disciplined himself to forgo the satisfaction of an immediate desire for the sake of a long-range good will also find it difficult to resist the sexual appeal of especially attractive members of the opposite sex whom he is likely occasionally to encounter.

Closely related to this last consideration is a fourth reason for premarital abstinence. Genuine love in married life presupposes mutual confidence, and this grows in large part out of the conviction that one's partner has controlled and can control his sexual impulses. Such confidence, or trust, is essential for the emotional security which is prerequisite to the total giving of the self to another which is implicit in the sexual relationship when it brings the largest measure of fulfillment and satisfaction. The basis for such confidence is strengthened—especially between couples who contemplate marriage—by the help which each has been able to give the other in the form of sympathy, encouragement, and firmness in finding the ability to control sexual desires prior to marriage.[51]

In the fifth place, it should be remembered that there is no absolutely effective contraceptive and that for this reason a couple who engage in premarital intercourse always run a chance, however small, of bringing children into the world. Children that are born under such circumstances are far less likely to receive that which they need most, namely, love and emotional security, for they are unwanted at the outset at least because they threaten the security and peace of the parents.

---

[49] Bertocci, *op. cit.*, p. 70.
[50] *Ibid.*, p. 74. Cf. Bergler and Kroger, *op. cit.*, pp. 25, 43–44.
[51] Bertocci, *op. cit.*, pp. 71–72.

Moreover, the fear of possible pregnancy weighs especially upon the woman so that it is difficult if not impossible for her to enter whole-heartedly into the relationship. Such fear of pregnancy frequently creates an additional barrier which has to be overcome in marriage.

Finally, it should not be forgotten that premarital intercourse has disintegrating effects upon the personalities of those who participate in it; for it increases the hold of sexual desire, it tends to weaken human creativity, and it contributes to the undermining of one's moral integrity and character. It also contributes to the development of feelings of guilt, anxiety, fear, and hostility, all of which furnish fertile soil for the development of various forms of neurosis. One participant in premarital relationships also shares the responsibility for the development of these traits in one's partner as well as in oneself.

For all of these reasons, then, it is evident that a couple who engage in premarital intercourse are not truly expressing their love. They are, rather, violating the dignity of themselves and endangering the future expression of their love within the structure of marriage where alone it can find adequate and complete manifestation and fulfillment.

In describing the Christian view of marriage thus far, we have spoken primarily of the intent of the Creator as evidenced in the sexual nature of man and in the intent of the Judge who has set man in a moral order which he violates only at the cost of many different kinds of penalties which he must pay for his selfishness and his sensuality. It remains now to indicate briefly the way in which God the Redeemer is encountered in marriage. According to Roman Catholicism, matrimony is a sacrament and as such it constitutes a means of grace, providing divine aid to those who receive it in leading a Christian life within the state of marriage. While Protestants generally do not consider it to be a sacrament, they nevertheless consider marriage to be sacramental in the sense that it may become a means of grace, not through the performance of a rite, but through the opportunities and encouragement which "the holy estate" itself affords those who enter it to grow in grace and love and the virtues pertaining to personal and social life. The community of the family is the one group in which such virtues and graces as patience and forgiveness are most effectively nourished and shared. It is in the family that man is most fully redeemed from his isolation and loneliness into a genuine community of love and acceptance wherein each person has a true sense of belonging. It is in the family—in the relationships of husband and wife, of parents and children, and of children with each other—that *eros* becomes most effectively transformed by *agape* in daily relationships wherein forgiveness, vicarious suffering, and the bearing of one another's burdens are nurtured by mutual dependence, a deep sense of gratitude, and the natural ties of kinship.

In a masterly survey of what Christians have said about "sex, love, and marriage," Professor Roland Bainton describes three main attitudes toward marriage which have characterized different groups and different periods: the sacramental, the romantic, and the companionable.[52] He uses the term "sacramental view" to refer to both the Roman Catholic and the Protestant positions insofar as both stress the religious nature of the relationship as requiring an exclusive, lifetime commitment. According to this view, marriage has two purposes: propagation and serving "as a remedy for sin" by restricting the gratification of passion to wedlock. This is the earliest of the Christian views, and it is basic to the other two.

The romantic view of marriage regards love between the sexes as ennobling, and falling in love is considered a prerequisite to marriage. The view of love which is associated with this concept of marriage first arose in the secular courts of love in France toward the end of the eleventh century.[53] At first this courtly love was a cult of adultery, but during the Renaissance the ideal of romantic love was taken over into marriage by the Church, and thus it added refinement and tenderness to the Christian view. The meaning of this change was not that people now began to fall in love for the first time in history but rather that now for the first time romantic love was given a new status and dignity.[54] It was considered ennobling, because the beloved was considered superior to the lover and bestowed something of her own worth upon her lover. This resulted in the idealization of women and required a certain humility on the part of man. A man must never take his conquest for granted; he must continually engage in courting his beloved. The incorporation of this view into Christian marriage meant that women received a higher status and the emotional needs of men and women were given more adequate recognition as the work of the Creator. The danger, on the other hand, was that this view by itself tended to make the marital union unstable.

The companionable view of marriage places the emphasis upon "a

---

[52] Bainton, *op. cit.*, pp. 16–19.
[53] See C. S. Lewis, *The Allegory of Love*, Oxford, The Clarendon Press, 1936.
[54] Bainton, *op. cit.*, p. 58.

partnership in a common set of ideals and aspirations and a common endeavor."[55] Such a partnership may center around children or the service of the Church or, in its secular forms, around common tastes and interests such as music, art, or golf. Such common concerns enrich marriage, but a relationship built upon them alone is relatively unstable.

Professor Bainton's analysis of the teachings of the Church on marriage indicate the extent to which Christians have from the beginning seen it as a means of saving men and women from the grossest and most destructive forms of sexual sin.[56] But the emphasis upon the value of marriage as a "remedy for sin" is essentially negative and obscures the positive purpose of the Creator. It partially recognizes the will of the Redeemer in regard to sinful man, but it does not take sufficient account of the goodness of the resources which the Creator has given man for meeting his genuine needs.[57] The attitude of Jesus toward sex, like that of the Old Testament as a whole, is more positive than this concept suggests. Jesus' understanding of the depth and pervasiveness of man's lust was as great as that of Paul and the early Church, but he nowhere implied that marriage and the sexual relations which are attendant thereto are on a morally lower level than celibacy or that permission to engage in the latter in itself represents a concession on account of the hardness of men's hearts.

There is of course implicit in Paul's conception of *agape,* or Christian love, a more positive understanding of the manner in which love redeems and restores and fulfills all human relationships than is actually spelled out in what he has to say about sex and marriage themselves. Such love never fails. At times Paul glimpsed the positive fulfillment—not just "the restraint"—that comes in Christian marriage (cf. Eph. 5:25–6:4). But Paul's eschatological expectations and the early Church's asceticism kept them from giving proper attention to the positive fulfillment of the sex relationship in marriage understood as an order of creation which, although corrupted by sin, is not meant to be relegated to the status of a secondary good but rather to be purified and restored. Recognition of a proper place for romantic love and of the need for common interests represents a fuller appreciation

[55] *Ibid.,* p. 18.
[56] Cf. I Corinthians 7:9, 36–38.
[57] Cf. Roberts, *op. cit.,* p. 92: "Some of the derangement which goes into sin has been due, not to the fact that man has tried to save himself, but to the fact that his religion has taught him to regard as liabilities what are actually latent assets."

of the positive will of the Creator and the Redeemer for sexual beings who need fulfillment and redemption in their sexual relationships as elsewhere. Here also the Redeemer is at work in the relationships which He has ordained between husband and wife, between parents and children, and among children in the home.

DIVORCE AND REMARRIAGE

According to the Christian teaching, it is intended by the Creator that marriage should be a life-long union. In reply to the question of the Pharisees as to whether it was lawful for a man to divorce his wife, Jesus asked what Moses had said upon this subject. They answered that Moses had permitted a man to write a certificate of divorce and put his wife away. Whereupon Jesus replied that the Mosaic rule represented a concession to the hardness of men's hearts and as such it ran counter to the will of God. "But from the beginning of creation, 'God made them male and female. For this reason a man shall leave his father and mother and be joined to his wife, and the two shall become one.' . . . What therefore God has joined together, let not man put asunder" (Mark 10:2–9). He added by way of explanation to his disciples, "Whoever divorces his wife and marries another, commits adultery against her, and if she divorces her husband and marries another, she commits adultery" (Mark 10:11–12). Thus, according to Mark, Jesus spoke of all divorce without exception as being a violation of God's will. According to the Matthean account, however, he permitted a single exception to this requirement, namely, divorce "on the ground of unchastity" (Matt. 5:32; 19:9). New Testament scholars are generally agreed that Mark's version reflects the original teaching of Jesus more accurately than does the Matthean account, which probably represented a later effort to adjust an extremely difficult requirement of Jesus to the hardness of men's hearts in the latter part of the first century A.D.

The question inevitably arises, therefore, whether divorce is ever permissible for the Christian. On the face of the matter, Jesus seems to be giving an absolute law here, but to interpret his teaching on this subject as a piece of legislation that is binding in its literal form upon all of his followers is to interpret it in a manner that is foreign to his usual method of teaching. His primary criticism of the Pharisees, it will be recalled, was directed against their legalism. But if we do not assume that Jesus was laying down such a requirement for all of his followers, how are we to interpret this "hard saying"?

In the first place, Jesus was concerned with making clear the eternal will of God, not with formulating a code of laws for his followers. "Who made me a judge or divider over you?", he asked on another occasion (Luke 12:14). In his reply to the Pharisees he wasn't interested either in justifying or in condemning Moses' legislation on divorce as a practical measure. Rather, he was intent upon making clear the divine will with regard to marriage. It must be remembered that Jesus lived in a society where women had relatively few rights. In marriage they were largely at the mercy of their husbands. It was the husband who took the initiative in securing a divorce. And according to the school of Hillel, which took an extremely liberal attitude in interpreting the Mosaic law, a man might divorce his wife for such a trivial thing as burning his dinner. Another school of interpretation of the Law—that of Shammai—was far more strict and held that only in the case of actual unfaithfulness could a man put away his wife. Jesus simply refused to participate in this kind of legal disputation. Instead, he placed the question of the Pharisees in its ultimate context of man's relation to the perfect will of God. In the words of A. D. Lindsay, Jesus was "in effect saying, 'Moses set some limits to your right to regard women as your property and to get rid of them when you are tired of them or have no further use for them or when they are childless. Moses said there must be a certain amount of decency about it. You must give them a writing of divorcement. But I say *the whole thing is wrong*. You have under no circumstances a right to dispose of women in that way, whatever the excuse may be.' "[58]

Jesus' categorical prohibition of divorce performs the function, then, of exposing men's need for forgiveness and summoning them to repent and accept the divine forgiveness. Such forgiveness does not serve merely as a balm to soothe the uneasy conscience; rather, it is the creative power of God coming into human life and opening up unlimited possibilities of creative and redemptive action to the repentant and forgiven sinner. This surely is the significance of Jesus' new definition of adultery: "But I say to you that every one who looks at a woman lustfully has already committed adultery with her in his heart" (Matt. 5:28). Obviously, he was not here seeking to broaden the grounds for divorce; rather, he was pointing to lust—i.e., to the desire to use another person as a means to one's own sexual gratification—as the root evil in man's sexual life. Clearly all men stand under the judgment of the Creator at this point, for all are guilty of the lustful

[58] A. D. Lindsay, *The Moral Teaching of Jesus*, New York, Harper & Brothers Publishers, 1937, p. 164. Italics added.

glance. But such precepts are more than standards by which human conduct is judged; they are also "guideposts" pointing the way men must travel in seeking to be children of their Father in heaven.

In the light, then, of Jesus' unambiguous teaching about the permanence of marriage as representing the will of the Creator, are we to conclude that it is never God's will that actual marriage in the sinful here and now be dissolved? May there not be marriages which are recognized by church and state but which do not represent "what . . . God has joined together"? Both church and state, for example, recognize certain conditions which may annul a marriage. The Roman Catholic Church recognizes many such circumstances, but it does not recognize divorce. Or, what if man has already "put asunder" those whom God has joined together? Indeed, how does man put them asunder? Only by the severing of an external tie? Or may those who are still united by an outward bond be in fact so far separated spiritually that the marriage itself is in actuality already broken?

As we have seen, marriage in the Christian sense is based upon fidelity and implies a "one flesh" union. Moreover, Christians recognize that they are incapable of fulfilling the will of God for their marriage without the aid of divine grace in forgiveness and renewal. Although an irrevocable bond is established by intercourse, the achievement of a genuine "one flesh" union involves a deepening of this bond. The realization of this goal requires time, patience, effort, and all that is implied by fidelity and love. If such an union were to take place to the point of perfect fidelity and perfect love that was mutually shared, it would doubtless endure, but in a sinful world actual marriages always fall somewhat short of this ideal. This is why Christians recognize the need for forgiveness and grace. These are powerful and creative resources for aiding those who are aware of their sin and weaknesses. But when such a "one flesh" union as has been possible becomes dissolved—as it sometimes does—through the failure of love understood in its threefold meaning of *eros, philia,* and *agape,* then the marriage itself has failed; it no longer has any inner meaning.

Since only the failure of love can cause the dissolution of the "one flesh" union, it ought, according to Bailey, "strictly speaking, to constitute the sole and sufficient ground of divorce."[59] But, while this is true with regard to the inner meaning of the relationship, Bailey recognizes that the community could never admit this as a ground for

[59] Bailey, *op. cit.,* p. 80.

divorce because it would be too hard to verify and too open to abuse. The recognition of this inward test of the reality of the marriage union should, however, serve as a warning against smugness and pride, for all fall short of the divine will. Countless more marriages are broken in this sense than ever reach the divorce courts, and obviously those which end in divorce were broken before the idea of getting a divorce ever seriously occurred to either party. From the standpoint of God's eternal will, all persons who are parties to such inwardly broken unions are *de facto* "put asunder."

On the other hand, society ought not to enact the absolute prohibition of divorce into a civil law binding upon Christians and non-Christians alike. "The worth of a law," as Brunner points out, "is to be measured not by its 'strictness' in the absolute sense, but by the wisdom with which the legislation is adjusted to reality, in order to attain a maximum of social health and decency."[60] If marriage laws are made excessively strict, they tend to encourage infidelity, untruthfulness, and even the deliberate commission of those acts which are admitted as reasons justifying divorce. The achievement of the Christian ideal in marriage is dependent upon a vital Christian faith, and it is both impractical and uncharitable to attempt to force those who do not hold that faith to accept the Christian ideal *in toto*. Indeed, it is also impractical and uncharitable to try to enforce it upon Christians themselves, for that which can be enforced by law is not the genuine, permanent, monogamous union but only an external form.

If society should neither admit the disintegration of the "one flesh" union as the one legitimate ground for divorce nor prohibit divorce entirely, it is thrown back upon the necessity of trying to discover under the particular conditions of a particular day and age what causes should be recognized as grounds for divorce, and it should do this by giving attention not only to the desires of the husband and wife but also to the emotional needs of the children involved and to the need of society itself for decency and stability. Just as marriage is not solely a matter of concern between two parties, so divorce does not concern only two people. The community is interested in the health of the family in general—not specifically in its conformity to the Christian ideal, but in the way in which its welfare affects the physical, intellectual, and moral growth of children; in the way it affects juvenile delinquency and adult crime; and in the way in which its integrity affects the moral life of the community as a whole. Here, as elsewhere, the

[60] Brunner, *op. cit.*, p. 363.

only absolute command which the Christian is required to follow in his effort to formulate the best civil laws is the command to love the neighbor.

Not only ought society to make provision for the granting of divorces under certain carefully examined circumstances, but individual Christians are also faced with the question as to whether they are forbidden under every circumstance to divorce their marriage partners. Does God under all circumstances require them above everything else to maintain their own marriages? In reply it needs to be emphasized that, in view of the divine will, every divorce regardless of its "cause" represents a failure of marriage. Divorce is a "concession to human weakness"[61]—that is, to human sin. Moreover, despite what is said in the divorce proceedings, it is almost always the case that both parties contribute to the breakdown of the marriage union. Hence, divorce is a concession to the weakness of both, but "cases are possible," as Brunner declares, "where not to divorce might be a sign of greater weakness, and might be a still greater offence against the Divine order."[62] However, in the attempt to decide whether, under the particular circumstances God wills a particular divorce, one must guard against such legalistic considerations as are common in civil law, including adultery. In itself adultery as a crude physical act need not present an insurmountable obstacle to restoring a genuine union. Here again the Christian must be guided by love, and that means by a sense of responsibility for one's mate and for the children involved in one's marriage. But from the standpoint of Christian ethics there is little to be said for maintaining the outward shell of a marriage when its inner meaning is gone and when love in its threefold relationship has disappeared, so that there is no real basis for rebuilding it, unless other more positive considerations make the preservation of the marriage a work of love.

Once a place for divorce is recognized, the question of remarriage of divorced persons is raised almost immediately; for divorced people want to remarry for much the same reasons that those who have never been married desire to marry for the first time. But, in view of the Christian conception of marriage as a life-long union, are couples who have obtained a civil divorce free to enter a new marriage, and should such remarriages be accorded the blessing of the church?

Many Protestant groups permit only the "innocent" party to a di-

[61] *Ibid.,* p. 362.
[62] *Ibid.*

vorce to remarry, but such a position is open to serious question on at least two grounds. In the first place, the assumption that one party is wholly innocent is entirely unrealistic in a relationship that is as intimate as marriage. And in the second place, the administration of such a law makes adulterers judge between adulterers, for according to the Christian view the lustful glance is essentially as evil as the outward act, and all are adulterers in this sense. A much more realistic approach to this matter of remarriage of the divorced would be, as Bailey suggests, to permit it for the repentant and only for the repentant.[63]

If reconciliation with one's former partner is impossible, it is highly legalistic to deny a person the right to enter a second marriage, provided there is indication that such a person seriously intends to establish a Christian union and provided also that there is sincere repentance for the causes which brought about the disintegration of the first union. When these conditions are genuinely met, the possibility is opened up for the making of a successful Christian marriage, for such a person is in a position to draw upon the resources of Christian faith, especially the divine forgiveness and love, to sustain the new union from the beginning and constantly heal such divisions as may develop as the marriage progresses. The final word of God, it should not be forgotten, is not judgment but redemption and renewal, and a second marriage may witness to this renewal.

What has been said does not mean that the Christian ideal of permanent marriage should be given up. It means rather that, given a broken marriage in a sinful world, the Christian is absolutely required only to love God and neighbor and that this love may lead him, in repentance and trust in the divine forgiveness and renewal, to seek a second marriage. It means also that for others, including the Church, to fail to take into account the human needs of the divorced—their biological and emotional needs, their need for fulfillment, the fact that it also is "not good that they should be alone"—is to treat them as "cases" rather than as persons. This failure in itself betrays a spirit of smugness and complacency that ill becometh those who claim to be motivated by Christian *agape*.

[63] Bailey, *op. cit.*, pp. 95–96. Cf. James A. Pike, *Doing the Truth,* Garden City, New York, Doubleday & Company, 1955, pp. 163–164.

THE SOCIAL CONTEXT OF THE FAMILY

In our discussion of the Christian views of sex and marriage we have referred to various social and cultural forces that have deeply affected the traditional patterns of Christian sex and marital relationships, but we have not said much about the extent to which society facilitates or impedes the realization of the essential Christian ideals in these areas. We have spoken of the primary importance of the family as a social institution, but little has been said about the way in which Christians can help make it easier to have Christian homes by bringing about changes in society in general—in the economic order, in the scale of values in a community as a whole, in the elimination of discrimination and the alleviation of racial tension, in the provision of more adequate recreational facilities and counselling services, in the kinds of divorce laws that a state adopts, in the prevailing attitude of society toward religion, and in the quality of the sex education and education for marriage which are provided in the schools. The list could be extended indefinitely. Christian ethics is vitally concerned with all of these aspects of society, and all of them help to determine the extent to which the realization of the Christian ideal in sex and marriage relationships is a genuine possibility. Moreover, in all of these areas Christian ethics is dependent upon the specialized knowledge and skills of the social sciences for the empirical data which it needs in the formulation of specific policies. For example, it is dependent upon sociological and psychological data in its search for the best divorce laws for a particular society at a particular time and in the development of strategy for preventing juvenile delinquency and reducing racial tension.

This is not, however, the place to develop all of these relationships between the family and society at large. Our primary concern at this point is to indicate the close connection which exists between personal and social Christian ethics even in the area of sex and the family. This fact will become clearer in our subsequent discussions of the economic and political life as well as in our study of race relations.

RECOMMENDED READINGS

Bailey, D. S., *The Mystery of Love and Marriage*, New York, Harper & Brothers, 1952.

Bainton, Roland H., *What Christianity Says About Sex, Love and Marriage,* New York, Association Press, 1957.

Bertocci, Peter A., *The Human Venture in Sex, Love, and Marriage,* New York, Association Press, 1949, ch. 2.

Brunner, Emil, *The Divine Imperative,* trans. by Olive Wyon, New York, The Macmillan Company, 1942, chs. XXXI, XXXII.

Cole, William Graham, *Sex in Christiantiy and Psychoanalysis,* New York, Oxford University Press, 1955.

Doniger, Simon, ed., *Sex and Religion Today,* New York, Association Press, 1953.

Geddes, Donald Porter, ed., *An Analysis of the Kinsey Reports on Sexual Behavior in the Human Male and Female,* New York, E. P. Dutton & Co., 1954.

Hiltner, Seward, *Sex and the Christian Life,* New York, Association Press, 1957.

Hiltner, Seward, *Sex Ethics and the Kinsey Reports,* New York, Association Press, 1953.

McCann, Richard V., *Delinquency: Sickness or Sin?* New York, Harper & Brothers, 1957.

Miller, Haskell M., *Understanding and Preventing Juvenile Delinquency,* New York, Abingdon Press, 1958.

Piper, Otto A., *The Christian Interpretation of Sex,* New York, Charles Scribner's Sons, 1941.

Roberts, David E., *Psychotherapy and a Christian View of Man,* New York, Charles Scribner's Sons, 1950, ch. IX.

Trueblood, Elton and Trueblood, Pauline, *The Recovery of Family Life,* New York, Harper & Brothers, 1953.

chapter 9

LOVE AND JUSTICE

CHRISTIAN ETHICS BEYOND PERSONAL RELATIONSHIPS

THERE are a great many people who would agree that as Christians they ought to seek to practice the Christian ethic in their own personal sex and family relationships but would reject the idea that they have a responsibility to apply this ethic to the social structures within the context of which they as individuals must seek to be Christian. Hence, they would not recognize any obligation on their part as Christians to work for more just divorce laws, for the provision of more adequate services for families in need, for better housing, and for the alleviation of those socio-cultural conditions which contribute to such social evils as the exploitation of one race by another, sexual perversion, and the rise and perpetuation of juvenile delinquency.

Such people generally restrict the Christian's moral duty simply to the following of Jesus' specific ethical teachings and the imitation of his own example. Jesus, they say, didn't get involved in the political and economic struggles of his day—he wasn't concerned about Supreme Court decisions and Sputniks but with the practice of love in his dealings with his fellowmen. These folk find the heart of Christian ethics in the Sermon on the Mount, which becomes for them a new law replacing the old Mosaic law. Where Jesus speaks, they speak; and where he is silent, they are silent. They are quite pessimistic about the possibility of transforming culture. All forms of culture, they insist, are sinful, and the Christian can only hope to remain "in the world" without being "of the world." There is no possibility of improving the social order until at least a majority of people become genuinely Christian. Moreover, the use of law seems to them to be in conflict with love, and the pursuit of social justice through the appeal to law seems to be un-Christian.

For these believers, love is a "new law," and its meaning is spelled out in terms of the content of the specific sayings of Jesus and his specific example in the first-century Palestinian culture. Arguing from the silence of Jesus upon principles of social justice and from the fact that he himself was not a social reformer, they conclude that the Christian ethic has nothing constructive to say upon political, economic, and social issues. It has no witness here except that of the condemnation of politics, business, and society to the realm of evil and the summons to Christians to separate themselves from the evil that is implicit in these aspects of culture.[1]

The result of such an interpretation of Christian ethics is to restrict it to personal relationships and make it irrelevant to the basic social problems of the present day. This is true despite the fact that the advocates of this position fervently proclaim that "Christ is the answer" to these problems and that love alone is the path to true brotherhood and the Kingdom of God. It is worth noting that those who speak of Christian ethics as the imitation of Jesus' example and the literal following of his specific ethical counsel are generally quite selective in their choice of those aspects of his example and teachings which they follow, and generally dismiss other aspects as not binding upon men today. For instance, they do not ordinarily follow his example of celibacy and itinerant preaching or his craft as a carpenter, and they do not imitate his martyrdom. In the main, they do not follow his teaching concerning so-called "nonresistance" either in relation to military service or in relation to the use of courts of law. In these and many other important respects they recognize that they are not called to "follow in his steps" but rather to make new paths and walk in quite different ways.

Such an interpretation of Christian ethics ignores the eschatological setting of Jesus' life and teaching as well as the vast differences between our democratic society and the autocratic regime under which he lived. Jesus' apparent indifference to questions of social justice must be seen in the light of his conviction that the entire social

---

[1] H. Richard Niebuhr calls those who hold this interpretation of Christian ethics the "Christ-against-culture" Christians. For an admirable appraisal of this position see his *Christ and Culture*, New York, Harper & Brothers, 1951, ch. 2.

order would soon be completely overthrown and the Kingdom of God would soon be inaugurated. Jesus looked upon his own deeds as a sign that the Kingdom was already becoming manifest. Partly for this reason he did not address himself to the political and social problems of his day. Moreover, to have done so would have resulted in a misunderstanding on the part of his followers concerning the nature of his mission and the Kingdom which he proclaimed. It was not his vocation to be a social reformer but rather to proclaim the coming of the Kingdom and the necessity for repentance (cf. Mark 1:14–15).

There is another difficulty with this effort to restrict the concern of Christian ethics to personal relationships, namely, the impossibility of being neutral in regard to questions of social policy. The very effort to avoid becoming involved in political and economic and social issues inevitably results either in the support and strengthening of the *status quo,* which is recognized as unjust, or in the creation of a power vacuum into which some other group is more easily able to move. Injustice that goes unchecked tends to become increasingly unjust, and corrupt power that is not held accountable tends to become increasingly corrupt, so that those who try to maintain their innocence by neutrality must in actuality share the responsibility for the evils in society which they deplore.

In addition to the foregoing difficulties with this tendency to restrict Christian ethics to personal relationships and to interpret it in terms of a literal following of the teachings and example of Jesus, Professor H. Richard Niebuhr has pointed out a number of weaknesses in this position considered from the standpoint of the theological assumptions upon which it is based.[2] In the first place, those who maintain this view tend to make too sharp a dichotomy between reason and revelation. They tend to use the term *reason* to designate the methods and the content of that knowledge which is found in cultural society—in sociology, in economics, and in the political life, for example. On the other hand, they tend to use the term *revelation* to designate that Christian knowledge of God and duty which is derived from Christ and Scripture. Thus, reason tends to be discredited and revelation tends to be exalted as the only path to the discovery of the divine will. Such a view fails to do justice both to the role of reason as a gift of God and also to the continuing revelatory action of God in history and the continuing manifestation of His will in the Christian community in terms of ever-changing social and cultural conditions.

[2] *Ibid.,* pp. 76 ff.

In the second place, those who interpret Christian ethics in these narrow terms have an inadequate conception of sin, for they fail to see the extent to which they are responsible for the sin of society. They tend to assume with Rousseau that it is society that corrupts the individual. They fail to see that the root of social sin is in the hearts and wills of sinful men. Hence, they are tempted to smugness and pharisaism because they are not aware of their responsibility for society and also because of their legalistic conception of personal ethics.

In the third place, the "Christ-against-culture" Christians have a tendency to obscure the grace of God because of their concentration upon precise rules and conformity to the precise example of the historical Jesus in an effort to maintain personal purity. They tend to be more concerned with saving themselves by the observance of such rules than with responding to the living God who calls men to serve the neighbor in his need and who freely forgives those who put their trust in Him and lose their lives for the Kingdom's sake. This is the meaning of the Pauline and Reformation emphasis upon salvation by grace through faith. Both those who try to keep themselves unspotted from the world by not getting involved in politics, for example, and those who out of love engage in the "compromises" that are necessary in the political order must be justified by the grace of God, for none can earn salvation. The Christian understanding of God's grace frees men, as Paul saw, from works-righteousness based upon the assumption that one must earn his salvation—and hence from self-centeredness in the ethical life. In view of God's grace, man is free to respond to the divine will on all fronts and to the neighbor's need wherever this is found. "Whoever seeks to gain his life will lose it, but whoever loses his life will preserve it" (Luke 17:33).

Finally, those who interpret Christian ethics exclusively in terms of personal relationships neglect the radical meaning of the Christian understanding of God both as Creator and as Redeemer. They fail to see the goodness that there is in corrupt society as in sinful individuals and also the possibility of its being redeemed. While the "orders of creation" as they actually exist in particular states and economic systems and marriages are corrupt, they nevertheless represent the intent of the Creator and they minister to human need; hence, they have a goodness and value which is to be affirmed. And since the will of the Redeemer is that everything that affects human need should be made to serve man's fulfillment rather than to bring about his defeat, it is the divine will that these orders shall be restored to their original purpose in ministering to man. God is the Lord of society as of individuals, and men continually confront both His creative and His transforming will in the social institutions which they inevitably establish and maintain. Men are responsible to God for these institutions and for the neighbors to whom they are related through these institutions as well as for the neighbors whom they meet directly face to face.

All of the foregoing criticisms may be summarized by saying that those who limit Christian ethics to personal relationships fail to take seriously the implications of the radical monotheism of Christian faith which rests upon the conviction that everywhere man is confronted with the will and the purpose of the One God who is active simultaneously as Creator, as Judge, and as Redeemer. He alone is the Creator; He alone is ultimately sovereign over all; and His will is to redeem and renew all that has been corrupted by sin. Men, therefore, are responsible to God in all of the relationships of one self with other selves, no matter how indirect these relationships may be and no matter how much this responsibility may be shared by other persons or selves. As H. Richard Niebuhr puts the matter: "Whatever is, is good in the world of this God-in-Christ. It may be perverted, sinful, broken; but it is not bad, for God-in-Christ has made it and maintains it. *Such universal responsibility is incompatible with a spiritualism* that limits the Church's concern to immaterial values, *with a moralism* that that does not understand the value of the sinner and the sinful nation, *with an individualism that makes mankind as a whole and its societies of less concern to God than single persons,* and with any of those particularistic and polytheistic theories of value and responsibility which substitute for God-in-Christ some other deity as the source of valuable being."[3]

THE BIBLICAL BASIS OF THE DEMAND FOR SOCIAL JUSTICE

That the responsibility of man for all areas of his social as well as his personal life is implicit in the monotheism of Hebrew-Christian faith is evidenced in both the Old and the New Testaments. It is implicit in the entire covenant relationship of Israel to Yahweh, but

[3] H. Richard Niebuhr, "The Responsibility of the Church for Society" in *The Gospel, the Church and the World,* III, Kenneth Scott Latourette, ed., New York, Harper & Brothers, 1946, pp. 119–120. Italics added.

it is spelled out most forcefully by the prophets of the eighth-to-the-sixth centuries and their successors. God, they declared again and again, is a righteous God and He demands justice of men. While it is true that two different words are used to designate the righteousness of God (*tsedeq*) and the justice of man (*mishpat*), it is clear that the standard by which human justice is judged is God's righteousness. Not only do individuals who are unjust fall under God's judgment, but the community of Israel is judged for her "transgressions" and unfaithfulness.

A piety and a ceremonialism that neglect justice are an offence to the Lord of Israel. Thus Amos represents Yahweh as saying to Israel:

"I hate, I despise your feasts,
 and I take no delight in your solemn assemblies.
Even though you offer me your burnt offerings
  and cereal offerings,
 I will not accept them,
and the peace offerings of your fatted beasts
 I will not look upon.
Take away from me the noise of your songs;
 to the melody of your harps I will not listen.
But let justice roll down like waters,
 and righteousness like an ever-flowing stream." (Amos 5:21–24)

Micah expresses the same demand of Yahweh for human justice when he declares:

"He [Yahweh] has showed you, O man, what is good;
 and what does the Lord require of you
 but to do justice [*mishpat*], and to love kindness,
 and to walk humbly with your God?" (Micah 6:8)

Here justice is one of two moral virtues which are to govern man's relationships with his fellowman just as humility is exalted in his relationship with God. Or, again, Jeremiah speaks of the doing of justice as the way whereby Yahweh is known. "Did not your father . . . do justice and righteousness? . . . He judged the cause of the poor and needy. . . . Is not this to know me?" (Jer. 22:15–16). And Isaiah of Jerusalem pictures Yahweh as saying to the rulers and people of Judah,

"Your new moons and your appointed feasts
 my soul hates;

> they have become a burden to me,
>   I am weary of bearing them.
> When you spread forth your hands,
>   I will hide my eyes from you;
> even though you make many prayers,
>   I will not listen;
>   your hands are full of blood.
> Wash yourselves; make yourselves clean;
>   remove the evil of your doings
>   from before my eyes;
> cease to do evil,
>   learn to do good;
> seek justice,
>   correct oppression;
> defend the fatherless,
>   plead for the widow." (Isa. 1:14–17)

Not only the prophets of the eighth-to-the-sixth centuries but also the codifiers of the law and the psalmists as well as the sages assumed that Yahweh demanded justice of His people. The laws and customs of the land were to embody the righteous will of Yahweh: "You shall appoint judges and officers in all your towns . . . and they shall judge the people with righteous judgment. You shall not pervert justice; you shall not show partiality; and you shall not take a bribe. . . . Justice, and only justice, you shall follow" (Deut. 16:18–20). The Lord "loves righteousness and justice" (Ps. 33:5). "To do righteousness and justice is more acceptable to the Lord than sacrifice" (Prov. 21:3).

The requirements of the covenant spell out the implications of God's righteousness in terms of the justice which He demands among men. Moreover, the central theme in the entire development of the messianic hope and the conception of the Kingdom of God is the idea of a people, a holy community, which incorporates in its life the will of the just and righteous Lord of that Kingdom. This concern for justice is implicit, of course, in the whole conception of God as King and Judge in both the Old and the New Testaments.

As we have noted, Jesus does not himself develop the implications of this monotheism and the Kingdom which he proclaims in terms of principles of social justice. Unlike Amos, for example, he addresses his teaching to the poor rather than to the strong and influential members of the community who are treating the poor unjustly. He is not primarily concerned about reforming the oppressors but rather with rescuing the poor and the outcast.[4] But throughout his teaching, Jesus stresses the value of every human being and the importance of those actions which affect the neighbor; moreover, he makes it quite clear that the neighbor is any member of that universal community of which the one righteous God is the sovereign. It is evident, furthermore, that the will of God is normative for human conduct. Jesus teaches his disciples to pray, "Thy kingdom come, Thy will be done, on earth as it is in heaven" (Matt. 6:10). And he admonishes his followers to emulate the love of God and to seek to be perfect as God is perfect (Matt. 5:44–48). Finally, there is implicit in the commandment of neighbor-love the demand that all those actions which affect the neighbor indirectly through the patterns of social life as well as directly through person-to-person relations be directed toward the service of the neighbor under God.

When account is taken of the social status of his followers and the lowly positions which they occupied in society during his earthly ministry, when it is recalled that he rejected the method of legalism in instructing his followers concerning the form their actions should take under all circumstances, and when it is remembered that he lived in a nondemocratic society and also that he shared the eschatological expectations of his Jewish contemporaries, it is not surprising that Jesus did not spell out the implications of his teaching for social reform.[5] But the basis for the later development of the concern for social justice was firmly laid in Jesus' fundamental conviction that God now rules this world and that His rule and justice will presently be made manifest. This faith, which became the faith of his followers, implied that those who accepted it would seek to make their Father's will a reality in the life of groups as well as of individuals insofar as they were able to influence these relationships.

While Paul did not develop a social ethic in the sense of applying

[4] Waldo Beach and H. Richard Niebuhr, *Christian Ethics*, New York, The Ronald Press, 1955, p. 34.

[5] However, there is, in addition to his words on divorce, at least one other exception to this general silence of Jesus regarding the institutional life of his day which should not be overlooked, namely, his criticism of the religious leaders of the time who set down rules and prohibitions which violated the purpose of the Sabbath, who placed heavy burdens upon the people, and who corrupted the Temple. By implication, these criticisms showed how the institutional religion should be reformed, although even here it was obviously not his purpose to set forth a handbook on church administration. He did, nevertheless, by implication point out certain kinds of reform which were needed in this particular pattern of institutional life in order to bring it into harmony with the righteous will of God.

the Christian faith to problems of institutional reform—except in regard to certain aspects of ecclesiastical and familial life—he took a step of great importance for this development in his interpretation of the cosmic significance of the life and work of Jesus Christ. Not only Paul but also the other writers of the New Testament were at one in affirming the lordship of Christ, a lordship which was unlimited. All things were created through the Logos (John 1:3; cf. Col. 1:16), and "in him all things hold together" (Col. 1:17). Moreover, the true followers of Christ are those who do his will even as he did the will of his Father. This means that they will *imitate his love* in their relationships with their neighbors—enemies as well as friends. Such love, which has as its source and norm the *agape* of God in Christ, is centered upon the neighbor and intent upon meeting his needs. That this ethical monotheism, which understands that the Creator and the Judge and the Redeemer are one and that God now exercises His rule over the present nations, races, and classes of mankind, has within it the most far-reaching implications for social justice, has been made evident, it is hoped, by our analysis of the theological principles of Christian ethics.

Not only is the basis for concern with social justice firmly laid in the radical monotheism of the Bible, but the content of this justice is itself derived from the biblical understanding of God's righteousness. Justice is not understood as an abstract formula of "giving to each according to his due," either in terms of retributive justice (that is, of meting out punishment in accordance with the seriousness of one's offense—"an eye for an eye," etc.) or of distributive justice (that is, of meting out rewards in proportion to one's contribution or merit); rather, it gains its content from the righteousness of God in His dealings with men. As Norman H. Snaith puts the matter, "Knowledge of God came first, and the understanding of right action second."[6] Human justice is to be patterned after the righteousness of God rather than after some rationalistic notion of justice conceived of either in terms of equality or in terms of earned rewards and punishments. God's righteousness has been made manifest in His refusal to deal with men on the basis of their merits. It has been revealed in the undeserved deliverance of the Israelites from bondage, in the especial concern which He shows in the law for the widow, the orphan, the poor, the needy, and the stranger. It is not that these are to be

[6] Norman H. Snaith, *The Distinctive Ideas of the Old Testament*, London, The Epworth Press, 1944, p. 60.

treated with special favor or that acts which are condemned in the privileged are to be condoned in the depressed and powerless groups. Rather, it is that the latter are in special need because they have no one in the courts and the centers of power to plead their cause. God's righteousness is manifest, therefore, in the partiality which He shows for the weak and the poor; and the justice which He demands of men differs from all other conceptions of justice in that it demands the same partiality for those in special need.

That God's righteousness constitutes the measuring rod of human justice is made clear in the Old Testament by the fact that *tsedeq* and *mishpat* are frequently used either in perfect parallelism or as interchangeable terms.[7] Thus, for example, Amos, in the passage already quoted, uses both words to express the same idea in poetic parallel lines:

But let justice [*mishpat*] roll down like waters,
and righteousness [*ts^edaqah*][8] like an ever-flowing stream. (Amos 5:24)

An example of the interchangeable use of the two words is found in the charge to the judges in the opening chapter of Deuteronomy:

"Hear the cases between your brethren, and judge righteously [*tsedeq*] between a man and his brother or the alien that is with him. You shall not be partial in judgment [*mishpat*]; you shall hear the small and the great alike; you shall not be afraid of the face of man, for the judgment [*mishpat*] is God's. . . . " (Deut. 1:16–17)

But in order to grasp the full meaning of the justice which is demanded of men according to the Bible, we must look somewhat more closely at the manner in which the divine righteousness—the prototype of human justice—is permeated by mercy, or as Snaith suggests, by the vocabulary of salvation.[9] The tendency to understand the righteousness of God as involving the intent of salvation and the action which was designed to bring it about—whether in the case of Israelites in bondage, of the poor, or of the transgressor nations—was present even in the eighth-century prophets, although there the divine righteousness had primarily an ethical meaning (retributive or distributive

[7] Paul Ramsey, *Basic Christian Ethics*, New York, Charles Scribner's Sons, 1950, pp. 7–8.
[8] The feminine form for *tsedeq*. There is no difference in meaning between the two words.
[9] Snaith, *op. cit.*, p. 87.

justice). But in the later prophets, particularly in the suffering servant passages of Second Isaiah, and in the Psalms the emphasis came to be upon "God's mighty work in saving the humble."[10] According to these later writings, the purpose of God's righteousness is to bring salvation, not to mete out to each person his due in terms of reward or punishment; the idea of human justice, moreover, is similarly transformed as the understanding of the divine righteousness is deepened.

In the teaching of Jesus, this transformation of justice by mercy and redemptive love is completed. According to Professor H. Richard Niebuhr, the special character of the ethical teaching of Jesus stems out of his conviction that "the God who rules nature and history is holy love."[11] For Jesus God is, emphatically, just. He judges men by their own standards (Matt. 7:2); but His justice is also evidenced by the manner in which He makes up for the unfair inequalities among men, granting to the poor, the meek, the hungry, and the mourners what they have lacked (Matt. 5:3–11). His justice is holy justice, demanding complete inward integrity (Matt. 5:17–6:6); but His justice is also holy love, for what He demands He gives before making any demands: love, mercy, forgiveness, kindness. His kindness is manifest in the indiscriminateness of nature, for "he makes his sun rise on the evil and on the good, and sends rain on the just and on the unjust" (Matt. 5:45). He bestows His good gifts upon those who turn to Him more generously than does a parent upon his children (Matt. 5:7–11). "The divine mercifulness is not for Jesus something added to God's justice; it is the very heart of the goodness with which God is good. *This is what he is, mercy, and this is what he requires in the character of his children.*"[12]

Thus, in the Bible, the justice which is demanded of men in the social order gets its meaning from the righteousness of God, and the latter can be understood only in terms which include both His justice and His mercy. The justice which God both manifests and requires is redemptive justice, or what Paul Tillich suggestively calls "transforming or creative justice."[13] Creative justice differs both from retributive and from distributive justice. Both of the latter represent

---

[10] *Ibid.*, p. 92.
[11] Beach and Niebuhr, *op. cit.*, p. 33.
[12] *Ibid.*, p. 34. Italics added.
[13] Paul Tillich, *Love, Power, and Justice,* New York, Oxford University Press, 1954, p. 64.

static conceptions of justice as something that can be measured in quantitative terms. Transforming or creative justice, on the other hand, recognizes that justice is dynamic and that the demands of justice cannot be determined in advance of the presentation of a claim or the appearance of a need. Such justice seeks the fulfillment of each and every being, and for this purpose it demands the resignation of proportionate (retributive and distributive) justice. Creative justice forgives in order to reunite those who are estranged and in order to achieve the fulfillment of the neighbor. "Justice in its ultimate meaning is creative justice, and creative justice is the form of reuniting love"—i.e., "the form in which and through which love performs its work."[14]

THE RELATIONS OF LOVE TO JUSTICE

Love and justice are related to each other in many ways. We have seen that in the biblical view the demand for justice is placed upon man by a just and righteous God who is both Judge and Redeemer as well as Creator. We have also seen that justice is transformed by love so that the tension between ideal justice and love is ultimately overcome. But it is nevertheless true that Jesus continues to speak of God as Judge, albeit the kind of judge that a father would be rather than as the kind of father that one who is first of all a judge would be. And the question still remains as to what extent the tension between love and justice can be overcome in actual systems of justice in the present sinful order.

Emil Brunner, for example, sees a strong dualism between love and justice. The latter, he declares, renders to each person what is "due" him, or "what is fitting" for him, in view of his place in the "underived, primal order of things."[15] "Justice belongs to the world of systems."[16] Love, on the other hand, belongs to the world of persons; it "knows nought of systems." Justice is essentially impersonal; it is not concerned primarily with persons as unique individuals but rather with the claims or rights which they have by reason of their relations to a particular structure. Love is personal; it is concerned with the special needs of each individual self. Justice is the supreme virtue

[14] *Ibid.,* p. 71.
[15] Emil Brunner, *Justice and the Social Order,* trans. by Mary Hottinger, London, Lutterworth Press, 1945, pp. 23–25.
[16] *Ibid.,* p. 116.

in the sphere of institutional ethics, but in the area of personal relationships it is inferior to love.[17] Yet justice is "as indispensable as love." On the one hand, the "nature" of justice is radically different from that of love; yet on the other hand, the former is "very closely akin" to the latter.[18] Since justice is supreme in its proper sphere, the man of love when he begins to act in the sphere of institutions "turns his love into justice."[19] Justice is "the pre-condition of love"; it "must never be neglected by love." Love goes "beyond justice." It "can only do more, it can never do less, than justice requires."

Despite the fact that Brunner sees that justice is indispensable and that love does not negate justice but rather goes beyond it, he exaggerates the dualism between the two. "Justice can make no use of this love, nor does it need to. Justice is never concerned with the human being as such, but only with the human being in relationships."[20] In this respect Brunner follows the Lutheran antinomy between the social and personal spheres of ethics. Like the "dualists"— or "Christ-and-culture-in-paradox" Christians—in general, he emphasizes the restraining character of the social institutions as agencies to keep sin in check and prevent anarchy rather than their positive character as agencies through which the neighbor is served and human life is enriched.[21] The Christian ruler or the Christian citizen, he recognizes, is responsible before God for seeking to make justice a present reality in the social order, but there is always a tension between this effort and the demands of love, which is the highest virtue for the Christian.

Brunner fails to give proper attention to the need for justice as grounded in the social nature of man by creation. Institutions are both a precondition of true community and an expression of such community quite apart from the need to restrain sin. Moreover, Brunner ignores the positive relationships involved in the pursuit of justice to the will of the Redeemer. This is evidenced both by his conception of the role of institutions and by his concept of the nature of justice. In the first place, he maintains, for example, that the attitude of Christian faith toward actual existing systems of justice is "essentially a conservative one."[22] While he recognizes that justice

[17] *Ibid.,* pp. 25, 116.
[18] *Ibid.,* p. 114.
[19] *Ibid.,* p. 117.
[20] *Ibid.,* p. 116.
[21] Cf. H. Richard Niebuhr, *Christ and Culture,* p. 188.
[22] Brunner, *op. cit.,* p. 97.

is dynamic in the sense that it must be adapted to changing historical conditions, he nevertheless thinks of it primarily in terms of its "fixed" character in relation to one's ordained place in the order of creation.[23] Thus, he underestimates the possibilities of transforming the present systems of justice, especially in democratic countries, by programs of social reform. Historical situations do change, he acknowledges, and justice must be adapted to these changes, but he overlooks the motivation which the Christian has for helping bring about such changes.

In the second place, Brunner assumes that justice is essentially impersonal in purpose because it is impersonal in the form which it takes in law. He fails to take account of the fact that there is wide agreement in modern penology that justice demands concern for the rehabilitation of the criminal rather than simple retribution. This is especially clear in the treatment of juvenile delinquents. Moreover, it is manifestly impossible to determine what a man's "due" is without first inquiring what his nature is by creation and what his destiny is. Unless justice is defined in terms of a metaphysical or theological understanding of the moral order, the concept is an empty formula which may be used to justify any social order whatever—absolute monarchy or democracy, private property or communism, slavery or desegregation.[24] Judged from the standpoint of Christian faith, it is impossible to determine what is "due" a man apart from an understanding of God's will that he be redeemed. The proper place for retribution or punishment can be determined only when this ultimate purpose for man is taken into account. Hence, all existing systems of justice need to be transformed by love which considers the neighbor's needs as a child of God. Love, therefore, ought not to be restricted to operating "between the lines" of systems of justice;[25] it ought, rather, continually to seek to transform all systems of justice so that they will better serve the needs of men, including the unjust. Within a sinful order there are obvious limits to the degree to which such a transformation can be achieved at any particular time without promoting greater injustice and undermining the social order; nevertheless, every system of social justice stands under the judgment of a

[23] *Ibid.*, pp. 90 ff.
[24] Cf. Hans Kelsen, "What is Justice?" in *What is Justice?: Collected Essays,* Berkeley, California, University of California Press, 1957, pp. 1–24. See especially pp. 11, 21.
[25] Brunner, *op. cit.,* p. 117.

justice which is completely transformed by love and which provides the form in which the needs of each individual can be met.

Among the relationships of love to justice, the following three are deserving of especial consideration. While they are neither exhaustive nor mutually discrete, taken together they show how inseparable the two concepts are for Christian faith.

LOVE IS THE FULFILLMENT OF JUSTICE, NEVER A SUBSTITUTE FOR JUSTICE

In view of the widespread tendency to restrict the concern of Christian ethics to personal relationships, and thereby dispense with the demand for justice as a part of Christian ethics, it is essential that the positive relationship between justice and love be reëxamined in the light of the monotheism which Christians profess. Despite the weaknesses to which we have referred in his analysis of justice, Brunner has done an important service in underscoring the urgency of the problem of justice in our day. Beyond this he has shown that the Christian as Christian is obligated to seek justice in the social order. Love in the area of personal relations can never be a substitute for justice in society. In 1937, the Oxford Conference on Church, Community and State had issued a similar warning: "Undue emphasis upon the higher possibilities of love in personal relations, within the limits of a given system of justice or an established social structure, may tempt Christians to allow individual acts of charity to become a screen for injustice and a substitute for justice."[26]

But Brunner obscures the positive relationship between justice and love. He also exaggerates "the higher possibilities of love in personal relations" because he overlooks the role of love in the pursuit of justice itself. It is true that he considers love which is not just in the realm of institutions to be "sentimentality";[27] he recognizes, moreover, that justice will remain "as indispensable as love" as long as men live in a world of institutions and systems. Hence, he is reluctant to say that justice is "inferior" to love. The end result of his analysis, however, is that it *is* inferior because it is impersonal whereas love is personal. Not only is this position indefensible insofar as it ignores the

---

[26] J. H. Oldham, ed., *The Oxford Conference: Official Report,* New York, Willet, Clark & Company, 1937, p. 78. Cf. "Churches and Segregation," an editorial in *Life,* 41, no. 14 (October 1, 1956), p. 46.

[27] Brunner, *loc. cit.*

indirect concern of justice with persons and the interest which *agape* has in meeting the needs which social institutions fulfill; it also fails to provide a sufficient motivation for the pursuit of justice.

It is impossible to apply love in a "wholesale and direct" manner in the sphere of institutional relationships. To attempt to do so is in effect to "bleat fatuously about love." [28] What does it mean, for example, to apply love to the settlement of a strike or to problems of international trade? Yet, without love as the determining principle of justice, justice degenerates into injustice which gives less than is "due" to others in view of the fact that they are persons made in the divine image and bear the claim for fulfillment and participation in the redeemed community symbolized by the Kingdom of God. As Tillich puts the matter, "Justice is just because of the love which is implicit in it."[29] This does not mean that justice is just only insofar as love replaces justice. Nor does it mean that love transcends justice in the sense that the former is added to the latter. Rather, it means that "ultimately love must satisfy justice in order to be real love, and that justice must be elevated into unity with love in order to avoid . . . injustice."[30] Why this is so will become clearer as we examine the manner in which justice serves as an instrument of love and the reason why love must be the norm of justice.

JUSTICE IS A NECESSARY INSTRUMENT OF LOVE

Neighbor love in the New Testament means ministering to the neighbor's need, and the neighbor is every man who is affected by what one does or leaves undone. The neighbor may be encountered both as an individual and as a member of various institutions by others who are also related to him both directly as individuals and indirectly through institutions. In all of these relationships his welfare and his dignity are at stake. Hence, as Daniel D. Williams warns, it is "a dangerous sentimentality to exalt a pure and unmediated meeting of subjects in the I-Thou relationship as the only true good."[31] Social justice, like love, seeks the welfare of all persons in community. It aims directly at the good of the group and indirectly at

[28] William Temple, *Christianity and Social Order,* London, Student Christian Movement Press, Ltd., 1950, p. 80.

[29] Tillich, *op. cit.,* p. 15.

[30] *Ibid.,* p. 14.

[31] Daniel D. Williams, *God's Grace and Man's Hope,* New York, Harper & Brothers, 1949, p. 98.

the good of each person in the group; and, since most of our relationships with our neighbors are necessarily indirect, the most effective way of ministering to their total welfare is through the pursuit of social justice.

In his Gifford Lectures, Professor Reinhold Niebuhr has analyzed the manner in which systems and principles of justice become the servants and instruments of love insofar as they extend the sense of obligation toward the neighbor in the following three ways.[32] In the first place, they may transform the awareness of an obligation that is immediately felt in the presence of an obvious need into a continuing sense of obligation that is expressed in fixed principles of social justice. An immediately felt obligation that is prompted by the emotion of pity in the presence of an obvious need such as an occasional encounter with extreme poverty is likely to be momentary and passing. It may on occasion call forth considerable generosity from a sensitive person, but such charity is a poor substitute for a persistent recognition of the continuing needs of the poor when one does not happen to be prompted by such "vagrant, momentary and capricious impulses." In the second place, systems and principles of justice may extend the obligation which one feels in relation to a single neighbor to the complex relations of the self and a group of neighbors. For example, a rule of justice extends the obligation one may feel to respect the integrity of a member of one's family or a friend to all of the members of the larger community of men, irrespective of race, nationality, or class. And, finally, principles of justice have a further positive relation to love in that they extend the obligations which are discerned by the single individual to include "the wider obligations which the community defines from its more impartial perspective." Thus rules and principles of justice serve both to supplement and to correct the insights of each agent into the needs of both his individual and his collective neighbors.

Accordingly, the principle of justice is frequently needed as an instrument of love in relationships involving only two individuals, by way of assisting one person to discern with greater clarity and disinterestedness the true needs of the other. Recognition of the claims of justice makes it clear, for example, that even in relation to a single neighbor love does not mean simply and always the renunciation of one's own rights and claims. To refuse to prosecute a criminal or a delinquent in the name of Christian love *may* actually

---

[32] Reinhold Niebuhr, *The Nature and Destiny of Man,* II: *Human Destiny,* New York, Charles Scribner's Sons, 1943, pp. 248 ff.

drive a person toward a criminal career. To renounce one's own claim when there is need for "punishment" in order to reveal the seriousness of a crime and the importance of the moral order is neither justice nor love but rather "injustice, covered by sentimentality."[33] There are other occasions, however, when it is not necessary for one person to employ the concept of justice in dealing with a single neighbor, as when the Samaritan is confronted by a single victim lying by the side of the road. But the situation changes the moment a third person is introduced into the relationship. If the Samaritan becomes confronted with two victims both of whose needs he is unable to meet, he must evaluate their respective claims in the interest of *agape*. Similarly, some rational estimate of conflicting needs and desires is necessary in the interest of love even within the family. Moreover, even if perfect love were presupposed, complex relations involving more than two people would still require some calculation of rights.[34]

Instead of contradicting the ethic of love, the provision for social justice is the indispensable means to the welfare of society as a whole and thus indirectly of the neighbor as an individual. Systems of social justice as exemplified in the laws of a state have a dual value. In the first place, they have the negative function of restraining egoism and aggressiveness on the part of the constituent members of a society, thus making social order possible (cf. Rom. 13:4). In the second place, they have a positive function to which the negative one is subordinate, viz., the provision of the structural framework in which all of the members of society may more effectively seek the fulfillment of their natures and purposes.[35] Both of these tasks must be taken into account in an ethic of love, for without some structure of justice and law there would be no order and no freedom, both of which are necessary to undergird man's efforts to fulfill his physical and social and spiritual needs.

Not only do systems of social justice provide the framework for the development of man's nature and the meeting of his needs, but this structural framework is itself dynamic and performs a work of love insofar as it is a constructive rather than a destructive element in the life of a community. Institutional structures, whether they take the form of law, of economic patterns, or of patterns of social rela-

---

[33] Tillich, *op. cit.*, p. 14.
[34] Reinhold Niebuhr, *op. cit.*, p. 252.
[35] George F. Thomas, *Christian Ethics and Moral Philosophy*, New York, Charles Scribner's Sons, 1955, p. 254.

tionships, are not simply static instruments of order; they also wield powerful social and psychological influences upon a community. On the one hand, they reflect the values of a society and provide a means for the balancing of competing claims and interests; on the other hand, they also help to mould the mind and spirit of a community and effect new patterns of group life. "The state," as Daniel D. Williams points out, "is always creative for good or evil."[36] And law, or the system of political justice, is an important instrument by which a community may educate and discipline itself for good or for evil.

Law marshalls the moral power as well as the political power of a state behind the ideal pattern of life which it seeks to establish. While there are obvious limits to the power of law to change patterns of behavior when the former is not supported by the public conscience, the existence of law together with the intention to enforce it constitutes a powerful social factor in the life of a community. A notable example of this educational and dynamic character of law is to be found in the history of legislation affecting the relationships between the races in this country in recent years. Stimulated by the example of President Roosevelt's executive order establishing a wartime agency to insure fair employment opportunities, many states have adopted fair employment practices legislation. These laws have accomplished a great deal by way of eliminating discrimination in employment and alerting the public to a serious form of injustice. The dynamic character of law is particularly well illustrated in the case of such FEPC legislation since the public authorities have generally relied upon the appeal to the moral force of public opinion through persuasion, investigation, and publicity rather than upon appeal to the courts. Other examples in the same general area are: the effect of the abolition of segregation in the Armed Services; the impact of a succession of decisions of the United States Supreme Court directing the abolition of segregation at various levels of public education, beginning with the professional and graduate schools of state universities and ultimately including the elementary grades; and the enactment of legislation implementing the protection of certain basic civil rights guaranteed to all citizens by the Constitution of the United States.[37]

[36] Williams, *op. cit.*, p. 102.

[37] Cf. Gordon W. Allport, *The Nature of Prejudice*, Cambridge, Massachusetts, Addison-Wesley Publishing Co., 1954, p. 477. Professor Allport concludes his analysis of the effect of law upon prejudice with the unequivocal judgment that legislative action is "one of the major methods of reducing, not only public discrimination, but private prejudices as well."

In the opinion which the Supreme Court handed down in the case of *Brown* v. *Board of Education*, Chief Justice Warren cited the dynamic character of legally enforced segregation in the public schools as the determining consideration of the Court in declaring compulsory segregation in such schools unconstitutional. Our system of public education, he argued, is of the utmost importance in the training of young people both for good citizenship and for personal fulfillment. He wrote: "Compulsory school attendance laws and the great expenditures for education both demonstrate our recognition of the importance of education to our democratic society. It is required in the performance of our most basic public responsibilities, even service in the armed forces. It is *the very foundation of good citizenship*. Today it is *a principal instrument in awakening the child to cultural values, in preparing him for later professional training*, and *in helping him to adjust normally to his environment*."[38] Continuing, Mr. Warren cited the language of the Kansas case (one of the original cases which had been appealed to the Supreme Court) to show why segregation in public schools on the basis of race deprives the children of a minority group of equal educational opportunities: " 'Segregation of white and colored children in public schools has a detrimental effect upon the colored children. *The impact is greater when it has the sanction of the law;* for the policy of separating the races is usually interpreted as denoting the inferiority of the Negro group. . . . Segregation with the sanction of the law . . . has a tendency to retard the educational and mental development of Negro children and to deprive them of some of the *benefits they would receive in a racially integrated school system.*' "[39]

Examples of the creative power of law and the systems of justice which are established thereby are so abundant that it is difficult to see how love and justice continue to be separated so sharply in the thought of large segments of contemporary Protestantism. Of course, the state cannot make men good. It can only bring about external conformity to a certain minimum level of morality and gradually effect a rise in this minimum level as the public conscience will support it. In a sense its primary function is regulatory. But the regulation itself presupposes a standard of ordering, and the process of selecting

[38] *Brown* v. *Board of Education*, Opinion of the United States Supreme Court, May 17, 1954. Quoted in *Southern School News,* I, no. 1 (September 3, 1954), p. 16. Italics added.
[39] *Ibid*. Italics added.

a standard and applying it under changing conditions of society is a creative one. This is true in the case of traffic laws, compulsory school attendance laws, laws protecting property, laws governing conditions of employment and the rights of labor and management, laws regulating marriage and divorce, and laws affecting relations between different racial and ethnic groups. The truth of this judgment is ironically confirmed by the fact that the very groups which insist most vigorously that "righteousness" cannot be legislated in one particular area, such as race relations, are frequently among the strongest supporters of similar efforts in other areas, such as prohibition, censorship, or the attempt to control juvenile delinquency by meting out more severe penalties to juvenile offenders or to their parents.

LOVE IS FOR CHRISTIANS THE ULTIMATE NORM OF JUSTICE

As Reinhold Niebuhr declares, love is "both the fulfillment and the negation of all achievements of justice in history."[40] Individualistic Protestantism is quite right in seeing a certain negative relationship between love and justice, for all actual laws and systems of justice contain contradictions to *agape,* but it errs in failing to see the positive relationship whereby love is at the same time the fulfillment of the justice which these historical systems seek. Because it fails to understand this latter fact, individualistic Protestantism is always confronted with the temptation to attempt to withdraw from culture.

Viewed, then, in relation to concrete systems of justice, love reaches beyond these and provides a standard for judging all historical schemes of justice. While recognizing the necessity for such systems, love always seeks to raise them to new heights, for it recognizes that each existing system represents something less than perfect justice or perfect love. Yet love does not attempt to take the place of justice in group relationships, for it recognizes that even in the family or the church the attempt to live by spontaneous love alone is self-defeating. For this reason love makes use of the structures of justice, not as "eternal norms to which life must perennially conform" but rather as "*ad hoc* efforts to strike a balance between the final moral possibilities of life and the immediate and given realities."[41]

[40] Reinhold Niebuhr, *op. cit.,* p. 246.
[41] Reinhold Niebuhr, "The Christian Faith and the Economic Life," in A. Dudley Ward, ed., *Goals of Economic Life,* New York, Harper & Brothers, 1953, p. 451.

For the Christian, the distance between what is actually possible in a particular situation and the divine will under which all human action stands in judgment is covered by grace. The central meaning of the classical doctrine of justification by faith is that no man— neither the pietist nor the monk nor the reformer—is justified by works, even works of withdrawal to avoid compromise, but only by faith. The person who withdraws from social responsibility in the name of a perfectionist ethic is always in danger of falling into pride and self-righteousness because he so narrowly limits the scope of the application of this ethic. Moreover, the attempt to withdraw from the pursuit of greater justice (greater equality, e.g.) just because perfect justice (perfect equality of opportunity, e.g.) is unattainable in the present represents a serious misunderstanding of the nature of love, for it starts at the wrong center. It seeks to save one's life in eternity by keeping oneself unspotted from the world. The New Testament *agape,* on the other hand, begins with an orientation of the self toward God's will and the neighbor's need: "For whoever would save his life will lose it, and whoever loses his life for my sake will find it" (Matt. 16:25). The service of the neighbor under God is what is required of man.

Not only does love seek the welfare of all through the pursuit of social justice, but it also seeks the welfare of each member of the group as an individual; moreover, it is in dealing with the needs of the individual neighbor in an I-Thou relationship that the highest possibilities for sacrificial love are found. "Naturally, the justice and harmony which is achieved in this way (social justice) is not the harmony of the Kingdom of God, nor yet identical with the highest possible harmony between individuals in their personal evaluations. For this reason," writes Reinhold Niebuhr, "there must always be a final distinction between what the Gospel demands of us in our individual and spontaneous relations and what is demanded in the institutions and structures of society."[42] Thus, in addition to—not instead of—the love which is expressed in the effort to provide an ever-increasing measure of justice in the community at large, the Christian is called upon to seek a fuller expression of *agape* above and beyond the law. To limit love to the relative justice of any historical system is to put love in a strait jacket. Love that is thus restricted and systematized becomes cold and prudential. It becomes

[42] Reinhold Niebuhr, "Christian Faith and Social Action," in John A. Hutchison, ed., *Christian Faith and Social Action,* New York, Charles Scribner's Sons, 1953, p. 241.

something less than *agape*. But, on the other hand, to divorce love from justice is to turn it into a pious sentimentality so that instead of being more than justice it ends up being less than justice.

RECOMMENDED READINGS

Beach, Waldo and Niebuhr, H. Richard, eds., *Christian Ethics*, New York, The Ronald Press, 1955, ch. I.

Brunner, Emil, *Christianity and Civilisation*, I: *Foundations*, London, Nisbet & Co., Ltd., 1948, ch. VIII.

Brunner, Emil, *Justice and the Social Order*, trans. by Mary Hottinger, London, Lutterworth Press, 1945, chs. 2–3, 8, 13–15.

Holbrook, Clyde A., *Faith and Community*, New York, Harper & Brothers, 1959, ch. 6.

Niebuhr, Reinhold, "The Christian Faith and the Economic Life," in *Goals of Economic Life*, A. Dudley Ward, ed., New York, Harper & Brothers, 1953.

Niebuhr, Reinhold, *The Nature and Destiny of Man*, II: *Human Destiny*, New York, Charles Scribner's Sons, 1943, ch. IX.

Oldham, J. H., ed., *The Oxford Conference: Official Report*, New York, Willett, Clark and Company, 1937, "Report of the Section on Church, Community and State in Relation to the Economic Order."

Ramsey, Paul, *Basic Christian Ethics*, New York, Charles Scribner's Sons, 1950, ch. I.

Robertson, D. B., ed., *Love and Justice: Selections from the Shorter Writings of Reinhold Niebuhr*, Philadelphia, The Westminster Press, 1957.

Temple, William, *Christianity and Social Order*, London, Student Christian Movement Press, Ltd., 1950, ch. VI.

Thomas, George F., *Christian Ethics and Moral Philosophy*, New York, Charles Scribner's Sons, 1955, ch. 11.

Tillich, Paul, *Love, Power, and Justice*, New York, Oxford University Press, 1954.

Snaith, Norman H., *The Distinctive Ideas of the Old Testament*, Philadelphia, The Westminster Press, 1946, chs. 3–4.

chapter 10

THE ECONOMIC ORDER

IN this and the following chapter we come to a consideration of two of the areas of modern life in which Christian responsibility is most urgently needed yet most generally neglected or denied, viz., the economic and political orders. Without doubt these represent two of the most influential and determinative aspects of modern society, and they confront us with many of our most perplexing problems.

As we shall use the term, the economic order—or the economic life—refers to all those relationships, decisions, and activities which are primarily concerned with the acquisition, possession, and use of material goods. The tremendous scope of such involvements is indicated by the well-known economist, Professor Howard R. Bowen. Economic activity of some nature, he writes, "fills most of our waking hours, and to it we devote much energy and talent. It supplies the goods (and bads) which make up our scale of living. It involves us in many of our most rewarding (and most difficult) human relationships. It requires us to meet competition. It places heavy responsibilities upon us. It influences our family life, our religious observances, and our cultural attainments. It partly determines our sense of personal tranquility (or fear and uncertainty). It provides us with opportunities for creative satisfactions (or monotonous drudgery). Altogether, economic activity places an indelible stamp on human personality and on the quality of human life."[1] Because of the magnitude and complexity of the problems relating to the economic life, it is impossible to deal with them effectively without utilizing the state

[1] Howard R. Bowen, "Ethics and Economics," in John C. Bennett *et al.*, *Christian Values and Economic Life*, New York, Harper & Brothers, 1954, pp. 183–184.

in some degree as an agency of regulation and control. The state, of course, has many other functions which are not directly related to the economic order, but we shall postpone consideration of these to the following chapter. Our present concern is with those problems which are basically economic rather than political in character, and in the present discussion we shall deal with the state only insofar as it is involved in the economic order.

ETHICS AND ECONOMICS

THE SEPARATION OF ETHICS AND ECONOMICS

In view of the importance of the economic life for human well-being, it perhaps seems strange that throughout much of the period of modern industrial development the former has been largely divorced from any sense of genuine ethical responsibility. While we cannot examine the reasons for this separation in detail, it will be helpful briefly to remind ourselves of a few of the major underlying causes which have helped to produce this state of affairs. Among the most significant of these factors are the following: a growing academic specialization, which has resulted in a breakdown of communication between scholars even in closely related fields; the tendency of many economists to convert their discipline into a science which would deal only with those values which are susceptible of quantitative measurement; the growing fragmentation of modern life, with the resultant loss of any integrating value-system or moral code; and the ascendancy of the economic doctrine of laissez faire, which rested upon a belief in the natural harmony of private self-interest with the general welfare. Through its faith in the preëstablished harmony between private self-interest and the common good, the doctrine of laissez faire served to divert attention away from ethics and away from consideration of the relationship of the economic processes to the larger goals of life itself.

These forces were also strengthened by others which affected the masses of industrial workers as well as the professional economists and the owners of industry. For example, the impersonal character of the relationships which dominate our modern technological economy and the one-sided individualism which has characterized much modern social thought since the Renaissance have also contributed to the separation of economic activities from considerations of ethics. The results have been, on the one hand, that professional economists have generally assumed that the goal of the economic life is to maximize the national income without taking into consideration values which are not measurable in monetary terms and, on the other hand, that businessmen have generally assumed that the economic order is essentially autonomous and self-regulating. Major reliance in the control of self-interest has been traditionally placed upon competition rather than upon restraints imposed by society through the state. Moreover, the traditional biblical and Protestant concepts of stewardship and vocation have become largely meaningless. For the layman—whether he be owner or employee—stewardship has come to be associated, not with the totality of life and the resources of the earth, but with appeals for support of churches; and only those who are engaged in religious activities in a professional way think of themselves as having vocations.

Their Complementary Character

Despite the difficulties posed by any attempt to relate ethics to economic activities, it gradually became evident from the practice of laissez faire that the economic order was not self-regulating and that competition was not a sufficient safeguard of the public interest. In practice, the owners of industry did not always follow even the minimal obligations of honesty, respect for property, observance of contracts, and abstinence from fraud and violence which were presupposed by the system.[2] But the breakdown of laissez faire as the dominant principle of economic organization was not due simply to the discrediting of the optimistic view of man upon which it rested. It was also due to a rediscovery of the significance of community and a recognition of the increased dependence of the individual upon society in an industrial age. The emergence of such pressing social problems as the concentration of economic power, business cycles, technological unemployment, disparities in economic opportunity and distribution of income, the personal insecurity of people with reference to sickness and old age, and exploitation of natural resources—problems which could not be dealt with adequately on the basis of laissez faire—caused the adequacy of both the theory and the practice to be called into question. As a result, within the past fifty to seventy-five years

[2] Howard R. Bowen, *Social Responsibilities of the Businessman,* New York, Harper & Brothers, 1953, pp. 17–21.

there has been a progressive decline of the laissez faire system of economic organization and a rapid increase in the social controls that have been placed upon economic activities. In some countries this has led to socialism, in others to communism, and in still others to some form of welfare capitalism or mixed economy.

As a result of the foregoing developments, there has come about a growing recognition of the importance of bringing economics and ethics into a closer relationship in an effort to come to grips with the problems left unsolved by laissez faire. Moreover, there has been general recognition of the fact that the reconstructive task, both in theory and in practice, needs to be a joint undertaking because any adequate attack upon these problems is dependent upon a competent understanding both of values (or goals) to be pursued in the economic order and of technical knowledge concerning the means of realizing such goals. What is needed, therefore, is neither that professional economists should become moral philosophers in the sense that they should attempt to become arbiters of value and prescribe what the goals of economic life should be, nor that moral philosophers should attempt to become specialists in economics.[3] This does not mean, of course, that an economist may not be well-versed in ethics or that a moral philosopher may not be a competent economist. It means, rather, that the characteristic methods and knowledge that are essential to competency in the science of economics are different from the methods and knowledge that are distinctive to the special concern of ethics. Economics is concerned with the question of what is possible, whereas ethics is concerned with the question of what the goals of the economic life should be. Specialists are needed in both these areas, although it is of the utmost importance to recognize that it is highly abstract to attempt to separate the two fields of theoretical concern as sharply as has generally been done in modern times, because they cannot be separated in practice. The ethicist has to make actual as well as ideal choices, and it is of the greatest importance for him to know whether a particular goal which he chooses as an ideal represents a genuine possibility in the economic life. Similarly, the economist has to choose among many ends or goals which are open to him as he arranges his own economic activity and participates in policy formation; hence, it is important for him to have some guidance in the choices which he must make among com-

[3] See Bennett, *et al., op. cit.,* pp. 196–197. Cf. Kenneth E. Boulding, *The Organizational Revolution,* New York, Harper & Brothers, 1953, pp. xv–xvi.

peting values. In the light of the decisions which are demanded by the economic order, it is evident that the economist and ethicist each has an important contribution to make to the other; moreover, the guidance of both is needed by those who are specialists in neither field but who are nevertheless faced with the responsibility of making economic choices affecting themselves, their families, and society as a whole.

In summary, the economist's responsibility is not to become an arbiter of values but rather to help "identify the values of society, define these operationally and with some precision, point out ambiguities and conflicts among them, appraise the operation of the economic system in terms of those values, and translate them into relevant economic policies."[4] The responsibility of the moral philosopher and theologian, on the other hand, is to determine what values should be pursued, to formulate these values in meaningful terms, to consider their practical implications and be prepared to reconcile the conflicts among them through compromise.

THE CHRISTIAN UNDERSTANDING OF THE ECONOMIC ORDER

It is of course possible to evaluate the moral significance of economic activities in terms of other systems of ethics and other faiths, but the task of Christian ethics is to examine the economic life in the light of biblical faith. Usually, however, when such an attempt has been made, it has taken the form of a simple reiteration of certain aspects of the economic ethic that is spelled out in the New Testament, especially certain of the teachings of Jesus which have direct reference to the acquisition, possession, and use of material goods. Moreover, the sharpest and most demanding of these are frequently dismissed as eschatological sayings or as hyperboles. In addition, the whole question of the possibility of developing economic structures and institutions that would be more in keeping with the demands of Christian faith is frequently ignored on the basis of the fact that Jesus did not deal specifically with the matter of institutional reform. As a consequence, the Christian ethic is understood in highly individualistic terms, and its demands are limited to the area of the personal encounter of one individual with another.

But all of these attempts to relate the Christian ethic to the eco-

[4] Howard R. Bowen, in Bennett, *et al., op. cit.,* p. 197.

nomic life are inadequate because they fail to understand the radical character of this ethic and also because they fail to take into account the concrete demands of different societies and different cultures. The result is that the divine will is related only to isolated parts of our economic activity and only certain aspects of the divine will appear to be concerned with the latter—e.g., the will of the Judge as over against that of the Creator and Redeemer. This does not mean, of course, that such specific sayings of Jesus as "You cannot serve God and mammon" (Matt. 6:24) and "Beware of all covetousness" (Luke 12:15) have no relevance to what our attitudes toward the acquisition of wealth should be in the present day. Such sayings have the most profound relevance. They remind man of his true nature and his true good, but they must be understood in the light of Jesus' total teaching and life; and the unifying element in the totality of his teaching and life, as we have seen, is God. When this fundamental unity is lost sight of, the significance of the isolated sayings themselves easily becomes distorted and corrupted.

AN AREA OF CREATION

From the standpoint of Christian faith the economic order must be understood as an area of activities and relationships which are permeated with religious and ethical meaning. Here, just as in connection with any other area of life, an adequate conception of this order must begin with a Christian understanding of God as Creator. According to Christian faith, God is the Creator of all, and all that He has created is essentially good. He created the material world in which man is set; and He created man with a body which has physical needs for food, clothing, and shelter. God is the One who in creation has made provision whereby these needs can be met, and He has so ordered the life of man that they must be met if life itself is to be preserved. In this sense the economic order may be spoken of most fundamentally as an order of creation. It is made necessary by the nature of man as he was created.

The Christian conception of the fundamental character of the economic order stands in sharp contrast, however, to all forms of materialism according to which the world is understood primarily in terms of material forces and values. The concept of creation by a personal God whose will can be understood ultimately only in terms of righteousness and love represents the strongest possible denial of the economic determinism upon which Marxist Communism is based. According to the biblical view, the most powerful force in history and in the universe is the righteous and sovereign God; according to Marxism, it consists of the economic processes involved in the production and distribution of goods. Judged from the standpoint of biblical faith, the Marxist faith is idolatrous. But the Christian doctrine of creation also represents an equally strong rejection of all other forms of secular materialism which conceive of life's highest values in material terms—not only of money but of the material things and pleasures which money can buy and the power and prestige which it can help one to attain—and which view the economic processes as the determining force in society. Non-Marxist capitalists are not necessarily more Christian in this respect than are Marxists. The biblical concept of man as made in the divine image and the warning of Jesus that "a man's life does not consist in the abundance of his possessions" (Luke 12:15) constitute a clear and explicit rejection of the secular materialism of Western culture with its faith in the primacy of material values just as clearly as biblical faith in God constitutes a denial of the atheism which Marxism avows.

It is important to see, however, that there is implicit in the biblical view of the economic life as a divine order far more than a mere denial both of asceticism, on the one hand, and of materialism, on the other. For while it is recognized that economic goods do have value, the Bible as a whole makes it quite clear that the purpose for which such goods exist is to minister to the needs of man; it insists, moreover, that man's needs can be adequately understood only in terms that take into account his divine image and not just his physical nature alone. The function of the economic life is not merely to meet man's physical needs, much less simply to provide the barest necessities for physical existence; rather, it is "to place at (man's) disposal a surplus of goods which alone makes a human civilized life possible." Its function is to enable man not just to live, but "to live in a *human* way."[5]

It is because of the function of the economic order to minister to human life—both to its preservation and to its spiritual enrichment—that Christian ethics places a high value upon efficiency in the production of goods. As a reminder of the importance of the task of providing goods and as a protest against utopianism, Brunner's

[5] Emil Brunner, *The Divine Imperative*, trans. by Olive Wyon, New York, The Macmillan Company, 1942, p. 402.

declaration that any adjustment which paralyzed the vitality of the economic life "would be every whit as wrong as the policy of laissez-faire, which releases its demonic energies" is justified.[6] But Brunner's dictum cannot be taken as a justification for the evils which arise out of laissez faire. Out of love for the neighbor the Christian must be concerned with efficiency in the production of goods to meet the neighbor's needs, but efficiency understood solely in terms of quantitative production cannot be made the sole or even the highest consideration in the economic order without doing violence to the persons whose needs this order is intended to serve. Out of love for the neighbor the Christian must also seek to prevent the processes of production and distribution themselves from violating other and deeper needs.

Hence, it follows that in response to the Creator the Christian must be concerned with justice in the economic order.[7] One of the most obvious facts about the economic life is the dependence of the individual upon the community. This is true of the producer who is able to produce only because of the order and resources which are provided by society. It is also true of the consumer who is dependent upon many kinds of producers and distributors of goods. It is true not only of individuals and small groups but of nations as well. From the standpoint of Christian faith, this interdependence of individuals and groups points to the will of the Creator that men should live together in community rather than in isolation, and the fact that each person has needs which can be met only in community places a claim upon society to recognize its actual oneness and its obligation to meet these needs through the establishment of economic institutions which will best serve man's highest capacities and true good. Some forms of economic organization are necessary for the preservation of life, and these institutional forms are the product of society as a whole. They are the responsibility of the group as well as of the individuals who constitute the group. It is the will of the Creator that such structures as are devised shall serve the fulfillment both of those who participate in the productive processes of the economic order and of those whose needs this order is intended to meet.

[6] *Ibid.*, p. 408.

[7] While justice frequently implies a reference to man's sinfulness and to the correction of injustice, the principle itself has also a more positive significance. It is primarily the latter concern which is involved in a response to the Creator whereas the former is involved in the response to the Judge and Redeemer.

What this response to the Creator means in terms of the ownership of property and in terms of man's daily work we shall examine in more detail in subsequent sections of the present chapter. Fundamentally, however, this response is characterized by gratitude to God for the material world and its bountiful resources for meeting the physical needs of men and by the effort to use these resources to minister to the needs of the neighbor.

AN AREA OF JUDGMENT

From a glance at the nature of the existing economic order it is apparent that man is confronted not only with the will of the Creator but also with a denial of this will. He is confronted not only with the intent of order but also with disorder. For here one sees material values being acclaimed as supreme in our own society, with its emphasis upon success defined in terms of economic rewards, with its "conspicuous consumption," and with its obsession with fashions and gadgets. Here one sees men threatened with the loss of their own souls in their worship of mammon. Instead of community there are divisions of class against class and extremes of poverty and wealth existing side by side in the same cities. Instead of justice there is injustice; instead of mutual service there is exploitation. The purposes of the Creator are being flouted by man the sinner who has rebelled against the divine will; therefore, man is confronted with God the Judge who has ordained that man cannot find his true good except in conformity with the moral order which He has established.

This does not mean that there is no community or justice or neighbor-love manifest in the economic life. Man still retains the divine image although it is marred by sin. What we have said means, rather, that because of the universality of human sinfulness all of man's economic activity is tainted with egoism, pride, and idolatry. There is a relic of community, for human life cannot exist except in community, but the latter is broken and partial. On the one hand, defenders of individualistic economic theory and practice are not able to isolate themselves completely from the remainder of society, and their efforts to ignore the claims of society hinder the achievement of genuine harmony and unity. The resulting disorder witnesses to the community which is intended in Creation and which man can never finally escape. On the other hand, in collectivist societies there is an outward shell of community based upon coercion and the subjection of men to the state, but the resulting uniformity and unity which is imposed by force does not represent genuine community. The former is, in fact, a denial of the latter; for the latter is based upon recognition of the uniqueness and the worth of each individual and upon the acknowledgment and free acceptance of the mutual dependence of each upon all and of all upon each. But neither collectivism nor individualism can escape the consequences of its attempt to deny the community of man. As long as man remains *human*—that is, as long as he bears the divine image—collectivism will be intolerable to the human spirit, which longs for freedom and creativity. And as long as he remains set in society, an individualism which ignores the claims of the community will breed disorder based upon injustice. The divine will is neither that individuals should exist in isolation nor that they should be forced into an anonymous collective mass; rather, it is that there should be between the individual and the community a mutual relationship which would provide for "a mutual limitation of the individual and of the community, the moulding of individuality within the intimate life of the community."[8]

From the perspective of biblical faith, the rise and spread of Communism represents the divine judgment upon the moral failure of Western civilization. The latter has professed to be Christian, but in reality it is its failure to establish genuine community and to achieve justice under the technical conditions of modern society which has brought about the rise of Marxism with its promise of community and social justice.

Thus, Reinhold Niebuhr, addressing the First Assembly of the World Council of Churches at Amsterdam in 1948, declared that in the midst of the disorder and crisis through which the contemporary world is passing the first task of the Christian Church is to interpret the "sorrows and distresses, the agonies and pains" of the present day and "to recognize the hand of God in them."[9] As Christians we must acknowledge, he continued, that there is "a divine judgment upon our sins in this travail." Moreover, if this divine judgment is recognized, it can transmute the despair of the present day, which arises out of suffering and confusion which have no meaning, into

[8] Brunner, *op. cit.*, p. 405.
[9] The World Council of Churches, *Man's Disorder and God's Design*, III: *The Church and the Disorder of Society*, New York, Harper & Brothers, n.d., p. 24.

the "godly grief (which) produces a repentance that leads to salvation" (II Cor. 7:10).

A decade prior to Amsterdam, Jacques Maritain, the well-known Catholic philosopher, had similarly seen the judgment of God in the growth of Communism. In reply to the question, "What is the cause of this (the atheism of Communism)?" he said: "It is, I hold, because it originates, chiefly through the fault of a Christian world unfaithful to its own principles, in a profound sense of *resentment,* not only against the Christian world, but—and here lies the tragedy—against Christianity itself. . . ."[10] And Nicolas Berdyaev, the eminent Eastern Orthodox interpreter of Christianity, himself an exiled victim of Russian Communism, had expressed the same conviction when he wrote:

> Christians, who condemn the communists for their godlessness and anti-religious persecutions, cannot lay the whole blame solely upon these godless communists; they must assign part of the blame to themselves, and that a considerable part. They must be not only accusers and judges; they must also be penitents. Have Christians done very much for the realization of Christian justice in social life? Have they striven to realize the brotherhood of man without that hatred and violence of which they accuse the communists? The sins of Christians, the sins of historical churches, have been very great, and these sins bring with them their just punishment.[11]

The judgment of God upon Christians and the churches and Western civilization can be discerned of course only by faith and only from the vantage point of a standard in terms of which all men and all human institutions and cultures are seen to be sinful and corrupted. When the contemporary social revolution in which the traditional religious, social, economic, and political structures of our civilization are being challenged by competing structures is viewed in relation to the will of God, Christians are summoned first of all, not to defend as "Christian" their institutions and their civilization which have never been Christian in their ethical attainments, but to confess the failures and injustices of their own institutions and of the social order of which they are a part. Those who know God to be the Creator, Judge, and Redeemer of all, ought to be able to recognize

[10] Jacques Maritain, *True Humanism,* London, The Centenary Press, 1938, p. 33.
[11] Nicolas Berdyaev, *The Origin of Russian Communism,* trans. by R. M. French, London, The Centenary Press, 1937, pp. 207–208.

that judgment begins "at the house of God" and that the divine judgment falls upon all human institutions and traditions. Only as they recognize their own involvement in the guilt of their own society and of the nations can they participate redemptively in the effort to establish brotherhood and justice in a divided and unjust social order.

In view of the perplexities of the problems with which we are confronted in the areas of race, economics, and politics, and in view of the temptation to despair and cynicism with regard to the possibility of discovering creative strategies for dealing with these problems, it is important to recognize that the Christian must inevitably make judgments among institutions, men, and nations; but such judgments ought never to be self-righteous and vindictive. Rather, they ought to be made in humility and in the awareness that one's own cause also stands under God's judgment. Nevertheless, the Christian is forced to act, and faith in the Creator and Redeemer ought to enable him to act with firmness and decisiveness, relying upon God to accept his decisions and actions as an expression of love which is offered in humility and in faith. Inaction which is prompted by too exclusive a focus upon man's sinfulness represents a lack of faith in the goodness and sovereignty of God. Moreover, it reflects an unbiblical view of man's rational and moral capacities and a failure to understand the moral character of all decisions, including the decision to attempt to remain neutral.

AN AREA OF REDEMPTION

Thus, beyond the judgment with which men are confronted in the disorder and suffering which characterize so much of modern economic life, the Christian sees the summons of the Redeemer who is at work to effect the reconciliation both of individuals and of groups which are presently alienated by competing economic interests through the establishment of genuine community based upon justice and *agape*. Hence, the present disorder in the economic sphere must be viewed finally in the light of the purpose of the Redeemer rather than that of the Judge.

As we have already seen, the Christian conception of salvation has two major dimensions: one individual and the other social. It has also been observed that the major emphasis of the New Testament, insofar as hope for fulfillment of this promise within history is concerned, is upon the individual experience of salvation. In view of the fact that the end of the present historical order was deemed imminent, it was expected that the transformation of society would take place eschatologically when God would overthrow the evil order and establish His Kingdom. When it became apparent, however, that the end would be "delayed" and as Christians came to have more potential power to influence the social order, increased emphasis was given to the transformation of the latter by the more prophetic voices in the Church.

This growing tendency to stress the social responsibility of Christians was an inevitable consequence of a profound understanding of the Church's faith in the Creator and Sovereign of history in view of the increasing number and influence of Christians and in view of the prospects for a longer historical future. Because of human sinfulness the transformation of human society will never be completed within history, but Christian faith affirms that it will be completed eschatologically and at the same time in such a way that the meaning of history will be fulfilled and not negated. The achievements that take place within history and the partial transformations that are made there are of lasting significance and point to a final transformation of life and an ultimate fulfillment of history in a Kingdom which transcends the bounds of earthly life.

Both elements in the Christian conception of salvation—the individual and the social—are essential; they are closely related to each other in a number of important ways. The beginnings of both are experienced in the present life and in earthly history, but the fulfillment of each lies beyond history in the coming Kingdom of God. In *Goals of Economic Life,* Professor John Bennett discusses two of the most important connections between the Christian experience of personal salvation and social salvation as the latter is related to the economic life.[12] Defining personal salvation in terms of (1) "the awareness of being forgiven or accepted by God" and (2) "growth in a life of obedience and love," he points out, in the first place, that economic conditions frequently become so oppressive that they constitute an almost insurmountable obstacle to the experience of salvation.[13] Hence, those who have received the divine forgiveness and have been renewed by the Spirit of God must seek to remove these obstacles to

[12] John C. Bennett, "A Theological Conception of Goals for Economic Life," in A. Dudley Ward, ed., *Goals of Economic Life,* Harper & Brothers, 1953, pp. 415–421.

[13] Cf. Paul Tillich, *The Protestant Era,* Chicago, The University of Chicago Press, 1948, p. xviii: "There are social structures that unavoidably frustrate any spiritual appeal to the people subjected to them."

salvation if they are to be effective in proclaiming the Gospel to their fellowmen. This does not mean that the poor and the oppressed cannot experience salvation in the most profound sense; nor does it imply that an abundance of economic goods and wealth may not also constitute an obstacle to salvation by tempting men to idolatry. It does mean, however, that the hypocrisy of a Church which preaches a gospel of love while it is at the same time indifferent to the physical needs of those to whom it ministers will be more likely to provoke resentment against the Church and a rejection of the faith which it proclaims than it will be to prove an effective instrument in the winning of men to an acceptance of that faith. It means also that hunger and poverty can become so oppressive as to be only crushing and destructive in their effects upon those who are caught in their grip.

Among the economic conditions which may constitute obstacles to the experience of personal salvation Bennett suggests the following: poor housing conditions, which may have disastrous effects upon family morale and thus adversely affect the emotional health of children in ways that are important for growth in the awareness of God's love; contrasts in a society between extreme wealth and extreme poverty, which may generate bitterness and hostility and constitute a serious barrier to fellowship; unemployment, which creates in the unemployed a sense of not being needed and wanted—a feeling of being rejected by society as well as a feeling of guilt for not being able to provide for one's dependents; and a corrupt moral climate in which undue emphasis is placed upon personal financial gain and success judged in terms of false standards. When these and other economic circumstances and policies become oppressive, they prepare the ground for totalitarian movements such as Communism and Fascism to arise with their promises of greater justice and equality. And totalitarianism brings in its wake the proscription of religious liberty and the denial of the claims of ethical monotheism. While it is true, as Bennett points out, that even under the most adverse conditions there will be some saints and heroes who will seem to be the greater because of the obstacles which they have had to overcome, it is likely that the majority of adults as well as most children will be their spiritual victims.

The second element to which Bennett refers as an essential feature of Christian salvation—namely, growth in obedience and love— implies an even broader reason for concern with the meeting of the fundamental economic needs of the neighbor. In response to the divine love which he has received the believer—when he is fully aware of the nature and the extent of this love—will not only be motivated to seek ways of bringing the neighbor to an awareness that the latter, too, is accepted by God but he will also be led to serve whatever needs the neighbor may have for his total fulfillment as a human being. He will not be intent merely upon the removal of obstacles to effective evangelism; he will seek to create economic institutions which will provide the physical conditions for the achievement of all of the values and goods which enrich life and which have been made possible by the Creator. Such an affirmation of the creative will of God is made possible by the action of the Redeemer who frees man from the egoism and idolatry into which he has fallen. In short, liberation from sin and growth in love and obedience, taken together, mean that one who is aware of God's *agape* will seek to affirm both the creative and the ordering, as well as the redemptive, purposes of God.

THE CHRISTIAN CONCEPTION OF PROPERTY

We have seen that the Christian doctrine of creation declares that the material world is good, and we have noted that man's proper response to the Creator is one of gratitude and thanksgiving for His good gifts. On the one hand, however, it is possible to conceive of these goods as being intended primarily for possession and control by isolated individuals; or, on the other hand, they may be conceived of as being intended primarily for possession and control by the community. In the former case, Christian faith would be identified with an individualistic conception of property; in the latter, with a collectivistic view. In face of the widely divergent consequences of these two conceptions of property for the entire cultural life of society, it is important that we ask what light Christian faith sheds upon the debate between these two views. More fundamentally, we need to examine what it says about ownership itself. In what sense may either an individual or a community be said to *own* anything?

From the standpoint of biblical faith, all property belongs to God who is its Creator.[14] He alone has absolute ownership over anything. Man's life, the earth, and all that man has or is able to create out of the raw materials with which he has been provided—all belong to God. "The earth is the Lord's and the fulness thereof, the world and those

[14] Cf. Charles L. Taylor, Jr., "Old Testament Foundations," in Joseph F. Fletcher, ed., *Christianity and Property*, Philadelphia, The Westminster Press, 1947, p. 12.

who dwell therein" (Ps. 24:1). "Whatever is under the whole heaven is mine" (Job 41:11; cf. Ps. 50:12; Ex. 19:5). God has freely given man the use of land, air, water, and even of other living creatures (Gen. 1:26–29), but the ultimate ownership of all belongs to the Creator alone. Man's relationship to them is one of stewardship, i.e., of using them in accordance with the will of the One who is sovereign over all.

Within the context of absolute ownership by God alone biblical faith assumes the necessity of some measure of individual ownership although it is keenly aware of the moral and social dangers of wealth and imposes severe limitations upon its acquisition and use in order to protect the welfare of less fortunate persons as well as that of society as a whole. In the Old Testament, the very existence of the commandment "You shall not steal" presupposes the right of individual ownership. Similarly, the frequent protests made by the prophets against the infringement of the prohibition of stealing implies that they assumed the right of individuals to own property. Also in the New Testament some measure of private ownership is presupposed as normal. Even the communism of love which was practiced for a time at Jerusalem after Pentecost (Acts 2:44–45; 5:1–5) does not provide an exception to this rule, for all were free either to place or not to place their property at the disposal of the community; moreover, there is no evidence that such a communal sharing of goods was followed in the other primitive Christian communities. This practice at Jerusalem seems to have been looked upon as a product of Christian fellowship rather than as a blueprint for the economic order.

Although the existence of the right of private property was generally assumed in the early Church, many of the Church Fathers believed that it had its origin in human sinfulness (i.e., in the Fall) rather than in Creation. In the medieval period, Aquinas insisted that private property was in accordance with natural law. In actuality his view differed little from that of the early Fathers who believed that property had been originally held in common and that private ownership had been instituted only after men had fallen into sin. He held that while this right is given in natural law, there is no requirement that men should exercise it; and, indeed, that they should find it necessary to allot property to particular individuals, on a permanent basis, at all results from man's fallen and sinful state in which he is lazy, greedy, and belligerent. Thus, in an unfallen world there would presumably be no necessity or reason for the exercise of the natural right of individual ownership.[15] It should be noted, moreover, that Aquinas was little closer than his predecessors to defending the modern notion that the right of property is absolute and unlimited, for he defined it as a right of *use*, i.e., of the individual ministering from what he has to the necessities of his fellows.[16] Like Aquinas, Luther and Calvin also accepted private property as a legitimate conditon of life in the order of creation as well as in that of the Fall.[17] Although they believed that the right to such ownership rested in God's munificence in creation, they did not believe that it implied a right of unconditional possession. In Lehmann's words, "According to the Reformation the right to use determines the right to possess. . . . Rightly understood, possession is in order to use; use is not in order to possess."[18] The Reformation concept of ownership implies a duty as well as a privilege, and the idea of ownership itself cannot be properly understood apart from the corresponding conception of stewardship.

While there were strong checks upon the right of individual ownership in the thought of Aquinas, Luther, and Calvin, there was a tendency in later Catholicism and to an even greater extent in later Puritanism (with its secularized doctrine of vocation and its tendency to regard prosperity as a sign that one was among the elect) to accept the highly individualistic notion, associated with laissez-faire capitalism, of the right to property as absolute and unconditional and to conceive of the state primarily as an instrument for the protection of this right. These developments have been vigorously challenged, however, in both Catholic and Protestant circles during the past century. At present there is a widespread consensus that the economic individualism which they reflect stands in direct contradiction to the teaching of Christian faith both as regards the nature of man as created-in-community and as regards the importance of social justice; moreover, there is growing recognition of the fact that the individualistic conception of production implied in the notion that the right of private property is absolute and unlimited ignores the role of society in the production of wealth.

In view of the manifest injustices which have been associated with the institution of private property and in view of the complete rejec-

---

[15] F. H. Smyth, "The Middle Ages," in Fletcher, *op. cit.,* pp. 86–87.
[16] *Ibid.*
[17] Paul L. Lehmann, "The Standpoint of the Reformation," in Fletcher, *op. cit.,* pp. 114–116.
[18] *Ibid.,* p. 114.

tion of this right by Communism, what justification—aside from the example furnished by biblical and historical tradition—can be given for private property in our day? Can any basis for it be found when the economic order is viewed in the light of the present creative, ordering, and redeeming will of God? In *Justice and the Social Order,* Emil Brunner grounds the right to private property in the right to freedom. Man was created to be responsible; responsibility presupposes freedom; and freedom presupposes the ability to make significant choices concerning the use of things over which one has a large measure of control. Hence, private property is a right established by creation.[19] Brunner writes: "The man who has nothing at his disposal cannot act freely. He is dependent on the permission of others for every step he takes, and if they so wish, they can make it impossible for him to carry on any concrete activity. Without property there is no power to act. . . . And the word 'property' must be taken literally as ownership, or, as we say to-day, private property. Without private property there is no freedom."[20] Moreover, collective ownership—whether it be by a corporation or by a union or by the state—can never replace the value of individual ownership in terms of freedom; for unless the individual has the right of disposal he becomes a slave of the collective will. Indeed, it is the lack of personal property, Brunner believes, which "is largely responsible for the reduction of the proletariat to an impersonal mass."[21] Brunner does not conclude from this requirement of human freedom, however, either that private property is "a purely individual concern" or that it is the only just form of ownership.[22] Although he tends to be strongly individualistic in his basic conception of property[23] he also stresses the communitarian nature of economic goods and the contribution which the community makes to the acquisition of wealth of all kinds. With respect to God man is always a steward with an account to render for the use of his property; and, from the standpoint of justice, all property is "held subject to the reservation of fellowship."

---

[19] Emil Brunner, *Justice and the Social Order,* trans. by Mary Hottinger, London, Lutterworth Press, 1945, pp. 58, 133.

[20] *Ibid.,* p. 42.

[21] *Ibid.,* p. 59.

[22] *Ibid.,* p. 133.

[23] *Ibid.,* p. 134: Brunner writes, "What a man has earned belongs to him, he has a right to it. . . . He is obliged, not by justice, but by compassion, to give to those in need out of what is entirely his property, but those in need have no right to it."

Professor George Thomas arrives at a similar justification of private property.[24] The individual can realize meaning and value in his life only as he adopts and carries out purposes of his own. Freedom is essential to this end, and material goods are necessary as instruments through which the personality may express and realize itself. In this sense provision for some individual ownership may be viewed as the intent of the Creator. Like Brunner, Thomas stresses the fact that in a collectivist society, in which all property is owned and controlled by the state, the governing authorities have almost unlimited power to determine the lives of the citizens and to prevent them from fulfilling any goals and needs which the rulers themselves do not approve.

Not only is private property essential for the fullest development of personality; it is also necessary, in view of human indolence and self-centeredness, for a second reason, viz., as an incentive to get accomplished the work which needs to be done in the economic order. There are many reasons why men work, but it is undeniable that many—perhaps most—are motivated to work most diligently and regularly by the promise of material possessions over which they can exercise control. The incentive of material reward is especially necessary in order that society may be able to recruit adequate numbers of persons to perform many monotonous, difficult, and dangerous jobs which must be done if the needs of society as a whole are to be met.

Recognition of the right of all people to private property raises the question whether the goal in the distribution of wealth should be absolute equality. It is obvious that there must be a greater amount of equality than exists at present, if all are to have enough resources adequately to meet their needs for physical nourishment, housing, clothing, medical care, education, and recreation. But it is also obvious that all people do not have the same needs for each of these goods and services. Hence, to provide all with the same amounts of food, shelter, clothing, medicine, and cultural and recreational facilities would be to treat them unequally in any except the most abstract sense of that term. Moreover, people differ vastly in the extent to which they have demands placed upon them by others who are dependent upon them for their physical needs and also in the demands which are placed upon them by the functions they perform in society. To permit the bachelor and the father of five children exactly the same income tax deductions would obviously be inequitable, and to make identical

[24] George F. Thomas, *Christian Ethics and Moral Philosophy*, New York, Charles Scribner's Sons, 1955, p. 312.

allowances for expenses connected with the performance of their official duties to the President of the United States and to the mayor of a city would be manifestly unjust.

From the standpoint of Christian faith, equality, like justice, can be properly understood only when it is viewed in relationship to specific individuals with specific needs. Abstract equalitarianism neglects individual differences between persons. It also ignores the social necessity of giving unequal rewards to people who make unequal contributions to the community. But, while some amount of inequality in the distribution of property is demanded by the inequality of men's needs and in the interest of social utility, it is clear that the vast inequalities of our present economic system are not justifiable on either of these grounds. In our own country, but especially in the world community, millions of people do not have even the barest necessities for physical existence while many others have many times that which their needs require. Moreover, often there is little relationship between either the social utility or the difficulty or the danger of the work which a person performs and the monetary reward which he receives in return for it.

Christian ethics, then, is not egalitarian; neither does it justify the vast inequalities of our existing economic system. The amount of equality which it demands in the distribution of wealth is determined by the extent to which men's needs are the same; the amount of inequality which it permits is determined by the extent to which their needs differ and the welfare of society as a whole demands such inequality.

While it needs to be recognized that the Christian ethic does not demand absolute equality, the greater danger lies in the tendency to rationalize the existing inequalities and to substitute fictitious forms of equality for a more realistic effort to provide a greater measure of actual equality. Thus, the Christian ideal is often alleged to be that of equality of opportunity. This in turn is interpreted in individualistic terms to mean that each person has the right to rise to whatever economic level he is able to attain on his own. Such a view of equality overlooks the *inequalities of circumstances* with which men are surrounded by accident of birth because of inequalities of social position, wealth, and environment. It also ignores those inequalities which are due to different physical endowments and different intellectual capacities. Provision for equality of opportunity, if this be genuine, must include provision for equality of circumstance.[25] Beyond this, Chris-

[25] Cf. *ibid.*, p. 317.

tian love recognizes the claim of all men, regardless of their abilities and circumstances, to those conditions which will make possible the fulfillment of their personalities as children of God. Moreover, since Christian faith perceives the purpose of God for man to be the creation of a community which is united in love and fellowship, great disparities of wealth which create barriers between groups and classes and prevent the participation of all in any genuine form of common life must be judged to be inconsistent with Christian love.

The foregoing view of the Christian conception of equality is more adequately summarized in the formula "equality of consideration" than it is in the phrase "equality of opportunity," since the latter is so widely understood in individualistc terms. Equality of consideration means that each person should be effectively taken into account in the distribution of social benefits and that each should be helped by society to develop his capacities and fulfill his needs to the greatest extent possible.[26]

It is difficult to define the Christian idea of equality in more precise terms because men differ so much in their capacities and needs. It is clear, however, that human need rather than an abstract notion of equality is the focal point in the effort to achieve an equitable distribution of goods. In practical terms, this would seem to lead inevitably to the idea of a floor, or minimum level, of income below which no families should be allowed to fall.[27] Even considerations of discipline for the shiftlessness of an employable father ought not to be allowed to penalize the whole family. The members of such a family have capacities and needs which ought to be taken into consideration equally with those of other members of society who are economically more advantaged, and these persons should receive equal *treatment* from society in terms of their capacities and needs insofar as this is possible.

THE CHRISTIAN CONCEPTION OF WORK

THE PURPOSES OF WORK

Not only is modern man faced with the necessity of achieving a more equitable distribution of wealth, he is also faced with a crisis as

---

[26] Cf. *ibid.*, pp. 317–318.

[27] Cf. John C. Bennett, "Christian Ethics in Economic Life," in Bennett, *et al., op. cit.,* p. 220.

regards the meaning of work. In our present-day industrial society, large masses of people find little or no ultimate meaning in the daily tasks which they perform. Their religious faith and worship are largely unrelated to the occupations by which they earn a livelihood. This is true to a great extent of employers as well as of employees.

This does not mean that people do not find some meaning or value in their work. On the contrary, they find many values, but these are not related to the Center of value in such a way that their work has ultimate religious meaning in their own understanding of it. Men work for material reward in the form of profits and wages. They also work because they find comradeship with their fellow workers on the job. They are motivated by the satisfaction which they find in the quality of workmanship they are able to achieve and in the prestige which work and excellence bring both with one's fellow workers and in the community at large. Moreover, those whose conscious goals in work are limited exclusively to their paychecks or their profits are generally motivated not so much by money as by those things which money can provide for their families and themselves and even for the larger circle of those for whom they feel a sense of responsibility.

The biblical view of work does not deny that most of these goals have a rightful place in work; but it does insist that work gets its final meaning from the relationship which it bears to the divine will. This will, however, is not understood in narrow terms, for the God to whom work is related is Himself at work in many ways. Moreover, according to biblical faith, it is also only in relation to the divine will that leisure and worship have final meaning or worth. In a word, the contribution which the biblical view of work makes to any effort to discover the meaning of this sphere of human activity is to provide a framework whereby the goals which men generally have in work may be related to the ultimate meaning of human life as a whole. Insofar as these goals are in keeping with the purpose of God for man in the created world, they are seen to have ultimate significance; insofar as they are inconsistent with this purpose, they must be rejected.

From the standpoint of Christian faith, daily work gets its meaning from the three primary functions which it serves. Each of these is related to the will of God for man. In the first place, it is *a necessary condition for human life*. Men must work in order that both their physical and their spiritual needs may be satisfied. On the one hand, they must work for food and for means for protecting themselves against many dangers which threaten them from without; on the other hand, they must also work in order to develop their capacities for creativity and culture and to make a fully human life possible. Work is necessary both for the achievement of goals that are self-centered and for the achievement of goals that are other-centered. Most men recognize this fact, and most men work; but they differ widely in their conceptions of the ends which they seek to achieve thereby. For some, work is primarily an instrument for the achievement of values for the self; for others it is also an instrument for the service of their families and their communities. In actuality, the motivation of most people represents a combination of self-interest, concern for their families, loyalty to fellow-workers and employers, and a desire to enrich the life of the community as a whole. The Christian and the secularist alike see work as a necessity for the realization of these ends. But the Christian differs from the secularist in viewing this necessity as part of the order which God has established and in which He has placed man for the achievement of a more ultimate end, viz., a life of love and service under the sovereignty of God.

Insofar as the goods and services which one provides through his daily work are intended to meet genuine human needs, these constitute *a practical expression of neighbor-love.* By the same token, the Christian ought also to recognize and gratefully accept the services which his fellowmen are similarly rendering to him through their occupations. Both recognition of the giving and recognition of the receiving aspects of work that is socially necessary are equally important, and both are equally difficult in the highly impersonalized society of our day. In order that the identity of the neighbor and the nature of the love which he needs may be made clear in terms of contemporary life, the traditional concept of the neighbor needs to be "translated into the customer or the client whom the worker perhaps sees once in his life, into the consumer of the goods he produces whom he will never know, into the fellow workers with whom he forms a team, into the enterprise or occupation in which he works, into the whole fabric of society of which his work is a function."[28] When the social significance of work is ignored and when men think only of their own rights and interests, they violate their own natures, and increased production and higher rewards come to be ends in themselves. From the standpoint of Christian faith, the primary purpose of the industrial order is the production

[28] Second Assembly of the World Council of Churches, *The Christian Hope and the Task of the Church,* New York, Harper & Brothers, 1954, Section on "The Laity—the Christian in His Vocation," p. 26.

of goods for the benefit of the community, and the primary purpose of work is the satisfaction of real needs.

In addition to the service of one's fellowmen, there is another purpose or goal for which man was created but which can be achieved only through work, namely, the *realization of the self through the exercise of its creative powers.* Man is endowed with capacities which can be developed only through their use. These talents are given to him both for service to his fellows and for the enrichment of human life as a whole. It is in the process by which these capacities are developed that the self is realized and meaning in life is discovered. Indeed, a person does not know the nature and extent of his talents and powers until he exercises them, trains them, and disciplines them in the course of applying them to some task such as the composition of music, the writing of poetry, or the seeking of truth in philosophy or science. We are able to recognize the abilities and occasional greatness of our fellowmen only as they express themselves in the work that they do. The desire to create new forms of being and of values is implanted in all men, although this power of creation is seen at the highest level only in the work of the very few great poets, artists, craftsmen, statesmen, scientists, and philosophers. But each person has an urge and need to express himself outwardly with some measure of individuality and freedom, whether it be in the building of sand castles on the beach, finger-painting in a kindergarten or at home, drawing on rocks or canvas, building model airplanes, making new designs of cars and buildings, or expressing himself in one of a thousand other ways. Ideally, each person's daily work ought to provide a major outlet for this urge toward creative self-expression.

It needs to be remembered, however, that while each person is given certain talents and held accountable by the Creator for their use, these are not to be developed and used primarily for the self but rather for the service and enrichment of others. In the biblical view, man's talents are to be understood first of all as gifts and secondly as instruments of service. It is in seeking to fulfill the needs of others that the self is realized. Fulfillment of the self is only a secondary, not the primary, purpose of work. Yet the nature of the self is such that it is realized most fully, albeit most surprisingly and paradoxically, when its primary aim is to serve the neighbor rather than the self. But the neighbor is served in many ways, by persons with different gifts; and the needs of the neighbor can be fully met only when they are fully understood in terms of all that contributes to the enrichment of his physical, intellectual, aesthetic, social, and religious life.

The foregoing three-fold way of defining the meaning of work as it is understood in Christian faith will seem to many to be abstract and far-removed from the realities and the possibilities of their daily activities. For this reason it is necessary to attempt to spell out the significance of these meanings or purposes of work in terms of more specific goals and objectives which are related more concretely to the daily tasks of men everywhere. If such an effort is to be helpful in bridging the gap between a theological conception of work and men's understanding of their daily tasks, an attempt must be made to relate the purposes of work which we have described above to a realistic appraisal of man's physical, psychological, social, and spiritual needs while at the same time bearing in mind the manifold ways in which these needs are interrelated. One of the most suggestive efforts to define the purposes of work in more specific terms is that of Professor Howard R. Bowen in *Christian Values and Economic Life*. According to Professor Bowen, man's economic life viewed as a whole has the following eleven "subordinate goals":[29]

1. survival and physical well-being
2. fellowship
3. dignity and humility
4. enlightenment
5. aesthetic enjoyment
6. creativity
7. new experience
8. security
9. freedom
10. justice
11. personality

Each person has need for each of these if he is to live a fully human life. Hence, work that is directed toward the meeting of any of these specific needs has significance from the standpoint of Christian faith when it is understood first of all as an expression of love in service of the neighbor and secondarily as a means of the fulfillment of the self through the development of its creative capacities as a way of glorifying God. If much modern work that is routine and irksome but still necessary is to have genuine significance for those who are called upon to perform such tasks, far more attention must be given to helping these workers see what needs are being served through these forms of work. In our day, the importance of identifying these needs in specific terms would seem to be equally as great as that of helping

[29] Howard R. Bowen, "Goals of Economic Life," in Bennett, *et al., op. cit.,* ch. 4.

the modern worker understand *who* his neighbor is. It is not sufficient abstractly to see all men as one's neighbors without at the same time recognizing *why* they are one's neighbors and without being made aware of the multiplicity of *claims* which the latter place upon one.

In view of the large portion of a person's energy and time that is devoted to his daily occupation (including that of the housewife), it would be desirable if all of the subordinate goals listed by Professor Bowen could be achieved in some measure in every work-situation, but this is manifestly impossible in many types of work that are especially monotonous and laborious. It is likewise highly impractical to make adequate provision for many of these goals in most work-situations, and indeed such a balance in one's job would not necessarily be desirable. But where sufficient opportunities are not available for any one of these goals in one's daily occupation, opportunity should be provided for it in some other phase of each person's round of living. The important point is that the purposes of the economic life should be seen in relationship to the goals of human life as a whole. Man's economic activity—his daily work, the conditions under which he works, the values he finds in his work—is an important part of his total experience, and ought to provide opportunity, directly or indirectly, for each individual to grow in the kind of life which represents the fulfillment of his destiny as a child of God. All work which directly or indirectly contributes to this goal has ultimate significance from the standpoint of Christian faith.

When the variety of human needs is recognized and when it is realized that these needs must be met in order to make possible the kind of life for which man was created, it is possible to go one step farther and affirm that man has a God-given right to the conditions which are essential to human fulfillment. This is to say that each person has a claim upon the resources available to a community to the extent that these are necessary to the living of a fully human life. Such rights are not absolute in the sense that each person's claim to them is unaffected by the claims of the group, but they are inalienable in the sense that they are grounded in the moral and spiritual relationships which men have by virtue of the humanity with which they are endowed. (See Chapter 11, pp. 326–328.) As an individual-in-community each person has responsibilities to all other members of the community, and, conversely, the community has responsibilities to each of its members. Beyond this mutual responsibility of each to the group and of the group to each, every man is related directly to

God and has responsibilities to Him. The rights of men are grounded in the claims which each person has upon the community for providing the conditions which make it possible for him to fulfill his needs and discharge his responsibilities. This does not imply that men have a right to identical amounts of property or leisure, but it does imply that all men have a claim to equality of consideration of their needs for each of these. It implies that they have a claim upon society to provide what Tillich calls "creative justice." Or, putting the relationship the other way around, it implies that society has an obligation to provide the conditions or circumstances which are essential to the fulfillment of each person's potentialities and responsibilities.

Any effort to list such rights in terms of the specific requirements of a particular economic system must be somewhat tentative. It is important, however, for society as a whole to recognize that it has an obligation to acknowledge and defend certain economic claims of every individual even though there may be disagreement as to the precise content of such rights. Apart from the recognition of such claims, the temptation is strong for those who are in a position to meet these needs to look upon any steps they may take in this direction as acts of charity or undeserved generosity when in reality they constitute only the fulfillment of the just claims of the economically disadvantaged. While the specific forms which man's economic rights will take at different times and under different economic systems will vary, a list of such rights stated in terms that are broad enough to be universal should probably include the following but would by no means be limited to these:

1. the right to a job
2. the right to a living wage
3. the right to maintain a home and family
4. access to adequate health facilities
5. economic security in old age
6. the right to private property
7. the right to be educated
8. the right to leisure
9. the right to participate in decisions affecting the terms and conditions of one's employment

THE PROTESTANT DOCTRINE OF VOCATION

The concept traditionally used by Protestants to express the religious meaning of work is *vocation*. In our day, however, this term has become largely secularized. Except for those who have found or expect to find their places of daily employment in various forms of religious activity as ministers or missionaries or perhaps as social workers or teachers, the idea of vocation in a religious sense has been largely replaced by the notion of an occupation in which one can earn a livelihood, gain prestige, and attain a desired standard of living. These latter goals rather than the answering of a summons from God to a life of service are the standards in terms of which most modern men choose their occupations.

Yet the idea of a "vocation" persists in a secularized form, as evidenced by our frequent usage of such terms as "vocational guidance" and "avocation," as well as the word "vocation" itself. The use of this idea in any of these forms implies a background of religious meaning according to which one's work was originally looked upon as an activity to which he was called in a personal way. Work had religious meaning because it pointed to the fact that the divine will was related in a personal and concrete way to the area of life to which each individual devoted the largest amount of his time and energy. In essence this concept represented a recognition of the fact that the whole of life—work as well as worship—is lived under the sovereignty of God. To the extent that this sense of divine sovereignty has been lost, the economic life has come to be looked upon as being autonomous and work has lost its ultimate dignity and religious significance.

Although the origin of the idea of "vocation" or "calling" is generally associated with Luther and Calvin, the notion itself is much older than the Reformation and is rooted in the biblical understanding of man's relationship to God. In actuality, what Luther and Calvin did was to give the term a distinctive meaning by combining the two biblical themes of *divine vocation* and *daily work* into the single concept of *vocation.* In the Bible, the primary summons of God to man is the call to repentance and faith and to a life of service within the community which God has chosen for His own purposes. In the Old Testament, of course, this community is Israel; in the New Testament it is primarily the Church, although Christians are called to remain in the world and not to withdraw from it. The main point in either case, however, is that the individual is called to a life of faith and service within the community which is also subject to God's rule and summoned to be a holy community. Only secondarily is the Bible concerned with the question of work, or the particular occupation in which one is engaged. God's summons to repentance, faith, and service comes to a man where he is—as a tentmaker, as a farmer, as a carpenter, as an engineer.

To modern Americans, with our emphasis upon the importance of vocational guidance, with our awareness of the social prestige which is attached to various forms of work, and with the comparative freedom which youth from the upper and middle classes in particular have in the choice of their life's work, this indifference of the Bible to the occupation in which one is engaged seems strange and even irresponsible. Yet, Canon Richardson goes so far as to maintain that the Bible "knows of no instance of a man's being called to an earthly profession or trade by God."[30] Indeed, the advice of John the Baptist to certain tax collectors that they "collect no more than is appointed" them and to certain soldiers that they "rob no one by violence or by false accusation, and be content with [their] wages" is typical of the standpoint of the Bible as a whole (Luke 3:12–14). So long as men's secular tasks do not conflict with loyalty to God the Bible does not seem much interested in how men gain a livelihood. What it is interested in is that all men—whatever their occupations may be—shall subordinate every motive to the will of God.[31]

This essentially was the attitude of the Reformers even though they identified a person's vocation with his occupation more explicitly than the Bible does. In opposition to the medieval church which, following Aquinas, had made a qualitative distinction between the values of different kinds of work and looked upon the monks and priests alone as having a divine vocation, Luther maintained that every Christian —whatever his task—is called into the service of God in his particular form of employment and that, for this reason, the work which he does becomes a divine vocation or calling insofar as it is done in faith and ministers to the needs of his fellowmen. To desire to change one's form of employment, Luther believed, was a sign of pride; and the Catholic concept of a hierarchy of works was to him a form of Pharisaism or works-righteousness. Justification is completely by faith, Luther held, and the desire to change the work in which one is called to the life of repentance and faith was a sign of the lack of

[30]Alan Richardson, *The Biblical Doctrine of Work,* London, Student Christian Movement Press, Ltd., 1952, p. 35.

[31] Paul S. Minear, "Work and Vocation in Scripture," in John Oliver Nelson, ed., *Work and Vocation: A Christian Discussion,* New York, Harper & Brothers, 1954, p. 77.

faith. Calvin similarly stressed the duty of each Christian—no matter how obscure or burdensome his employment—to regard his particular form of work as "a post assigned him by the Lord."[32] In keeping with his more activistic ethic in general, Calvin stressed the duty of the Christian to glorify God *through* his vocation somewhat more than Luther, whose emphasis was upon serving God *in* one's calling. For both Luther and Calvin, however, one's work was assigned him by the Lord. Both rejected the Catholic idea that one could earn merit, much less accumulate a surplus of merit, through any works whatsoever. Man remains an unprofitable servant at best and must rely upon God's grace alone for forgiveness and salvation. Both were fundamentally true to the biblical idea of the basic equality of men's occupations as opposed to the Greek idea that manual labor is degrading. Both had a strong sense of the Providence of God which sustained the largely feudalistic order of society in which it was appointed them to live and in which each person had a job to do which gained its meaning in relation to the whole. They accepted the fact that men were not generally free to choose the form of work which they would do, and they considered this arrangement to be providential in that it served as a restraint upon their pride and upon the restlessness which they might otherwise feel with their particular tasks.

The biblical themes of divine vocation and daily work were held together in dynamic relationship during the period of early Protestantism. But for a variety of reasons they fell apart again after the middle of the seventeenth century as they had done in the Middle Ages. Through its identification of daily work with one's vocation, the Protestant concept of a calling itself contributed in some degree to the later development of secularism,[33] for diligence in one's work and thrift in one's expenditures produced prosperity, and prosperity in turn dulled men's apprehension of what had originally been intended by dedicating one's work and one's possessions to the glory

[32] John Calvin, *Institutes of the Christian Religion*, 2 vols., Philadelphia, Presbyterian Board of Education, 1936, bk. III, ch. X, par. vi.

[33] It is widely agreed, however, that Max Weber exaggerated the contribution which was actually made by the "Protestant ethic" to the development of the spirit of capitalism in his *The Protestant Ethic and the Spirit of Capitalism*, New York, Charles Scribner's Sons, 1930. See Georgia Harkness, *John Calvin: The Man and His Ethics*, New York, Henry Holt & Company, 1931; Amintore Fanfani, *Catholicism, Protestantism and Capitalism*, London, Sheed & Ward, 1935; and R. H. Tawney, *Religion and the Rise of Capitalism*, New York, Harcourt, Brace and Company, 1937.

of God and the service of the neighbor. A number of other factors, however, also contributed to the secularization of work. The spread of free thought and revolt against authority, the growth of the industrial revolution, and the rise to power of a new middle class of merchants, manufacturers, bankers, and small landowners resulted in the disintegration of the old feudalistic economy and the breakup of the traditional ways of life.[34] Moreover, stress upon the individualistic tendencies in Protestantism at the expense of its great unifying principles of the universal reign of God and the corporate character of the Christian life contributed to the loss of a vivid sense of an entire community living under God. As a result of all of these forces work came to be understood in individualistic terms, and the idea of a calling came generally to mean merely human work, with God left out. Daily work became more and more isolated from worship, and life increasingly seemed to be divided into two separate spheres: the sacred and the secular (profane, godless). In this context, the traditional Protestant doctrine of daily work as a religious vocation appeared remote and naive.

This is the position which the idea of a "calling" continued to hold generally throughout the nineteenth century and into our own time. In view of the fact that it has become so emptied of its once powerful religious content, one is tempted to wonder, with Brunner, whether it should not be renounced altogether. On the other hand, in its biblical sense it is still "full of force" and "pregnant in meaning." It includes God's acts of grace toward men and the concrete character of His command to man in terms of the world in which he is placed. For this reason we are forced to agree with Brunner that to give up this concept would be to lose "a central part of the Christian message." Therefore, we must not throw it away; rather, we must seek to regain its authentic meaning.[35] Today of course no one would advocate a return to the conditions of the seventeenth century—its feudalism, its hierarchical and hereditary social structure, its serfdom, and its autocratic rule—but the Protestant and biblical sense of a community living under the sovereignty of God must be recovered if the common tasks of men are again to be suffused with religious meaning.

If the concept of vocation is to be relevant to our own day, it must

---

[34] Robert L. Calhoun, "Work and Vocation in Christian History," in Nelson, *op. cit.,* p. 84.
[35] Brunner, *The Divine Imperative,* pp. 205–206.

be restated in a way that will take into account the far-reaching economic changes that have taken place since the seventeenth century. The most important of these have been related to the industrial revolution and include the rise of such phenomena as mass production, the increasing specialization of labor, the impersonalization of the relationships between employers and employees, and the separation of ownership from management. Resulting largely from the transformation that has taken place in the economic order, there has been, on the one hand, an exaltation of the profit motive as the standard of success for managers and owners of industry; and there has been, on the other hand, a subjection of the industrial worker to a huge industrial process over which he has little or no control and in which he is able to find scant opportunity for the expression of the whole self. Under such circumstances the revival of a genuine sense of vocation among owners and managers of industry would involve their becoming more socially oriented, more service-motivated, and more concerned with the welfare of their employees and the community as a whole. As we have seen, this does not mean that profit would cease to be *a* motive in business, but to make it the *only* motive or the overriding consideration represents a denial of the Protestant conception of work as a way of glorifying God and serving the neighbor.

The industrial worker needs to be assisted in relating his particular task to the total industrial enterprise by helping him understand the total process and the contribution which he makes to it. Such assistance might take the form of providing a fuller understanding of why work—even that which appears as drudgery—is socially necessary and hence may be viewed as service of God. There is need also realistically to examine the reasons why men work and to seek to meet these needs in modern industrial situations to the fullest extent possible. It is often assumed, for example, that men work effectively only if they are working for monetary rewards. But there is much evidence to support the view that the worker is not so exclusively an "economic man" as this belief supposes. Managerial groups are frequently aware of this fact, as evidenced by their widespread interest in programs of "human relations in industry." Factors other than economic return play an important role both in making employees better satisfied and in making them more productive. More attention to human relationships and to the values which are associated with them offers a promising way of restoring religious significance to one's daily work by setting it in a context of personal relationships to management and to one's fellow workers.

The modern industrial worker also needs to be given a greater chance to express his creativity and freedom through the provision of more opportunities for him to participate responsibly in the making of those decisions which affect his welfare and determine the circumstances under which he works. This, of course, is one of the major goals in the unionization of labor. In view of the social and political consequences of large concentrations of economic power in the hands of owners and managers of industry, provision also needs to be made for the safeguarding of the political and social as well as the economic rights of the worker in the total life of the community as a whole. Protection of these rights would seem to be one of the major functions of labor unions in the struggle for social justice.

Finally, a conception of vocation that is meaningful in our day needs to be related to areas of human relationships other than one's daily occupation. Today we hear predictions of a thirty-hour work week, and it is estimated that there will be eighteen million unemployed people over sixty-five living in the United States in 1975.[36] Under such conditions, it is essential that the concept of a calling be broadened to include man's responsibility for what he does in his leisure and in his retirement. The biblical idea of a divine vocation implies that each person is summoned in both his daily task and his off-duty hours, as well as in his retirement, to use his gifts and abilities to meet all the genuine needs of his neighbors. These needs are many, and an effort ought to be made to discover what they are and find ways of meeting them both through individual and group-centered activities. In our discussion of the values of work we noted what some of these needs are. Here, we are concerned to emphasize the fact that they represent continuing needs, and many of them must be met on a voluntary basis by people who devote part of their free time in periods of leisure and retirement to various forms of community service and to fulfilling their responsibilities as citizens. In this sense marriage, parenthood, citizenship, and participation in the institutional life of the Church ought to be understood as vocations just as much as the summons to some remunerative form of daily work.

[36] E. A. Friedmann and R. J. Havighurst, *The Meaning of Work and Retirement,* Chicago, University of Chicago Press, 1954, p. 188.

THE ECONOMIC TASK OF THE CHURCH

The Church is the community of all those who share a common faith in God as revealed through Christ. Its membership is drawn from all economic classes and from people who participate in different economic systems. This is true not only of the "holy catholic Church" of faith but also to a considerable extent of the "mainline Protestant denominations"—such as the Baptist, the Methodist, and the Presbyterian churches—in America today.[37] However, in contrast to the inclusiveness that is professed by all Christians in their creeds and is at least partially exemplified in the over-all membership of the major denominations, there is abundant evidence that a similar inclusiveness is generally lacking at the level of the local congregation. Thus, Dean Liston Pope, for example, declares: "Differentiation within Protestantism corresponds fairly closely to class divisions. Individual Protestant churches tend to be 'class churches,' with members drawn principally from one class group."[38]

In view of the contradiction which exists between the inclusiveness of the Church of faith and the exclusiveness of most churches, it is urgent that each congregation make every effort to exemplify in its own life the supra-class character of the Christian fellowship in the recruitment of membership and in the assignment of responsibility for leadership in the local church. If local churches as well as denominations are to be true to their own nature as embodiments of the Church universal, each must seek ways to manifest the oneness of all classes in its total ministry. Specific steps in this direction include the manifestation of concern for all economic groups and the encouragement of members of groups with conflicting economic interests to come together to seek solutions to their conflicts upon the basis of their common faith and worship. The provision of a genuine

[37] For a comparison of the class distribution of membership in the major religious bodies in the United States see "Christianity and the Economic Order. Study No. 10: Social-Economic Status and Outlook of Religious Groups in America," *Information Service*, XXVII, no. 20 (May 15, 1948), pt. 2. See also David W. Barry, "The Fellowship of Class," *The City Church*, VI, no. 1 (January–February, 1955), pp. 5–8.

[38] Liston Pope, "Religion and the Class Structure," *The Annals of the American Academy of Political and Social Science*, 256 (March, 1948), p. 89. Cf. Waldo Beach, "The Protestant Church and the Middle Class," *Social Action*, XV, no. 3 (March 15, 1949), pp. 16–26. See also August B. Hollingshead, *Elmtown's Youth*, New York, John Wiley & Sons, 1949, pp. 248–250.

community of worship that transcends social and class lines is one of the most important contributions which the churches can make to the resolution of the economic problems and conflicts of our day.

Secondly, the Church has a responsibility to help people understand the intrinsic relationship between Christian faith and their daily work. This is a task for laymen as well as for ministers. In recent years large numbers of laymen have begun to rediscover the essential meaning of their work in terms of its vocational character. In Europe, for example, there have sprung up many groups composed largely of laymen which have as their objective the effort to relate their Christian faith to their occupational life. The *Kirchentag* movement in Germany, The Christian Frontier Council in England and Scotland, and similar movements in Sweden, Holland, France, and Greece are showing what can be done in this direction. At occasional conferences sponsored by these groups, Christians and non-Christians, trained theologians and experts on industry and other social issues, come together to discuss matters of common interest and to seek a more adequate understanding of their common problems by sharing their specialized experiences and insights. Through these conferences it is becoming clear that the Christian message concerns not only the inner personal life of man but also his responsibilities in his occupational, social, and political life. Evaluating the significance of groups such as these shortly before the Evanston Assembly, a preparatory commission of the World Council of Churches concluded that two important changes are taking place as a result of these conferences. The report of this commission said: "Non-Christians . . . have been becoming more aware of the fact that virtually all so-called secular matters and relationships have a spiritual dimension without which they are not recognized fully, even in their more technical aspects. Christians, on the other hand, are beginning afresh to take worldly things seriously as the concern of Christianity, and to take their fellow men seriously, not only as potential converts but as human beings."[39]

Similar concern with the vocational character of daily work is beginning to be manifest in the United States. Four important conferences on Christian economic responsibility have been held at Pittsburgh in 1948, Detroit, Buffalo, and again at Pittsburgh in 1956, under the auspices of the Department of the Church and Economic

---

[39] Second Assembly of the World Council of Churches, *op. cit.*, p. 41.

Life of the Federal (now National) Council of Churches.[40] At least two major denominations—the Evangelical and Reformed Church and the Methodist Church—have held national conferences on this theme. Other denominations have also given major attention to the same topic in the national conferences of their men's organizations.

As already noted, the task of relating Christian faith to the economic life cannot be done effectively and realistically without the participation of both laymen and clergy. By themselves ministers can never gain a full appreciation of the difficulties and tensions that laymen encounter as they are exposed to the pressures and demands of their manifold jobs in the largely secular business world. Such an understanding is necessary, however, if the clergy are to offer guidance that is relevant and if they are to provide leadership that is worthy of trust and confidence in dealing with economic problems. Laymen, on the other hand, frequently need the objectivity that a minister is able to provide by reason of his different occupational status. Moreover, because of their training and experience, the clergy have much to contribute in terms of their more specialized and systematic comprehension of the Christian view of God, of man, of history, and of community.[41] The Church, it needs to be remembered, consists of both laymen and clergy; and the task of transforming the economic order is a joint one. To the laymen, however, falls the primary responsibility for technical knowledge and for the Christian witness and action on the job where the transformation itself must ultimately be made.

Thirdly, the Church must refrain from identifying itself with any particular economic system or program, whether this be capitalism, communism, socialism, or the coöperative movement. Sincere Christians who are well-informed on economic matters differ widely in their judgments as to which system is the most equitable and the most congenial to Christian faith. Each type of economic organization exists in many different forms, and each is subject to corruption. The Church as such does not possess the technical knowledge that is necessary for the solution of economic problems essentially technical in character. For these reasons, the Church as a whole ought not to

[40] The monumental Series on the Ethics and Economics of Society, produced by a Study Committee of The Federal (National) Council of Churches, provides further striking evidence of this same concern.

[41] See Cameron Parker Hall, *The Christian at His Daily Work,* New York, National Council of Churches, 1951, p. 42.

identify itself with any one economic system or program. This does not mean, however, that individual Christians and groups of Christians ought not to seek solutions to the many economic problems with which they are confronted—solutions that will be both technically sound and in keeping with Christian principles. On the contrary, Christian businessmen, labor leaders, economists, and political leaders have a special duty to do this in relation to the areas in which they have particular responsibilities—for example, in the formation of policies governing relationships between employers and employees; in decisions concerning the goals of labor unions and the strategy to be employed in securing these goals; in the task of discovering how the goals of human life as these are understood in Christian faith can be most effectively related to the economic life; and in the task of formulating specific proposals and organizing political support for those policies which will best promote economic justice in the community as a whole. In addition to the special responsibilities of particular individuals and groups, each citizen has an obligation to support the political party and candidates which seem to him to offer the best solutions to the economic issues at stake in a particular campaign. Individuals cannot escape their responsibility by refusing to take sides. If they fail to support efforts to achieve a better economic order, in effect they support the one which already exists. In this process, however, the Church ought to avoid giving an unqualified endorsement to any human economic program or system, and it ought to avoid identifying itself with any one economic or political group. When it is true to its own nature, the Church is neither pro-labor nor pro-management; by the same token it must be pro-justice.[42]

Fourthly, the Church should seek to improve the moral and spiritual climate in which economic institutions function. The value-judgments which underlie a culture are more important than all particular efforts to improve its institutions. In our society these are to a very large extent secular, and as long as this circumstance prevails, it cannot be expected that our economic institutions will be transformed in such a way as to reflect a Christian ordering of values. To seek to transform the prevailing moral climate of society is one of the major continuing challenges confronting the Church. A deeper awareness of the moral and spiritual dimension of human life, a vital comprehension of the nature of life in community, and a more

[42] Victor Obenhaus, *The Responsible Christian*, Chicago, The University of Chicago Press, 1957, p. 52.

adequate understanding of the urgency of the demand for social justice—all of these are needed to undergird efforts to bring economic institutions into greater harmony with Christian faith.

RECOMMENDED READINGS

Bennett, John C., *et al., Christian Values and Economic Life,* New York, Harper & Brothers, 1954, chs. 4, 12–14.

Boulding, Kenneth E., *The Organizational Revolution,* New York, Harper & Brothers, 1953.

Bowen, Howard R., *Social Responsibilities of the Businessman,* New York, Harper & Brothers, 1953.

Brunner, Emil, *Christianity and Civilisation,* II: *Specific Problems,* New York, Charles Scribner's Sons, 1949, chs. V, VII.

Brunner, Emil, *The Divine Imperative,* trans. by Olive Wyon, New York, The Macmillan Company, 1942, chs. XXXIII–XXXV.

Fitch, John A., *Social Responsibilities of Organized Labor,* New York, Harper & Brothers, 1957.

Fletcher, J. F., ed., *Christianity and Property,* Philadelphia, The Westminster Press, 1947, chs. 1–2.

Galbraith, John Kenneth, *The Affluent Society,* Boston, Houghton Mifflin Company, 1958.

Hall, Cameron Parker, *The Christian at His Daily Work,* New York, National Council of Churches, 1951.

Heimann, Eduard, "The Economy of Abundance," *Social Action,* XXIII, no. 5 (January, 1957), pp. 6–12.

Husslein, Joseph, ed., *Social Wellsprings,* 2 vols., Milwaukee, The Bruce Publishing Company, 1940–42, vol. I, ch. 9; vol. II, ch. 7.

Muelder, Walter G., *Foundations of the Responsible Society,* New York, Abingdon Press, 1959, chs. I, VII–XII.

Munby, D. L., *Christianity and Economic Problems,* London, Macmillan & Co., Ltd., 1956.

Nelson, John Oliver, ed., *Work and Vocation: A Christian Discussion,* New York, Harper & Brothers, 1954.

Obenhaus, Victor, *The Responsible Christian,* Chicago, The University of Chicago Press, 1957, chs. II–IV, VI–VII, XI.

Oldham, J. H., ed., *The Oxford Conference: Official Report,* New York, Willett, Clark and Company, 1937, "Report of the Section on Church, Community and State in Relation to the Economic Order."

Richardson, Alan, *The Biblical Doctrine of Work,* London, Student Christian Movement Press, Ltd., 1952.

Visser't Hooft, W. A., ed., *The Evanston Report: The Second Assembly of the World Council of Churches,* 1954, London, Student Christian Movement Press, Ltd., 1955, The Report of Section VI on "The Laity: The Christian in his Vocation."

Ward, A. Dudley, ed., *Goals of Economic Life,* New York, Harper & Brothers, 1953.

Wilcox, Walter W., *Social Responsibility in Farm Leadership,* New York, Harper & Brothers, 1956.

chapter 11

THE POLITICAL ORDER

THE CHRISTIAN AND POLITICAL AUTHORITY

THE OLD TESTAMENT

THE starting point of the Christian's understanding of the political order is the belief in the radical monotheism of Judaic-Christian faith. It is belief in the one God who is the Creator of the ends of the earth, the present Ruler of the nations, and the active Lord of history. As we have seen, He is a God who demands justice and righteousness of men in their dealings one with another in the social order at large—in economic affairs, in the exercise of the authority of the king, in the dispensing of justice in the courts, and in the dealings of nations with each other. This conception of the universality and righteousness of God was the great contribution of the Hebrew prophets of the eighth-to-the-sixth centuries before Christ. Amos (5:24) and Micah (6:8) perhaps expressed the divine demand for justice in the life of the community most unforgettably, but Hosea and the Isaiah of the Exile were at one with them in calling both the individual Israelites and the nation as a whole to repentance and to a renewal in righteousness. Each prophet addressed his message both to kings and to subjects, for each saw all men standing under the divine judgment and the community as a whole as responsible to the divine will.

THE NEW TESTAMENT

As we turn to the New Testament, we are impressed with the different attitudes which we find reflected there in relation to the political authorities. Whereas the primary word of the prophets concerning the rulers of Israel was that God demanded justice of them, the characteristic word of the New Testament in this regard is that the political order should be accepted as the work of divine providence and hence the rulers should be obeyed. There is little concern in the New Testament either to reform the existing political structures or to influence the policies of the governing authorities. This difference in attitude reflects a major difference between the situations to which the prophets on the one hand and the writers of the New Testament on the other hand addressed themselves. Unlike the early Christian community, Israel was a political state, or theocracy, and throughout much of her history her religious leaders exercised political as well as religious authority. In this capacity her rulers had a responsibility and an opportunity to govern the internal and foreign affairs of the state in accordance with the will of Yahweh, whereas the early Christians were subject to pagan rulers. Hence, it is not surprising that the writers of the New Testament assumed a different attitude toward the political authorities from that exhibited by the prophets who had been able to appeal to the rulers of their day on the basis of their common participation in the Covenant.

The dominant attitude of the New Testament toward the civil rulers, then, was one of acceptance and obedience. It is represented by Paul and the author of First Peter. In his letter to the Romans, Paul wrote, "Let every person be subject to the governing authorities. For there is no authority except from God, and those that exist have been instituted by God. Therefore he who resists the authorities resists what God has appointed, and those who resist will incur judgment" (Rom. 13:1-2). And the author of First Peter wrote, "Be subject for the Lord's sake to every human institution, whether it be to the emperor as supreme, or to governors as sent by him to punish those who do wrong and to praise those who do right" (I Pet. 2:13-14). This attitude of obedience to the political authorities is supported conditionally by the words of Jesus: "Render to Caesar the things that are Caesar's, and to God the things that are God's" (Mark 12:17). But Jesus' own words can also be used to support the other attitude found in the New Testament, namely, that expressed in Revelation 13, where the Roman Empire is described as a blaspheming beast because it required worship of the emperor.[1] Thus

[1] Professor Oscar Cullmann contends that the difference between Romans 13 and Revelation 13 is to be understood entirely in the light of the demand

Jesus' words "and [render] to God the things that are God's" may be interpreted to demand the rejection of the claims of Caesar when he usurps the place of God. In any event, Jesus did not advocate a program of political reform, and neither did any of the writers of the New Testament. When the author of Revelation 13 admonished Christians to reject the demands of the empire and its rulers, there was no thought of organized political resistance. All that was envisaged—indeed, all that was possible—was nonviolent spiritual resistance and faithful endurance under persecution.

There were two basic reasons why Christians adopted this attitude of acceptance of, and obedience to, the civil authorities in the first century. In the first place, the Christians constituted a very small minority which had no political power and no opportunity to influence the ruling authorities in the empire. In the second place, they expected the present age of history to come to an end in the very near future when God would overthrow the forces of evil and establish His Kingdom. In view of this expectation, political issues seemed relatively unimportant. Effective reform was manifestly impossible in the short-run, and there was no long-run anticipated before the divine intervention.

Moreover, the early Christians believed that, on the whole, the civil authorities represented the divine will for the provision of order in society. Since men are sinful, there is need of the coercive power of the state to restrain them from the grossest forms of evil and injustice. Paul, writing before the severe persecutions of the Christians by the Roman rulers had begun, expressed his belief in the justice of the state in the most unreserved fashion when he declared: "For rulers are not a terror to good conduct, but to bad. Would you have no fear of him who is in authority? Then do what is good, and you will receive his approval, for he is God's servant for your good. But if you do wrong, be afraid, for he does not bear the sword in vain; he is the servant of God to execute his wrath on the wrong-doer. Therefore one must be subject, not only to avoid God's wrath but also for the sake of conscience" (Rom. 13:3–5). Although the author of First Peter wrote in the midst of an organized persecution of Christians by the Roman authorities, he similarly urged his readers to be

for emperor worship which underlies the latter passage and which constitutes an example of the state's going beyond the sphere in which it has a right to claim obedience. (*The State in the New Testament,* New York, Charles Scribner's Sons, 1956, ch. IV.)

"subject for the Lord's sake to every human institution, whether it be to the emperor as supreme, or to governors as sent by him *to punish those who do wrong and praise those who do right"* (I Pet. 2:13–14). The sentence which follows suggests that the author believed that the persecution which was being waged against the believers would stop once it had become clear that Christians were neither lawless nor rebellious and that their only crime was that of being Christians. He wrote: "For it is God's will that by doing right you should put to silence the ignorance of foolish men" (I Pet. 2:15). Hence, because of the importance of the state as a dike against anarchy, Christians not only might but indeed ought to obey the civil authorities except in those instances where it was impossible to obey the laws of men without at the same time disobeying the commandments of God. In the latter cases they were to endure the injustices of the present order patiently and accept the consequences of disobedience even if this meant martyrdom, for the end of the present age would soon come.

RESPONSIBLE PARTICIPATION IN DEMOCRATIC GOVERNMENT

Not only is there a vast difference between the situation which is presupposed by the prophetic demand for political reform and that which provides the background for the writing of the New Testament, but the latter situation also differs greatly from that which prevails in our own day in democratic countries where the authorities are at least in some degree responsible to the people and in which Christian citizens do have political power. Where such democratic forms of government do exist, the concepts of acceptance of the ruling author- ities and obedience to them are by themselves inadequate to define the duties of citizens in relation to their rulers. Under such circum- stances the *particular* rulers can no longer meaningfully be under- stood as exercising their authority by divine appointment except in a very general sense.[2] To be sure, the state may still be viewed as existing by divine appointment, and the democratic process of govern- ment whereby the people appoint particular rulers may be considered providential; but the people themselves are responsible in some meas- ure at least for the specific government which is in power at a particular time.

[2] Cf. John C. Bennett, *The Christian As Citizen,* New York, Association Press, 1955, p. 51.

It is important to recognize the differences between the situation confronted by the early Christians in the first and second centuries and that confronted by ourselves, for unless we do so we are likely to suppose that concern with political problems is alien to Christian faith. If we understand these differences, however, we are able to see that such concern is implicit in the heart of this faith—in the belief in the sovereignty of God and in the injunction to love the neighbor.

The primary basis for Christian concern with the political order and the chief motivation for any effort to institute political reform are to be found, therefore, not in the few isolated bits of political counsel in the New Testament but rather in the faith which undergirds the teaching and practice of Jesus and the writers of the New Testament. Jesus, like the prophets before him, points men to God who is the Lord of heaven and earth, and he teaches them to pray that His will may be done "on earth as it is in heaven." He reveals the power and the goodness and the love of God, and he teaches men to love God with heart, mind, soul, and strength and to love their neighbors as themselves. Behind the teaching and the actions of Jesus in relation to the political authorities and the political factions of his day is his faith in the living God whom he meets even here as Creator, as Governor, and as Redeemer. This is the God whom he trusts as his Heavenly Father and whose will he undertakes to do in every situation. Always this means trusting God and loving the neighbor in his need. The Christian's orientation toward the state and his understanding of political responsibility in a democratic country begin, therefore, with the consideration of what it means for one who has political power to be responsible before a righteous God for the exercise of this power. Or, putting the matter another way but a way which means the same thing, what does it mean for one who has political power to love the neighbor who is affected by the exercise or the failure to exercise this power?

In view of the rise and growth of democracy in many countries, the Pauline-Petrine doctrine of obedience to the governing authorities needs to be converted into new concepts which are more relevant to the existing relationship between the state and the people. Professor John Bennett suggests that the words "responsibility" and "participation" are more adequate at this point than the word "obedience."[3]

---

[3] *Ibid.*, p. 52.

This does not mean that the citizen in a democratic country will not sometimes find it necessary to obey a law simply because it is law. But under such circumstances he must recognize his own responsibility —not just that of the governing authorities—for upholding the sanctity of law and for maintaining the orderly processes of community life even though he may personally wish that the particular law were not in effect. If the occasion arises when he believes that he must disobey a specific law for the sake of conscience, he has a responsibility to do so in such a way as not to undermine respect for all law and civil authority. Moreover, whenever he believes a law to be unjust, he has a duty to do what he can to change it by participation in the normal and legal processes whereby laws are made, amended, and repealed. In those countries where citizens have an opportunity to participate in the processes of government, obedience to God is not the same thing as mere submission to those who are in authority at a particular time. Rather, it involves the responsibility to assist those in authority in performing their appointed tasks by giving them support, by keeping their actions under continuous criticism, and by preparing to replace the governing authorities themselves when this seems necessary in the interest of better government.

THE NATURE AND PURPOSE OF THE STATE

At this point, before turning to an analysis of the relationships between Christian faith and democracy as a form of government on the one hand and the relationships between Christian ethics and responsible citizenship on the other, it will be helpful to consider briefly the nature and purpose of the state from the standpoint of biblical faith. And here a distinction needs to be made between the political order and the state. In the sense that man is destined by the nature with which he is endowed to live, not as an independent solitary individual, but in community with other men, and indeed as a member of the community which includes all human beings, *the political order is an order of creation.* Just as marriage and economic exchange and coöperation stem from man's divinely given nature, and thus represent the intent of the Creator, so man's tendency to be drawn together into groups in order that he may achieve that community or oneness with his fellows to which his incompleteness points is an expression of the purpose of the Creator for man. The community which is intended in marriage and in the economic order needs to find expression also in the formation of a more comprehensive and inclusive association wherein the manifold relations and interdependencies of men are recognized and their conflicts resolved. In this sense man is a "political animal" by creation; and considering the process from the standpoint of biblical monotheism and the biblical understanding of the nature and destiny of man, we ought to "regard the growth of ever larger circles of community to the very limit of a unity which will include all who bear the name of *man*, not as a merely historical fact but as an indication of the Divine Will of the Creator."[4] This does not mean that the divine will can be equated with every form of world order but, rather, that the intent of the Creator is that the essential oneness of humanity should be effectively manifest while at the same time the dignity and the freedom of the individual are preserved and adequate provision is made for many less inclusive groups with natural interests and ties.

Whereas the political order must be understood, first of all, as an order of creation in that it represents the intent of God quite apart from sin that men should live in political communities rather than as isolated, independent beings, *the state*—insofar as it is an instrument of coercion—must be theologically understood, first of all, as *an order for sin* in that its coercive character is made necessary by sin. As such, it represents the will of the Judge, or Orderer, rather than the Creator; for the necessity that what is required for the welfare of the people as a whole must be forced upon a reluctant citizenry is the result of sin and not of the nature of man as he is by creation. Apart from sin there would doubtless be many conflicts of interests stemming out of the variety of relationships existing among men as social beings, but if it were not for sin such conflicts could be resolved without resort to compulsion.

In order for the state to perform its ordering function effectively, it must have *sovereign power*. Indeed, so essential is sovereign power to a state that the latter may in fact be defined as that "organ of the community which lays down laws and enforces them with supreme power for the purpose of furthering the common life."[5] In a sinful society, man as a "political animal" needs the state as an instrument of coercion in order to secure the order and the harmony which are

---

[4] Emil Brunner, *The Divine Imperative*, trans. by Olive Wyon, New York, The Macmillan Company, 1942, p. 444.

[5] George F. Thomas, *Christian Ethics and Moral Philosophy*, New York, Charles Scribner's Sons, 1955, p. 265.

necessary for the mutual development of his individual and social capacities and relationships. It is needed as an instrument for the preservation of the unity which already exists in fact and also for the achievement of a more perfect community. Insofar as it performs both of these functions the state represents the will of God for a sinful order. It is clear, moreover, that the purpose of the Judge and the purpose of the Creator are ultimately one in this regard. Fallen man is still a "political animal" by creation; and, although the order and community which are effected by the state represent perverted forms of that order and community which God wills for man in creation, they are far better than anarchy. Man does not cease to be man because of his sin; neither does he cease to be destined to find his fulfillment in community with all other human beings. Insofar as the state ministers to this end for sinners it represents the divine will for sinful man.

This view of the nature of the state is, however, diametrically opposed to all forms of political absolutism according to which the state possesses absolute sovereignty. In the biblical view the claims of the state are always limited by the claims of God. The state stands under the will and purposes of God. Its function is to minister to the needs of man, and man is always understood as a free spiritual being who exists in relationship to many other free spiritual beings with many interests and needs. The existence of the state as the sovereign or supreme authority presupposes the existence of many voluntary and autonomous groups within a community—the family, economic organizations such as labor unions and associations representing management, churches, schools, a free press, and numerous other social and philanthropic groups. The state is not a substitute for these voluntary centers of community life; rather, it is that agency of a people which is designed to maintain a proper balance among these less inclusive groups through the enactment and enforcement of laws. The function of the state is not to replace the free activities of its citizens as individuals and as members of voluntary associations with prescribed patterns of conduct; rather, it is to coördinate and harmonize them. The state as an institution which is ordained because of sin is subservient to the will of the Creator that man shall live in a community based upon freedom and love. A state which shackles the freedom of its citizens through a process of regimentation makes the achievement of genuine community impossible since it deprives man of his essential dignity and violates his true nature.

Moreover, because of its primary concern with the needs and interests which its citizens share in common, the state is by its very nature inadequate to express the deepest and richest levels of human community which stem out of men's freely chosen interests and loyalties and out of a recognition of the uniqueness of each person's endowments.

In view of the nature of the state as an instrument of the community for the protection of its members and for the harmonizing of their activities, the state may be said to have two main purposes: the provision of *order* and the provision of *justice*. Of these the first is clearly the more fundamental; for order, or peace, is prerequisite to the achievement of justice. But the ultimate end of the state as a sovereign power is not the achievement of order but the establishment of justice. God does not will that man as a free moral being should live under an order that is based upon coercion alone, for such an order would ignore man's true humanity. Order is indispensable to prevent human life from becoming a "war of every man against every man," but justice is equally essential if the state is to be a true instrument of the community for the promotion of the common welfare. Not only is the state necessary to defend the lives and liberties of its citizens by the order which it provides, but it is also needed positively to further the common good by the encouragement which it gives to the pursuit of an increasingly fuller measure of justice in the social order in view of the general reluctance to pursue the good of the people as a whole when the latter conflicts with one's own narrower interests.

CHRISTIANITY AND DEMOCRACY

In seeking to understand the relationship of Christianity to democracy, we need to be on our guard against two common misconceptions. In the first place, there is a frequent tendency to equate Christianity with democracy as if the latter were the only form of government which could possibly be considered Christian. But, as James Hastings Nichols points out, for over fifteen hundred years Christians never suspected that political democracy was the natural or even a possible implication of their faith and ethic.[6] And even within the relatively recent period since the rise of Western democratic ideals and institutions only a minority of Christians have been genuine advocates of

[6] James Hastings Nichols, *Democracy and the Churches,* Philadelphia, The Westminster Press, 1951, p. 17.

political democracy. Indeed, Professor Nichols goes so far as to say that only those forms of Christianity which have been associated with what he calls "Puritan Protestantism"—i.e., the Calvinistic and "Free Church" or sectarian forms of Protestantism—have made any real contribution to the development of democracy and have consistently sought to realize it through the political institutions which they have adopted.

In the second place, there is an even more common tendency to suppose that democracy is independent of any religious foundation. A great many people believe that such a conclusion is implied by the doctrine of the "separation of church and state." The fallacy of this view was brought home to many Americans, however, following World War II, when an effort was made to transplant democracy to Japan, Germany, and Italy as well as to other countries in Asia. It soon became evident that the religious and moral roots which are needed to provide vitality to democratic institutions were lacking, and without such rootage the constitutions and parliamentary processes which were introduced failed to show the vigor which they had exhibited in the older democracies of Western Europe and America.

But if we must reject both the tendency to identify Christianity in general with democracy and the tendency to view the latter as independent of the former, we must inquire more carefully into the relationship which exists between the two. According to Professor Nichols, Anglo-American democracy was the creation of Puritanism in England in the 1640's and 1650's.[7] Nichols does not deny that other groups and forces contributed to the growth of democratic ideas—e.g., Greek and Roman political thinkers, Roman Catholic ideas of natural law, and certain secular thinkers of the enlightenment; but he does contend that the spiritual roots of Anglo-American democracy are to be found in Puritanism rather than in Lutheranism or Anglicanism or Roman Catholicism.[8] Moreover, the way had been prepared for the birth of democracy in England by the constitutional reforms and writings of the earlier Calvinists on the Continent and in Scotland. In all of their efforts to limit the power of the rulers through the institution of constitutional government, Nichols declares, the religious motive was primary, viz., the duty to resist the state's encroachments in areas of religious belief and practice. But

[7] *Ibid.*, p. 29.
[8] For a brief evaluation of Nichols' thesis see John C. Bennett, *Christians and the State*, New York, Charles Scribner's Sons, 1958, p. 147.

while the religious motive was primary, political expediency was also a factor in this struggle; for the Calvinists generally constituted minorities in the countries where Roman Catholicism, Anglicanism, or Lutheranism enjoyed an established status. Because of their minority status the Calvinists generally demanded constitutional government. For this reason, too, Nichols points out, Roman Catholics, particularly in England and France, also attempted under similar circumstances to impose limitations upon the Protestant monarchs, and thus their contribution to the development of constitutional government was second in importance only to that of the Calvinists.[9]

Despite the fact that some of the early Calvinists on the Continent do not seem to have been as strong advocates of the ideas of popular sovereignty, government by consent, natural rights, and the duty to resist tyranny as he implies, Nichols' over-all account of the historical development of constitutional government is generally sound. He does, however, fail to do justice to the insistence of Christians from the beginning that the sovereignty of rulers is limited by the sovereignty of God. To be sure, this belief does not necessarily lead to the development of constitutional governments; it may only mean that the state is subordinate to the church which in turn exercises absolute power. Moreover, it is also true, as Nichols recognizes, that the principle of constitutional government may itself be used as an instrument of tyranny on the part of the majority or even of a strong religious minority. Indeed, sixteenth-century Calvinism, although it prepared the way for the development of democracy in England in the seventeenth century, was not itself democratic. Puritanism became democratic in England only after the Nonconformists there had added to the Calvinist tradition three additional elements: the concept of a "gathered church," the belief in the presence and guidance of the Holy Spirit in the fellowship of the church, and the doctrine of the separation of church and state.[10] The first of these concepts issued in the development of the congregational form of church government and contributed to the growth of political democracy—especially to the rise of the contract theory of political government—by its emphasis upon the consent of the governed. Implicit in the belief in the continuing guidance of the Spirit was a genuine trust in the value of group discussion as a way of discovering truth and also a recognition of the duty of each to participate in this process. Finally, there was implicit

[9] Nichols, *op. cit.,* p. 20.
[10] *Ibid.,* pp. 32 ff.

in the doctrine of the separation of church and state the belief that each of these institutions is autonomous in its own sphere. Recognition of this fact was necessary before an effective safeguard could be provided against the theocratic control by any religious group of the instruments of government.

Looked at in terms of its historical development, then, liberal democracy in its Anglo-Saxon form has owed a great deal to the Puritan form of Protestantism. And in view of subsequent developments in such countries as England and Sweden, where Anglicanism and Lutheranism have prevailed respectively, there is reason to believe that the latter traditions can, at least under some circumstances, also provide genuine support for democratic institutions although under other conditions they may support other forms of government. Similar support for democracy may also be provided by Roman Catholicism in those countries where Roman Catholics constitute a minority; although, in general, Roman Catholicism is not opposed to the use of the state as an instrument of the church to secure the propagation of Roman Catholic faith.

While it is important to appraise the historical contributions of different groups of Christians to the development of democracy, it is also important to guard against an uncritical projection of these relationships into the future, especially insofar as most of the major Protestant denominations are concerned.[11] As Professor Bennett points out, the ecumenical experience of the churches provides a meeting ground in which the mutual influence of most of the leading Protestant churches—together with a number of Eastern Orthodox groups—is constantly being felt. Here a single tradition has an opportunity to bear witness to the implications of the Gospel in such a way as to affect deeply the attitudes and insights of other groups. In this way they may be led to a more genuine appreciation of the relationship of the Christian faith to the development and support of democratic institutions. Insofar as the present and the future are concerned, therefore, it will be more fruitful if, instead of focusing our attention exclusively upon the historical relationships of the churches to democracy in the past, we examine the nature and purpose of democracy and some of the contributions which Christianity may make toward the realization of these goals.

Democracy means, essentially, government *by* the people and *for*

---

[11] Bennett, *The Christian As Citizen*, p. 69.

the people. Usually, of course, the people are not able in a literal sense to govern themselves; rather, they do so indirectly through the representatives whom they select. The people retain the final authority in a democracy, and their representatives are responsible to them. The people govern themselves in the sense that they choose those who will represent them, and they give their consent to be ruled by the latter. This obviously does not mean that all of the people give their consent to a particular candidate or a particular policy, for if this were required the election of candidates and the making of policy decisions would be impossible. Indeed, democracy presupposes the freedom to disagree, but it is government by consent in the sense that the elected officials have the general approval of the majority or at least of a plurality of the electorate.

Democracy also means government *for* the people. Its purpose is to serve the common good of all of the people without conferring special advantages upon any privileged group. Its aim is to serve the individual in the community. On the one hand it rejects the anarchic view that the individual is independent and sufficient unto himself; on the other hand, it rejects the collectivist view that the good of the individual person is subordinate to a superpersonal state, or race, or class, membership in which alone bestows worth upon the individual. Democracy, therefore, is neither essentially individualistic nor essentially collectivistic. Rather, it views the individual as having worth in himself, and at the same time it views him as being a member of the community in which he finds fulfillment and for which he is also responsible.

An essential corollary of the concept of government *for* the people, as this idea has developed in Western democracy, is the recognition of the rights of minorities. Democracy is not simply government *of* the majority *for* the majority. As a practical device for enabling the community to make decisions which rest upon the approval of as many of its citizens as possible, democracy takes the form of majority rule. But the majority does not have absolute sovereignty. Rather, the authority of the majority is limited by the welfare of the people as a whole, all of whom have inalienable rights stemming out of their inescapable duties. Hence, democracy in its Western form guarantees the protection of certain rights of all of the people by law and constitutional provisions which are accepted by the people as a whole. Among these rights is the freedom of the minorities of today to speak and organize and seek to become effective political majorities of tomorrow. The safeguarding of this freedom of minorities is essential as a check upon the power of majorities and also as an expression of the essential dignity—the individuality, the responsibility, and the creativity—of man as man rather than of some men as members of some particular aristocracy.

If democracy rests upon the convictions that the best form of government is that in which the people govern themselves, that the purpose of government is to serve the common welfare of all of the people equally, and that the rights of the majority are limited by the rights of the minority, the question naturally arises, upon what basis do these convictions rest? They are sometimes held to be "self-evident," but as Professor John H. Hallowell suggests, they are not self-evident to positivists, who tend to regard all value judgments as expressions merely of subjective individual preferences.[12] And such positivists are not limited to the Machiavellis, the Hitlers, and the Stalins alone; they also include those liberal jurists who prepare the way for such tyrants by their interpretation of the rights of man, not as natural rights which belong to him by virtue of his humanity, but simply as legal rights which belong to him by virtue of their having been conferred upon him by the state. From the standpoint of positivism, man has no rights as man. In this view, what have traditionally been called "rights" are in reality only concessions granted to man by the state. Rights are simply the product of law, and as such they merely represent the recognition on the part of the state of certain claims which individuals make. The implication of this view is that "rights" may be withdrawn or limited as the state desires. Such a conception of the rights of man leads inevitably to the destruction of liberal democracy and to the rise of some form of tyranny.

Far from being self-evident, the fundamental beliefs upon which democracy is based rest ultimately upon certain theological convictions about the nature of man and the moral universe in which man is placed. And, while each of these beliefs can be defended upon some basis other than that of biblical faith, it is important—in view of their historical connections with this faith—to ask what contributions biblical faith makes to the continuing vitality of these beliefs and thus to the nurture of the democratic form of government. Without attempting to exhaust the contributions which Christianity may make to the undergirding and strengthening of democracy, we may

---

[12] See John H. Hallowell, *The Moral Foundations of Democracy*, Chicago, The University of Chicago Press, 1954, pp. 76–80.

consider three which are perhaps of greatest importance. In the first place, there is a striking kinship between the Christian conception of man and the view of man which underlies Western democracy. Indeed, the relationship between the two concepts is so close that Reinhold Niebuhr has maintained that the real strength of democracy lies in the Christian view of human nature.[13] The strength of democracy depends upon the preservation of a proper balance between an excessive optimism regarding the motives of men and an excessive pessimism regarding their potentialities. As Niebuhr declares:

> A free society requires some confidence in the ability of men to reach tentative and tolerable adjustments between their competing interests and to arrive at some common notions of justice which transcend all partial interests. A consistent pessimism in regard to man's rational capacity for justice invariably leads to absolutistic political theories; for they prompt the conviction that only preponderant power can coerce the vitalities of a community into a working harmony. But a too consistent optimism in regard to man's ability and inclination to grant justice to his fellows obscures the perils of chaos which perennially confound every society, including a free society. In one sense a democratic society is particularly exposed to the dangers of confusion. If these perils are not appreciated they may overtake a free society and invite the alternative evil of tyranny.[14]

Or, putting the matter in an unforgettable epigram, he writes, "Man's capacity for justice makes democracy possible; but man's inclination to injustice makes democracy necessary."[15]

Belief in man's capacity for justice is strongly supported by the Judaic-Christian conception of the rationality and goodness of man as a being made "in the image of God." The biblical concept of man provides ground for confidence in his ability to govern himself and to provide a tolerable degree of justice in the political order. On the other hand, the democratic understanding of man's inclination to injustice is confirmed by the Christian conception of man's sinfulness. The biblical view of the sinfulness of all men constitutes a warning against all unrestrained forms of power—whether it be the power of the legislature, the executive, the courts, or even of the majority itself. Effective checks upon all human concentrations of power are needed, not because power itself is evil, but because sinful men tend

---

[13] Reinhold Niebuhr, *The Children of Light and the Children of Darkness*, New York, Charles Scribner's Sons, 1949.

[14] *Ibid.*, pp. x–xi.

[15] *Ibid.*, p. xi.

to use power as an instrument of injustice. The greater the power, the greater the possibilities of injustice become. The system of checks and balances in the various branches of the federal government and the division of powers between the federal and state governments as well as the limitations upon the powers of Congress in the making of laws are excellent examples of the kinds of restraints upon all which are necessary both from the standpoint of democracy and from the standpoint of a Christian understanding of the universality of sin.

Moreover, the biblical estimate of man's goodness by creation and of the possibility of his redemption provides ground for belief in his capacity to make real although tentative progress in the realization of the welfare of the people as a whole. It is apparent that the ideals or goals of democracy—liberty, equality, justice—have never been completely achieved. But it is the democratic faith that these goals are constantly to be striven after and that they may be more perfectly realized for all of the people. However, the biblical estimate of man's sinfulness constitutes a warning against utopianism. The laws of a state must be based upon the moral standards which most of its citizens are prepared to accept. In this respect, the aim of democracy is perfectly consistent with the Christian understanding of the purpose of the state, viz., to promote the welfare of the people as a whole. Its aim ought not to be to enact the most idealistic legislation or to embody the highest Christian norms of personal conduct in the law of the land. To attempt to do so is unrealistic and leads inevitably to hypocrisy and cynicism with regard to the possibility of achieving even more modest goals. In this sense and to this extent, "politics is the art of the possible; it is not a science of perfection."[16] This does not mean, of course, either that politicians should settle for what a majority of the people actually prefer or that they should be content with the level of justice and equality which is now possible. The function of political leaders is to lead. But it is, nevertheless, far better for a society to be governed by laws which can reasonably be expected to be implemented in practice and to have these firmly enforced than for it to have more idealistic laws which are violated with impunity or effectively circumvented, for the failure to enforce a law results in the undermining of the authority of all law as well as in the encouragement of the violation of the particular perfectionistic statute.

[16] Cf. Hallowell, *op. cit.,* p. 108.

It would be unwise, for example, as well as uncharitable, to prohibit all divorce simply because the majority of citizens believed that divorce is contrary to God's will. Such a law would ignore the sinfulness of men and the moral and spiritual corrosiveness of homes which are filled with strife and hostility.

A second contribution of Christianity to the strengthening of democracy lies in the Christian understanding of liberty and rights. A major weakness of democracy has been the tendency to interpret liberty exclusively in the negative terms of freedom from restraint while understanding rights primarily in individualistic terms. When the liberty of one citizen or one group is defined without reference to the liberty of other citizens and groups, the liberty of the people as a whole is threatened, and the way is prepared for the emergence of a new tyranny of the strongest. Similarly, when rights are understood in exclusively individualistic terms, the basic equality of men is jeopardized. Moreover, such a conception of liberty and rights leads to the loss of that real sense of unity which is essential if there is to be genuine government for the people as a whole, as well as government by the people.

An authentically Christian approach to the concept of the rights of man does not begin with the empirically observable nature of man but rather with an understanding of his obligations to God and to his neighbors under God.[17] According to this view, the rights of man are grounded in the biblical conception of the nature and destiny of man, with emphasis placed upon the underlying duties upon which the rights of the individual are based. Men have rights—e.g., freedom of speech, the ballot, and freedom of religion—because they have responsibilities which stem out of the moral and spiritual relationships with which they are endowed.[18]

Biblical faith thus provides strong support for the democratic doctrine that *all* men have certain inalienable rights regardless of whether or not they are recognized as such by the laws of a particular

---

[17] See Paul Ramsey, *Basic Christian Ethics*, New York, Charles Scribner's Sons, 1950, pp. 353 ff.

[18] Professor John H. Hallowell maintains that democracy can remain viable in the long-run only if its conception of the rights of man is theologically grounded: "Because we have a destiny that transcends time and, as a consequence, responsibilities that transcend the demands of the particular time and society in which we live, we must have the freedom proportionate to those responsibilities *and the rights that are derived from those obligations.*" (Hallowell, *op. cit.*, p. 84. Italics added.)

state. There is implicit both in biblical and in democratic faith recognition of the demand that the genuine humanity of all of the people —their absolute worth and true dignity as individuals—be safeguarded. This demand implies, in turn, the duty to provide those conditions under which it is possible for each person to be genuinely human in the fullest sense of that word. Thus, through its emphasis upon the responsibilities of man before God and in relationship to the neighbor, Christianity indirectly provides the strongest possible support for the democratic conception of the rights of man which exist prior to and independent of the positive laws of particular states.

Moreover, through the emphasis which it places upon the obligation of each citizen to use his "rights" in the service of the neighbor under God, biblical faith undergirds the democratic notion that the purpose of the state is to promote the welfare of the people as a whole. The vitality of democracy depends upon a genuine sense of oneness among the citizens of a country. Unless there is recognition of the responsibility of each for the people as a whole and of all for each there is little possibility that conflicting interests will be resolved in terms of the common welfare. Effective pursuit of the common good presupposes recognition of the fact that each person is by birth a member of society and shares in the responsibility for it. The individual does not incur responsibilities for his fellows simply by wilfully entering into a "contract" with them. Individuals do not intentionally create society; they are born into it and participate in it of necessity. Recognition of this unity of the community and free commitment to the common good as over against the special interests of the individual or of less inclusive groups is indispensable in a democracy. Without such loyalty to the common good, one will not seek liberty and equality for all. Though it is frequently supposed that enlightened self-interest provides a sufficient basis for community in a democracy, enlightened self-interest is inadequate, for it cannot cause men to respect and defend the rights of others when it is not to their advantage to do so, neither will it lead them to devote themselves to the service of their country in government and civic causes in time of peace or risk their lives for it in time of war.

Christian faith, as we have seen (Chapter 7, pp. 174–186), goes far beyond the norm of enlightened self-interest in its conception of each person's obligations both to his individual and to his collective neighbors. Biblical faith as a whole supports the democratic sense of unity and commitment to the common good in many ways—e.g., through its concept of the oneness of mankind in creation, through its emphasis upon the obligation to establish social justice as this is spelled out in terms of the Covenant and by the prophets, and through the idea of the Kingdom of God. But the contribution which Christian faith makes in this regard is epitomized in its concept of *agape*. The support which Christian love gives to democracy at this point is so important because the acceptance of this norm involves the faith that the fullest life is to be found in the subjection of the desires and interests of the self to the service of the neighbor and also because this love is all-inclusive and therefore excludes no class or race or nationality. For both of these reasons, Christian love serves to strengthen the basis of community within democracy while at the same time it provides a safeguard against making an idolatry of nationalism.

The contribution which Christianity can make to democracy at this point does not depend upon all or even a majority of the citizens being Christians. As we have previously observed, the laws of a state must be based primarily upon the moral standards which a majority of the citizens accept, but Christian love exhibited by even a minority serves as a leaven which influences the community as a whole. Moreover, it may in time bring about a gradual conversion of the public conscience to a higher moral standard and a higher level of social justice. Thus, it is difficult to conceive how our country, for example, although the majority of its citizens have never been more than nominal Christians, could have made the progress which it has made toward economic justice and racial equality, in prison reform and the provision of better care for the mentally ill, and in gaining recognition of our international responsibilities if it had not been for the great reservoir of good-will and humanitarian concern which has been in large part a product of Christian faith.

A third major contribution which Christianity makes to democracy lies in its concept of the church as an autonomous institution which exists alongside the state and limits the powers of the state. By reminding the state that it, too, stands under the sovereignty of God, the church provides a strong bulwark against totalitarianism. Despite many important differences in their conceptions of the proper relationship between these two institutions, Christians have always recognized that both are ordained of God and that each has a sphere of its own. Moreover, Christians have always insisted that man's primary responsibility is "to obey God rather than man." On the one hand, the state has a legitimate sphere of authority where it is autonomous in relation to the church, but it is nevertheless subject to the will and sovereignty of God. The church, on the other hand, also has a sphere of authority where it is autonomous in relation to the state although the church, too, is responsible to the will and judgment of God. There have of course been sharp disagreements as to where Caesar's sphere ends and the church's sphere begins, but recognition of the fact that Caesar's just claims are limited is an indispensable precondition for the acceptance of the democratic concepts of the rights of man and the democratic goal of government for the people viewed as individuals-in-community. This recognition has taken many forms—the duty of disobedience to civil authorities, the Thomistic concept of Natural Law, the right of revolt, the right to assassinate a tyrant, and the duty to seek to limit tyrants by constitutional and parliamentary reform. Frequently, of course, there has been a desire to set up a theocratic state in which the church could control the state; but in the main it has been recognized, in theory at least, that the state is autonomous in the temporal realm and the church in the spiritual realm.

Emphasis upon the parallel and autonomous functions of the church and state is more congenial to Protestantism than it is to Roman Catholicism because of the latter's doctrine of the Catholic Church as the only true church and because of her dogma of Papal Infallibility. On the whole, Catholicism has not championed the religious liberty of the individual to follow his own conscience so much as it has the liberty of the church over against the control of the state. As the history of intolerance in the relations of church and state in the early Protestant period clearly shows, Protestantism may also be theocratic and intolerant. However, when it is true to its principles of the primacy of conscience as over against institutionalized religious authority, and when it is true to its understanding of sin as a power which corrupts the church as well as the state, Protestantism provides strong support for the principle of the separation of church and state. Thus, it represents an even stronger safeguard against totalitarianism than that provided by Catholicism, whose primary protest is against secular totalitarianism rather than against totalitarianism of every form.[19]

[19] Cf. M. Searle Bates, *Religious Liberty: An Inquiry*, New York, International Missionary Council, 1945, pp. 376–377.

REASONS WHY PROTESTANTS FAIL TO EXERCISE
POLITICAL RESPONSIBILITY

In view of the importance of the state from the standpoint of Christian faith and in view of the kinship between Christianity and democracy, it is somewhat ironical that Protestants in general tend either to neglect or to deny their political responsibilities. Frequently this neglect or denial is due to certain very non-Protestant conceptions of Christian ethics and a certain naïveté concerning the nature of the political processes. It will help to make our preceding analysis more concrete if we examine some of the most common reasons why Protestants in particular neglect their political duties.

THEY BELIEVE THAT POLITICS IS A DIRTY BUSINESS. Protestants generally share the common American belief that politics is a dirty business. Professor George A. Graham describes the traditional attitude toward politics in this country as one of "mingled pride and shame."[20] The typical American venerates such political heroes of the past as Washington, Jefferson, Jackson, Lincoln, and Wilson, but he habitually abuses the political leaders of his own day—just as his fathers before him did. On the one hand he is proud of his democratic heritage and the democratic way of life which he enjoys; on the other hand he looks upon government as being inherently evil. Those who are active in the processes of policy formation are "politicians"; and both politicians and bureaucrats, as well as lawyers generally, are held in low repute in their own day. This inconsistency in the attitude of the typical American toward democracy becomes most obvious when those who hold it equate "the American way of life" with "the Christian way," as uncritical Protestants in particular are inclined to do.

Commenting upon the effect of this derogatory view of politics, Francis P. Miller says that, if the persons and the activities which it describes "continue to be thought of by most Americans in this way, the future of the Republic is not bright. No republic will long survive if those charged with its maintenance are regarded by their fellow citizens with contempt, or if the activities required for its maintenance are considered unworthy of the ablest and best citizens."[21]

[20] George A. Graham, *Morality in American Politics,* New York, Random House, 1952, p. 5.
[21] Francis P. Miller, "Our Participation as Christians in Politics," *Social Action,* XX, no. 3 (December, 1953), p. 2.

Such an attitude makes it difficult for a nation to recruit as public servants its most able citizens. As we have seen, however, the need of man for some form of government is universal. Without it human life would be "nasty, brutish, and short," as Hobbes pictured it to have been before the emergence of organized society.[22] The provision for some measure of order and justice is the most basic need of society, and in a democracy the people undertake to make this provision themselves through their representatives. In view of the importance of the state and in view of the greatness of the debt which each individual owes to it, those who are charged with representing the people in this endeavor ought to be among the most capable and responsible citizens which a democracy produces, and politics—i.e., "the business of providing, maintaining, and changing government"—ought to be one of the most honorable of all human endeavors.

Not only does the derogatory view of politics which we have been considering make it more difficult to persuade able citizens to enter government service, but it also overlooks the fact that corruption in politics and government generally represents a reflection of common practices in business and other relationships carried over into government. Frequently the incentive for such corruption comes from private citizens, especially from men in private industry who provide the temptations to which government officials sometimes succumb. Public officials do not corrupt themselves. As Senator Paul H. Douglas remarks, "For every bribe-taker, there generally is a bribe-giver. For ever public official who goes wrong, there is at least another private citizen who has helped him in that direction."[23] Corrupt legislators and public officials go hand in hand with corrupt private citizens, and they reinforce each other. Especially at the national level, Douglas maintains, the initiative is taken by private interests seeking to influence or control government. Paradoxically, public opinion has concentrated its indignation upon the guilty public officials and left the equally guilty private corrupters relatively unscathed. This attitude is essentially unfair and fails to get to the root of the problem. As Douglas points out, in any moral indignation which is developed and any reforms which are initiated, account needs to be taken of the corrupter as well as of the corrupted and of the enticer as well as of the enticed, and the former ought to be deterred and punished as well as the latter.

[22] Hobbes, *Leviathan,* pt. I, ch. XIII.
[23] Paul H. Douglas, *Ethics in Government,* Cambridge, Harvard University Press, 1952, pp. 22–26.

From the standpoint of responsible citizenship, what is needed to clean up politics is not cynicism and self-righteous withdrawal from the political process but more concern and participation in it by those Christians and others who deplore the existing corruption. This participation can take place at many levels, and it does not demand that everyone run for office. All of the citizens share the responsibility for government, but relatively few actually represent the people in the process of governing.

THEY DO NOT UNDERSTAND POLITICAL POWER.   There is a general failure on the part of Protestants to understand the nature of political power. It is widely assumed that voting represents the full duty of citizenship and that it is in itself an effective way of exerting political influence. E. E. Schattschneider calls this the "old maid's view of politics," and he points out that by itself voting does not really influence the formation of public policy to any very marked degree.[24] Voting is a last-minute choice or taking of sides after the issues have been selected, the platforms adopted, and the candidates chosen. By itself it ignores the party caucuses, the informal agreements that are worked out by the party leaders at the ward level, the party conventions, the organization of support for the party, and the wide variety of ways that issues are clarified and aired and that support is gathered for the opposing platforms and candidates. In a word, the individual voter who limits his political action to registration and voting never becomes involved in the real process of policy formation. He just steps up and gets counted—and then rejoices or laments over the outcome. This does not mean that voting is unimportant; it does mean that what people will vote upon, whether they will vote, and how they will vote is pretty well decided before election day.

This tendency to ignore the real political process is interestingly illustrated by our daily use of such phrases as "They ought to pass a law," "They ought to do something about that," and "They ought not to allow that." It is also illustrated by our common tendency to blame the incumbents in office—the members of the legislature or the present administration—with little or no recognition of the part we and our fellow-citizens played in deciding who the present representatives and administrators would be and what policies they would be authorized to pursue.

[24] E. E. Schattschneider, "Our Unrecognized Governmental Crisis," *Social Action*, XVI, no. 8 (October 15, 1950), p. 13.

THEY FAIL TO ORGANIZE TO INFLUENCE GOVERNMENT POLICY. Protestants generally are prejudiced against organized and coöperative efforts to influence government policy. This prejudice stems from a highly individualistic understanding of man and society and a highly moralistic conception of ethics. According to this view, the social and political ills of society will be effectively overcome only as individuals become persuaded in increasing numbers to practice the good private virtues of sobriety, thrift, honesty, justice, and love—all understood in terms of each person's individual relationships to other individuals. In this view, a good society is simply a collection of upright citizens. Its organic character is overlooked, and the indirect relationships of men to each other through various special interest groups as well as through the common body politic are ignored.

Implicit in the concept of Christian ethics which underlies this prejudice is the assumption that Christian love is unrelated to the demand for social justice. Love and justice may even be viewed as being in contradiction to each other because the establishment of justice rests upon the appeal to political power and also because justice appears too impersonal and calculating whereas love appears to be personal and self-giving. For Christians who are motivated by love, the requirement of justice is alleged to be unnecessary; moreover, it is often assumed that, unless men are motivated by love and personal commitment to the social virtues, they will not actually accept and practice justice. "You can't legislate morals," so the argument runs. The only effective appeal is to the individual's private conscience; and, indeed, any other appeal is counter to the Christian ethic of love.

This individualistic and moralistic approach to political problems causes many Protestants to pride themselves on staying aloof from party affiliation. They prefer to be independents on principle, thus ignoring the role of political parties in sharpening and clarifying the alternatives in an election and in fixing responsibility for public policy. Sometimes these individualists seek to exercise their political responsibility merely by casting a protest vote for a third party which has no chance of winning; they may even be proud of the fact that they have never voted for a winning candidate. By simply registering their preferences as individuals and by neglecting the organizational and promotional work that are essential to winning elections, Protestants generally fail to marshal their potential strength. Thus their influence remains disorganized, diffused, and feeble, and by default they permit other better-organized and more active groups to dominate the government and establish the policies by which the lives of all the citizens are regulated. By their inaction they create a low pressure area into which other pressures soon move. Through their failure to use their political strength in the cause of social justice, they contribute to the spread of injustice. Because of their failure to organize their strength and transform the existing political institutions which have become corrupt, they share the responsibility for the perpetuation of the corruption against which they inveigh.

THEY FEAR CONTROVERSY. Protestants—along with many others —sometimes fail to fulfill their political obligations because they fear controversy and its possible penalties. This fear is not limited to Protestants, of course, nor is it restricted to the area of political controversy. Insofar as the latter is concerned, however, it represents a failure to recognize how dependent our democratic form of government is upon free and vigorous debate on issues of vital concern. Moreover, it is a peculiarly inconsistent attitude for Protestants to hold in view of their belief in the priesthood of all believers. The vitality of both democracy and Protestantism depends upon the freedom of men to discuss those matters about which there are disagreements and upon the faith that out of this process there will emerge a fuller conception of truth than any one person or group can apprehend alone.

Recently, some parts of the South have hailed the prospective development of a genuine two-party system, because it is recognized that this would strengthen the democratic process by encouraging debate and providing real issues to be decided in elections. But it now seems doubtful that a genuine two-party system will come into being in the near future. The pressures toward conformity are of many types: political, economic, social, religious. They operate upon the liberal press, upon teachers in the public schools, upon the clergy, upon legislators, and upon employers. They operate upon whites and Negroes. No one is free from them. Fear of opposition—from which stem efforts to restrict freedom of speech, press, and pulpit—and fear of the penalties which nonconformity might bring represent two of the greatest obstacles to the exercise of genuine political responsibility in the South today; and they no doubt have their parallels in every other section of the country.

THEY FEAR COMPROMISE.   In a sense politics is an art of compromise. From the standpoint of a legalistic morality, all compromise involves moral taint. Therefore, politics is best left to those whose consciences are less strict—those who are willing to settle for the expedient. It is argued that the morally sensitive person who is dedicated to high goals and lofty ideals cannot maintain them in the practical game of politics. One must compromise his principles in order to be elected, and one must also compromise them if he is going to be effective as a lawmaker or as an administrator of the law.

But such a view of politics stems out of an unbiblical understanding of Christian ethics. It starts out with the self and the desire to maintain one's own personal purity rather than with God's will and the neighbor's need. It rests upon the assumption that one's salvation depends upon the preservation of his personal purity rather than upon the grace of God which accepts the service of those who in love seek to minister to His children's needs. Such a view overlooks the fact that the effort to escape the necessity of compromise also involves sin and a lack of faith in the goodness and love of God. Both those who compromise out of love for the neighbor and those who out of self-love seek to avoid compromise stand in need of the divine forgiveness.

As we have noted earlier, the use of the term *compromise* is misleading if it is made a primary category in Christian ethics, for it suggests a legalistic, or moralistic, conception of morality. When Christian ethics is understood, not in terms of abstract laws and absolute principles primarily but in terms of responsive love to God, it becomes clear that it is misleading to speak of compromising one's Christian ethic in the political arena simply because one has to settle for something less than the ideal. We are summoned to love the neighbor—i.e., to minister to his needs in the kind of world in which he and we live. The will of God for us is related to the neighbor's needs in a particular, concrete situation; and Christian love implies a willingness to do the best that is possible for the neighbor now and a persistent effort to make it possible to take further steps in his behalf at the earliest possible moment. Compromise of abstract moral laws and principles of justice, which serve as guides but not as final norms in Christian ethics, is not only permitted but demanded to the extent —but only to the extent—that it is required by the neighbor's needs.

THEY CONFUSE ISSUES BY GENERALIZING POLITICAL PROBLEMS. Another serious obstacle to the exercise of political responsibility is the general tendency to stereotype political problems and thus cover up the real issues at stake in a campaign. The rank-and-file voter tends to think in terms of voting for or against "states' rights," for or against corruption in government, for or against integration, for or against prosperity at home and peace abroad, or for or against militarism. He is encouraged to think in terms of pat slogans and clichés which obscure the basic differences in policy between the opposing parties. Some corruption—five-per-centers or mink coats or men who profit from various kinds of deals—is discovered in one administration, and a campaign is built around the "mess in Washington" under the Democrats or under the Republicans as the case may be. The impression is given that a change in the administration will bring an end to corruption; and little is said about the more basic matters of foreign policy, tariffs, the relation of private economic groups to government, labor policies, social security, income tax policy, and farm policy. This is not to say that tax scandals and influence peddling should be condoned in the least. There is no substitute for personal integrity; but individual corruption should not be allowed to obscure the organized injustice and the organized corruption involved in high tariffs, in granting of special concessions to favored groups in tax revisions, in legislation relating to private utilities, or in immigration policies.

Similarly, the voter is frequently led to choose between parties and candidates on the basis of their being for or against a reduction of taxes or for or against big government. The voter isn't told, nor does he bother to inquire, how the candidate can perform all of the things he has promised to do and still reduce taxes; but the credulous voter hopefully casts his ballot for the man who promises the biggest giveaway for home consumption. Or one votes against big government and for Jeffersonian democracy without asking whether these are live options in our time. Big government, it seems clear, is here to stay. The only real question is, how responsible can it be made to be?

THEY EMPHASIZE PERSONALITIES AND SINGLE ISSUES. A closely related reason why Protestants generally fail to fulfill their political obligations lies in their tendency to decide political matters on the basis of personalities and single issues. Sometimes it is a matter of the candidate's personal life—the fact that he has or has not been divorced, his religious faith (Is he a Jew or a Roman Catholic?), or his habits with regard to drink or tobacco—that shoves all other considerations into the background. Uncritical citizens are often beguiled into supporting a particular candidate on the basis of personal considerations such as these which are largely irrelevant to the weightier matters of social justice and the public welfare. In reality, under our two-party system of politics, the party which a candidate represents— the organization, the policies it stands for—is generally far more important than the individual who happens to be its standard-bearer.

On other occasions, attention is focused throughout a campaign upon a single issue such as race relations, federal aid to education, farm policies, small businesses, alcohol, or Communism. Obviously each of these issues is important, but each needs to be seen as a facet of the total problem of promoting social justice and fostering the total well-being of society. Exaggerated and exclusive attention to only one such issue serves as a kind of smoke screen behind which many other forms of evil may go unchallenged. Moreover, such an approach to single social problems ignores the many interrelationships between the different social evils and prevents an effective attack upon the fibrous roots of the particular ill one has selected as "the number-one social problem."

In *The Decline and Revival of the Social Gospel,* Professor Paul A. Carter makes a provocative evaluation of the effect of the alliance of the Protestant churches with the Prohibition movement. He points out that in the championing of this cause they came inevitably to be identified with the conservative political policies of right wing groups.[25] The Protestant churches generally had to pay a price for this alignment in terms of loss of the support of liberal forces and labor groups in the years which followed. But there were two other consequences which were even more serious, Carter declares. In the first place, "The emotional heat generated by the wet-dry controversy destroyed, in the minds of many supporters of Prohibition, any sense of the *proportionate importance* of social issues other than the Demon Rum."[26] As one "old-fashioned parson" wrote in the *Churchman,* "One wondered whether there were not other and greater evils against which a valiant Christian knight could tilt his word."[27] And, secondly, "The general prestige and moral influence of the churches suffered unprecedented damage, so that all of their teaching—religious as well as

---

[25] Paul A. Carter, *The Decline and Revival of the Social Gospel,* Ithaca, New York, Cornell University Press, 1954, p. 41.
[26] *Ibid.* Italics added.
[27] *Ibid.,* p. 42.

social—was rendered less effective."[28] The same "old-fashioned par-son" complained of the tendency to substitute Prohibition for the Gospel when he asked, "Are we to be content with a merely negative religion? . . . These glad young folk do not like the thing which they know as religion . . . from what they see of the reforming army of the Lord, and they say . . . 'We don't want to be like them.' " Thus, Carter declares, the dry leaders contributed greatly to the "secularist bias of the rising generation by causing it to associate the Church simultaneously with a joyless legalistic morality and with dubious ethical practices" used by some in order to achieve the success of The Cause.[29]

These dangers, of course, are not peculiar to the championing of Prohibition or temperance; but they are implicit in the championing of any single issue in such a way as to divert attention from other equally important or more fundamental ones. In Jesus' day it was the Sabbath laws and ceremonial requirements. In a day that is not altogether gone in this country it is sometimes blue laws. In the 'thirties it was "peace at any price" in Europe. Frequently it is some form of peace and prosperity at home—to distract attention from our obligations abroad.

THEY MISUNDERSTAND THE DOCTRINE OF THE SEPARATION OF CHURCH AND STATE. The founding fathers of our country wisely provided that there should be no established church on the national level. The first step in this direction was taken with the adoption of the original Constitution which stipulated that "no religious test shall ever be required as a qualification to any office or public trust under the United States" (Article VI, Section 3). There was an immediate demand, however, that this provision be supplemented by a more explicit guarantee of religious freedom. Accordingly, the First Amendment, which constituted part of the Bill of Rights, provided that "Congress shall make no law respecting an establishment of religion, or prohibiting the free exercise thereof." This amendment meant that no one church could be given preferential status or government support at the national level through the levying of taxes for its support or through the requirement of attendance at its services and the imposition of penalties for nonattendance. It also meant that Congress

---

[28] *Ibid.,* p. 41.
[29] *Ibid.,* p. 44.

could not give such support to all of the churches any more than to a single one, for this, too, would be a form of establishment.

But while the founding fathers were intent upon preventing any organic or institutional connection between the state and the church, they did not seek to separate the state from religion. Indeed, they believed that the vitality of democratic government and the welfare of the country depended to a large extent upon the strength and support which were made available through religious faith.[30] According to Dean Luther Weigle, "It was not unbelievers, but believers, who brought religious freedom into American life and established it as a national principle. The separation of church and state in this country was intended not to restrict but to emancipate the churches, not to impair but to protect religious faith."[31] The purpose of the founding fathers was to grant an equal legal status to all religious groups and guarantee full religious liberty to all of the people. They believed, moreover, that disestablishment would prove beneficial to the churches themselves.[32]

The term "separation of church and state" emphasizes the negative aspect of religious freedom, but it fails to do justice to the positive meaning of this concept. The former is essential to the latter, but religious freedom is incomplete if it does not safeguard the latter. In the words of Dean Weigle, religious liberty not only includes "the right to dissent in the name of religious belief, reason and conscience, from an act or requirement of the state, and to express this dissent in action or in refusal to act as well as in speech," but it also includes "a right greater than that of dissent; it is the right of responsible participation in the making and executing of public policy. The religious freedom of the citizen includes his right to hold the state itself responsible to the moral law and to God, and the right to labor to this end through appropriate judgments, witness, and constructive participation in the activities of citizenship."[33] From the standpoint of our democratic heritage, the right of responsible participation is a right which every individual and group has; from the standpoint of man's responsibility before God such participation is a duty for each.

[30] See Anson Phelps Stokes, *Church and State in the United States,* 3 vols., New York, Harper & Brothers, 1950, vol. I, pp. 514–517, 556.
[31] Luther A. Weigle, "The American Tradition of Religious Freedom," *Social Action,* XIII, no. 9 (November 15, 1947), p. 8. Cf. Stokes, *loc. cit.*
[32] Stokes, *op. cit.,* p. 556; Merrimon Cuninggim, *Freedom's Holy Light,* New York, Harper & Brothers, 1955, p. 99.
[33] Weigle, *op. cit.,* pp. 11–12.

When discussion of the relationship between religion and politics is focused exclusively upon the separation of church and state, the impression is given that the predominant relationship between religion as a whole and the political life as a whole is one of separation. In the long run this negative approach tends to defeat the deeper interests of Protestants in combatting the secularization of American culture. As Thomas Keehn and Kenneth Underwood point out, "The clearest indication of this danger is the alliance which some Protestants have made with secular and conservative forces in support of the 'wall of separation' doctrine. What the secularists want is a state which is avowedly free from all religious pretensions and a society in which religion is limited to private life. Protestants are thus encouraged to revert to their worst selves—to a negative, irresponsible program based upon an individualistic ethic."[34]

Clearly, there is need for a careful examination of the meaning of the concept of separation of church and state, and there is need to seek out ways in which religious forces can coöperate across church and even faith lines in the effort to achieve common goals and ends. Only thus can secularism be effectively combatted and the forces of religion be effectively marshaled in the struggle for such common objectives as social justice and the strengthening of the foundations of peace.

RECOMMENDED READINGS

Barth, Karl, *Against the Stream,* London, Student Christian Movement Press, Ltd., 1954.

Bates, M. Searle, *Religious Liberty: An Inquiry,* New York, International Missionary Council, 1945.

Bennett, John C., *Christians and the State,* New York, Charles Scribner's Sons, 1958.

Bennett, John C., *The Christian as Citizen,* New York, Association Press, 1955.

Brunner, Emil, *The Divine Imperative,* trans. by Olive Wyon, New York, The Macmillan Company, 1942, chs. XXXVI–XXXVII.

Cadoux, C. J., *Christian Pacificism Re-examined,* Oxford, Basil Blackwell, 1940.

Calvin, John, *Institutes of the Christian Religion,* 2 vols., Philadelphia, Presbyterian Board of Education, 1936, bk. IV, ch. XX.

[34] Thomas Keehn and Kenneth Underwood, "Protestants in Political Action," *Social Action,* XVI, no. 6 (June 15, 1950), p. 33.

Cullmann, Oscar, *The State in the New Testament*, New York, Charles Scribner's Sons, 1956.

Cuninggim, Merrimon, *Freedom's Holy Light*, New York, Harper & Brothers, 1955.

Evans, Joseph W. and Ward, Leo R., eds., *The Social and Political Philosophy of Jacques Maritain*, New York, Charles Scribner's Sons, 1955, chs. 4, 7–12.

Hallowell, John H., *The Moral Foundations of Democracy*, Chicago, The University of Chicago Press, 1954, chs. IV–VI.

Husslein, Joseph, ed., *Social Wellsprings*, 2 vols., Milwaukee, The Bruce Publishing Company, 1940–42, vol. I, chs. 4–5; vol. II, chs. 14–15.

Lefever, Ernest W., *Ethics and United States Foreign Policy*, New York, Meridian Books, 1957.

Luther, Martin, "Secular Authority: To What Extent It Should Be Obeyed," in *Works of Martin Luther*, vol. III, Philadelphia, A. J. Holman Company, 1915.

Maston, T. B., *Christianity and World Issues*, New York, The Macmillan Company, 1957, chs. VI–X.

Miller, William Lee, *The Protestant and Politics*, Philadelphia, The Westminster Press, 1958.

Muehl, William, *Politics for Christians*, New York, Association Press, 1956.

Nichols, James Hastings, *Democracy and the Churches*, Philadelphia, The Westminster Press, 1951. See especially ch. I.

Niebuhr, Reinhold, *The Children of Light and the Children of Darkness*, New York, Charles Scribner's Sons, 1959.

Niebuhr, Reinhold, *Christian Realism and Political Problems*, New York, Charles Scribner's Sons, 1953.

Stokes, Anson Phelps, *Church and State in the United States*, 3 vols., New York, Harper & Brothers, 1950. See especially vol. I, ch. VIII, secs. 1–2.

Visser't Hooft, W. A., ed., *The Evanston Report: The Second Assembly of the World Council of Churches*, 1954, London, Student Christian Movement Press, Ltd., 1955, The Report of Section IV on "International Affairs: Christians in the Struggle for World Community."

Voorhis, Jerry, *The Christian in Politics*, New York, Association Press, 1951.

West, Charles C., *Communism and the Theologians*, Philadelphia, The Westminster Press, 1958.

chapter 12

RACE RELATIONS

THE RACE PROBLEM

WHEN we turn to a consideration of the relationships among the races, we are faced with one of the most complex and stubborn problems of the contemporary social order. While differences between various groups of men and individuals have always been recognized and while the tendency toward ethnocentrism has apparently been perennial, discrimination on the basis of alleged racial or biological differences is a relatively modern phenomenon. In earlier times, discrimination against various out-groups rested primarily upon such factors as religious differences, nationality differences, or differences in language rather than upon differences in physical traits.

According to Dean Liston Pope, "a well-articulated theory of racial superiority" first made its appearance in the writings of Comte Arthur de Gobineau, who between 1853 and 1855 published a four-volume work entitled *Essai sur l' Inégalité des races humaines.*[1] De Gobineau was primarily interested in bolstering the declining position of the nobility not of one nation alone but of all civilized countries by identifying them as Aryans and proclaiming them to be superior to all other racial groups. De Gobineau's pseudoracial theories were further developed by Houston Stewart Chamberlain, who applied the concept of a superior race to the Teutonic (Germanic) peoples in order to support the national aspirations of the Germans. Chamberlain also proclaimed that the Jews were a degenerate race. Both of these ideas were in turn taken over by Adolf Hitler, who used them

[1] Liston Pope, *The Kingdom Beyond Caste,* New York, Friendship Press, 1957, pp. 22 ff.

to demonstrate the superiority of the Nordic peoples and to justify the extreme anti-Semitism of Nazism which issued in the extinction of millions of European Jews. The race theories of de Gobineau and Chamberlain were also disseminated in other countries where they were given different applications for different purposes. In the United States, they were used to exalt the "older American stock" and to restrict immigration of non-Nordic peoples to this country. They were also used to assert the superiority of white Americans over Negroes and to justify segregation and the subjection of Negroes to the dominant white group. They have also been used in South Africa as the basis for the maintenance in practice of white supremacy, although the official policy of the government there has been that of seeking to preserve the complete separation of the races (*apartheid*) without asserting either the superiority or the inferiority of one racial group. In actual practice, however, *apartheid* implies the superiority of the dominant group in South Africa just as, according to the Supreme Court, segregation in public schools as well as in parks and on playgrounds and golf courses means an inferior status for the Negro in the United States.

Exploitation of the colored peoples as slaves had been going on in different parts of the world for more than two hundred years prior to the time of de Gobineau. It had followed in the wake of the colonial expansion of the countries of Western Europe. Throughout this period Christians both in England and in America were divided in their attitudes toward slavery. While most white Westerners who subdued the colored peoples of Asia and Africa professed to be Christians, there were some voices (John Woolman in America and John Wesley, Granville Sharp, and William Wilberforce in England, for example) which were raised in protest against the slave trade and also against slavery itself. The number and influence of the latter increased until they became at length an important factor leading to the abolition of both of these evils throughout the civilized world.

Following the abolition of slavery, however, new methods of controlling and ostracizing the Negro by custom and law were devised in the South,[2] and indeed in other sections of the country comparable

[2] See C. Vann Woodward, *The Strange Career of Jim Crow*, New York, Oxford University Press, 1955. Professor Woodward shows that the Jim Crow laws which established the present pattern of rigid segregation were not enacted until the closing decade of the nineteenth century and the opening years of the twentieth century. Prior to that time relations between the Negroes and whites in the South were much less rigidly defined.

methods of controlling other minorities—the Jews, Orientals, and Mexicans—were contrived. The churches themselves generally followed the patterns of segregation in the community at large, and hence came to be racially exclusive. Sometimes this exclusiveness of the churches was the result of the Negroes being forced out of the white churches; more frequently it was the result of the Negroes' withdrawal in order to escape the inferior status which they had in the predominately white churches. This pattern has persisted on down to the present with relatively slight modification. "It is still true," writes Pope, "that 94 per cent of the Negro Protestants are in Negro denominations, having few religious relationships with other Protestants."[3] The church is still "the most segregated major institution in American society."[4]

While the churches are now vigorously wrestling with the question of race relations, it must be confessed that they have not taken the lead in focusing national interest upon racial issues in the last two decades—especially since the end of World War II—in this country. Rather, the greatest national attention has been centered upon a series of Supreme Court decisions culminating in the declaration that segregation in the public schools is unconstitutional. Other decisions of this same body pertaining to the political and civil rights of Negroes and members of other minorities have also focused attention upon additional important facets of race relations. The efforts of certain labor unions to organize all qualified workers without regard to race has served both to raise the economic position of the Negro and also to call widespread attention to the effects of discrimination in employment upon the economy as a whole. The integration that has taken place in the Armed Services and the breakdown of segregation in the area of sports have likewise contributed greatly to the progress made by the Negro in recent years, and these changes have served to challenge the churches to a more rigorous examination of their own practices. The major denominations, including those which are predominately Southern such as the Southern Baptist Convention and the Presbyterian Church, U.S., have endorsed the decision of the Supreme Court declaring segregated public schools to be unconstitutional, and in their national assemblies they have called upon their constituent agencies and churches to reëxamine their life and practices to see whether these are Christian. The national assemblies of the

[3] Pope, *op. cit.*, p. 109.
[4] *Ibid.*, p. 105.

major denominations have generally declared segregation to be un-Christian.

In view of the different concerns which have led various groups to be interested in racial issues in the last two decades, it becomes clear that the race problem is not an isolated one.[5] It is closely related to many other issues which cannot be adequately dealt with apart from consideration of the manner in which segregation, discrimination, and racial prejudice affect them. Recent developments and findings in the fields of sociology, criminology, economics, genetics, psychology, psychiatry, political science, and international relations have all contributed to a deeper insight into the nature of social problems and the extent to which all of these problems are interrelated. These disciplines have contributed a deeper understanding of the injustice of segregation and the *human* cost of prejudice and discrimination, both in terms of those who are the object of these evils as well as of those who practice them. Moreover, in the years since World War II it has become increasingly apparent that the flagrant gap between the American democratic creed and the actual treatment of minorities in the United States poses a serious handicap to us in our national effort to win the support of other countries in the battle against Communism. Realization of this fact has given a tremendous impetus to the endeavor to achieve a larger measure of practical democracy at home. Similarly, recognition of the social consequences of the fundamental changes that have taken place in our economy—e.g., the rapid industrialization of the South, the increased need for skilled industrial workers especially during World War II, and the rapid urbanization of our society—has encouraged labor unions, the churches, and many other groups, both Negro and white, both North and South, to attack the various facets of segregation and discrimination with increased confidence and vigor.

In many quarters this deep and widespread concern with the racial problem has led to an examination of existing patterns of relationships between the races, with the result that these relationships have been found to be both undemocratic and un-Christian. While the pattern of segregation is most deeply entrenched in the South, since there it is defined and enforced by state and municipal law as well as by firmly established custom, other forms of discrimination have become deeply engrained in the patterns of community life in other sections

[5] Cf. Charles F. Marden, *Minorities in American Society,* New York, American Book Company, 1952, pp. 16–24.

of the country—in the churches, in housing, and in employment, for example. Hence, there has been a general need to examine at a deep level the meaning and the implications of the American democratic creed and of biblical faith for the manifold aspects of the racial problem. It has not been sufficient to appeal to the general practice of our society or of the churches, for there has been the uneasy feeling that this practice has fallen far short of the fundamental norms which have been professed. In the political realm we have been forced to reconsider the meaning of the Constitution itself. In the religious realm we are being forced to go back and examine the meaning and implications of the fundamental tenets of Christian faith concerning the nature of man, man's relationship to God and his fellowmen, and the nature of the Church. The traditions of men who have profited from segregation are not a trustworthy guide to God's will. For this reason these traditions must be examined in the light of the experience and insight of the larger community of those who share the Christian faith. This means, above all, that Christians must seek to discover God's will in the area of race relations by beginning with God rather than with themselves and their customs.

THE CHRISTIAN UNDERSTANDING OF RACE

The starting point of Christian ethics as it seeks to deal with the racial problem, therefore, is the effort to understand what God is doing in this area of human relationships as Creator, as Judge, and as Redeemer. Man's action in this sphere, as in every other, should be a grateful and obedient response to the will of God who is the Lord of history.

We have emphasized the fact that, while it is impossible to divide the divine action into three distinct forms of behavior, it is possible to discern a three-fold purpose in God's activity. Man's action, we have insisted, should always be a three-fold response to this ever-present three-fold intent of God. It is particularly important to remind ourselves of the total character of the divine action in the area of race relations, for here perhaps more than elsewhere in our day many voices are raised in the name of religion which seek both to defend and to attack segregation by appealing to the partial will of the Creator or the Judge or the Redeemer with little or no effort to relate this partial will to the total purpose and action of God. Thus, segregationists widely appeal to the intent of the Creator as this is expressed in Acts 17:26 (King James Version): "[God] hath made of one blood all nations of men for to dwell on all the face of the earth, and hath determined the times before appointed, and the bounds of their habitation." Or, again, they confuse the judgment of man with the judgment of God when they appeal to the "curse" which Noah, recovering from a drunken stupor, placed upon Canaan: "Cursed be Canaan; a slave of slaves shall he be to his brothers" (Gen. 9:25). A careful reading of this passage in its proper context shows that it was Noah rather than God who placed this curse upon Ham's son, and that Noah was scarcely in a condition to be the Lord's spokesman under the circumstances. The defenders of segregation and white supremacy see God's judgment as being passed almost exclusively upon the Negro and not upon the white. Moreover, when they take account of the redemptive will of God, they do so almost exclusively in the narrow terms of personal and spiritual salvation with no reference to the application of love understood as including justice and righteousness to the social order in the area of race relations. In an effort to justify their defense of segregation, they frequently appeal to the strongly deterministic social philosophy of William Graham Sumner and the social psychology of William McDougall (dominant in America in the early part of the twentieth century but greatly modified in the direction of voluntarism since about 1940), and thereby obscure the power of God to change human life and to transform intergroup relationships.[6]

The opponents of segregation and other forms of racial discrimination have also frequently failed to see their goals and their strategy in the light of the full implications of the Christian understanding of God's will. They have overlooked the work and power of the Redeemer in making the beginnings of a present transformation of individuals and of the group life possible. Like the defenders of the *status quo*, they have often exaggerated the deterministic character of cultural patterns and institutions, and have used their belief in the inflexibility of these social forces to justify passive submission to the existing order. They have seen God's judgment upon prejudice and discrimination clearly, but they have frequently not understood the

[6] See, for example, George Eaton Simpson and J. Milton Yinger, *Racial and Cultural Minorities: An Analysis of Prejudice and Discrimination*, New York, Harper & Brothers, rev. ed., 1958, pp. 500–501; Robert M. MacIver, *The More Perfect Union*, New York, The Macmillan Company, 1948, pp. 170–171; and Gordon W. Allport, *The Nature of Prejudice*, Cambridge, Massachusetts, Addison-Wesley Publishing Company, 1954, pp. 469 ff.

depth of their own involvement in these forms of sin and their own responsibility for them. Hence, they have often failed to see the inclusiveness of God's judgment, which falls upon all—integrationists as well as segregationists, minority groups as well as dominant groups.[7] They have frequently denounced others; but they have often failed to see that the motive for the divine judgment is love, both for the oppressed and for the oppressor. They have also frequently failed to relate actual racial differences effectively to the creative will of God; hence, they have often dismissed these as meaningless and valueless.

RACE AND CREATION

The first great biblical affirmation about the action of God in the area of race relations is that God has created all men in His image and for fellowship and communion with Himself. All men have a common ancestry, for all are descended from Adam and Eve; and all are ultimately dependent upon the same Creator. Regardless of race, all human beings are sacred because all are created in the divine image (Gen. 5:1). In a word, the human race is, according to the Bible, one in its origin and one in its essential nature. The exclusiveness of the Hebrews was based upon the covenant which God had made with Abraham, not upon any supposed racial superiority of the Hebrews over their neighbors who, incidentally, were of the same racial stock (Semites) as themselves. Abraham was to be the father of a "multitude of nations" (Gen. 17:4), all of which were included in the promise of the covenant which Yahweh made with him. Moreover, provision was made for males who were not descendants of Abraham to enter the Hebrew community and become participants in the covenant by being circumcised (Gen. 17:10–13).

The prohibition of mixed marriages in the Old Testament likewise rested upon religious considerations rather than upon any notion of the racial superiority of the Israelites. When the Hebrews were about to cross the Jordan at the end of their wanderings in the wilderness after their flight from Egypt, they were forbidden to marry the inhabitants of the land because "they would turn away your sons

---

[7] Cf. "We Should Quit Singing the Blues," an editorial in the Norfolk *Journal and Guide,* a leading Negro newspaper. This editorial is reprinted in Maurice R. Davie, *Negroes in American Society,* New York, McGraw-Hill Book Company, 1949, pp. 473–474.

from following me, to serve other gods" (Deut. 7:4). This same demand for religious purity also underlay Ezra's requirement that the exiles who had returned from captivity in Babylon put away their foreign wives (Ezra 10:10–11).[8] As Pope declares, "Racial intermarriage as such does not seem to be either prohibited or advocated in the Bible."[9]

The election of Israel for the covenant relationship with God did not imply any special privileges for her. God had chosen her for His own purposes. Her people were "like the Ethiopians" to Him (Amos 9:7). The destiny for which she had been chosen demanded of her special humility and faithfulness, for her mission was by her sufferings to bring salvation to all nations and peoples. This fuller understanding of her vocation and her destiny was made clear by the prophets, especially by Isaiah of the Babylonian exile who represented God as saying,

"Turn to me and be saved,
 all the ends of the earth!
For I am God, and there is no other.

. . . .

'To me every knee shall bow,
 every tongue shall swear.' "   (Isa. 45:22–23)

The inclusiveness of God's love for all peoples was dramatized and popularized in the stories of Ruth and Jonah. Ruth was a Moabitess who was received into the national heritage of Israel. As the great-grandmother of David she held an important place in the messianic tradition. The postexilic story of Jonah represents a strong condemnation of Israel's failure to live up to the full implications of her monotheistic faith and the universalism of the prophets.

Despite a few passages which are sometimes used to support the view that Jesus thought of his ministry in particularistic terms as being intended primarily for the Jews, the overwhelming testimony of the Gospels is that his mission was universal in its purpose and included Gentiles as well as Jews.[10] The story of the healing of the daughter of the Syrophoenician woman (Mark 7:24–30) is some-

[8] The same consideration applies to other verses frequently cited as prohibiting interracial marriage—e.g., Genesis 28:1, 8; Hosea 5:7; Amos 3:2; Matthew 10:5-6.

[9] Pope, *op. cit.*, p. 148. In this connection see also Everett Tilson, *Segregation and the Bible*, Nashville, Abingdon Press, 1958, ch. 2.

[10] See Tilson, *op. cit.*, ch. V.

times cited to show that Jesus did not conceive of his mission as universal in scope; but the most significant part of this account is generally lost sight of by those who use it in this manner. The most important fact about this story is not that Jesus is represented as classifying these Gentiles with "the dogs" but, rather, that in the end he actually does respond to the mother's faith and heal her daughter! Another passage that is frequently used to show that Jesus held an exclusivist view of his work is the Matthean version of Jesus' missionary charge to the twelve (Matt. 10:5–6). Matthew includes the injunction, "Go nowhere among the Gentiles, and enter no town of the Samaritans, but go rather to the lost sheep of the house of Israel." Many scholars do not accept this prohibition as part of Jesus' charge because it does not appear either in the Markan or in the Lukan versions of this incident. Even if it is accepted as authentic, however, it is nevertheless significant that the First Gospel concludes with the narrative of a post-resurrection appearance in which Jesus is quoted as saying, "Go therefore and make disciples of all nations, baptizing them in the name of the Father and of the Son and of the Holy Spirit" (Matt. 28:19). The inference is clear: even if Jesus' missionary charge before his death did include a directive against activity beyond the borders of Israel, the disciples soon became convinced that this mandate was meant to be only temporary—whatever the reason for it may have been—and that it was now replaced by the charge to proclaim the Gospel to all nations.

The testimony of the Gospels that Jesus' mission and message were universal in purpose is fully confirmed by the rest of the New Testament. Agreement was soon reached among his followers that the Church which was built upon faith in him as the Christ must be open to people of all ethnic and social groups on the same basis if it was to be true to its Lord. There was, to be sure, a brief but heated debate as to whether Gentiles must first submit themselves to the Jewish ceremonial laws before they became Christians; but, due largely to Paul's refusal to accept any sort of legalistic requirements upon the believer, the Church came, within a generation after the death of Jesus, to affirm with an almost unanimous voice that God "shows no partiality" and that "in every nation any one who fears him and does what is right is acceptable to him" (Acts 10:34–35).

The Gospels themselves contain abundant references to events and teachings associated with the historical Jesus which make it quite evident that his disciples were true to his spirit in interpreting his mission and the Church in inclusive terms. The Jesus of the Gospels always treated each individual as a person of dignity because he looked upon each as a child of God. He mingled with publicans and sinners. He was denounced by the Pharisees for dining with publicans. He healed the servant of a Roman centurion and marveled at the latter's faith because he had not found anything to compare with it in all Israel (Matt. 8:5–10, 13). He refused to grant the Jews any special claim upon the Kingdom. Many will come from the east and the west and sit down at the table with Abraham, Isaac, and Jacob in the Kingdom of God, he declared, while "the sons of the kingdom" (i.e., the Jews) will be cast out into outer darkness (Matt. 8:11–12). And, in an equally surprising and pointed way, when he wanted to make clear the meaning of neighbor-love, he told his Jewish audience a story about a merciful act of a despised Samaritan.

Recognition of the dignity and fundamental equality of all men has been part of the general witness of historical Christianity. As we have previously noted, the idea of a superior race is a relatively modern one. Although it has been defended by some on religious grounds, it has never gained general acceptance in the Church at large. The position of historical Christianity as a whole was well summarized by the Oxford Conference in 1937: "The existence of black races, white races, yellow races, is to be accepted gladly and reverently as full of possibilities under God's purpose for the enrichment of human life. And there is no room for any differentiation between the races as to their intrinsic value. All share alike in the concern of God, being created by him to bring their unique and distinctive contributions to his service in the world."[11]

The testimony of science strikingly confirms the Christian conceptions of both the oneness of mankind in its origin and the essential equality of the races. Scientists generally agree that all men belong to

[11] J. H. Oldham, ed., *The Official Report of the Oxford Conference,* New York, Willett, Clark and Company, 1937, p. 60. Compare the Preliminary Report for the Second Assembly of the World Council of Churches at Evanston, *The Christian Hope and The Task of the Church* (New York, Harper & Brothers, 1954), section entitled "Intergroup Relations—the Church Amid Racial and Ethnic Tensions," p. 27: "The Churches agree that since mankind . . . is created and sustained by God, the human race is of one blood, possessing a fundamental unity in spite of secondary differences." Roman Catholicism grounds the equality of men in natural law. See John LaFarge, *The Catholic Viewpoint on Race Relations,* Garden City, New York, Hanover House, 1956, p. 77.

the same species, Homo sapiens, and, further that all are probably derived from the same common stock.[12] While there are obvious hereditary differences between certain groups of men, these differences are "always few when compared to the whole genetic constitution of man and to the vast number of genes common to all human beings regardless of the population to which they belong. This means that the likenesses among men are far greater than their differences."[13] There is no authentic evidence so far as science is concerned that the three major racial groups—Mongoloid, Negroid, and Caucasoid—differ either in the average or in the range of their innate mental capacities. Inherited genetic differences do not seem to be a major factor in producing the differences between the cultural achievements of different ethnic groups. Rather, it is the history of the cultural experiences which varying groups have undergone that constitutes "the major factor" in explaining differences between cultures.[14] Finally, there is no convincing evidence that miscegenation is biologically harmful. From the standpoint of science, the term "pure race" is a meaningless one; for the mixing of racial and ethnic groups has been going on from earliest times.

It should be noted in this connection, however, that while the Christian conceptions of the unity of men and of the fundamental equality of the races are confirmed by science, the former do not depend for their validity upon such empirical verification. There is perhaps a closer correlation between the Christian and the scientific affirmations of the unity of man than there is between the two affirmations concerning the essential equality of the races. The Christian conception of the creation of man by a sovereign and purposive God who out of love made man in His own image for fellowship with Himself obviously goes far beyond the available scientific data. Moreover, while biologists, anthropologists, and psychologists find no basis for affirming the superior moral or intellectual capacity of any one race over another, they do not necessarily conclude that all men are essentially equal in worth. Long before the rise of the modern conception of a superior race, the notion of an aristocracy

---

[12] Ashley Montagu, *Statement on Race*, New York, Henry Schuman, 1951, p. 11. The UNESCO Statement on Race is reprinted in its entirety in this volume, pp. 11–18.

[13] *Ibid.*

[14] *Ibid.*, p. 14.

based upon intelligence or virtue was common. Aristotle believed, for example, that, quite apart from considerations of race, some men are born to be slaves while others are born to be free. Those who are superior in virtue, whoever they are, should be the masters. Similarly, Plato believed that the philosophers, those who are superior in wisdom, should be the rulers. Neither science nor Christianity denies that there are many differences both between racial groups and between individuals. Neither affirms that all men are equal in natural endowment. But, whereas science discredits the idea of a superior race, Christianity makes a far more sweeping claim, namely that "those who are naturally unequal are still equal before God, and that he is concerned about them equally, just as a father cares for his children whether they have few talents or many and is perhaps especially concerned about those who are weaker."[15]

The starting point, therefore, of the Christian understanding of relationships among the races is the conviction that God has created all men and that they share equally in His love. He has created them to dwell with Him in one great family or Kingdom. As we have seen, the response of the Christian to God's work as Creator is praise and gratitude to the Creator and love of His creation. This means, insofar as relationships among the races are concerned, that man is called to love his fellowmen and recognize his own responsibility for, and the privilege of, establishing fellowship and community with all of God's children. The Kingdom of God, as Liston Pope declares, is a "kingdom beyond caste."[16] As Creator, God is forming a universal community which transcends the lesser communities of family, class, race, and nation; and men are summoned to work together with Him in making His will to "be done on earth as it is in heaven."

In actuality, however, our response to the Creator in the area of human relationships is usually only a very limited response. Frequently, it is not so much hatred of the out-group or pride of one's own race as it is a narrow love of family or community or race which causes us to defend these smaller groups against what we perceive to be threats to their security, integrity, and well-being, even when this defense involves violence and manifest injustice to others.[17] It

[15] Pope, *op. cit.*, p. 155.
[16] *Ibid.*, p. 159.
[17] Rachel Henderlite, "The Christian Way in Race Relations," *Theology Today*, XIV, no. 2 (July, 1957), p. 200.

is our love and loyalty to our children, to our neighborhood, to our traditions, or to our race that cause us to seek above all else to protect these from deep-cutting social changes which seem to threaten them, without recognizing the will of the Creator who is equally concerned about the well-being of all families and all races and with the participation of all in a community of righteousness and love.

But Christian love—that is, *agape*—is by its very nature all-inclusive. As Professor Henderlite reminds us, it can neither be established nor maintained at one point if it is denied at another. "The very child we seek to protect, the very community we seek to preserve are diminished and finally destroyed by the narrow loyalty that causes us to strike out in their defense."[18] Narrow loyalties betray men and groups into isolation and hostilities; they lead to intellectual and spiritual impoverishment and decay. They keep the Christian's love from being genuine *agape*, for they focus man's love upon exclusive human groups rather than upon God. From the standpoint of biblical religion, these groups become idols. To give one's primary loyalty to them rather than to the Creator is to betray the monotheism of Christian faith.

RACE AND JUDGMENT

But here as elsewhere the Christian sees not only the intent of the Creator but also that of the Judge or Governor. For while it is evident that God wills a community of universal love, it is also apparent that such a community has not yet come into being. Since man lives in a moral order, he reaps the consequences of his rejection of the law of his being; and to the eyes of faith these consequences constitute God's judging or ordering action in history. Racial tension and strife are part of the judgment of God upon the failures of men to achieve genuine community and brotherhood. The Christian also sees the ordering and governing action of God in the many costs of segregation in the southern region of the United States—in the economic drain upon the region resulting from discrimination in employment opportunities and wages and from the effort to provide "separate but equal" educational facilities; in the increased difficulties involved in the integration of schools because of previous inequalities between the educational facilities and opportunities provided for Negro and

[18] *Ibid.,* pp. 200–201.

white children; in the political problems which arise out of a one-party system; and in the use of the race issue as a tool for political advantage. As a result of these last two characteristics of Southern political life, the race problem is itself intensified; and concern with fundamental political issues gives way to primary concern with person-alities and issues of race, thus making constructive political approaches to racial problems almost impossible. In all of these ways and in many others which affect the personalities—the emotional, the moral, and the spiritual development—of both Negroes and whites reared in the South, in ways that affect the region itself, in ways that affect the nation as a whole, and in ways that affect other peoples of the world the "wrath" of God is evidenced in His judgment upon men's narrow loyalties, their prejudices, and their discrimination.

But God's judgment does not fall upon one region alone. While there are important differences between the general pattern of Negro-white relations in the North and the South, much discrimination against the Negro has nevertheless taken place in the North; and this has brought its inescapable harvest of intergroup tension, blighted areas in large cities, and a high incidence of crime and disease in such areas. Whereas the Negro has constituted the major minority group in the South and often the only one, other sections of the nation have variously discriminated against recent immigrants from parts of Europe, Puerto Rico, and the Orient, and against the American Indians and the Jews. Moreover, as Professor Vann Woodward shows, one reason for the South's adoption of an extreme racism toward the end of the nineteenth century was the declining effectiveness of Northern liberalism—in the press, the courts, and the government—as a restraining force in preventing the growth and spread of bigotry and discrimination by law during that period.[19] For example, in 1890 the United States Supreme Court ruled that a state could *require* segregation on common carriers; in 1896 in *Plessy* v. *Ferguson* it laid down the "separate but equal" principle as justifying segregation; and in 1898 it opened the door to the disfranchisement of the Negro by approving the Mississippi plan for depriving Negroes of the right to vote. In addition, as a consequence of the fact that some eight million colored people were brought under the jurisdiction of the United States as a result of the Spanish-American War, the nation as a whole took up many of the Southern attitudes on race in relation

[19] C. Vann Woodward, *op. cit.*, pp. 51–56.

to these subject peoples who were widely held to be inferior to the white man and therefore unworthy of having the right to vote. For this reason, too, Northern liberals became more willing to accept the Southern practices without protest.

What has been said about the involvement of the country as a whole in our contemporary problem of race relations does not justify the widespread tendency of Southerners to say that they should be left alone in dealing with this problem in the South; because the North contributed to the South's problem in many ways, including the slave trade; and also because other parts of the country have similar problems of their own. As we have previously noted, response to the governing will of God begins with repentance and with humility, not with self-righteous denunciation of the sins of others or with the effort to justify or excuse one's own action when it is seen to represent a denial of God's will. The final purpose of the divine judgment is not to punish but to redeem. Hence, the response of faith is to accept God's judgment upon the self and the actions of the self; it is to confess one's own sins. And, since our decisions are so closely bound up with our neighbors' decisions through numerous groups in which we share the responsibility for action, the confession of our sins leads us to reëxamine all of our actions and relationships. Moreover, our response to the divine judgment involves both repentance on the part of the self and the responsible restraint of others inasmuch as our action inevitably affects their choices of good or evil. The Christian is not really concerned about who has the greater guilt but rather about what he can do and must do in order to make his action and the common life a faithful response to God to the end that His will may be done on earth. Recognition of the responsibility of each for all is implicit in the belief in the genuine oneness of mankind in its destiny by creation as well as in its fall and redemption.

Finally, God's "judgment" is manifest in the effects of prejudice and discrimination upon both the victims and the perpetrators of these evils. Not only does discrimination thwart the aspirations of its victims, but it produces bitterness and hostility in those against whom it is directed. Because they are denied a sense of real dignity and the normal sense of security which comes from being genuinely accepted on the level of equality and importance with other members of the community, the victims of discrimination frequently develop unrealistic inferiority feelings, a sense of humiliation in the face of the inferior social status to which they are restricted, and a psychological constriction of their potentialities for self-development.[20] Being constantly told that they are inferior, members of minority groups frequently develop an image of themselves that closely resembles that held by the dominant group, and consequently fulfill the expectations of the dominant group by actually becoming inferior. This often leads to self-hatred and the rejection of one's own group. These attitudes in turn frequently find expression, on the one hand, in anti-social action that is directed against one's own group and, on the other hand, in similar action directed against the dominant group. In any case, the underlying feelings of inferiority and humiliation greatly affect one's level of aspiration, his capacity to learn, and his capacity to relate himself to others in all kinds of interpersonal situations. In all of these ways the social ills which result from prejudice and discrimination inevitably lower the level of well-being of the community as a whole.[21]

Although less obvious than the effects upon the members of minority groups, the effects of discrimination upon members of the dominant group are, both from the religious and from the psychiatric points of view, equally serious. The imposition of minority status upon another group leads to the development of an unrealistic feeling of superior personal worth in the members of the dominant group. This feeling of superior worth rests basically upon the artificial down-grading of the minority group. Although the latter is held to be inferior by heredity, the dominant group usually deems it necessary to reënforce this alleged inferiority by numerous means of social control—legal, economic, educational, and religious—in order to keep the minority group inferior. For the dominant group the result of this effort is an uneasy and hollow sense of superiority which is frequently shot through with feelings of anxiety and guilt. The need to justify the discriminatory treatment of an entire group frequently leads to a reaffirmation and entrenchment of the myth of racial superiority. In this way reality is further distorted, and it becomes increasingly difficult to deal constructively with the genuine needs of each racial or ethnic group. Not only is the facing of the basic problems involved in race relations impeded by this process, but the generalized issue of race itself is often used as a screen to avoid the facing of other social

---

[20] Group for the Advancement of Psychiatry, *Report No. 37: Psychiatric Aspects of School Desegregation*, New York, 1957, p. 10. Cf. Allport, *op. cit.*, ch. 9.

[21] *Psychiatric Aspects of School Desegregation*, p. 11.

problems essentially unrelated to it or related to it only peripherally. Thus, in those areas where the issue of race is exploited by political leaders for demagogic purposes, it becomes exceedingly difficult to deal directly and constructively with such basic problems as how to provide the best education possible for all children, how to achieve better law enforcement, how to raise the level of well-being for the community as a whole, and how to strengthen democracy at home and abroad.

As a result of the development of a false sense of superiority and feelings of guilt, anxiety, and fear in members of the dominant group, it is extremely difficult for persons who are reared in an environment in which prejudice and discrimination are socially sanctioned to acquire a genuinely democratic outlook. Such an environment tends to foster either a bullying or a paternalistic attitude in members of the dominant group. In the former instance it tends to encourage government by fear, by the denial of freedom of speech and press, by the restriction of the ballot to keep the minority from wielding its proportionate political power, and by the denial in practice if not in law of equal protection of the law to members of the minority group. In the latter instance it tends to encourage a condescending attitude on the part of the dominant group and results in the substitution of charity for justice. Such paternalism fails to take into account the real needs of the members of the minority for an opportunity to become mature and independent. It ignores the right of the minority to have a real voice in the determination of its own destiny.

In all of these ways, then, racial prejudice and discrimination exact their toll both in the development of individuals, whether they be the victims or the primary perpetrators of these evils, and in the general health of the community as a whole. The Christian sees in the inevitably resulting spiritual and social impoverishment and corruption the judging action of God upon the racial sin of our society. The white Christian sees in the rise of aggressive Negro leadership which demands equal rights and equal status a divine chastisement upon the pride and cumulative injustice of the whites in their dealings with the Negroes. He sees, moreover, in the churches' loss of moral leadership and inability to minister spiritually to the victims of racial and economic injustice God's judgment upon their failure to serve as the conscience of society in protesting against injustice and in providing an example of brotherhood in their own life. The sensitive Negro also sees God's judgment as falling upon his own apathy, his resentment and bitterness, his tendency toward escapism in religion and in sexual indulgence, his tendency to ingratiate himself to the white group by clowning and exaggerated flattery, and his conservatism which sometimes seeks to protect a vested interest in segregation.[22] While these attitudes are understandable, they are nevertheless not the proper responses of faith and love. They warp and harden the personalities of those who practice them, and they contribute to the preservation of the barriers of separation between the races.

RACE AND REDEMPTION

But the judgments of God upon the racial life fall within a process that is ultimately redemptive. As we have seen, it is the Creator who judges in order that He may redeem and heal man in and through the suffering which attends evil. To the eyes of faith the costs of prejudice and discrimination are seen to be the consequences of man's denial of the brotherhood and community which the Creator intends, and these costs provide an increasingly urgent incentive for men to accept their common destiny of dwelling together in a relationship of equality and mutuality lest they destroy themselves in their rebellion against the moral order.

The Christian understanding of the destiny of man as intended by the Creator and the Redeemer is most clearly revealed in the life and teachings of Jesus and in the experience of the Church which is built upon faith in him. We have noted that Jesus practiced and taught an inclusive love of all without regard to their race or their reputation. The central conviction of the New Testament is the faith that Christ came to bring salvation to all men, and this salvation is understood to mean, on the one hand, reconciliation between man and God and, on the other hand, reconciliation among men. The Church, which was built upon faith in Christ as the Lord of those who are united in this common faith, is summoned by its very nature to be "an inclusive and integrated community."[23] As Paul, writing to the churches at Galatia, declared, "For as many of you as were baptized into Christ have put on Christ. There is neither Jew nor Greek, there is neither slave nor free, there is neither male nor fe-

---

[22] Cf. George D. Kelsey, "Racial Patterns and the Churches," *Theology Today*, IX, no. 1 (April, 1952), 75. See also Martin Luther King, Jr., *Stride Toward Freedom*, New York, Harper & Brothers, 1958, pp. 211–213, 222–223.

[23] Pope, *op. cit.*, p. 157.

male; for you are all one in Christ Jesus" (Gal. 3:27–28). And this new unity and oneness which men found in Christ was not only a spiritual oneness; it was manifest in the common life of the local congregations. To be sure, the general acceptance of this concept of the Church was not won without much searching of heart on the part of the early Christians, many of whom felt that the Gentiles ought first to become incorporated into the Jewish community before being accepted into the Christian fellowship. But the important fact is that due to the experiences and labors of such men as Stephen, Peter, and Paul the Church came, within the lifetime of the Apostles, to acknowledge its supraracial and supranational character.[24]

The Christian thus sees that God is at work in the common life to bring into being a new, inclusive community. This is His intent as seen in Creation; it is His intent as seen in the judgments which He metes out upon all of men's denials of their oneness; and it is His intent as seen in His revelation of His love in Christ and in the fellowship of the Church. As Redeemer, God is seen to be offering forgiveness to men who are unworthy of His love; and He is seen to be giving men freedom and power to practice love in the common life. In response to the Redeemer's action, the love which is revealed to be God's attribute and His gift is seen also to be a requirement upon man in relation to his fellowmen; but the requirement does not represent a new law as much as it does a new understanding of reality, a new understanding of God. A new kind of love is seen to be required of men, but it is given to man before it is required of him; for it is only in the receiving of it that it is known to be required of him, just as it is only in this receiving of it that it becomes a possibility for man in his relationships with his neighbors.

The first response of the Christian to the love and forgiveness of God is, therefore, the acceptance of this love and forgiveness in humility. Because he knows that his salvation—his experience of God's love and companionship—is entirely unmerited, he is forbidden to judge the neighbor and to assume that he is more righteous than the neighbor. He is called, rather, in humility to confess his own sin— his own individual acts of evil, his own indifference to the neighbor's need, and the poverty of his own love. He is summoned also to confess his own responsibility for the common guilt; for although he may not personally engage in or endorse the grosser acts of injustice,

[24] See W. A. Visser't Hooft, *The Ecumenical Movement and the Racial Problem,* Paris, UNESCO, 1954, pp. 53–55.

he nevertheless must acknowledge his own involvement in the social system which permits such injustices and encourages and even requires other forms of discrimination.

The Christian is called by the Redeemer, in the second place, to manifest the love which he has received in his relationships with the neighbor. This means that he is summoned to meet the neighbor in his needs with the kind of action which will minister to his needs for acceptance on a level of dignity and equality, for the establishment of a relationship of mutual fellowship and service, for justice in the social life, and for freedom from fear of humiliation as well as from fear of economic and legal disadvantage or even of physical violence. Action that is directed toward these ends represents the concrete reality of love in the realm of race relations; and the Christian who is aware of the depth of God's forgiving love is free to devote himself henceforth to the service of the neighbor without fear of the guilt which he may incur by throwing himself into the concrete struggles of good with evil in the political, economic, ecclesiastical, and social life of the day. He is able to accept the fact that many of the choices which he will need to make if he is to be an effective worker for the amelioration of social evils will be choices between alternatives all of which involve some evil consequences. If he is not willing to participate in the struggle for racial justice on this basis, his only remaining option is the futile one of seeking to wash his hands of any responsibility for the evils he deplores. This problem confronts the Negro and the white in the South today in a particularly poignant way, but it also confronts many who live in other sections of the country and who are faced with segregated churches, restricted neighborhoods, and discriminatory employment policies. Shall those who feel the tension between the patterns of discrimination and their own ideals move to areas or situations where their actions will not be restricted by the prejudiced attitudes and practices of segregated communities? Shall the person with political ability and interest and with a desire to make the political structures of a city or state the instruments of greater justice be willing to "compromise" and engage in a process of gradual change? Or, should the morally sensitive person refuse to get involved in the compromises that are demanded if the effort to promote greater social justice through political action is to be successful? Should the minister who believes that all local churches should receive persons into their membership without regard to race refuse to become the pastor of a congregation which will not as yet adopt such a policy? Without attempting to lay down a rule in regard to these matters, the person who is aware of the reality of the divine forgiveness and *agape* and who in response to this love is seeking unselfishly to meet his neighbor's needs knows that whatever is required by *agape* is acceptable in God's sight as an offering of love. This is all that God requires of man in relation to his fellow-man, but He does require that this *agape* shall be genuine. The Christion knows that salvation—in the present life and in eternity—is always dependent upon the divine goodness. As Paul and the Reformers expressed the matter, salvation is by grace through faith. This is true without exception. And, while works of love will be the fruit of a vital faith, one is free to *love* the neighbor according to the latter's concrete needs and in accordance with the demands and the possibilities of the specific situation in which the neighbor and the self are placed. Moreover, one is forbidden by love to seek to maintain his own personal purity at the cost of by-passing the neighbor.

The response of the Christian to the redemptive action and will of God, therefore, is a double response. In the first place it involves the work of alleviation of evil within a segregated social system, and in the second place it involves the effort to reconstruct the present order of society by the abolition of segregation and the establishment of an order of equality and mutuality. Even when the system of segregation has been abolished, there will still be need for both of these responses of alleviation and of reconstruction, for no social institution is—or is likely to be—completely just; all are subject to corruption and all need to be continually readapted to changing social conditions. But even in a corrupt system of segregation—whether or not this is supported by local laws—there is room for the pursuit of greater justice and the fuller expression of *agape* in numerous unconventional ways without waiting for the removal of segregation; and these acts have an important role in preparing the way for the elimination of segregation itself. But, although much can be done within the framework of a system of segregation, the achievement of genuine equality and mutuality demands the abolition of this system. It is through the outward relationships effected by integration that the recovery of true interpersonal community—rather than the mere meeting of Negro and white groups that remain self-conscious of their own racial identity—can best be realized.[25] It is in an integrated so-

[25] Cf. Waldo Beach, "A Theological Analysis of Race Relations," in Paul Ramsey, ed., *Faith and Ethics*, New York, Harper & Brothers, 1957, p. 224.

ciety that the "kingdom beyond caste" can be most fully manifest "upon earth as it is in heaven." It is for this reason that the Christian rejoices in the progress which is being made in this direction, although the progress itself is frequently painful. For this reason the churches generally have seen an opportunity for the fuller realization of equality and genuine community in the new possibilities created by the Supreme Court decisions relating to abolition of segregation in the schools as well as in many other areas of public life.

THE ROOTS OF PREJUDICE

The person who is seriously interested in helping reduce racial prejudice and discrimination must seek to understand as fully as possible the roots of these evils. In this effort the Christian can learn a great deal from the social sciences.

Although there have been attempts to account for the rise of prejudice and racial discrimination in terms of a single causal factor such as economic forces or historical circumstances or the need for a scapegoat, there is a general consensus among students of prejudice that no single explanation is adequate. As yet, the roots of prejudice are by no means fully understood; but a growing body of sociological and psychological evidence tends to show that many factors in the experience of the individual contribute to the development of prejudiced personalities and many factors in our society contribute to the discriminatory behavior of persons who themselves have little or no prejudice. It is important, therefore, that the many sources of prejudice and injustice be understood so that the struggle to reduce them may be waged as effectively as possible.

In *The Nature of Prejudice* Gordon Allport describes six different approaches to the etiology of prejudice.[26] Each, he believes, illuminates a different dimension of the subject, but all of these approaches must be taken together in order to understand the pattern of causation involved in prejudice and discrimination. In the first place, there is the *historical* approach which seeks to explain the rise of these ills in terms of the distinctive history of a particular region. Thus, it is sometimes argued that the racial attitudes of Southern whites are the result of the system of slavery and the bitterness that was produced by the reconstruction policies imposed upon the South

[26] Allport, *op. cit.*, ch. 13.

by the North following the Civil War. While it is no doubt true that a historical understanding of the social forces which provide the broad context in which personality is shaped sheds light upon the present-day attitudes of people who live in a particular region, it is clear that other factors are also involved; for within a single geographical area some persons develop prejudices while others who have been nurtured in the same general context do not. The different historical factors involved in Negro-white relations in the South and in the North should not be lost sight of, but the historical process does not operate inevitably. As Pope points out, the history of a region is the story of human choices many of which could have been made otherwise.[27] For example, the present patterns of segregation in the South were deliberately prescribed by law, and there was considerable opposition to these laws among the whites when they were first proposed.

In the second place, there is the *sociocultural* approach to group conflict. Sociologists and anthropologists tend to ascribe primary importance to various social and cultural forces in their analysis of the etiology of prejudice. Like the historian, they seek to understand the broad social context in which people develop attitudes of hostility toward others; but, whereas the historian is more largely concerned with the historical background of present attitudes and conflicts, the sociologist and the anthropologist give greater attention to an analysis of the dynamic and interlocking character of the cultural forces which influence social change in different societies. Within the framework of this approach (which may easily be combined with the historical approach) some writers stress the importance of the relative density of the populations involved; others emphasize the effects of a one-crop agrarian economy and a one-party political system upon the South; others, the relative upward mobility in in-groups and out-groups; others, the kinds of contacts that exist between the groups involved; and still others, the importance of industrialization and urbanization.

The third approach which Allport describes places the emphasis upon the *situation*. Here the primary concern is with the current forces which act upon an individual rather than with the historical background of these forces—with the immediate effects of the situation rather than with an attempt to explain how the situation itself

[27] Pope, *op. cit.,* p. 44.

came to be as it is. Thus Lillian Smith, in *Killers of the Dream,* presents what Allport refers to as an "atmosphere theory" of prejudice. According to this view, the Southern white child—which obviously has no knowledge of the historical background of the contemporary patterns of race relations and which also has no understanding of the economic and political factors involved—very early begins to mirror the prejudiced attitudes which it sees in the world around it because it soon learns that it must conform to the patterns of race relations even when it senses that they are quite inconsistent with its own inner feelings of love and with the moral teachings of Christianity.[28] Other situational approaches stress the impact of the current level of employment and various aspects of economic competition. Still others stress the influence of the present types of contact between the different groups and the importance of the relative density of the groups without attempting to explain the reasons why the present situations have come into being or why they are so resistent to change. Clearly, both the sociocultural and the situational theories, like the historical theory, shed light upon the origin of prejudice and group hostility, but none of these types of causation operates in a completely deterministic way.

In addition to the foregoing approaches, which place the emphasis upon the broad social context in which personality develops, Allport describes two other methods of causal analysis which focus attention on the agent and one which focuses it upon the object of dislike and hostility. *Psychodynamic* theories of prejudice stress the importance of the structure and dynamics of personality. It may be argued, for example, that prejudice is caused by frustration. When the fulfillment of a person's basic needs is denied, he experiences deprivation and frustration which lead to the development of hostility. If this hostility is not controlled and directed against the object which has caused the frustration, it comes to be directed against some other object by a process of transference. Thus, a minority group is frequently used as a scapegoat upon which the blame for one's own failures or the failure of the dominant group is transferred. As the result of this process, members of the dominant group come to hate members of the minority group. The Jews in Germany served as such a scapegoat under the Nazis prior to and during World War II. By the somewhat different mechanism of projection, a minority group frequently serves

---

[28] See Lillian Smith, *Killers of the Dream,* New York, W. W. Norton & Company, 1949, pp. 17 ff.

as a convenient screen for the projection of feelings of anxiety and guilt on the part of the dominant group. In this way ethnic hostility appears as "a projection of unacceptable inner strivings onto a minority group."[29] Other psychological theories of prejudice point out that persons who are basically insecure and anxiety-ridden tend to exclude and fear groups that are unfamiliar and seem to threaten their relatively secure relationships and customary way of life.

Like the preceding method, the *phenomenological* approach focuses attention upon the prejudiced person; but here the emphasis is upon his view of the situation which confronts him. For example, a person may develop hostility toward members of a particular group because he believes them to be lazy, dirty, inferior, repulsive, aggressive, or threatening. The important thing is not whether these characteristics are typical of the group but whether the individual believes them to be typical. Thus the stereotype which a person has of members of another group plays a prominent role at the level of immediate causation. However, if analysis at this level is not supplemented by the previous approaches, there is danger that the underlying dynamic factors in the personality and society which cause one to view the world as he actually does view it may be overlooked.

Finally, there is a sixth approach which puts the emphasis upon the *stimulus object* itself. Here attention is focused upon the actual characteristics of the group against which prejudice and hostility are directed. While recognizing that the actual differences between groups are much less—and even quite other—than they are generally imagined to be, some analysts point out that at times hostility is directed toward a minority *in part* because of the earned reputation of that group. Without ascribing the major blame to such a minority, these writers warn against assuming that every minority is necessarily blameless. But in view of the tendency that the dominant group has to rationalize its own hostility toward the minority and to project its guilt upon the latter, Allport's word of caution in this regard needs to be emphasized. "It would be impossible," he writes, "to find any social scientist today who would subscribe completely to the *earned reputation* theory."[30] This approach has its greatest validity when it is used to point up the interaction of a great many causal factors in-

[29] Bruno Bettelheim and Morris Janowitz, *Dynamics of Prejudice: A Psychological and Sociological Study of Veterans,* New York, Harper & Brothers, 1950, p. 42. Cf. Allport, *op. cit.,* pp. 199–200.
[30] Allport, *op. cit.,* p. 217.

cluding the relevant characteristics of the minority group itself—characteristics, which in turn are frequently the result of the other factors we have been considering but which also form part of an "interactive complex" which serves to perpetuate intergroup hostility.

From the standpoint of our concern with general principles of strategy for improving relationships between the races, Allport's emphasis upon the fact that many factors are involved in the etiology of prejudice and discrimination is an important one. Allport does not, however, give sufficient attention to the interdependence of the different factors which he describes.[31] These factors do not operate as isolated, independent units: rather, they constitute an interactive complex which needs to be understood in terms of the dynamic relationships among the various parts. Allport recognizes this fact to a certain extent, but it needs to be made clearer. He points out, for example, that there is a tendency on the part of the minority group to fulfill the dominant group's expectations with regard to its behavior. If they are expected to be dirty, lazy, dishonest, inferior, or clownish, members of the minority group frequently tend to exhibit such characteristics, which in turn serve to perpetuate the dominant group's expectations. But the dominant group's expectations are also affected by other factors such as the changing contacts between the groups involved, significant changes in the relative size of the groups, the attitudes of leaders of the dominant group toward the minority group, the tradition of a region, the economic opportunities open to members of the minority group, and the personality structure of members of the dominant group. These interrelationships are obviously important when one faces the question of the kind of attack upon prejudice and discrimination that will be most effective. Failure to recognize the interactive character of the various causal factors results in a false abstraction of one from the others and frequently leads to the effort to advocate one type of strategy as a panacea for the elimination of intergroup hostility.

Simpson and Yinger remind us that effective strategy is based upon a precise knowledge of the goals which one wants to achieve and upon a thorough understanding of the obstacles in the way of achieving them.[32] We have already examined the nature of the Christian's

[31] Otto Klineberg, *Social Psychology,* New York, Henry Holt and Company, rev. ed., 1954, pp. 536–537. Cf. Robert M. MacIver, *Social Causation,* New York, Ginn and Company, 1942.

[32] Simpson and Yinger, *op. cit.,* p. 726.

long-range objectives in the area of race relations. It should perhaps be noted that pursuit of these ideals by the Christian does not preclude his coöperation with others whose goals fall far short of his ultimate objective of genuine equality and mutuality. Indeed, the Christian who accepts the latter goal should be prepared to coöperate with others in taking the best step that is possible (for example, the promotion of economic or political equality) both as a way of improving conditions of life for the minority and as a means of preparing the way for a further step (for example, genuine equality in the schools and churches).

An adequate understanding of the obstacles in the way of the realization of the goals which one is seeking in the area of race relations involves consideration of (1) the types of persons to be affected, and (2) the types of situations with which one must deal. Different strategies are effective with different types of persons and in different types of situations. Robert Merton, for example, distinguishes between four types of persons for each of whom a different group of strategies is indicated.[33] In the first place, there is the unprejudiced nondiscriminator, or all-weather liberal, who is inclined to underestimate the importance of organized, collective action in effecting a social adjustment which would encourage nondiscrimination. Because he fails to recognize the social roots of intergroup hostility, he is likely to insist that all that is needed is for each individual to "put his own house in order." In the second place, there is the unprejudiced discriminator, or fair-weather liberal. Although without prejudice himself, such a person complies with and supports discriminatory practices if it is easier or more profitable to do so under the circumstances. This kind of person is likely to have a sense of guilt about his conduct, and the all-weather liberal may effectively appeal to him on this basis to desist from his discrimination, especially if this appeal is reinforced by a change in the weather so that he will find rewards (e.g., approval of the more liberal groups, the support of respected leaders, the moral support of laws providing for fair employment and various civil rights) for abiding by his own convictions. Thirdly, there is the prejudiced nondiscriminator, or fair-weather illiberal. While this type of person is prejudiced, he reluctantly conforms to a pattern of

[33] Robert K. Merton, "Discrimination and the American Creed," in *Discrimination and National Welfare,* Robert M. MacIver, ed., Institute for Religious and Social Studies (distributed by Harper & Brothers, New York), 1949, pp. 103–110.

equal treatment if he believes that he would be penalized for treating people unequally. Such a person would not be motivated to cease from discrimination by appeal to his value creed, but he would be influenced by legal measures which made such practices costly if these measures were strictly administered. Finally, there is the prejudiced discriminator, or all-weather illiberal. Appeal to this type of person's value creed obviously would be ineffective in reducing his prejudice. A commitment to a new set of values or loyalties is needed, but under some circumstances his discrimination might be reduced if the group norms were changed and if the legal and economic supports of discrimination were removed.

Not only are there different types of persons, there are also different types of situations to which strategy must be adjusted if it is to be effective. For example, in some areas discrimination is reinforced by state and municipal laws; in other areas such laws forbid the unequal treatment of different ethnic groups. In some situations, immediate decisions and action are called for; in others, there is time for discussion and the preparation of a community for the facing of important issues. Or, again, there is considerable variation from one situation to another with regard to the educational, economic, and social differences between the ethnic groups involved. It is also important to know what groups are supporting the pattern of discrimination and what their reasons for doing so are. To what extent, for example, is the question of racial inequality an issue that is used to keep certain political groups in power, or to what extent is it a tool in the hands of conservative economic forces to prevent the organization of labor unions?

Christian ethics is greatly indebted to the social sciences for the light which the latter have shed upon the complexity and the variety of the roots of prejudice. They have greatly illuminated both the social and the individual sources of racial hostility, and in so doing they offer valuable guidance as to the kinds of attack upon prejudice and discrimination that have the greatest likelihood of being effective.

THE TASK OF THE CHURCH IN THE AREA OF RACE RELATIONS

In view of the fact that effective strategy must take into account the different types of persons and the different kinds of situations with which one is dealing, no effort will here be made to prescribe detailed tactics for the great variety of specific problems which call for attention in the broad area of race relations. Neither will an attempt be made to draw together the results of a growing amount of important research with regard to certain principles which must underlie the development of any effective strategy for reducing prejudice and discrimination.[34] Rather, our primary concern at this point is to emphasize the fact that the Christian is motivated by gratitude to God and by love for the neighbor to use the knowledge, instruments, and skills provided by the social sciences in an effort to realize the goal of equality and mutuality in human relationships. The Kingdom for which he prays and labors is a "kingdom beyond caste," and it is to be manifest in the daily relationships of men as well as in the spiritual oneness which they profess.

Although we have disavowed any attempt to prescribe the tactics which Christians should employ in dealing with any of the social problems which we have examined, consideration of four general obligations which the Church faces in the field of race relations will indicate something of the breadth of responsibility which Christians share in this area, both as members of the Church and as citizens in society.

In the first place, Christians in and through the Church have a responsibility to make clear the relevance of Christian faith to issues of social concern in general and to intergroup relationships in particular. The Church must seek to understand the faith to which she has been summoned to witness, and she must be faithful in proclaiming and interpreting it to the world. It is not sufficient to speak vaguely of the fatherhood of God and the brotherhood of man and of the obligation to love the neighbor. What these mean in the present-day economic, educational, political, and religious areas of life must be squarely faced, for it is here that the neighbor is to be loved. While there will be sincere differences of opinion with regard to the specific ways in which Christian love can best be expressed in dealing with these social problems, the Church ought to make it clear that responsible Christian action in these areas begins with the acknowledgment that God's will is normative in all of these relationships and with a per-

---

[34] The reader is referred to such discussions of strategies for influencing intergroup relations as the following: John P. Dean and Alex Rosen, *A Manual of Intergroup Relations,* Chicago, University of Chicago Press, 1955; Simpson and Yinger, *op. cit.,* pt. III; MacIver, *The More Perfect Union;* and Allport, *op. cit.,* pt. VIII.

sistent effort to discover the meaning of this will in the concrete situations which are confronted in the daily life.

In the second place, along with this proclamation of the radical monotheism of Christian faith and this witnessing to the relevance of the Christian's understanding of the divine righteousness and *agape* to all of life, the Church needs to interpret its own mission in the world. Unless the Church's own understanding of her prophetic ministry as well as of her priestly ministry is made clear, many Christians will continue to assume that she ought not to get involved in the problems of the social order and many other Christians will continue to suppose that she ought to endorse the norms and standards of culture as representing the norms and ideals of the Gospel for these areas. If, however, a congregation or a community is led to reëxamine its expectations of the functions of a church and a Christian ministry in its midst, the way may be prepared for the receiving of the prophetic and redemptive message of the Church. This does not mean that the Church's witness and prophetic word will always be heeded, but it does mean that if a congregation and a community expect the Church to exercise moral leadership and proclaim judgment and serve as a redemptive leaven in the community, she will be better able to fulfill these functions. If men are not aware of their need for a prophetic word and if they do not expect it, it is likely to be only an offence; if, however, they are aware of their need for it and if they expect it and hear it in humility, they may respond with repentance. If men are not aware of their need for radical renewal and strength beyond their own, the announcement of the possibility of these is foolishness; if, however, they are aware of this need and if they expect such renewal and power to be mediated through the Church, they may be led to open themselves to its healing ministry.

The task of interpreting the function of the Church cannot, of course, be separated from the message which the Church proclaims; but in many communities where the Church has become conformed to the standards and practices of society and where her prophetic voice has long been silent, she needs not only to prophesy but to first of all make it clear why she must prophesy. This can be done—and indeed can best be done—without direct reference at first to such concrete social problems as race relations and economic issues if the latter are charged with strong emotional feelings and if the discussion of these topics puts people on the defensive. But once there is some understanding of the nature and task of the Church in relation to its Lord and to men in society, then the Church must undertake to carry out her mission by being both prophetic and redemptive.

In the third place, the Church has a responsibility to manifest in her own life the unity and the brotherhood which she proclaims. As the Amsterdam Assembly of the World Council of Churches declared, racial segregation in the Church is a "scandal" in the Body of Christ.[35] It is in clear violation of the nature of the Church as a supraracial community of those who share a common faith in Christ. In this sense the Church's primary responsibility in the area of race relations is "to be the Church." This does not mean that every congregation ought self-consciously to attempt to become interracial, but it does mean that every church should be racially inclusive in the sense that its membership should be open to members of all racial groups. Many factors contribute the actual character of a particular congregation. Generally speaking, churches tend to reflect the constituency of the neighborhoods in which they are located, and neighborhood churches are not likely to become interracial until the communities in which they are located become integrated. All churches can, however, welcome visitors, and all can open their membership to persons of other races. Churches in down-town and transitional areas of cities, in rural communities, and in integrated urban communities have a special opportunity to demonstrate the sincerity of their commitment to the Lord of the Church and to realize in their own life the richness and depth of fellowship which transcends the boundaries of race. Moreover, all churches have a responsibility to work toward the elimination of segregration in the life of the communities in which they are located —in schools, on public transportation facilities, in hospitals and restaurants, in employment, and in housing. As these barriers are broken down, it will become increasingly possible, not just to overcome segregation in the churches, but to achieve a genuine unity of fellowship and mutuality. In the words of the National Council of the Churches of Christ, churches have a double responsibility to "work for a non-segregated church and a non-segregated community."[36]

It is important, in this connection, to make certain that emphasis upon the obligation of the churches to become inclusive in their mem-

---

[35] *First Assembly of the World Council of Churches, Amsterdam, Holland, August 22nd–September 4th, 1948: Findings and Decisions,* p. 19. Available from The World Council of Churches, Geneva.

[36] From a statement adopted in 1952. Quoted in *The Christian Hope and the Task of the Church,* Section on "Intergroup Relations—The Church Amid Racial and Ethnic Tensions," p. 39.

bership shall not be allowed to hide the fact that the realization of this goal is ultimately a means of grace and spiritual enrichment. Those who have participated in the life and activities of the World Council of Churches and the National Council of the Churches of Christ in the U.S.A., as well as in other genuinely interracial organizations which are no longer self-conscious about their inclusiveness, are aware of the freedom and the enrichment which such fellowship brings. And one of the most striking aspects of the experience of those individual churches which have become racially inclusive is their testimony that the rewards in terms of their spiritual growth and vitality far outweigh the difficulties involved in breaking down the racial barriers and achieving an inclusive brotherhood.

In the fourth place, the Church has a responsibility to work for the realization of justice in the entire social order. Not only must she seek to bring about the transformation of personal relationships by a larger measure of good will and *agape,* but she must also out of love seek the transformation and reconstruction of the institutional structures through which the needs of men are either met or denied. Moreover, she needs to make clear the dynamic character of the relationship between personal ethics and social justice. Not only do transformed persons affect the moral quality of the institutional life of society, but the moral quality of these institutions affects the ethical and spiritual development of those individuals who participate in them and are subjected to them. It is impossible to separate personal from social ethics for the very reason that they are not separated in life. Man is social by nature; he inevitably exists in community; and his behavior is largely determined by the character of the community in which he lives.

Recognition of the obligation to work for the realization of justice in the social order as well as for the transformation of personal relationships implies the need to attack the many problems which stem out of racial prejudice and discrimination by a variety of methods which are adapted to the different types of problems—discrimination in voting, in employment, in civil rights, in education, in housing, and in the churches. It implies the need to work for the elimination of discrimination as well as for the eradication of prejudice. As we have seen, these two social evils are not unrelated; but strategy that is aimed directly at the former may have only a long-range, indirect effect upon the latter; and, conversely, strategy that results in the reduction of personal prejudice may have little effect upon one's discriminatory practices.[37] A continuous struggle on both fronts is needed, and this involves a determination to use a variety of forms of strategy which will supplement and undergird each other. It involves a willingness on the part of churches and Christians to supplement exhortation with the best educational methods available and also with the utilization of law and other methods of establishing and influencing public policy. Christian love, when it is genuine, provides the most adequate motivation for the effort to realize social justice; it also provides the final measure of justice in the social order when the latter is understood from the standpoint of Christian faith.

RECOMMENDED READINGS

Allport, Gordon W., *The Nature of Prejudice*, Cambridge, Massachusetts, Addison-Wesley Publishing Company, 1954.

Beach, Waldo, "A Theological Analysis of Race Relations," in *Faith and Ethics*, Paul Ramsey, ed., New York, Harper & Brothers, 1957.

Group for the Advancement of Psychiatry, *Report No. 37: Psychiatric Aspects of School Desegregation*, New York, 1957.

Haselden, Kyle, *The Racial Problem in Christian Perspective*, New York, Harper & Brothers, 1959.

King, Martin Luther, Jr., *Stride Toward Freedom*, New York, Harper & Brothers, 1958.

LaFarge, John, *The Catholic Viewpoint on Race Relations*, Garden City, New York, Hanover House, 1956.

Loescher, Frank S., *The Protestant Church and the Negro*, New York, Association Press, 1948.

Mays, Benjamin E., *Seeking to be Christian in Race Relations*, New York, Friendship Press, 1957.

Montagu, Ashley, *Statement on Race*, New York, Henry Schuman, 1951.

Myrdal, Gunnar, *An American Dilemma*, New York, Harper & Brothers, 1944.

Oldham, J. H., ed., *The Official Report of the Oxford Conference*, New York, Willett, Clark and Company, 1937, "Report of the Section on Church and Community" and "Additional Report of the Section on Church and Community."

Pope, Liston, *The Kingdom Beyond Caste*, New York, Friendship Press, 1957.

Simpson, George E. and Yinger, J. Milton, *Racial and Cultural Minorities: An Analysis of Prejudice and Discrimination*, New York, Harper & Brothers, rev. ed., 1958.

[37] See Simpson and Yinger, *op. cit.,* pp. 728 ff.

Visser't Hooft, W. A., *The Ecumenical Movement and the Racial Problem,* Paris, UNESCO, 1954.

Visser't Hooft, W. A., ed., *The Evanston Report: The Second Assembly of the World Council of Churches,* 1954, London, Student Christian Movement Press, Ltd., 1955, The Report of Section V on "Intergroup Relations: The Churches Amid Racial and Ethnic Tensions."

Tilson, Everett, *Segregation and the Bible,* Nashville, Abingdon Press, 1958.

INDEX

Absolutism, ethical, 186 ff.
Agape, and justice, 188–189, 248–270, 373–374
  and law, 84 ff., 186 ff.
  and love for God, 84–86, 88, 174
  and mutual love, 183 ff.
  and sacrificial love, 184–186
  and self-love, 175 ff.
  nature of, 87 ff., 175 ff.
  norm of neighbor-love, 164 ff., 173, 176 ff.
  relation to *eros,* 179 ff., 219, 231–232, 234, 239–240
  relation to faith, 84 ff., 179 ff.
  source of, 87–88, 175–176, 182
  See also Justice
Allport, Gordon W., 266 n., 363 ff.
Ambrose, 215–216
Antinomianism, 81, 83, 186
Apocalypticism, 43–45
  See also Eschatology
Aquinas, Thomas, 13, 215–216, 286–287, 299, 329
Aristotle, 5, 13
Asceticism, 103, 186, 277
  See also Sex, asceticism
Aspiration, 5, 25–27, 98–99, 161–162
Augustine, 14–15, 103–105, 121–122, 131, 135, 141, 143 ff., 159, 215–216

Bailey, D. S., 231 ff., 242–243, 245
Bainton, Roland H., 238–239
Barry, F. R., 200 n.
Barth, Karl, 136–137, 153
Bennett, John C., 153, 191, 197, 283 ff., 314–315, 321
Benoit, Hubert, 221
Berdyaev, Nicholas, 220–221, 281
Berry, Brewton, 9
Bertocci, Peter A., 219 n.
Bible, diversity in moral thought, 22–23
  primary source book for Christian ethics, 21
  relation of Old Testament to New, 21–24
  unity in moral thought, 22–24
Birth control, 210, 222 ff.
Bonhoeffer, Dietrich, 193 n.
Bowen, Howard R., 271, 295–296
Bright, John, 50 n.

Brunner, Emil, concept of love, 158 n., 189
  divorce, 243–244
  doctrine of vocation, 301
  dualism between love and justice, 259 ff.
  fall of man, 145–146
  function of economic life, 277–278
  justification of private property, 288
  man as creature, 104, 127, 132
  man's response to God, 163 n., 170 n., 189
  marriage, 226–227, 229 ff., 234 n.
  orders of creation, 207, 226–227
  personal character of divine command, 199
  relation of philosophical to Christian ethics, 11 ff.
  relation of redemption to creation, 114
  role of law in Christian ethics, 194–196
  sin, 145 ff.
Buber, Martin, 219
Bultmann, Rudolf, 59 n.
Burrows, Millar, 119 n., 142 n.
Bushnell, Horace, 79 n.
Butterfield, Herbert, 108–109

Calhoun, Robert L., 111, 122–123, 165 n.
Calvin, John, 121–122, 143 n., 148 n., 149, 222, 287, 298, 300, 319–320
Capitalism, 274, 306
Carter, Paul A., 337–338
Casuistry, 201
Celibacy, 215–217, 220, 222 ff., 225–226, 249
Chamberlain, Houston S., 342–343
Christian ethics, guiding principles of, 93–205
  in Jesus' teaching, 47–67, 163, 175
  in Paul, 68–91
  method of response to divine action, 95 ff., 161 ff.
  Old Testament background, 21–46, 162–163
  relation to Christian theology, 16 ff., 66 n.
  relation to philosophical ethics, 10 ff., 186

CONCORDIA COLLEGE LIBRARY
2811 N. E. HOLMAN ST.
PORTLAND, OREGON 97211

BJ1251 .G28   CU-Main
c.1
Gardner, Edward Cli/Biblical faith and social ethi

3 9371 00034 2410